OUR GUARANTEE: If you are not satisfied with the **PUBLIC EMPLOYMENT LAW REPORT** for any reason, we will refund the unused portion of your subscription payment.

Use the attached order cards to order your own or extra subscriptions to the **PUBLIC EMPLOYMENT LAW REPORT** ... the monthly newsletter service reporting the very latest public employment cases and late-breaking legislation.

The attached order cards may be removed from the book for your order.

Yes, please send me ______ subscriptions to the **PUBLIC EMPLOYMENT LAW REPORT** ... the monthly newsletter service reporting the very latest public employment cases and late-breaking legislation.

☐ Send two years at $175.00 (your best price)

☐ Send one year at $95.00

Name ____________________

Title/Organization ____________________

Address ____________________

City ____________________ State_____ Zip __________

Purchase Order Number, if needed____________________

Send order and check payable to: DATA RESEARCH, INC.,
P.O. Box 490, Rosemount, MN 55068

Yes, please send me ______ subscriptions to the **PUBLIC EMPLOYMENT LAW REPORT** ... the monthly newsletter service reporting the very latest public employment cases and late-breaking legislation.

☐ Send two years at $175.00 (your best price)

☐ Send one year at $95.00

Name ____________________

Title/Organization ____________________

Address ____________________

City ____________________ State_____ Zip __________

Purchase Order Number, if needed____________________

Send order and check payable to: DATA RESEARCH, INC.,
P.O. Box 490, Rosemount, MN 55068

DESKBOOK ENCYCLOPEDIA OF PUBLIC EMPLOYMENT LAW

SECOND EDITION

Published by
Data Research, Inc.
P.O. Box 490
Rosemount, Minnesota 55068

OTHER TITLES PUBLISHED
BY DATA RESEARCH, INC.:

Handicapped Students and Special Education
Private School Law in America
Deskbook Encyclopedia of American Insurance Law
U.S. Supreme Court Education Cases
Deskbook Encyclopedia of American School Law

Library of Congress Cataloging-in-Publication Data

Deskbook encyclopedia of public employment law. -- 2nd ed.
p. cm.
Includes bibliographical references and index.
ISBN 0-939675-27-7
1. Civil service--United States--Digests. 2. Employee-management relations in government--law and legislation--United States-Digests. I. Data Research, Inc. Rosemount, Minn.
KF5336.A75D47 1992
342.73'068--dc20
(347.30268)

91-35806
CIP

PREFACE

The ***Deskbook Encyclopedia of Public Employment Law*** is an up-to-date compilation of state and federal court decisions which affect public employment. These decisions have been selected and edited by the editorial staff of Data Research, Inc., publishers of Public Employment Law Report. From hiring and employment practices to suspensions and termination of employment, this volume examines a broad spectrum of legal issues.

Public employment law is a blend of well-settled principles which are unlikely to change and new ideas finding their way into courts. For example, it is well-settled that discrimination will not be tolerated in the workplace, but affirmative action plans are meeting with greater resistance as the requirements for their adoption change. This volume will give the reader a comprehensive guide to the direction public employment law is moving toward.

EDITORIAL STAFF
DATA RESEARCH, INC.

INTRODUCTORY NOTE ON THE JUDICIAL SYSTEM

In order to allow the reader to determine the relative importance of a judicial decision, the cases included in ***Deskbook Encyclopedia of Public Employment Law*** identify the particular court from which a decision has been issued. For example, a case decided by a state supreme court generally will be of greater significance than a state circuit court case.

Almost all the reports in this volume are taken from appellate court decisions. Although most insurance law decisions occur at the trial court level, appellate court decisions have the effect of binding lower courts and administrators so that appellate court decisions have the effect of law within their court systems.

State and federal court systems generally function independently of each other. Each court system applies its own law according to statutes and the determinations of its highest court. However, judges at all levels often consider opinions from other court systems to settle issues which are new or arise under unique fact situations. Similarly, lawyers look at the opinions of many courts to locate authority which supports their clients' cases.

Once a lawsuit is filed in a particular court system, that system retains the matter until its conclusion. Unsuccessful parties at the trial court level generally have the right to appeal unfavorable determinations of law to appellate courts within the system. When federal law issues or Constitutional grounds are present, lawsuits may be appropriately filed in the federal court system. In those cases, the lawsuit is filed initially in the federal district court for that area.

On rare occasions, the U.S. Supreme Court considers appeals from the highest courts of the states if a distinct federal question exists and at least four justices agree on the question's importance. The federal courts occasionally send cases to state courts for application of state law. These situations are infrequent and in general, the state and federal court systems should be considered separate from each other.

The most common system, used by nearly all states and also the federal judiciary, is as follows: a legal action is commenced in **district court** (sometimes called a trial court, county court, common pleas court or superior court) where a decision is initially reached. The case may then be appealed to the **court of appeals** (or appellate court), and in turn this decision may be appealed to the **supreme court**.

Several states, however, do not have a court of appeals; lower court decisions are appealed directly to the state's supreme court. Additionally, some states have labeled their courts in a nonstandard fashion.

In Maryland, the highest state court is called the Court of Appeals. In the state of New York, the trial court is called the Supreme Court. Decisions of this court may be appealed to the Supreme Court, Appellate Division. The highest court in New York is the Court of Appeals. Pennsylvania has perhaps the most complex court system. The lowest state court is the Court of Common Pleas. Depending on the circumstances of the case, appeals may be taken to either the Commonwealth Court or the Superior Court. In certain instances the Commonwealth Court functions as a trial court as well as an appellate court. The Superior Court, however, is strictly an intermediate appellate court. The highest court in Pennsylvania is the Supreme Court.

While supreme court decisions are generally regarded as the last word in legal matters, it is important to remember that trial and appeals court decisions also create important legal precedents. For the hierarchy of typical state and federal court systems, please see the diagram below.

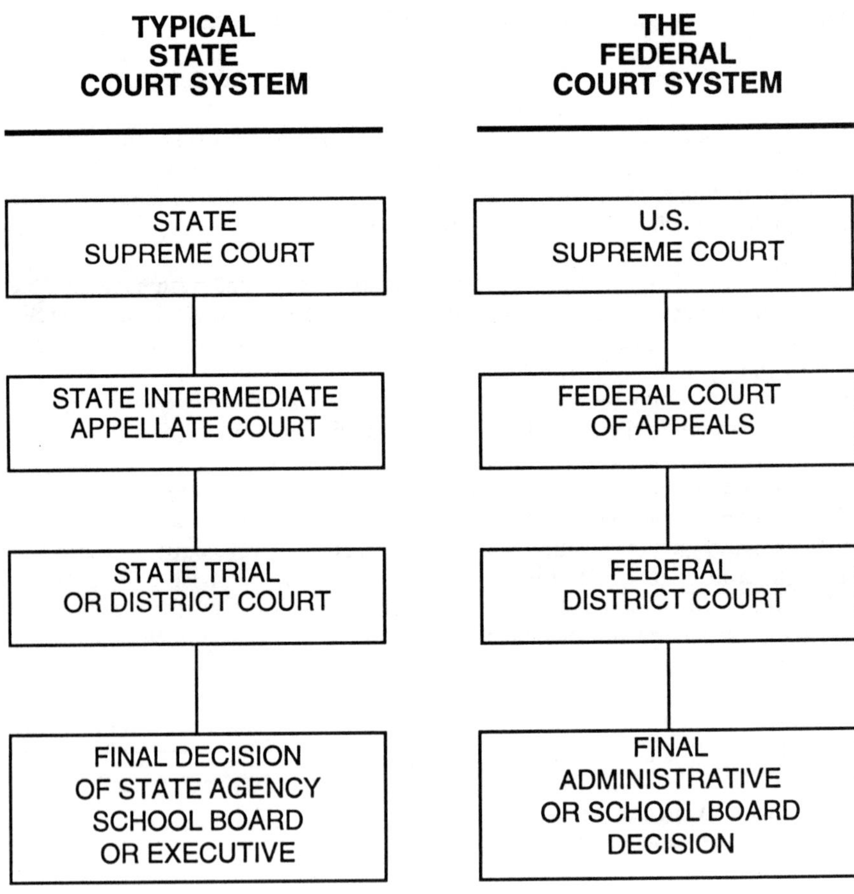

Federal courts of appeals hear appeals from the district courts which are located in their circuits. Below is a list of states matched to the federal circuits in which they are located.

First Circuit	--	Puerto Rico, Maine, New Hampshire, Massachusetts, Rhode Island
Second Circuit	--	New York, Vermont, Connecticut
Third Circuit	--	Pennsylvania, New Jersey, Delaware, Virgin Islands
Fourth Circuit	--	West Virginia, Maryland, Virginia, North Carolina, South Carolina
Fifth Circuit	--	Texas, Louisiana, Mississippi
Sixth Circuit	--	Ohio, Kentucky, Tennessee, Michigan
Seventh Circuit	--	Wisconsin, Indiana, Illinois
Eighth Circuit	--	North Dakota, South Dakota, Nebraska, Arkansas, Missouri, Iowa, Minnesota
Ninth Circuit	--	Alaska, Washington, Oregon, California, Hawaii, Arizona, Nevada, Idaho, Montana, Northern Mariana Islands, Guam
Tenth Circuit	--	Wyoming, Utah, Colorado, Kansas,Oklahoma, New Mexico
Eleventh Circuit	--	Alabama, Georgia, Florida
District of Columbia Circuit	--	Hears cases from the U.S. District Court for the District of Columbia.
Federal Circuit	--	Sitting in Washington, D.C., the U.S. Court of Appeals, Federal Circuit, hears patent and trade appeals and certain appeals on claims brought against the federal government and its agencies.

TABLE OF CONTENTS

TABLE OF CONTENTS

Page

Page

TABLE OF CASES

TABLE OF CASES

CHAPTER ONE
SEARCHES AND SEIZURES

I. SEARCHES OF HOMES, OFFICES AND PERSONS

The Fourth Amendment to the U.S. Constitution guarantees the "right of the people to be secure in their persons, houses, papers, and effects, against unreasonable searches and seizures..." Searches and seizures are generally supposed to be performed only where officials have a warrant based upon probable cause describing with particularity the things or persons to be seized. In the context of public employment, searches and seizures implicate the Fourth Amendment only if the employee has a reasonable expectation of privacy in a place to be searched. In cases involving work-related misconduct, searches taking place in government offices do not resemble searches of a private home, where Fourth Amendment protections are in full effect.It is true, however, that under certain circumstances government employees may have reasonable privacy expectations at work. The courts suspend the general requirement of a search warrant supported by probable cause for cases involving searches of public offices and utilize a reduced standard of "reasonableness."

A. Applicable Standard of Reasonableness

A leading case on the standard for public employer searches is *New Jersey v. T.L.O.*, 469 U.S. 325, 105 S.Ct. 733, 83 L.Ed.2d 720 (1985), a school case which established a two-part inquiry into whether the action by the public official was justified at its inception, and whether the search itself was reasonable in scope and circumstances.

In the *T.L.O.* case, a New Jersey high school teacher found two students smoking in the lavatory, in violation of school rules. The teacher brought the students to an assistant vice principal's office where one of the students admitted smoking in the lavatory. The other student denied being a smoker, and the assistant vice principal then asked her to come to an inner private office where he opened her purse and found a pack of cigarettes. In removing the cigarettes, he discovered rolling papers and decided to thoroughly search the purse. He also found marijuana, a pipe, empty plastic bags, a number of one dollar bills and a list of "people who owe me money." The assistant vice principal then summoned the local police, who prosecuted the student in juvenile court, resulting in a delinquency adjudication. The student appealed the adjudication, contending that the search of her purse had violated her constitutional rights under the Fourth Amendment. Her attorney made a motion to exclude the evidence seized from her purse from the juvenile court proceeding. Her appeals within the New Jersey court system were unsuccessful until she reached the state's supreme court, which reversed the lower court rulings and suppressed the evidence seized from the student's purse. The state supreme court ruled that the search had been unreasonable.

The prosecution appealed the case to the U.S. Supreme Court, which first noted that school officials should not be held to the probable cause standard to which law enforcement officers are held. The legality of student searches by teachers and other school officials should depend simply upon the reasonableness of the search under all the circumstances. In each case, the court should inquire into whether the search was justified at its inception and whether the search was reasonably related in scope to the circumstances which justified the search in the first place. Ordinarily, the search of a student by a school official is justified at its inception where there are reasonable grounds for suspecting that the search will turn up evidence that the student has violated or will violate the law or rules of the school. Under these conditions, a search is permissible in scope when the measures adopted are reasonably related to the objectives of the search and not excessively intrusive in light of the student's age and sex, in view of the suspected violation. In this case, the search was not unreasonable under the Fourth Amendment. This is because the initial search for cigarettes was reasonable, based on the assistant vice principal's reasonable suspicion that the student had cigarettes in her purse. When the assistant vice principal discovered rolling papers, he held a reasonable suspicion that the student was carrying marijuana as well. Because the reasonable suspicion in the assistant vice principal's mind justified further search of the purse, the search was reasonable and it was improper to suppress the evidence in the juvenile delinquency adjudication. The Supreme Court reversed the New Jersey Supreme Court's decision. *New Jersey v. T.L.O.*, 469 U.S. 325, 105 S.Ct. 733, 83 L.Ed.2d 720 (1985).

A physician and psychiatrist at a California state hospital was primarily responsible for training young physicians in psychiatric residency programs. He occupied the same office for seventeen years, when hospital officials became concerned about possible improprieties in his management policies. The officials were concerned that the doctor had sexually harassed two female hospital employees, had taken inappropriate disciplinary action against a resident, and had acquired a personal computer for use in the residency program under questionable circumstances. The hospital's executive director requested the psychiatrist to take paid administrative leave during an investigation of the charges. The director then formed an investigative team composed of an accountant, a physician, a hospital security officer and a hospital administrator. The administrator determined to make a search of the doctor's office, which was allegedly in compliance with the hospital policy of conducting routine inventory of state property in terminated employee offices. However, when the search was conducted, the psychiatrist remained on administrative leave and had not yet been terminated. Prior to the search, the investigators suspected that the psychiatrist had taken the computer to his home, but the search involved several entries into the office and seizure of items from the doctor's desk and file cabinets, including personal items such as photos and a valentine's card. The investigators put the remainder of the doctor's personal property in storage and placed it at the psychiatrist's disposal. The employer used the seized items in a proceeding before a state personnel hearing officer to impeach the psychiatrist's credibility.

The psychiatrist filed a separate lawsuit against the hospital administrators in a federal district court for violation of his Fourth Amendment rights. The court granted the administrators' motion for summary judgment, ruling that the search was proper. However, the U.S. Court of Appeals, Ninth Circuit, reversed and remanded this decision, ruling that the psychiatrist had a reasonable expectation of privacy in his office. According to the court, the hospital had improperly utilized its inventory procedure for terminated employees and violated the Fourth Amendment. The U.S. Supreme Court granted the administrators' petition for certiorari.

The court considered the case in view of *New Jersey v. T.L.O.*, above, which it considered in detail. As in the *T.L.O.* case, the Fourth Amendment governed the conduct of public employees making searches. The court of appeals was correct in ruling that public employees had an expectation of privacy in their offices, a standard which warranted a case by case analysis. Offices were not private enclaves and the government had the right to make reasonable intrusions in its capacity as an employer. Some government offices also were so open to fellow employees or the public as to involve no expectation of privacy. In this case, the psychiatrist had occupied the same office by himself for seventeen years and had a reasonable expectation of privacy in his desk and file cabinets.

However, the psychiatrist's reasonable expectation of privacy was to be balanced against the public employer's interest in supervision, control and efficient operation of the workplace. The Court refused to impose a search warrant requirement for public employers, because such a requirement would frustrate the governmental purpose behind the search. Under *T.L.O.*, exceptional circumstances going beyond the normal need for law enforcement made the warrant and probable-cause requirement impracticable. The warrant requirement would unduly interfere with work-related searches by public employers and the warrant requirement should only be imposed in searches that were not work-related. This was because obtaining a warrant would disrupt the daily work routine of government business and would require officials to become familiar with probable cause standards. The governmental interest in efficiency outweighed the psychiatrist's privacy expectation.

The probable cause standard was rooted in criminal investigations and had little meaning in the context of public employment. Instead, the reasonableness standard established in *New Jersey v. T.L.O.* was the appropriate standard for work-related non-investigatory intrusions of work-related misconduct. The reasonableness of such a search involved inquiry into whether the action was justified at its inception and reasonably related in scope to the circumstances which justified the interference in the first place. Generally, a search could be justified at its inception when there were reasonable grounds for suspecting that it would turn up evidence that a public employee was guilty of work-related misconduct, known as "individualized suspicion." Both the district court and the court of appeals were in error and summary judgment was inappropriate. The court reversed and remanded the case to the court of appeals to resolve factual disputes about the reasonableness of the search. *O'Connor v. Ortega,* 480 U.S. 709, 107 S.Ct. 1492, 94 L.Ed.2d 714 (1987).

A security guard employed by a state hospital which was operated by the Florida Department of Health and Rehabilitative Services (HRS) smelled marijuana smoke coming from the office of a hospital employee. Eight months later, the guard recalled the incident and mentioned it to an undercover sheriff's deputy. The two then searched the employee's office using a hospital passkey. They searched a locked file cabinet and a bathroom closet adjacent to the office. The searchers found a substance resembling marijuana in the closet and, hoping to obtain a sample, they searched the employee's desk drawer for an envelope. In the desk, they found a two-year-old prescription bottle with the employee's name on it. Along with prescription medicine, the searchers found a packet of cocaine in the bottle. The state prosecuted the employee for possession of cocaine and he moved to suppress the evidence, claiming that it had been unconstitutionally seized. The court denied his motion to suppress evidence and the employee appealed to the District Court of Appeals.

Citing *Ortega* and other Supreme Court cases, the court noted that warrantless searches performed by law enforcement officers are usually unreasonable. Public employees did not forfeit their Fourth Amendment protections merely by consenting to work for the government rather than private employers. HRS regulations which were outlined in the employee handbook reserved to the HRS the right "to make inspections of employee's personal property on departmental premises when there is reasonable cause to believe such items might serve to conceal contraband." Reasonable cause under the HRS regulations was further limited to a standard resembling probable cause, limiting searches to the person with ultimate authority to take a personnel action or his written designee. The regulations also stated that the public employee in control of the general area to be searched must expressly consent to the search and be advised about the consequences of failing to allow a search. These consequences included disciplinary action for insubordination and possible criminal charges.

The appeals court determined that the employee's rights had been egregiously violated in this case, because the official instituting the search was a law enforcement officer. Law enforcement officers, unlike public employers, were expected to be familiar with the requirements for a search warrant and to obtain one except in the most exigent circumstances. In this case, there were no exigent circumstances sufficient to justify the failure to obtain a search warrant. The employee had a reasonable expectation of privacy in his office as he had occupied it for nineteen years and had never shared it with other employees. The reasonable cause standards outlined in the department's own regulations had not been observed. The mere fact that the employee had accepted employment at the public hospital did not mean he acquiesced to an unconditional waiver of his constitutional rights. The court reversed the judgment and sentence imposed by the trial court. *Bateman v. State of Florida,* 513 So.2d 1101 (Fla.App.2d Dist.1987).

Two Los Angeles police officers responded to a radio call regarding a disturbance at the scene of an automobile accident. At the scene they encountered an intoxicated man who had sustained minor injuries. The officers arrested him because a computer check revealed he was wanted on an outstanding misdemeanor arrest warrant. Before booking him, however, the officers took him to the hospital for treatment. The man told a physician at the hospital that the officers had taken over $600 from him. The man later reduced the amount to $60 when questioned by a police sergeant. The police sergeant searched the patrol vehicle and each officer's pockets, wallet and weapon belt, and failed to discover any evidence of wrong-doing. However, the watch commander at the station ordered the sergeant to strip search the officers. The officers objected to the proposed strip searches. The officers were then searched without their consent. Later, the officers sued the city under 42 U.S.C § 1983 alleging that the searches violated their Fourth and Fourteenth Amendment rights. A federal district court dismissed the suit, concluding that the searches were reasonable. The officers then appealed to the U.S. Court of Appeals, Ninth Circuit.

The court of appeals stated that the permissibility of a particular law enforcement practice is judged by balancing its intrusion on the individual's Fourth Amendment interests against its promotion of legitimate government interests. The court stated that the city's argument that the government's interest in the integrity of its police force was sufficient to justify the search of its officers absent individualized suspicion was unsound. Strip searches of police officers must be supported by a reasonable suspicion that evidence will be uncovered. Here, there was no reasonable suspicion that the officers had taken any money. A reasonable suspicion exists when the person responsible for the search is aware of specific articulable facts that evidence will be uncovered. In this case, there were no facts indicating that money would be found on the officers. However, the court stated that the police officials who conducted the search could not be held personally liable for the constitutional violation since it was not clearly established at the time of the search that a strip search without articulable suspicion was a constitutional violation. The court of appeals remanded the case for further proceedings. *Kirkpatrick v. City of Los Angeles*, 803 F.2d 485 (9th Cir.1986)

B. Expectations of Privacy

An investigator for a Louisiana district attorney was fired following a dispute over unauthorized telephone calls which he had placed. The district attorney ordered him to clear his desk and leave. The investigator then spent the day moving out of his office. He made several trips in and out of the building and then told his secretary that he would not be coming back. He turned in his office keys and never returned. The district attorney went to the office the following Sunday and decided to check the investigator's former office. He checked desk drawers and found bank statements in envelopes bearing the investigator's name but addressed to the district attorney's office. The envelopes were bound only with a rubber band. Because the statements were addressed to the district attorney's official business address, he assumed that the statements were related to official business. He opened the envelopes and found that the statements pertained to a personal bank account of the former investigator. The district attorney also noted that there were deposit slips on the account showing many entries of $36 or multiples of $36. The district attorney seized the bank slips and randomly looked through the department's worthless check files. In the worthless check files, he found copies of letters from the former investigator to the sheriff's department closing many of the files. This was a job duty not assigned to the former investigator and the district attorney brought criminal charges for forgery against him. At trial, the district attorney testified that he had no probable cause to believe that the envelopes contained evidence of a crime, but had opened them under his duty to find out if the statements pertained to district attorney official business. The former investigator testified that he had simply forgotten them due to being upset about being fired.

The trial court determined that the former investigator was guilty of forgery. The former investigator appealed to a Louisiana Court of Appeal, claiming that the search of his former desk was invalid and unreasonable and that evidence seized from it should be suppressed. The court noted that the Fourth Amendment applied to the district attorney's office under the *Ortega* case. Searches and seizures by government employers or supervisors involving private property were subject to the Fourth Amendment reasonableness standard. The court of appeals also noted that employees may have a reasonable expectation of privacy in their desks and offices and that public employers must perform searches under the reasonableness standard.

The former investigator had no reasonable privacy interest in the bank statements because the envelopes were unsealed and bound only with rubber bands. From the outside, the envelopes indicated that they were the district attorney's property rather than being private property. Since the former investigator had no reasonable expectation of privacy in the envelopes, the search was not intrusive. The district attorney was justified in determining what was inside the envelopes and it was necessary to view their contents to resolve his doubts. The search was justified at its inception and reasonable in scope under *New Jersey v. T.L.O.*, above, and the court of appeal denied the former investigator's motion to suppress the evidence. *State v. Lambright,* 525 So.2d 84 (La.App.3d Cir.1988). *Application for writ of certiorari denied,* 530 So.2d 83 (La.1988).

A Michigan deputy sheriff's duties included handling bail bonds at the county jail and returning bail money and documents to the recorder's court. An audit revealed that he was delivering bonds to the recorder's court in a delinquent manner. The deputy's supervisors reassigned him to other duties. The department then investigated the matter and questioned the deputy about his procedures. In the course of questioning, the deputy claimed he was ill and left the office. A sheriff's department sergeant seized documents and receipts from the deputy's desk and bookshelf. The sergeant had not obtained a search warrant. Three weeks later, a citizen complained that two $1,000 bonds which he had posted for a relative were missing and that he had receipts for the bonds. At the request of the sheriff's department, the citizen petitioned the recorder's court for return of his money, but the court told him there was no record of the bonds. After a full investigation, the department issued a warrant and arrested the deputy, suspending him from his job duties.

In a trial at which the prosecution sought to charge the deputy with two embezzlement counts, a Michigan trial court excluded evidence of materials seized from the deputy's office without a search warrant. The prosecution appealed to the Michigan Court of Appeals which considered whether the search and seizure complied with the U.S. Constitution's Fourth Amendment. As in all search and seizure cases, the question was whether the person accused had a reasonable expectation of privacy in the place to be searched. The appeals court held that the deputy should have no such reasonable privacy expectation at his workplace. The question depended upon the facts of each case because some offices were so open to the public as to allow no privacy expectations at all. In this case, the search did not involve the deputy's own private property; he had no reasonable privacy expectation in his office. The facts of this case could be distinguished from the *Ortega* case because in that case personal items were seized from a private office. The deputy in this case shared his office with two other sheriff's deputies and there had been no evidence of any of his personal items in the office. Nothing but work-related papers had been seized. No warrant was required in this case due to the burden and disruption which would have resulted. Public employers should be able to have access to employee offices and desks for work-related reasons incident to the agency's business. The search in this case was not part of a criminal investigation because, at the time of the search, the deputy was not suspected of any criminal activity. The court reversed the trial court's suppression of the evidence. *People v. Duval,* 428 N.W.2d 746 (Mich.App.1980).

A naval reservist was employed by the Navy in a civil service engineering position in California. General Dynamics provided security services for the plant. A security investigator employed by General Dynamics entered the engineer's locked office, searched his locked desk and credenza, and seized personal photographs and correspondence that involved sexual matters. On the following day, the inspector and Naval employees conducted a second search and seized similar items. Those searches were conducted without a warrant. The engineer contended they were not authorized by Naval regulations. The Naval employees who conducted the second search informed the Postal Service that the engineer was receiving and sending pornographic materials through the mail. They also informed the Naval Reserve that the engineer was involved in sodomy and homosexual activities. The Naval Reserve discharged the engineer and sent a letter describing the reasons for the discharge to the engineer's home, where it was read by his family. The engineer sued the Navy and General Dynamics, claiming violations of his constitutional rights as well as emotional distress and anguish. A federal district court dismissed the constitutional claims because the engineer had failed to establish a reasonable expectation of privacy in his desk. The engineer appealed to the U.S. Court of Appeals, Ninth Circuit.

The court of appeals noted that the district court's ruling that the engineer could not have a reasonable expectation of privacy in his desk was primarily because the desk was not property of the employee. The court noted, however, that according to *Katz v. United States*, 389 U.S. 347 (1967), Fourth Amendment privacy interests do not turn on property interests. An employee need not have a property interest in something to have a privacy interest. The court also noted the holding in *Ortega v. O'Connor* (see above), in which the Supreme Court held that a public employee may have a reasonable expectation of privacy in his desk and filing cabinets. It held here that the engineer would enjoy a reasonable expectation of privacy in areas given over to his exclusive use unless he was on notice that searches might occur from time to time. The case was remanded for determinations of the engineer's privacy interests and the breadth of the search. *Schowengert v. General Dynamics Corp.*, 823 F.2d 1328 (9th Cir.1987).

An Illinois university's police officer was accused of gambling while on duty in violation of the orders of the chief of police. During an investigation of the accusation, a hidden video camera was installed to observe the officer in the police office. University officials observed the officer playing poker in the office and he was discharged. An Illinois circuit court upheld the discharge and the officer appealed to the Appellate Court of Illinois.

On appeal, the officer argued that the video tape should not have been allowed into evidence since no search warrant had been obtained. The officer argued that he had a reasonable expectation of privacy in the police department office and so a warrantless search violated his Fourth Amendment right against unreasonable search and seizure. The court stated that the Fourth Amendment only protects against unreasonable intrusions. If there is no intrusion, there is no search or seizure. In considering whether an expectation of privacy is reasonable, the court stated that it must examine whether the officer exhibited an expectation of privacy and whether society is ready to recognize that expectation as reasonable. Although the officer exhibited an intention to keep his activities private, the court did not believe that that expectation was reasonable. The office under surveillance was used by all officers and was not a private office. The search was also conducted with the police department's permission. The search was not unreasonable and the discharge was affirmed. *Thornton v. Univ. Civil Service Merit Bd.*, 507 N.E.2d 1262 (Ill.App.1987).

C. Use of Evidence

The estranged wife of a California state employee called the employee's supervisor to report that her husband was bringing home things which she thought were state property. The materials included video materials, clothing, a telephone, and some electronic equipment. A security officer was assigned to investigate the report. The officer contacted the estranged wife and arranged to meet with her. The officer went to the wife's home, which was separate from her husband's home. With the aid of the local sheriff's office, the security officer and the wife then broke into the husband's home. The wife led the officer through the house, identifying things taken from the husband's employer. The officer seized the items as identified. Two intercoms and nine T-shirts were later identified as stolen state property. At a subsequent criminal hearing, the search of the house was held to be illegal, and the evidence suppressed. As a result, the criminal charges were dismissed. The state began disciplinary proceedings against the employee, utilizing the evidence gained in the illegal search. A California superior court upheld the dismissal and the employee appealed to the California Court of Appeal.

On appeal, the employee argued that illegally seized evidence should not have been allowed in the disciplinary hearings. The court held that there was no justification for admitting the evidence in this case. The deterrent effect of the exclusionary rule would be undermined by allowing its use. The court also stated that since the illegality of the search had already been determined at the criminal trial, the state would not be allowed to deny its illegality in the disciplinary proceedings. *Dyson v. California State Personnel Bd.*, 262 Cal.Rptr. 112 (Cal.App.1989).

A St. Louis man was employed by his city as an emergency medical technician. The technician lived with his mother in an apartment above a store-front. Three St. Louis police officers went to his residence to investigate a report that the technician had city property stored there. The officers observed a stretcher and other hospital supplies through a window. They spoke to the technician and sought permission to search the residence. After some discussion, the technician allowed the officers to search and the evidence was seized. Apparently, the officers initially claimed to have a search warrant, but soon revealed that they did not. The technician was suspended for five days and dismissed the next month. Among other things, the city based his dismissal on his appropriation of city property. The technician claimed that the only evidence to support the city's charges was seized illegally, and that the Civil Service Commission, which upheld his dismissal, should not have used this evidence. The technician appealed to the Missouri Court of Appeals.

The court stated that in considering the totality of the circumstances, the technician voluntarily consented to the search. The police never placed the technician under arrest, nor did they make any show of force. The police merely stated that they wanted to talk to retrieve city property. Since the evidence was seized pursuant to a consensual search, the use of the evidence to support the technician's dismissal was not in error. *Jarrett v. Hill,* 648 S.W.2d 170 (Mo.App.1983).

II. BLOOD AND DRUG TESTING

It is no longer disputed that compulsory urinalysis or blood testing of public sector employees qualifies as a "search and seizure" within the meaning of the Fourth Amendment. This is true whether or not the urinalysis procedures involve direct visual inspection of urination. In

***Shoemaker v. Handel*, 795 F.2d 1136, an early case on the subject of the "reasonableness" of mandatory drug testing, the U.S. Court of Appeals, Third Circuit, upheld the random drug testing by urinalysis of jockeys, trainers, groomers and race officials under the administrative search exception. Courts generally followed the *Shoemaker* decision only in employment areas involving security and public safety. More recently, in two cases decided on the same day, *Skinner v. Railway Labor Executives' Ass'n* and *Nat'l Treasury Employees Union v. Von Raab* (see summaries which follow), the U.S. Supreme Court set out some general principles for determining the legitimacy of drug testing programs. Individualized suspicion of a particular employee is not necessary under the Constitution, nor does a drug problem need to be documented at a particular workplace. Rather, when the testing serves a special need beyond the scope of normal law enforcement, it is necessary to balance government interests against the individual's privacy expectations. The Supreme Court has recognized at least three interests it feels sufficiently compelling to justify a search of all employees: 1) maintaining workplace integrity; 2) enhancing public safety; and, 3) protecting truly sensitive information.**

A. Balancing Public and Individual Rights

Railway labor organizations sued the U.S. Secretary of Transportation in a federal district court for an order which would prevent enforcement of regulations under the Federal Railroad Safety Act of 1970. The regulations required testing after major train accidents and permitted railroads to administer breath or urine tests after serious incidents and where supervisors had reasonable suspicion from observing individual behavior. A U.S. district court concluded that the public and governmental interest in safety outweighed the labor organization members' interest in privacy. The U.S. Court of Appeals, Ninth Circuit, held that the testing was unconstitutional. It reversed the district court decision, ruling that government action was not sufficient to implicate the Fourth Amendment for the permissive tests, and that the required tests failed to use particularized suspicion to confine the tests to actual detection of currently impaired employees.

The Supreme Court ruled that even private railroads acting with the government's encouragement in taking of blood and urine samples were performing searches and seizures under the Fourth Amendment. The appeals court had failed to balance the interests among the employers, employees and the public. The public interest was strong enough to constitute a "special need" beyond normal law enforcement and justified departure from the usual warrant and probable cause requirements. Obtaining a warrant was likely to frustrate the government effort to reveal drug use, and privacy interests were minimal. The Court reversed the appeals court and affirmed the district court's decision for the secretary. *Skinner v. Railway Labor Executives' Ass'n,* 489 U.S. 602, 109 S.Ct. 1402, 103 L.Ed.2d 639 (1989).

U.S. Customs Service employees contested the service's right to implement a drug-testing program for employees seeking transfer or promotion to some positions. Employees seeking jobs requiring direct involvement in drug interdiction and enforcement, use of firearms, or handling of classified material were to be tested under the program. The testing required applicants to give urine samples under observation by a same-sex monitor. Employees who tested positive were subject to dismissal from the service but would not be turned over to agencies for criminal prosecution without written consent by the employee. The employees' union sued the customs service in a federal district court, claiming that the testing program violated the Fourth Amendment. The court ruled in the employees' favor and the service appealed to the U.S. Court of Appeals, Fifth Circuit. The appeals court vacated the lower court's order prohibiting enforcement of the testing program. The union appealed to the U.S. Supreme Court.

The Supreme Court followed the *Skinner* case (above) in finding that the taking of urine constituted a search or seizure under the Constitution. The customs service testing program served a special government need beyond normal law enforcement. The program was designed to deter drug use among persons eligible for sensitive positions. The special need to keep drug abusers from these positions justified departure from the usual warrant and probable cause requirements. The government's need to conduct searches without reasonable suspicion outweighed the employee privacy interest for employees engaged in drug interdiction and for employees required to carry firearms. However, the record was insufficient to assess the government's reasonable interest in testing employees required to handle classified material. Accordingly, the court affirmed the appeals court decision in part and remanded for a determination of the necessity to test employees who handled classified material. *National Treasury Employees Union v. Von Raab,* 489 U.S. 656, 109 S.Ct. 1384, 103 L.Ed.2d 685 (1989).

The U.S. Secretary of Transportation announced a drug testing program for some transportation department employees. The testing was for unlawful drug use only and divided employees and applicants into seven categories depending on safety and security matters. Employees in positions having a direct impact on public health, safety or national security could be required to submit to random testing. Employees in this category include air traffic controllers, mechanics, inspectors and engineers involved in air, rail, highway and water transportation. The testing involved two separate tests, and employees who tested positive could insist on being retested. Employees with positive results would be assigned to nonsafety or nonsecurity duties but generally could not be removed from federal employment unless testing positive a second time. A federal district court upheld the program, and the employees' labor organization appealed to the U.S. Court of Appeals, District of Columbia Circuit.

The appeals court referred to two U.S. Supreme Court decisions, *Skinner v. Railway Labor Executives' Association*, and *National Treasury Employees Union v. Von Raab* (see above). In these cases, the Court ruled that suspicionless testing constituted a search but was reasonable by Fourth Amendment standards. Federal employee drug testing did not require a probable cause standard where the program tested only those employees whose jobs were directly related to public health and safety, protection of life and property, law enforcement or national security. In this case, over ninety-four percent of employees subject to random testing worked for the Federal Aviation Administration, and most of these were air traffic controllers. The government interest in protecting the public safety was more compelling than employee privacy interests. The deterrent effect of random urinalysis was a reasonable means for detecting and preventing drug related injuries. The district court had appropriately granted summary judgment for the transportation department. *American Fed. of Gov't Employees v. Skinner,* 885 F.2d 884 (D.C.Cir.1989).

On September 15, 1986, President Reagan issued Executive Order No. 12,564, which called for various measures designed to create a drug-free federal workplace. That order required the head of each executive federal agency to establish a program to test for the use of illegal drugs by employees in sensitive positions. The Department of Justice (DOJ) implemented a plan which subjected five categories of DOJ employees to random drug testing. Under the plan, testing was to be conducted for marijuana, cocaine, opiates, amphetamines, and phencyclidine. The employee to be tested was to be notified "the same day, preferably within two hours, of the scheduled testing." The DOJ followed the Department of Health and Human Services (HHS) guidelines for obtaining the sample. The employee would be monitored by a supervisor of the same sex, but would be allowed to urinate in an enclosed area. The specimens would then be subjected to two tests. If both tests were positive, a Medical Review officer would review and interpret the testing, "examining alternate medical explanations" for any positive result. Before verifying the positive result, the employee would be consulted in order to discuss the test results. Possible penalties ranged from reprimand to dismissal, and always resulted in removal from any sensitive position. A group of DOJ employees challenged the rule as unreasonable under the Fourth Amendment since there was "no nexus between fitness for duty, security and integrity on the one hand, and compulsory random urinalysis drug testing on the other, where no drug problem is believed to exist." A federal district court enjoined the implementation of the tests on this basis and the DOJ appealed to the United States Court of Appeals, District of Columbia Circuit.

The court of appeals based its decision on certain general principles from the United States Supreme Court's holding in *Skinner v. Railway Labor Executives' Assoc.*, and *Nat'l Treasury Employees Union v. Von Raab.* Urinalysis, if compelled by the government, is a search subject to the restrictions of the Fourth Amendment. However, individualized suspicion of a particular employee is not required by the Constitution. Nor is it necessary that a documented drug problem exist within the particular workplace at issue. Rather, where the Fourth Amendment intrusion serves special governmental needs, beyond the normal need for law enforcement, it is necessary to balance the individual's privacy expectations against the government's interest in carrying out such an intrusion. The Supreme Court had recognized three interests sufficiently compelling to justify testing all employees: integrity of its work force, enhancing public safety, and protecting truly sensitive information.

The court of appeals stated that, in this case, maintaining the integrity of the work force was an insufficient interest to support the testing. There was no nexus between the nature of the employee's duty and any feared drug violation, whereas in *Von Raab* the tested employees were those involved in drug interdiction. Federal employment alone does not justify such a test. The court of appeals also stated that the public safety rationale adopted in *Von Raab* and *Skinner* focused on the immediacy of the threat. No such immediacy was apparent here. The court also held that the government's interest in protecting sensitive information was sufficient to support the testing, but only with respect to those DOJ employees with access to top secret national security information. The court of appeals affirmed the injunction with respect to the remaining employees. *Harmon v. Thornburgh,* 878 F.2d 484 (D.C.Cir.1989).

A New York county personnel office announced several vacancies for corrections officers. This announcement included a warning that a drug test may be required as part of a necessary background check. An applicant for the position was told that during the twelve-month probationary period, he would be required to take part in the county's drug screening program. The applicant was later made a probationary officer. As a trainee, the officer was again informed of the drug testing program. After taking the test, the officer was terminated due to a positive result for marijuana use. The officer sued seeking reinstatement on the grounds that the test was an unlawful search and seizure since it was not based on reasonable suspicion. The trial court dismissed, relying on the exception to the reasonable suspicion rule set out in *Patchogue-Medford Congress of Teachers v. Bd. of Educ.* (see below). The officer then appealed to the New York Supreme Court, Appellate Division.

The appellate court stated that the officer's awareness of the fact that undergoing random drug testing was necessary to maintain the integrity of his public employment significantly lowered his expectation of privacy.

The court also stated that public employees already have some diminished expectation of privacy in respect to inquiries by the state into their physical fitness. The privacy expectations of corrections officers were even further diminished by virtue of their membership in a paramilitary force. These factors all reduced the officer's expectation of privacy to an insubstantial level. The court also noted that the drug testing only occurred during the probationary period, when an officer does not yet have a property interest in his position. The court stated that the state's interest in safeguarding the security of its prisons was substantial. Since the state's interest was substantial and the officer's interest minimal, the urinalysis and discharge were reasonable. *McKenzie v. Jackson,* 547 N.Y.S.2d 120 (A.D.1989).

A New York school district signed a collective bargaining agreement with a teacher's union. The agreement required probationary teachers to submit to a full physical examination in their first year of employment and again when they became eligible for tenure. The school district later informed a number of probationary teachers that they must also submit to urinalysis. The test was required for all employees eligible for tenure. The teacher's union sued to prohibit the test claiming that it was unauthorized and constituted an unreasonable search and seizure in violation of the teachers' constitutional rights. The school district argued that the test was authorized by the collective bargaining agreement and was a reasonable requirement to impose on a tenure candidate. The trial court granted the union's request for a stay and the appellate court affirmed. The school district appealed to the New York Court of Appeals.

The court of appeals stated that the urinalysis was definitely a search and, therefore, needed to meet a standard of reasonableness. It said that the state had a legitimate interest in seeing that its employees were physically fit and their performance was not impaired by drug use. The court also noted that this goal would be easier to achieve if the state were able to search everyone periodically in an all-inclusive dragnet. However, random searches of this type need to be closely scrutinized and should only be allowed if the privacy interests implicated are slight. In this case, they were not. The urinalysis order was found to be unreasonable and the lower court's order was affirmed. *Patchogue-Medford Teachers Congress v. Bd. of Educ.*, 510 N.E.2d 325 (N.Y.1987).

The members of an elite voluntary corps within the New York City Police Department, the Organized Crime Control Bureau (OCCB), sued the Police Commissioner upon his announcement of a periodic random urinalysis drug-testing program affecting them. The program would require random submission to urinalysis and, thus, differed from the department's existing drug-testing program. Previously, OCCB members were subject only to testing during their academy training, probationary period, or upon reasonable suspicion of drug use. Those unwilling to participate in the new program could transfer out of the Bureau without loss of rank or salary. A New York trial court and appellate court found the program to be unreasonable under the New York and Federal Constitutions. The New York Court of Appeals reviewed the case.

The court noted that in *Patchogue-Medford Congress of Teachers v. Bd. of Educ.*, it had held that testing all teachers, absent reasonable suspicion, was forbidden. The court stated, however, that there were factors which took this case beyond *Patchogue* and which rendered the officers' privacy interests insubstantial. The privacy expectations of police officers are lower than those of teachers. In addition, the state's power to regulate the conduct of its officers extends to conduct which involves constitutionally protected rights. The officers had already been subjected to earlier drug tests, unlike the teachers in *Patchogue*. The teachers in *Patchogue* did not carry an obvious drug risk, as do police officers. The department's justifiable interest in performing the drug test outweighed the minimal privacy expectations of the officers. *Caruso v. Ward,* 534 N.Y.S.2d 142 (Ct.App.1988).

A police officer was hired by the Honolulu police department and submitted to a preemployment physical and urinalysis drug test. After the officer served for roughly two years, the department instituted an additional drug testing plan. The officer refused to be tested and was forced to surrender her badge and gun while reassigned to a desk job. The officer's challenge of the plan eventually reached the Hawaii Supreme Court.

The court needed to determine the extent of the officer's rights to privacy and then weigh those in comparison to the state's interest. An individual's interest in privacy is guaranteed by the Hawaii Constitution. It provides an individual with the means to avoid disclosure of personal matters, and allows freedom in making personal decisions. The state must carry a heavy burden to justify the testing. The Hawaii court noted that the U.S. Supreme Court and many other courts have upheld drug testing of police officers. Urinalysis is the only effective, and therefore also the least restrictive, method of achieving the state's interest in attempting to ensure the public's safety. The testing procedures in this case were narrowly tailored for this purpose and included safeguards for accuracy and against overdisclosure or use in a criminal trial. Additionally, random testing was allowed in order to ensure against off-duty drug use. This was found to be necessary to protect the integrity of the department and because the officer could be called upon at any time. The court upheld the plan. *McCloskey v. Honolulu Police Dep't.,* 799 P.2d 953 (Hawaii 1990).

A bus driver for the Greater Cleveland Regional Transit Authority (CRTA) rear-ended an automobile. CRTA's drug testing policy mandates post-accident testing, and the employee tested positive for marijuana. The employee was terminated, but had the discipline reduced on appeal. The employee agreed to be suspended for thirty days, and to submit to future testing.

Following his reinstatement, the employee again tested positive in a routine scheduled physical. He was then terminated. The employee filed a lawsuit in a federal district court alleging numerous violations of his rights. The issue was later determined to be whether the drug testing procedures violated the employee's right to privacy. CRTA moved for summary judgment.

When examining a drug testing policy a court must balance the government interests against the individual's right to privacy. The court explained that although drug testing constitutes a search for Fourth Amendment privacy purposes, a warrant is not needed in the following situations: when there is little discretion involved in invoking a test, when it is used for administrative purposes only (non-criminal), and when a warrant requirement would add little to the protection of privacy interests. An important factor in weighing the government's interest is the possibility for disastrous consequences which could result from a momentary lapse of attention. In this case, there was medical testimony that the use of marijuana may have "residual impairment effects" on a driver. Further, the employee was aware of the upcoming test, and the testing procedures used minimized the intrusion to the employee's privacy. The court held that the policy did not violate the employee's privacy rights. CRTA was granted summary judgment. *Holloman v. Greater Cleveland Regional Trans. Auth.*, 741 F.Supp. 677 (N.D.Ohio 1990).

The federal Research and Special Programs Administration proposed a drug testing plan through the Department of Transportation (DOT). It required extensive drug testing of employees involved in what the DOT felt were safety sensitive positions. Despite a generally adverse reaction from employees, the plan was issued and required testing in many situations. These included preemployment, postemployment, random testing, and testing for reasonable cause. Two labor unions challenged the appropriateness and constitutionality of the plan. A federal district court ruled for the DOT and the unions appealed.

The first issue the court dealt with was the appropriateness of the plan in this situation. If the DOT was found to have acted in a way that was "arbitrary and capricious" the plan could be set aside under the Administrative Procedure Act. It was not disputed that the DOT was unable to show a specific drug use problem among the employees to be tested. In fact, the employees pointed to the safety record as an argument against the need for the plan. It was the burden of the DOT to explain the rationale for the rule, and the rationale must be found reasonable by the court. The DOT argued that the plan protected against the potential for catastrophic harm to the public's safety. The court found this reasonable. The unions' novel arguments of "over-inclusiveness" and cost ineffectiveness were considered to be without merit. The court found the plan to be appropriate. The next issue for the court was the constitutionality of random testing. The court balanced the employees' interest in privacy against the DOT's interests in public safety. In this case, the potential safety concerns led to diminished privacy expectations even absent other regulations of the employees' functions. The court upheld this plan and the decision of the district court. *I.B.E.W., Local 1245 v. Skinner,* 913 F.2d 1454 (9th Cir.1990)

A Nebraska human services agency providing services to mentally disabled persons adopted a chronic infectious disease policy which required blood testing for AIDS and hepatitis B viruses for certain personnel. It also required employees to notify personnel officers when they knew or suspected they had one of the diseases. The policy applied to personnel having the most frequent contact with clients. The agency justified the policy by stating that it was concerned for clients who were violent or aggressive and might become infected by biting or scratching infected employees. Employees of a county subagency challenged the policy in a federal district court, claiming it violated their constitutional rights. The court accepted evidence that the chances of transmission from staff members to clients from the clients' scratching or biting or from clients' personal hygiene was near zero. There was no evidence of drug abuse or sexual abuse by the agency's personnel. The agency appealed to the U.S. Court of Appeals, Eighth Circuit.

The appeals court ruled that mandatory blood testing was a search or seizure under the Fourth Amendment which must comply with its reasonableness standard. This required balancing the personnel members' privacy rights against public and client interests and safety. The court rejected the agency's argument that employees had a reduced expectation of privacy because they worked in a highly-regulated state agency. It also accepted the district court's finding that the risk of transmission from employees to clients was miniscule. Therefore, the agency's blood testing policy was unreasonable from its inception and was unjustifiable under the constitution. The appeals court affirmed the district court's order preventing enforcement of the policy. *Glover v. Eastern Nebraska Comm. Office of Retardation,* 867 F.2d 461 (8th Cir.1989).

In 1985, the police department of a Georgia city received reports that some of its officers were smoking marijuana in public. The chief of police was unable to find the offending officers through conventional investigative means. It was decided to conduct urinalysis in a nonselective manner in order to ascertain the offending officers. The city decided to test all city employees who had police powers. A fire department captain with fire inspector duties was required to submit to urinalysis. The captain tested positive under one of the three tests conducted and he was subsequently discharged. The Georgia Court of Appeals reversed the discharge, holding that the city could not require the captain to submit to the urinalysis test without a reasonable individualized suspicion of drug use. The city appealed to the Georgia Supreme Court.

The Georgia Supreme Court determined that the city's urinalysis testing of all employees with police power was reasonable under the Georgia state constitution. The court stated that the city had a compelling need for urinalysis testing of its employees since normal investigative means to root out drug-users had been unsuccessful. The court also stated that although the urinalysis would infringe on the employees' expectations of privacy, the intrusion was not so great as an invasion of the home or of a strip or body cavity search. Taking notice of *Shoemaker v. Handel*, the court stated that the city's interest in ensuring the integrity and safety of employees with police powers is at least as strong, if not stronger, than the interest involved in ensuring the safety and integrity of horse racing. The court stated that in light of the justification for the city's use of urinalysis coupled with the protective aspects of the city's urinalysis program, the program was reasonable under the Georgia constitution. *City of East Point v. Smith*, 365 S.E.2d 432 (Ga.1988).

The United States Department of Education (DOE) instituted a drug-free work force plan which included reasonable suspicion testing and random testing of sensitive employees in specified positions. The American Federation of Government Employees (AFGE), sued the DOE in the U.S. District Court, District of Columbia, seeking an order to disallow the tests. The AFGE questioned the reasonableness of the testing when the privacy concerns of its workers were balanced against the government's interests in conducting the tests. The sensitive employees category included law enforcement personnel, motor vehicle operators and employees with access to sensitive data.

The court held that random testing was constitutionally permissible with respect to law enforcement personnel, motor vehicle operators, and some of the employees with access to sensitive information. Because law enforcement personnel carry guns, they present a potential risk to the public if impaired by drug use. Random testing was allowable because the government's interest outweighed the employee privacy interests. The motor vehicle operators come into direct contact with other drivers and pedestrians and therefore are in a position where a momentary lapse of attention could result in harm. The court also held that employees with access to truly sensitive information could be randomly tested under the Constitution. It was not required that employees be suspected of using drugs on the job. A reasonable suspicion that an employee used drugs was sufficient. The court found that the deterrence rationale behind the testing outweighed the privacy rights of individual employees. *American Fed'n of Gov't Employees v. Cavazos*, 721 F.Supp. 1361 (D.D.C.1989).

A New York Regional Transit Authority (RTS) bus driver gave a urine specimen during the course of a routine back-to-work physical. It was discovered that his urine sample contained cocaine. He was offered the opportunity to take a new test, but declined to do so, indicating that he had used cocaine the night before and would now test positive if he submitted to a new exam. As a result, he was fired. The bus driver brought a § 1983 action against RTS in a U.S. district court challenging the RTS's drug testing policy as a violation of his Fourth Amendment right to privacy.

The court held that safe transportation of passengers outweighed any individual employee privacy expectations. Further, the court noted that the bus driver's privacy expectation was diminished because the drug screen was conducted during a routine back-to-work physical. These physicals had been conducted for many years and included urine testing. The testing for drugs imposed only a minimal intrusion on his privacy. Therefore, the RTS's mandatory drug testing policy did not violate the bus driver's Fourth Amendment rights. *Moxley v. Regional Transit Servs.*, 722 F.Supp. 977 (W.D.N.Y.1989).

The District of Columbia school system initiated a mandatory drug testing program for employees in its transportation branch. Those employees included bus drivers, mechanics, and bus attendants whose primary duty was the daily transportation of handicapped students between their homes and schools. The drug testing program had been implemented because of a growing concern among school officials over a perceived "drug culture" in the transportation branch. There were repeated incidents of bizarre or dangerous drug-related behavior by drivers and attendants while on duty. Syringes and bloody needles were found in restrooms used by the transportation branch employees. The head of the branch estimated that sixty percent of the branch's employees were using narcotics to some extent. The program required mandatory urinalysis testing of all employees who were to undergo medical examinations to determine physical fitness for licensing and other employment-related reasons. Refusal to submit to the test or a positive result would result in termination. Twenty-six employees tested positive and were terminated. One employee sued the school system in federal court seeking damages under 42 U.S.C. § 1983 for violation of her Fourth and Fifth Amendment rights and for injunctive relief. A federal district court held that her termination on the basis of a single unconfirmed test, without a hearing, was arbitrary and violated District of Columbia law. The court ordered the employee reinstated with back pay, seniority and benefits. It ordered all mention of termination to be expunged from her record and enjoined the system from terminating her on the basis of urinalysis without confirmation. It also ordered the system not to administer any drug test to her without first establishing probable cause. The school system acquiesced to the district court's decision, except it appealed the issue of probable cause to the U.S. Court of Appeals, District of Columbia Circuit.

The court stated that in order to determine whether a search is a reasonable one, it must balance the individual's privacy interest against the government's interest in conducting the search. In striking this balance, the court stated that it must consider both whether the search was justified at its inception, and whether it was actually carried out in relation to its objectives and was not excessively intrusive. The court stated that the government had a compelling interest in protecting the physical safety of its employees and others when impairment of an employee might result in harm. The intrusion into the employee's privacy interests by conducting urinalysis as part of a routine medical exam was small in comparison. The court of appeals reversed and held the test to be legitimate. *Jones v. McKenzie*, 833 F.2d 335 (D.C.Cir.1987).

The city of Newark, New Jersey, issued a directive ordering all members of the police department's Narcotics Bureau to submit to urine testing for drug abuse both upon transfer into the bureau and at least twice a year thereafter. The program was motivated by concern that there was drug abuse among members of the police department as well as the public perception with respect to drug abuse among members of the police department. The department director also said that he had received specific information from citizens in the community and from street people that police officers were using controlled substances. A police union sued the department seeking an order invalidating the directive as a violation of the Fourth Amendment to the U.S. Constitution, and of Article 1, para. 7 of the New Jersey Constitution. The trial court sustained the directive and the union appealed to the New Jersey Superior Court, Appellate Division.

The appellate court stated that it is uniformly recognized that taking of urine is both a search and seizure under both constitutions' provisions. The court stated that warrantless searches are presumed invalid unless there is a specific exception to the warrant requirement, such as exigent circumstances, or individualized suspicion. The court refused to follow *Shoemaker v. Handel*, stating that police officers are not members of a highly-regulated industry. The court stated that under the New Jersey Constitution, the state's interest in promoting public confidence and ensuring public safety is not strong enough to justify this intrusion into the police officers' private lives. The court also stated that it based its holding exclusively on the New Jersey Constitution, and not on the Federal Constitution. It noted that the New Jersey Constitution protected its citizens' rights independently, and that it would not venture to guess whether the U.S. Supreme Court would uphold the same program under the Fourth Amendment alone. *Fraternal Order of Police v. Newark*, 524 A.2d 430 (N.J.Super.A.D.1987).

B. Standards for Reasonable Suspicion.

The Army began testing some of its civilian employees for drug use with a mandatory random urinalysis program. Applicants who tested positive for drug use were denied further consideration for employment and active employees who refused to submit to testing could be removed from federal service. Employees testing positive could then become eligible for counseling or treatment. A federal employee labor organization sued the Secretary of Defense and other officials in a federal district court, challenging the legality of the random part of the testing program. The court ruled that suspicionless urinalysis constituted an unreasonable search which violated the Fourth Amendment. The court ordered the Army to end all random testing under the program. The secretary appealed to the U.S. Court of Appeals, District of Columbia Circuit.

In this case, the government interest went beyond law enforcement purposes as it pertained to employee fitness and national security. The Army had a compelling safety interest in ensuring that its civilian employees were not drug impaired. The positions covered included air traffic controllers, pilots, aviation mechanics and other employees for whom a single drug-related accident could mean disaster. A second category of civilian employees included nuclear reactor operators, weapons technicians, ammunition maintenance specialists, secretaries, engineering technicians, research biologists and laboratory workers. From the record, the court was unable to tell whether all persons in the latter category were assigned to such sensitive positions that the government had a compelling safety and security interest. The court remanded the case for a determination on the reasonableness of the second category of employees. It also noted that a final category of tested positions for Army drug counselors and forensic drug testing laboratories presented no risk of irreparable harm. There was nothing to indicate that these employees had a diminished expectation of privacy which would justify random searches. The district court had correctly determined that the government interest in testing these employees did not outweigh their privacy expectations and the court affirmed that portion of the district court decision. The random urinalysis testing for aviation, police and service staff was reasonable, but drug testing for the other categories would be considered on remand. *Nat'l Federation of Federal Employees v. Cheney*, 884 F.2d 603 (D.C.Cir.1989).

A Philadelphia police officer was found off his beat in the company of a fellow officer, who was alleged to be selling drugs and who was later dismissed for the use of illegal drugs. The officer submitted to urinalysis following the incident, and the results were negative. He was, however, suspended from the department for fifteen days because he had been off his beat on three occasions while reporting otherwise in his patrol log. The officer's former girlfriend, also a police officer, accused him of having used drugs in her presence. She made this accusation to the officer's commanding officer. In response to this allegation, an investigation was launched. Two months passed and no drug use was uncovered. The girlfriend retracted her allegations and also denied having accused the officer. The officer, however, was forced to submit to urinalysis. The results showed marijuana or hashish in the officer's urine. When confronted with the results the officer explained that the results could have been from passive inhalation since he also worked as a security guard in a hotel where the hallways were filled with marijuana smoke. The lab report, however, said the levels of cannabinoids in the urine were too high to be consistent with passive inhalation. The officer was discharged and he sued the department seeking reinstatement, compensatory and punitive damages, and a declaration that his constitutional rights had been violated. A federal district court held for the department and the officer appealed to the U.S. Court of Appeals, Third Circuit.

The court, applying the standard of *New Jersey v. T.L.O.*, (see above) stated that the department must have had a reasonable suspicion that the officer was using illegal drugs. The standard required an objective evaluation of whether reasonable suspicion existed. The court stated that factors that may affect the reasonableness of the suspicion are: 1) the nature of the tip or informant; 2) the reliability of the informant; 3) the degree of corroboration; 4) other facts contributing to the suspicion or lack thereof. The court of appeals stated that the girlfriend's statement was sufficient to support a finding of reasonable suspicion. *Copeland v. Philadelphia Police Dep't*, 840 F.2d 1139 (3d Cir.1988).

The Philadelphia police department received an anonymous phone call from a "community leader" that numerous residents had observed police officers congregating behind some tennis courts in their neighborhood. The officers were reportedly "behaving unusually." The caller stated that people were afraid of the officers, as they were apparently using drugs and "acting crazy." After conducting an investigation, a surveillance team determined that four particular officers were spending a substantial amount of time behind the tennis courts. Although the team was able to identify the officers, it was unable to tell what they were doing. On one occasion, the team observed a small flash of fire, which burned for a few seconds. Returning to the scene the following day, the team discovered a partially burned police report, a burned bottle cap, and a straw. A narcotics unit officer stated that such items were consistent with the use of "crack." The officers were asked to voluntarily submit to urinalysis. They refused. The officers were then ordered to submit to urinalysis. Again, they refused. The officers were suspended for thirty days without pay pending dismissal. The department also issued a press release, including photographs of the officers, stating that they had been suspended for refusing to submit to urinalysis based on suspected drug use. The officers were formally notified that they were to be dismissed for failure to submit to urinalysis and for being off sector and falsifying logs.

The officers challenged the dismissals, and the matter was submitted to binding arbitration. The arbitrator ruled that under the city's collective bargaining agreement with the police union, the officers could not be ordered to submit to urinalysis, and that the officers had therefore been improperly dismissed for refusing that order. The arbitrator did find that a thirty-day suspension was appropriate for the other charges. The arbitrator's decision was affirmed by the Pennsylvania Court of Common Pleas, and the Commonwealth Court. The officers then sued the department in federal court alleging that they had been deprived of their Fourth Amendment right to be free from unreasonable searches when the department ordered them to submit to urinalysis. They also claimed damages to their jobs and good names, without a meaningful opportunity to respond to the charges. The district court dismissed the Fourth Amendment claims. After a trial, it held for the department on the other charges. The officers then appealed to the U.S. Court of Appeals, Third Circuit.

The court noted that in cases where the urinalysis is not conducted pursuant to a random drug program of the type approved by the Third Circuit in *Shoemaker v. Handel* and *Policemen's Benevolent Ass'n of New Jersey v. Township of Washington*, then the standard to apply to the test is that of *Copeland v. Philadelphia Police Dep't* . The *Copeland* standard is whether the department had a reasonable suspicion that a particular officer was a user of illegal drugs. This standard required an objective evaluation of whether reasonable suspicion existed. Factors important to such an evaluation include the nature of the tip or information, the reliability of the informant, the degree of corroboration, and other facts contributing to suspicion. The court held that the Fourth Amendment rights of the officers were not violated since the complaint which precipitated the investigation came from an apparently reliable source, including detailed accounts of different observations made by various people, and which was corroborated by subsequent surveillance of the area. The court reversed, however, the district court's holding on the other issue. It found that although the officers had been afforded the opportunity to challenge the department's order, they had not been provided a meaningful pretermination hearing since they had not been given a full explanation of the department's evidence. *Fraternal Order of Police v. Tucker*, 868 F.2d 74 (3d Cir.1989).

A firefighter for the city of Atlanta was informed that his department had been conducting an administrative investigation into drug use and sales within the department. He was informed that he had been named by another firefighter, who had been selling drugs from his home, as someone who had purchased drugs within the previous three months. The firefighter was ordered to submit to a urinalysis test. He refused. The department immediately suspended him and following a hearing, terminated his employment. The firefighter sued for violation of his civil rights, seeking damages and reinstatement. A federal district court granted summary judgment to the department and the firefighter appealed to the U.S. Court of Appeals, Eleventh Circuit.

The court stated that the department had reason to suspect that the firefighter was a drug user. The other firefighter, who was a confirmed drug dealer, had named him as a user, and previous information he had given regarding other drug users had been reliable. The city had a compelling interest in having its firefighters free from drugs. Under these circumstances, the request of the department was reasonable. The court stated, however, that the firefighter's suspension without pay before the first hearing violated his due process rights. The stoppage of pay required a hearing. The court, therefore, reversed the district court's judgment only with respect to the issue of suspension without pay. *Everett v. Napper*, 833 F.2d 1507 (11th Cir.1987).

The New York City Transit Authority (TA) utilized urine testing procedures to test for the use of marijuana. The policy was to take urine from TA employees in four circumstances: following an extended absence or suspension; as part of a periodic physical examination; as part of a physical examination for promotion; and when directed by a superior or manager following an incident which occurred while on duty. The employees and applicants who tested positive for marijuana and also denied drug use instituted this action in a federal district court alleging violations of the Fourth Amendment to the U. S. Constitution.

Drug testing of safety sensitive employees and applicants does not violate the Fourth Amendment. However, the court noted, when safety sensitive work was not involved, the balance of private and government interests mandates a higher standard than mere reasonableness to satisfy the Fourth Amendment. It must be individualized suspicion. The TA argued that its testing satisfied a reasonable suspicion standard based upon nationwide statistics for drug use and evidence that there were drug users on the TA work force. The court ruled, however, that these statistics were insufficient to impute a reasonable suspicion of marijuana use to all workers and applicants. The court ruled that it was only reasonable to conduct testing of an employee who may have been the cause of an incident or accident shortly after the event occurred. However, the testing of non-safety employees for the reasons the TA advanced was insufficient to meet the reasonableness requirement. *Burka v. New York City Transit Auth.*, 739 F.Supp. 814 (S.D.N.Y.1990).

The employees then sought monetary and injunctive relief for violations of the Fourth Amendment, specifically, violations of the search and seizure and due process clauses. The court found that violations of the search and seizure clause entitled victims to only monetary relief. Injunctive relief halting the use of the products of an illegal search is almost never granted.

The exclusionary rule is involved only when a court feels that excluding evidence would have a positive deterrent effect on the officials' conduct in the future. Any other relief granted must come by way of due process violations. A due process violation would occur only when an employee could prove that the hearing would have produced a different result absent the use of the drug test result. Because of their own intervention, employees who later admitted drug use would not be able to prove a due process violation. However, any employee who tested positive but did not later admit to drug use did experience a violation of the due process clause. Those employees were granted injunctive relief and were to have all record of the test or any hearing expunged from their records. They were also to receive monetary damages. The court ordered each party to submit a settlement proposal in light of the rulings made at this hearing. *Burka v. New York City Transit Auth.*, 747 F.Supp. 214 (S.D.N.Y.1990).

The federal Office of Personnel Management (OPM) implemented a drug testing plan for its 5,800 employees. The employees contended that the plan constituted an unlawful search and seizure in violation of the Fourth Amendment. Earlier litigation and settlement had left two issues undecided: the legality of testing after accidents causing at least $1,000 damage, and testing based on reasonable suspicion. Both parties moved for summary judgment on each issue. First addressed was the post-accident plan. The OPM employees were mostly office employees whose only dangerous function was driving an automobile. The court felt that driving did not impose an unreasonable risk to the public, and noted an absence of evidence showing a current drug problem. Importantly, there was no causation factor under the plan, and the $1,000 minimum damage requirement was comparatively low. The court found that the post-accident testing would not further the public's interest enough to justify the intrusion to the employees' privacy. The reasonable suspicion portion of the plan, however, included confidential results and guarantees against use in criminal trials. It was found to be based on reasonable factors and included sufficient safeguards against abuse of the plan. The court stated that the inclusion of off-duty conduct was permissible. It granted summary judgment to the employees on post-accident testing and to OPM on reasonable suspicion testing. *Connelly v. Newman,* 753 F.Supp. 293 (N.D.Cal.1990).

The American Federation of Government Employees sued the government over a drug testing plan in the U.S. District Court for the District of Columbia. The employees then asked the court to grant a preliminary injunction to stop drug testing until the suit was resolved. In examining their request for a preliminary injunction, the court tried first to predict the employees' chances for success, and then to balance the possible harm to the employees, the government, and the public. President Reagan's drug testing order specified the testing methods to be used and also specified certain groups of employees to be subjected to testing. The court examined each method and each of the groups separately.

Because the methods involved very private functions, the court noted that the government must have a great need for testing each group. The government proposed testing employees with top-secret security clearances and motor vehicle operators, as well as testing any employee after any accident or upon reasonable suspicion. Employees with top-secret clearances were subjects of a recent U.S. Court of Appeals decision (*Harmon v. Thornburgh*, 878 F.2d 484), holding that the government's interests outweighed the privacy interest of the individuals. Likewise, the public safety interest is of more importance than individual privacy interests with respect to motor vehicle operators. However, the court notified the government that it must narrow this category to exclude employees who drive infrequently. The standard for testing an employee involved in an accident was also found to involve more employees than was necessary. Next, reasonable suspicion testing was addressed. Again, the court found this proposed standard to be overbroad, and cited numerous problems. High among the court's concerns was that the government would be in violation of the Fourth Amendment when testing based on off-duty suspicion absent an on-duty impairment. The court denied the proposed injunction to halt drug testing of the top-secret clearance employees and motor vehicle operators, and granted the injunction halting drug testing after accidents and for reasonable suspicion. *American Federation of Government Employees v. Sullivan*, 744 F.Supp. 294 (D.D.C.1990).

C. Testing and Unemployment Benefits

A Pennsylvania man worked for a transit authority as a bus driver for over five years. He was then discharged for "discourtesy and conduct unbecoming a SEPTA employee." He was later reinstated on the condition that he successfully complete a standard reinstatement medical exam, including a drug screen. The reinstatement was made pursuant to a union-employer negotiated agreement. He returned to work, but was removed from his route that same day and informed he had failed the drug screen. The results showed traces of cocaine in his urine. He was then discharged for violating the authority's drug policy and for failure to pass a drug screening test. Upon applying for unemployment benefits, the driver was denied benefits since his discharge was based on "willful misconduct." The driver sued, asserting that he could not be denied benefits for willful misconduct when the discharge was pursuant to an unconstitutional policy. He also claimed that he could not be denied benefits for willful misconduct based on his failure to pass the drug screen without evidence of job impairment.

The Pennsylvania Commonwealth Court disagreed and upheld the denial of unemployment benefits. The bus driver had waived his Fourth Amendment rights by voluntarily submitting to the urine test. Additionally, as shown in *Skinner v. Railway Labor Executives Ass'n* and *Nat'l Treasury Employees Union v. Von Raab*, drug-testing as a precondition to a safety-related public service position is reasonable. The court also held that evidence of job impairment was unnecessary to deny benefits on grounds of willful misconduct. *Singleton v. Unemployment Comp. Bd. of Review*, 558 A.2d 574 (Pa.Cmwlth.1989).

A Florida sheriff's department initiated a program requiring urinalysis for all new employees. It did not have a policy requiring employees who were under suspicion of drug use to submit to a test, nor did it have a random testing program. It did have a policy forbidding off-duty drug use by its employees and it was a general requirement that all employees obey lawful orders as required or directed by superiors. Two supervisors noted adverse changes in a dispatcher who worked in the department. The supervisors suspected drug abuse. Later, the department received an affidavit from a person who was involved in a disturbance at the dispatcher's apartment. The affiant claimed that he had seen the dispatcher snorting lines of cocaine in her apartment. The sheriff ordered the dispatcher to submit to a urinalysis test. She was immediately suspended. The dispatcher refused to be tested, and consulted an attorney. The sheriff sent the dispatcher a letter inviting her to furnish him with a reason why she should not be discharged. She did not respond, and her employment was terminated. An appeals referee found the discharge unwarranted since the sheriff's department had no testing policy in place and had not made testing a condition of continued employment. The referee held that the dispatcher was entitled to unemployment compensation since the refusal to submit to this test was not misconduct. The Florida Unemployment Appeals Commission reversed the referee's award, stating that the dispatcher's refusal to submit to the sheriff's order was misconduct. The dispatcher appealed to the District Court of Appeal of Florida.

The court of appeal stated that drug testing based on a reasonable suspicion that an employee was using drugs was legitimate. The court said that in this case, the suspicion was reasonable. Since the test was legitimate, failure to submit to the test, after being warned that such a refusal may result in dismissal, constituted a deliberate disregard of the employer's interests. As such, it was misconduct. The court of appeal affirmed the commission's denial of unemployment benefits. *Fowler v. Unemployment Appeals Commission*, 537 So.2d 162 (Fla.App.1989).

A Florida city engineer's drug use came to his employer's attention. The employee, with the city's assistance, enrolled in a treatment program. However, the engineer was discharged from the program because of a disputed drug test result. The engineer was allowed to return to work under the condition that he submit to random drug testing, and also on the condition that any positive drug test result would result in his voluntary resignation. The city later advised the engineer that one of his drug tests proved positive for cocaine use and that he was being terminated. Subsequently, a claims adjudicator determined that the engineer was qualified for unemployment compensation benefits. The Florida Unemployment Appeals Commission (UAC) affirmed on the grounds that there was insufficient evidence that the engineer had tested positive for cocaine use. The city appealed to the District Court of Appeals of Florida.

The court stated that the sole evidence against the engineer was a lab report procured by the city. No one from the laboratory was called as a witness to establish the lab report as a business record, the only way such a report could be entered into evidence under Florida's hearsay rule. Since the report was hearsay, it could not alone be sufficient to prove the engineer's cocaine use. As such, the engineer was entitled to unemployment compensation. *Fort Lauderdale v. Unemployment Appeals Commission,* 536 So.2d 1074 (Fla.App.1988).

A Massachusetts city had a policy of subjecting firefighter probationary recruits to urinalysis at random times during their training. A recent graduate of the city's training program was required to provide a urine sample when he reported for duty. He was fired after his urine tested positive for cocaine. The employee then sued the city manager and the chief of the fire department for violation of his civil rights as guaranteed by the state. A Massachusetts trial court held that the city manager was immune from suit under state law, but that the chief of the fire department did not qualify for such immunity. The chief and the employee both appealed to the Supreme Judicial Court of Massachusetts.

The supreme court agreed that qualified immunity existed for the city manager. It concluded that the state legislature intended for public employees to have the same immunity against state civil rights claims as they do for claims brought under 42 U.S.C. § 1983. It stated that public officials are not liable for their discretionary acts under a civil rights claim unless they have violated a right which was clearly established at the time. However, it was not clearly established at the time of the employee's urinalysis that drug testing violated constitutional rights. The supreme court ruled that the acts of the city manager in formulating the policy were discretionary, and he was therefore immune from the employee's suit. The chief's acts were also discretionary because he was a subordinate carrying out official directions. Both the city manager and the chief were immune from the employee's termination suit. *Duarte v. Healy*, 537 N.E.2d 1230 (Mass.1989).

In 1988, the Urban Mass Transportation Administration (UMTA) issued regulations to require recipients of federal mass transit funds to implement an anti-drug program for employees who perform sensitive safety functions. The required anti-drug program included urinalysis testing of employees prior to employment, after an accident, when reasonable suspicion of drug use exists, randomly, and before returning to duty after a positive drug test. The union and transit employees filed suit in a federal district court. They challenged UMTA's statutory authority to enforce a testing program. The district court concluded that UMTA had the authority to specify the particular elements of the plan to deal with an identified safety hazard. The labor organization and the individual employees appealed to the U.S. Court of Appeals, District of Columbia.

The issue was whether Congress intended to permit UMTA to address mass transit safety hazards by imposing a uniform national solution. The court determined that a close reading of the act revealed that Congress did not grant UMTA the statutory authority to instigate general safety regulations. The act permitted UMTA to investigate conditions within its authority which created a serious hazard. Once the investigation was completed, however, the statute explicitly stated that the local public body had the responsibility for drafting a plan to eliminate any identified hazard. Congress chose not to give UMTA direct regulatory authority over urban mass transit safety to the extent that would justify imposing the mandatory drug testing program. The court of appeals reversed the district court's decision with instructions to vacate the anti-drug program. *Amalgamated Transit Union v. Skinner*, 894 F.2d 1362 (D.C.Cir.1990).

The Nebraska Public Power District (NPPD) is a public corporation and political subdivision of the state. It owned a nuclear power plant which, like all nuclear power plants, was heavily regulated by the Nuclear Regulatory Commission. The NRC maintained resident inspectors at the plant and periodically sent teams to review the plant's security. Access to the plant was restricted, but once inside, a person was free to move about unescorted. The NPPD adopted a drug-testing program in response to a number of developments. First, the NRC required the adoption of a drug-testing program. Second, the NRC reported an increase in the number of drug-related accidents at nuclear power plants, including alcohol use by guards at the Nebraska plant. Finally, at the time of the issuance of the NRC rule and report, the plant was temporarily shut down. The plant's managers feared the plant would not be allowed to reopen absent assurance that the personnel were drug-free. The plant's program called for the testing of all employees with access to protected areas of the plant. The plan called for preemployment, pretransfer, annual, and "for-cause" testing. If a positive result was obtained, the employee was given an opportunity to appeal and take a second confirmation test. Later, the plan was modified to include random testing. Two employees who visited the plant six to seven hours per month refused to comply with the test and were fired as a result. A federal district court held for the plant and the employees appealed to the U.S. Court of Appeals, Eighth Circuit.

On appeal, the employees argued that the drug-testing program violated their First Amendment right to the free exercise of their religion. The employees did not object to urinalysis itself, but rather to a statement made by the plant's program: "Alcoholism is recognized as an illness for which there is treatment and rehabilitation." The employees were conservative Christians who believed alcoholism is a sin, not an illness. They argued that by participating in the program they would be giving their support to a heretical idea. They also claimed that the program violated their Fourth Amendment right to be free from unreasonable searches. The court, however, affirmed the judgment against the employees. The court stated that the plant's program was the least restrictive method of assuring the safe operation of the power plant. The burden on the religious beliefs of the employees was insufficient to outweigh the need for the program, or to exempt them from it. The court also accepted the Third Circuit's standard set out in *Shoemaker v. Handel*, and held that the search was not unreasonable under the Fourth Amendment. *Rushton v. Neb. Pub. Power Dist.*, 844 F.2d 562 (8th Cir.1988).

The Philadelphia police commissioner issued a directive establishing a drug detection policy with guidelines and procedures for screening officers by urinalysis. The testing was limited to routine physical exams and situations in which there was a reasonable suspicion of illegal drug use. Routine exams were scheduled in cases of promotion, reinstatement, return from extended leave, transfer and special assignment. A labor organization representing Philadelphia police officers sought an order from a Pennsylvania court to prevent the commissioner from implementing the program. The court ruled for the commissioner and the association appealed to the Pennsylvania Commonwealth Court.

On appeal, the association argued that the program could not be implemented because it was issued as a directive rather than a civil service regulation. The commissioner responded that it had complied with Pennsylvania law by publishing a detailed written notice in advance of the testing regulations. The commonwealth court agreed with the commissioner, finding no requirement that police department procedures be subject to civil service regulations. There was no probability that the association would prevail on the merits of the case and the trial court had properly denied the association's request for an injunction. Alternatively, an adequate legal remedy existed for the police officers, who could avail themselves of a grievance procedure for adverse decisions under the program. *FOP Lodge No. 5 v. City of Philadelphia*, 557 A.2d 805 (Pa.Cmwlth.1989).

An Illinois police officer's girlfriend told the police department that the officer smoked marijuana both on and off duty. Although she later recanted the allegation, the department ordered the officer to submit to a urine test. His urine tested positive for marijuana. After a hearing, the police board discharged the officer for violating its rules against illegal conduct. The officer then challenged the urine testing in an Illinois trial court which found for the officer, ruling that the board had not established a chain of custody for the urine specimen. The court questioned whether the specimen was safe-guarded while it was transported from the police department to the testing laboratory. The police board then appealed to the Appellate Court of Illinois.

The board argued that it had sufficiently established the specimen's chain of custody. It had presented the testimony of each person who had control of the specimen during the testing procedure. The officer contended that the person who transported the specimen to the testing lab did not testify and therefore there was no evidence that the seal had not been tampered with during that time. The appellate court reversed the trial court's reinstatement of the officer. It ruled that the board had only to demonstrate that reasonable protective measures were taken to ensure that the urine taken from the officer was the same as that tested in the laboratory. Mere speculation that the specimen had been altered was not enough to invalidate the testing procedure. The court held that the board had sufficiently established a chain of custody and affirmed the officer's dismissal. *Williamson v. Police Bd. of Chicago*, 537 N.E.2d 1058 (Ill.App.1st Dist.1989).

The Washington Metropolitan Area Transit Authority (WMATA) formulated rules which required all employees who were involved in on-the-job accidents or unusual operating incidents to be tested for the presence of alcohol, illicit drugs, and other controlled substances in their systems. Blood tests were taken to determine the presence of alcohol. Two urine tests were performed to test for illicit or controlled substances. Eighteen employees who had been involved in on-the-job incidents and had tested positive sued in a federal district court, claiming that they had been negligently discharged from their employment. They also claimed violation of their Fourth and Fourteenth Amendment rights, deprivation of their right to privacy, violation of the Rehabilitation Act of 1973, and violation of 42 U.S.C. § 1983. WMATA asked the district court for summary judgment. The district court granted the request, concluding that WMATA was entitled to invoke immunity under the Eleventh Amendment because the activity involved a governmental function as to which WMATA's immunity had not been waived. The employees appealed to the U.S. Court of Appeals, District of Columbia Circuit.

The court of appeals held that WMATA was immune from suit on all the employees' constitutional and 1983 claims. Since these are general attacks on the testing plan itself, and not on the manner of particular cases, it would require judicial "second guessing" of governmental regulatory functions. The court stated that the remaining claim for negligent termination also was properly dismissed. Fourteen of the employees had already pursued administrative review under their collective bargaining agreement with WMATA and had been granted some relief. The other four had never sought administrative review and could not now ask for redress in court on claims that could have been grieved. *Sanders v. WMATA*, 819 F.2d 1151 (D.C.Cir.1987).

CHAPTER TWO
TERMINATION AND SUSPENSION

I. DUE PROCESS: PROPERTY AND LIBERTY INTERESTS

The Due Process Clause of the fourteenth Amendment provides that no state shall "deprive any person of life, liberty or property, without due process of law." In order to establish that a termination or suspension violates an employee's constitutional rights, the employee must first establish that he or she has a liberty or property interest in continued employment. As *Board of Regents v. Roth* and *Perry v. Sindermann,* below, illustrate, a property interest must be more than a mere expectation of continued employment. An employee must show a legitimate claim of entitlement to it or, as in *Perry*, a common understanding between employer and employee.

The Wisconsin state university system hired an assistant professor under a one-year contract. As the year drew to a close, the university notified the professor that his contract would not be renewed. The notice conformed to university rules, which did not require any reason for nonretention or any hearing for the teacher. Wisconsin tenure law required teachers to have four years of service before becoming "permanent" employees. The teacher sued the state college board in a federal district court, alleging that he was being terminated for making critical statements about university administrators. The teacher also claimed that the failure of university officials to give any reason for nonretention violated his procedural due process rights. The court held for the teacher on his due process claim and the U.S. Court of Appeals, Seventh Circuit, affirmed this decision. The U.S. Supreme Court agreed to hear the university board's petition.

In dismissing the teacher's due process claims, the Supreme Court stated that no liberty interest was implicated because in declining to rehire the teacher, the university had not made any charge against him such as incompetence or immorality. Such a charge would have made it difficult for the teacher to gain employment elsewhere and thus would have deprived him of liberty. As no reason was given for the nonrenewal of his contract, the teacher's liberty interest in future employment was not impaired and he was not entitled to a hearing on these grounds. The Court declared that because the teacher had not acquired tenure he possessed no property interest in continued employment at the university. The teacher had a property interest in employment during the term of his one-year contract, but upon expiration the interest ceased to exist. The Court stated: "To have a property interest in a benefit, a person clearly must have more than an abstract need or desire for it. He must have more than a unilateral expectation of it. He must, instead, have a legitimate claim of entitlement to it." Because the teacher's contract secured no interest in reemployment for the following year, he had no property interest in reemployment. The Court reversed the lower court decisions and remanded the case. *Board of Regents v. Roth,* 408 U.S. 564, 92 S.Ct. 2701, 33 L.Ed.2d 548 (1972).

A Texas junior college employed a professor for four years under a series of one-year contracts. At the end of his fourth year, he was not rehired. He was not given a reason for his nonrenewal, and the college did not offer him a hearing to challenge its decision. He sued in a federal district court, asserting that his due process rights had been violated. The court ruled for the college and he appealed successfully to the U.S. Court of Appeals. The college then appealed to the U.S. Supreme Court. The Supreme Court ruled that although the professor was not tenured, he might still have a due process right to a hearing. If the professor could show that a common understanding existed which essentially made him a tenured professor, then he had a property interest sufficient to require a hearing. The Court affirmed the court of appeals' decision, and remanded the case to the district court to determine if such a mutual understanding of continued employment existed between the college and the professor. *Perry v. Sindermann*, 408 U.S. 593, 92 S.Ct. 2717, 33 L.Ed.2d 570 (1972).

A Virginia deputy sheriff was dismissed from the sheriff's department in 1987. He received no formal written notice of the reasons for his dismissal and no hearing was held. The deputy sheriff then sought to have his dismissal heard through a grievance procedure, as called for in the employee handbook. The sheriff responded that the grievance procedures in the handbook were inapplicable to deputy sheriffs. The deputy sheriff then instituted an action in federal district court alleging deprivation of constitutional due process rights. The court granted summary judgment to the sheriff, stating that the deputy sheriff had no protectable property interest in continued employment. The deputy sheriff appealed the case to the U.S. Court of Appeals, Fourth Circuit.

In Virginia, a sheriff is an independent constitutional officer whose duties and authorities are defined by statute. State law is clear that a sheriff's deputies are terminated at will and serve at the discretion of the sheriff. The Virginia Code makes a deputy an employee of the sheriff, not an employee of the local governing body, and provides that he may be removed from office by the sheriff. The deputy sheriff claimed that the sheriff's adoption of the employee handbook gave rise to a constitutionally protectable interest. To support such a claim state law must provide a sufficient expectation of continued employment.The appellate court found insufficient expectation here and agreed with the trial court in determining that the sheriff's adoption of the employee handbook did not give rise to a constitutionally protectable interest. *Jenkins v. Weatherholtz*, 909 F.2d 105 (4th Cir.1990).

The mayor of a city in Georgia obtained the fire chief's affidavit in an investigation aimed at discharging the city clerk. In a later hearing, the chief testified that he had made false accusations against the clerk under duress because the mayor had threatened his job. After the city clerk was reinstated, the mayor began an investigation of the chief. The investigation produced a list of unsubstantiated charges and the chief was dismissed without a pretermination hearing. The chief claimed that he was improperly discharged as well as denied due process and sued the mayor and the city in a federal district court.

The court needed to determine whether the fire chief had a property interest in continued employment. If so, a pretermination hearing would be required. A city ordinance allows termination of a fire chief only for failing to perform to the standards of the position. The court found the ordinance analogous to allowing termination only for cause. This created a property interest in continued employment and an entitlement to a pretermination hearing. After this determination, the court examined the city's monetary liability for denial of due process. The city would be liable if the mayor was found to be following, or had the power to create, city policy. All of the mayor's decisions were subject to review by the city council. The court rejected the chief's argument that the mayor effectively had policy making authority because the council's custom was to follow the mayor's decision. The court found that the chief was entitled to a pretermination hearing, but that the city was not monetarily liable for the mayor's actions. *Payung v. Williamson,* 747 F.Supp. 705 (M.D.Ga 1990).

A Chicago firefighter suffered injuries to his back, head and neck while fighting a fire. The injuries forced him into an extended medical leave. One year later, the firefighter's doctor informed the fire department that the firefighter remained physically unable to return to work. Despite his inability to return to active duty, the firefighter received full pay for a year following his injuries. After the year was up, the department removed him from the active payroll, and notified him that he could apply for pension benefits. He was granted disability benefits equal to seventy-five percent of his salary at the time of disability. He then sued the city and the fire department in a federal district court, asserting that his due process rights had been violated.

The city acknowledged that all its firefighters possessed a property right in their continued employment. A municipal ordinance provided that firefighters could only be discharged when there was just cause for their dismissal. However, the city asserted that the firefighter was currently on the inactive roll of the fire department and had not been terminated. The court agreed with the city, finding that the firefighter would be reinstated to the active payroll if and when he became physically capable of performing a firefighter's duties. Since he had not been discharged, the court held that his claim essentially amounted to a deprivation of his full salary. However, the court determined that he had no property interest in continuing to receive his salary. Since he was unable to return to work, he was only entitled to disability pay. The court found no due process violations, and ruled for the city. *Schroeder v. City of Chicago,* 726 F.Supp. 1142 (N.D.Ill.1989).

An engineer for the Indiana Department of Highways (IDOH) was reprimanded in writing for discussing business matters outside the IDOH. A less than satisfactory performance appraisal followed. The engineer then conducted a performance appraisal of a subordinate, and this appraisal was alleged to be inflated. Demotion was recommended for the engineer. A predemotional hearing before an administrative law judge (ALJ) resulted in a recommendation of demotion, and that recommendation was accepted by the IDOH. The engineer claimed that his position was vested with a property interest and that the true reason for demotion amounted to a restriction of free speech. He also petitioned for judicial review in the Court of Appeals of Indiana.

The court explained that a legislature may decide not to confer a property interest in a position of public employment. After examining the relevant status and the employee handbook, the court agreed with the ALJ that the engineer held no property interest in his position. The engineer was not entitled to a warning, improvement plan, or probationary period. He was only entitled to a predemotional hearing. which he had received. Turning to the free speech issue, the court noted that internal office affairs are not always protected free speech. The topic of the engineer's speech was not found to be of vital public interest. Accordingly, the speech was not granted protection. Even if the speech had been the true reason for his demotion, the court found that this was allowable. The ALJ's findings were upheld. *Phegley v. Indiana Dep't of Highways*, 564 N.E.2d 291 (Ind.App. lst Dist.1990).

An Oregon elementary school principal was employed under a probationary employment contract. The district school board voted to dismiss him. It gave him a letter stating the reasons for dismissal, but did not publicly disclose them. The principal was formally notified of his dismissal and his right to have a posttermination hearing upon request. He never requested a hearing, but sued the district in an Oregon federal district court, claiming the dismissal was in violation of 42 U.S,C. § 1983 and the Due Process Clause. The district court entered summary judgment for the school district, and the principal appealed to the U.S. Court of Appeals, Ninth Circuit. The appellate court noted that procedural due process only applies where a person has been deprived of a liberty or property interest. The principal's dismissal implicated no liberty interest since the reasons for his dismissal were not disclosed to the public and did not jeopardize his interest in future employment. The court of appeals affirmed the district court's decision. *Hayes v. Phoenix-Talent School Dist.*, 893 F.2d 235 (9th Cir.1990).

An Alaska city manager ordered cash payments to himself representing compensation for unused accrued vacation and sick leave time. He claimed his subordinates had told him the city permitted this. He later gave the city 30 days' written notice prior to his resignation, as required by his contract. The contract also required the city to give him 30 days' notice if it wished to terminate him. Two days after this notice, the city council met at the mayor's house to discuss the cash payments and the resignation. The city manager was invited, but declined to attend. They then scheduled a special meeting for the following day, which he apparently did not know about, and at that time voted to terminate his employment immediately and to seek reimbursement of the cash payments he had received in excess of his entitlement. The city then sued him for reimbursement in an Alaska trial court, and he countersued, alleging a violation of his due process rights. The court held for the city, and he appealed to the Supreme Court of Alaska.

The supreme court ruled that the "30 day notice" requirement created a property interest which was protectable by law. It found that the city manager had not been given due process because he had been terminated prior to the 30 days necessary under the contract. However, it held that the city was entitled to recover the excess monies paid to him. The court affirmed that part of the trial court's decision, but reversed on the due process claim, and required that the city either pay him wages for the 27 days for which he had been deprived, or conduct a hearing to show why he had been discharged in violation of the contract. *Breeden v. City of Nome,* 628 P.2d 924 (Alaska 1981).

An Illinois woman was elected to a four year term as village clerk of an Illinois village. When the woman was sworn in as clerk the salary was $37,060 per year. Shortly after the woman won the election the Board of Trustees of the city enacted a new ordinance which created the office of village collector at a salary of $100 per year. The woman who had been elected to the office of village clerk was also designated to hold the office of village collector. The new ordinance did not reinstate the office of village clerk, thus, that office was eliminated and only the office of village collector existed. The woman brought a § 1983 action against the village, certain trustees and the village president. The woman alleged that the city had violated her First Amendment rights and deprived her of a property interest in a job as clerk without due process of law. Further, the woman alleged the the ordinance which essentially repealed the village clerkship was in retaliation for the woman's speeches in support of nonpartisan elections in the city. A federal district court ruled in favor of the village, and the woman appealed to the U.S. Court of Appeals, Seventh Circuit.

The court of appeals found that to prevail under the due process clause and the employment contracts the woman must establish a property interest in the employment. The woman must have more than an abstract need or desire for the position. She must have a legitimate claim of entitlement to the position. The appellate court stated that the village did not violate any of the woman's rights. Further, the employee had failed to show sufficient facts to support her First Amendment claim. It affirmed the district court's decision that the woman had no right to her continuance in the office of clerk. Thus, the woman had no recognizable property interest protected by the Fourteenth Amendment. The court affirmed the district court's decision. *Wolf v. Larson,* 897 F.2d 1409 (7th Cir.1990).

A New Hampshire man worked as a night guardian at a youth development center. One night, after he had conducted a bed check and was talking with his co-worker, eight "highly delinquent" juveniles escaped. He was asked to appear before an investigation commission in an effort by the center to determine how the escape had occurred. He was assured that the purpose of the interview was not to discipline him. However, he refused to answer questions without his lawyer being present and left the room after being warned not to leave. The center dismissed him for willful insubordination, and he appealed to the Supreme Court of New Hampshire.

The supreme court ruled first that public employment in New Hampshire is not a constitutionally protected property right of the employee. The court further ruled that since there was no rule or law which entitled the employee to have a lawyer present at such an interview, the employee had no right to demand this. The court upheld the employee's dismissal for insubordination. *Appeal of Parker*, 437 A.2d 283 (N.H.1981).

A Missouri city hired a man as a garbage truck driver. He worked in the street and alley maintenance department for 10 years as an employee at will. The employee's supervisor conducted a meeting in November of 1984 between himself and his employees. At the meeting, the man behaved in an insubordinate manner, and his supervisor decided to terminate his employment. After an investigation and meetings between the supervisor, the mayor and the city administrator, the city administrator met with the employee and eventually dismissed him for insubordinate conduct. He sued for wrongful discharge in a Missouri trial court. After the court ruled for the city, he appealed to the Missouri Court of Appeals.

On appeal, he argued that he could only be terminated for cause, and only with proper notice and a chance for a hearing. The court disagreed, ruling that as an at-will employee, the city could discharge him "at any time, without cause or reason, or for any reason." Further, the court held that he could not successfully bring an action for wrongful discharge against the city because he had no contractual right in continued employment. A hearing was not necessary for the discharge of such an employee. The court affirmed the trial court's decision, and upheld the man's dismissal. *Moon v. City of Sedalia*, 723 S.W.2d 597 (Mo.App.1987).

A North Carolina woman was hired as a social worker trainee. Eleven months later, she was told her employment would be terminated, and was given a letter stating that her performance was not up to the required level of the social services department. She requested and received a hearing where she presented witnesses and made a statement on her own behalf. Nevertheless, her dismissal was upheld. She then sued unsuccessfully in a North Carolina trial court, and appealed to the Court of Appeals of North Carolina.

The appellate court first noted that without a legitimate claim to job tenure, an employee can be dismissed without hearing or cause, so long as the reason is not unconstitutional. In this case, the employee was in a trainee position. The state did not confer any tenure or protectable property interest on her, so her claim of due process violations was not valid. Further, the court held that she need not even have been given a hearing upon her dismissal. The court affirmed the trial court, finding that the employee had no protectable interest in continued employment. *Yow v. Alexander County Dep't of Social Servs.*, 319 S.E.2d 626 (N.C.App.1984).

A North Carolina man, employed by the department of transportation, was involved in an accident while driving a state owned truck. An investigation revealed that he had been exceeding a safe speed, and that he had been out of his work area without proper authorization at the time of the accident. He was discharged. In accordance with the department's personnel manual, he presented his case to a five member committee. The committee recommended reinstatement, but the department head upheld dismissal. The employee asked for judicial review in a North Carolina trial court, which dismissed the case, and he appealed to the Court of Appeals of North Carolina.

The appellate court first stated that it was without jurisdiction and that the case had been properly dismissed. It further noted that even if it did have jurisdiction, the employee did not have a protectable property or liberty interest. Unless he had been employed for five years or more at the time of the accident, the state could terminate his employment at will. He had no automatic tenure by virtue of public employment. Since he had been employed for less than five years, he had no protectable interest. Finally, the court held that the department head was not required to abide by the committee's recommendation in determining whether to reinstate the employee. The department was free to agree or disagree with the committee. The court affirmed the trial court's decision, and upheld the employee's dismissal. *Dyer v. Bradshaw*, 282 S.E.2d 548 (N.C.App.1981).

The superintendent of a South Carolina school district had an employment contract with the school board by which he was to be employed as a superintendent until June 30, 1983. However, on January 11, 1983, he was notified by the board that effective immediately he was being relieved of his duties. The board stated that he would receive full pay and benefits until June 30, the date of the expiration of his contract. No reasons were given by the board for its decision. The superintendent brought suit against the board under the federal civil rights laws, contending that he should have been allowed to perform his duties until June 30. He asserted that he possessed a property right under the Fourteenth Amendment to continue in his capacity as superintendent, due to the fact that his contract did not expire until June 30. The U.S. Court of Appeals, Fourth Circuit, disagreed. The superintendent did possess the right to full monetary compensation under the terms of his contract, stated the court, but he possessed no property right in the actual performance of his duties. All that is required when a school district employee is dismissed for reasons outside the contract is that the employee be compensated in full for the duration of his contract. The court held that the superintendent had no right to continue performing his duties. *Royster v. Bd. of Trustees*, 774 F.2d 618 (4th Cir.1985).

A principal employed by a school district under a two year contract, sued the school district when his contract was not renewed. The principal claimed that Texas's term contract nonrenewal act created a property interest in continued employment beyond his contract term. He claimed that he had been deprived of the interest without due process of law. A federal district court dismissed the principal's claims, holding that he had no property interest in continued employment. The principal appealed to the U.S. Court of Appeals, Fifth Circuit. The court of appeals held that the act did not create a property interest in continued employment beyond the contract term for Texas teachers employed under term contracts. The act creates procedural safeguards for teachers whose contracts are not being renewed, and such procedural safeguards do not create a property interest. The court of appeals affirmed the trial court's decision. *English v. Hairston*, 888 F.2d 1069 (5th Cir.1989).

A Virginia school board removed its school superintendent for ineffective leadership and failure to carry out directives. The school board agreed upon the superintendent's removal in a closed executive session, giving no notice to the superintendent that his removal would be discussed. The board then held a public meeting and removed the superintendent. The superintendent appealed the school board decision to a Virginia trial court where he complained of constitutional violations including failure of the school board to afford him procedural due process and deprivation of his constitutional liberty interests. The trial court granted the superintendent's summary judgment motion and ordered the school district to reinstate the superintendent or give him a new hearing. The school board appealed the reinstatement to the Supreme Court of Virginia and simultaneously allowed the new hearing directed by the trial court. New charges were made at the hearing including improper expenditure of school funds, neglect of maintenance and failure to carry out school board directives. The school board again voted to remove the superintendent. The superintendent again appealed to a trial court and received a favorable decision. On the school board's appeal the Supreme Court of Virginia noted that employee discharges do not involve constitutional liberty interests unless the employer makes specific charges of "moral turpitude, criminal activity, or serious character defects." In this case the school board had not made charges which might seriously damage the superintendent's reputation in the community. Although a Virginia statute requires a new trial by reviewing trial courts, Virginia courts should not disturb school board decisions unless the board acted in bad faith or clearly made a mistake. The evidence of improper expenditure of school funds, neglect of school buildings and failure to carry out school board directives were sufficient to support the superintendent's dismissal. *Bristol Virginia School Bd. v. Quarles*, 366 S.E.2d 82 (Va.1988).

A Colorado school warehouse foreman was a classified employee. He received a classified employees' handbook from the school district which stated that the district would discharge classified employees only for good cause after attempts to improve employee performance by progressive discipline. After the foreman returned from a leave of absence, the district fired him. He then sued the district in a Colorado trial court, alleging breach of contract and deprivation of property without due process of law in violation of 42 U.S.C. § 1983. After the trial court dismissed both of the foreman's claims, he appealed to the Colorado Court of Appeals.

On appeal, the school district maintained that the employee handbook did not create an employment contract. The court reversed the trial court's decision, ruling that the employee handbook given to the foreman may have created an employment contract requiring termination only for good cause. The court concluded that an employee who cannot be suspended except for cause has a property interest in continued employment. Deprivation of this property interest by the school district without procedural due process as guaranteed by the Fourteenth Amendment gives rise to a claim under § 1983. The court ruled that the foreman must be given a trial and remanded the case. *Dickey v. Adams Cty. School Dist. No. 50*, 773 P.2d 585 (Colo.App.1988).

A man was hired as a police officer in 1968 and was promoted to second in command and the rank of captain in the early 1970s. The captain began to experience difficulty in satisfactorily completing his duties. Three successive chiefs of police reported that the captain experienced problems in meeting deadlines, understanding duties, following directives, and was often found to be sleeping or not locatable while on-duty. The officer also was obese, and would not remain on weight loss programs as ordered. The captain was demoted and later discharged. The chief listed reasons for the demotion and discharge, which included being overweight. The captain unsuccessfully appealed to a state administrative panel, and later filed suit in a federal district court. The captain alleged that the chief had violated his due process and equal protection rights.

The captain's first claim concerned his demotion and alleged that he was deprived of a property interest in his supervisory position without procedural due process. The court ruled that the captain held an interest in employment, but not to a certain position; no procedural due process was necessary. The captain next claimed his discharge unlawfully deprived him of a liberty interest in his good reputation. The court disagreed; the captain was afforded an opportunity for a hearing, cross-examination, and a chance to present evidence and arguments. The captain lastly claimed that his right to equal protection was violated as a result of his demotion for being overweight. The court found that this claim failed for three reasons. First, there was found to be just cause for demotion concerning the captain's performance of his duties. Second, evidence showed that other overweight officers were subject to weight loss programs. Third, the court felt that the chief could hold an officer who was second in command to higher standards. Higher standards or regulations must be rationally related to a legitimate public concern, and the chief's concern over respect for the department and for the position of second in command was found valid. The court entered judgment for the city. *Johnson v. City of Tarpon Springs*, 758 F.Supp. 1473 (M.D.Fla.1991).

A Rhode Island man was hired as the supervisor of the state law enforcement telecommunications unit. Over a year later, his supervisor dismissed him "for the good of the service." Although the position was an unclassified civil service position, which meant that it was terminable at-will, the employee asserted that his dismissal was unlawful, and sued in a Rhode Island trial court. He maintained that he had been deprived of a property interest, a liberty interest, and that he had been discriminatorily discharged. The trial court dismissed his claim, and he appealed to the Supreme Court of Rhode Island.

The supreme court held that as an unclassified civil service employee, regardless of what he had been told about continued employment, he was an at-will employee. It also stated that his mere dismissal, without a public statement of the reasons for his discharge, could not be a violation of his liberty interest. Finally, the court determined that the employee's discrimination claim failed because he did not show a conspiracy intended to deprive him of equal protection under the law, which was motivated by a class-based or racial animus. The court affirmed the trial court's decision, and dismissed the employee's claims. *Salisbury v. Stone,* 518 A.2d 1355 (R.I.1986).

An Arkansas man worked for the state department of human services and eventually became the director of a county office. However, the department then began receiving complaints about the services provided by that county office, and it began an investigation into the director's administration of the office. After finding nineteen alleged violations or irregularities in the running of the office, the department notified the director of its decision to terminate his employment. After his termination, the director appealed to a hearing officer, who reversed the decision to terminate him. A meeting was then held, and the department again decided to terminate the director. He appealed to a federal district court, which ruled that he had both a property and a liberty interest which had been violated. The department then appealed to the U.S. Court of Appeals, Eighth Circuit.

The appellate court stated that the director did not have a property interest in his continued employment because he was an at-will employee. However, the court agreed that the director had a liberty interest because he had shown that the reasons for his discharge stigmatized him. The court noted that unless those reasons had been made public, the director could not recover damages for the violation of his liberty interest. Further, it ruled that the director would have to show that the reasons for his discharge were false in order to recover damages. The court reversed the trial court's decision, and remanded the case to the trial court for a determination of the liberty interest issue. *Hogue v. Clinton*, 791 F.2d 1318 (8th Cir.1986).

II. PRETERMINATION DUE PROCESS RIGHTS

Generally, where an employee has a protectable property interest, the employer must provide a hearing of some sort before discharging the employee. The extent of the hearing necessary will be determined by the extent of the posttermination process available. Usually, notice of the charges against the employee and a chance to reply to them will be sufficient so long as a posttermination hearing is held.

Ohio law protected all civil service employees from dismissal except for "misfeasance, malfeasance, or nonfeasance in office." Employees who were terminated for cause were entitled to an order of removal stating the reasons for termination. Unfavorable orders could be appealed to a state administrative board whose determinations were subject to state court review. A security guard hired by a school board stated on his job application that he had never been convicted of a felony. Upon discovering that he had in fact been convicted of grand larceny, the school board dismissed him for dishonesty in filling out the job application. He was not afforded an opportunity to respond to the dishonesty charge or to challenge the dismissal until nine months later. In a second case, a school bus mechanic was fired because he had failed an eye examination. The mechanic appealed his dismissal because he had not been afforded a pretermination hearing. A federal district court rejected both of the employees' claims and they appealed to the U.S. Court of Appeals, Sixth Circuit, which reversed the district court's decisions. The U.S. Supreme Court consolidated the appeals by the school districts.

The Supreme Court held that the employees possessed a property right in their employment and were entitled to a pretermination opportunity to respond to the dismissal charges against them. The pretermination hearing, stated the Court, need not resolve the propriety of the discharge, but should be a check against mistaken decisions essentially a determination of whether there are reasonable grounds to believe that the charges against the employee are true and support the proposed action. The Supreme Court upheld that portion of the lower court decisions which found that the delay in the guard's administrative proceedings did not constitute a separate constitutional violation. The Due Process Clause requires a hearing "at a meaningful time," and here the delay stemmed in part from the thoroughness of the procedures afforded the guard. On the matter of the right to a pretermination hearing, however, both cases were remanded for further proceedings, consistent with the Court's decision. *Cleveland Board of Education v. Loudermill*, 470 U.S. 532, 105 S.Ct. 1487, 84 L.Ed.2d 494 (1985).

A policeman in a North Carolina city was dismissed by the city manager upon the recommendation of the chief of police. A city ordinance allowed for the termination of a permanent employee, which the officer was, if he failed to perform work up to the standard of his classification. Upon being discharged, the officer sued, asserting that he had a constitutional right to a pretermination hearing. He also argued that he had been deprived of property and liberty interests by his dismissal. The district court ruled against the officer and the court of appeals affirmed. The officer then appealed to the U.S. Supreme Court.

The Supreme Court held that the district court was correct when it concluded that the officer "held his position at the will and pleasure of the city." The Supreme Court also ruled that no liberty interest had been violated because no stigma attached through a public communication. The reasons for the officer's dismissal had been kept private. Also, since he was an at-will employee, he had no property interest to be protected. The court affirmed the lower court decisions, and held that no pretermination hearing had been necessary. *Bishop v. Wood*, 426 U.S. 341, 96 S.Ct. 2074, 48 L.Ed.2d 684 (1976).

An Illinois police officer missed a scheduled court appearance and was ordered to be examined by a doctor. The officer refused and the police chief then notified him that he was suspended without pay. The chief submitted a memorandum which informed the officer that a hearing had been scheduled for the following day at 1 p.,m. to afford the officer an opportunity to show cause why disciplinary action should not be taken. The memorandum charged the officer with violations of sick leave, neglect of duty, and a failure to comply with a lawful order by the chief requiring the officer to be examined by a doctor. The next day the chief and the officer appeared at the meeting but the officer declined to respond to any questions, asking for a continuance in order to have his attorney represent him at the hearing. The chief agreed to a one hour continuance but the officer countered that one hour was not enough since his attorney was in the midst of a trial. The meeting ended and the chief prepared a letter to the officer terminating his employment. The officer then instituted an action in a federal district court alleging that he was denied his right to procedural due process. The trial court granted summary judgment to the defendant. The officer appealed to the U.S. Court of Appeals, Seventh Circuit.

Due process requires that an employee be given oral or written notice of the charges against him, an explanation of the employer's evidence, and an opportunity to present his side of the story. The police officer contended that the receipt of the notice of the pretermination hearing less than a day in advance was insufficient to satisfy the U.S. Supreme Court's notice requirement. He also contended that he was not informed of the rules which he had allegedly violated and that he was not given his constitutional right to counsel at a pretermination hearing. The court, however, ruled against the officer on all counts. It determined that explicit written notice received the night before a scheduled hearing is sufficient. The court also determined that the allegations were sufficient to notify the officer of the evidence on which they were based. In response to the officer's right to counsel, the court determined that an employee has no constitutional right to counsel at a pretermination hearing. Therefore, the court affirmed the district court's decision. *Panozzi v. Rhodas*, 905 F.2d 135 (7th Cir.1990).

A routine traffic stop in Los Angeles resulted in the recovery of a weapon which had been reported stolen from a Mississippi police department. A further trace revealed that the weapon was traded to a pawnbroker by a narcotics officer of that department. The chief of police informed the narcotics investigator of an ongoing criminal investigation, but the officer could not recall where he got the weapon. He guessed that he probably obtained it through a confiscation. The officer feared the stigma of termination, and voluntarily resigned. After no criminal charges were brought, the officer unsuccessfully sought reinstatement. He then filed suit alleging a denial of due process and constructive discharge. The case eventually reached the Supreme Court of Mississippi.

The supreme court first ruled on the due process claims. All disputes concerning any preterminations or appeals hearings were resolved by the court stating that no hearings are available to employees who voluntarily resign. It next noted that a constructive discharge occurs when the employer has made conditions so intolerable that the employee reasonably feels compelled to resign. The court stated that humiliation or embarrassment which results from the criminal investigation will not satisfy this standard. Further, the chief testified that he did not intend to recommend the officer's dismissal. The court found no evident to support the officer's claims of constructive discharge. Earlier dismissals of the claims were upheld. *Bulloch v. City of Pascagoula*, 574 So.2d 637 (Miss.1990).

An Arkansas county deputy sheriff with ten years experience was asked to supply negative information about the incumbent sheriff during an election. The deputy was told by the sheriff's opponent that he would lose his job if he did not comply with the request. The request was denied, and the deputy later received a letter from the newly elected sheriff notifying him of his termination. The sheriff denied the deputy's request for a pretermination hearing. A lawsuit was filed by the deputy for procedural due process violations. A court ordered a pretermination hearing to be held, and awarded backpay until a hearing could be held. The sheriff then appealed to the U.S. Court of Appeals.

The issues reviewed were whether the employee was entitled to a hearing, and if the award of backpay was proper. Arkansas law provides that employment contracts are terminable at will unless a contract or handbook expressly states otherwise. The county handbook in effect stated that termination would be allowed only for cause. The court found that the employee should have been afforded a pretermination hearing. The court then questioned whether an award of backpay was proper. Procedural due process violations were distinguished from other due process violations. Procedural due process violations were defined as a shown absence of a hearing and were to be remedied with nominal damages. Other due process violations are found when employees show an absence of a hearing, and that they would not have been fired if a hearing had been held. These should be remedied with nominal, compensatory, and occasionally punitive damages. The court ruled the the award of backpay was not precluded by current law, and that this award would encourage a policy of suspension with pay until a hearing could be held. The decision of the district court was upheld. *Brewer v. Parkman,* 918 F.2d 1336 (8th Cir.1990).

A married Illinois police officer picked up a seventeen-year-old college student and took her for a ride on his motorcycle. Another policeman saw the college student riding on the motorcycle and he reported what he had seen to the chief of police. The chief obtained a statement from the college student concerning the ride. He mentioned the statement to members of the city council committee but they did not read it. At the meeting, the chief read aloud the incident and the list of charges. After the police officer responded to the charges, the chief gave the committee members a brief written statement that the chief had prepared concerning the police officer's conduct. At the conclusion of the deliberations, the committee voted to suspend the police officer until the next meeting of the city council. The council then voted to discharge the officer, on the ground that the motorcycle incident was damaging to the good relationship the police and the city had with the college. The discharged police officer brought civil rights actions against the city and various individuals involved in his discharge in a federal district court, which dismissed the action. The officer appealed to the U.S. Court of Appeals, Seventh Circuit.

The court felt that the important issue was the officer's right not to be deprived of his job without minimum safeguards. As a tenured employee, the officer had certain procedural rights. He was given an opportunity to respond to the formal charges that the police chief read to the public safety committee, but no opportunity to respond to the written statement that the chief submitted to the committee before he and the officer were excused. Also, the failure to show the college student's statement to the officer and allow him to comment on it was a separate infringement of his rights. Even though the statement was not shown to members of the public safety committee, they relied on it. The committee members had formed the idea that the statement was damaging. The court noted that public employees have a constitutional entitlement to a fair hearing which includes the right to be shown the evidence on which the council relied. The court of appeals reversed and remanded the case for further proceedings. *Swank v. Smart,* 898 F.2d 1247 (7th Cir.1990).

A Nevada building inspector visited a construction site approximately twenty-five times over a two-month period. He initially determined that a permit for construction existed, but did not ascertain the scope of the permit. The casino which was engaging in the construction (remodeling) finished up the kitchen area and called the inspector to get approval of the kitchen and dining areas for occupancy, even though there was no indication of which area was to be occupied for a dining area. Nevertheless, the inspector approved the area for occupancy and ceased his inspections of the site. Construction continued as the casino worked to get its dining area completed. Another city employee noticed several serious defects and notified the city's building department. As a result of an investigation, the inspector was suspended with pay, and terminated one week later. He appealed to the civil service board, which conducted a full posttermination hearing and upheld his discharge. He unsuccessfully appealed to a Nevada trial court and further appealed to the Supreme Court of Nevada.

The supreme court first noted that the inspector had a property interest in his job, which entitled him to a pretermination hearing unless "extraordinary and exigent"circumstances existed to justify a posttermination hearing only. Here, there was potential danger from structural collapse and fire hazards sufficient to warrant immediate termination. The court also rejected the inspector's claims that he had not been negligent because he had not even inspected the dining area. It held that his duty was to assure safety within his whole territory. Just because he had failed to inspect one area, he could not claim that he was not responsible for it. The court determined that there was substantial evidence to warrant his dismissal, and found that the posttermination hearing satisfied the due process considerations in this case. The court affirmed the trial court's decision. *State ex. rel. Sweikert v. Briare*, 588 P.2d 542 (Nev. 1978).

A village in New York employed a police officer trainee. The officer trainee successfully completed a police officer examination. The village was notified of the successful examination and appointed the trainee to a permanent police officer position. Eight months later, the village fired the officer. He sued the village in a New York trial court, alleging that the termination occurred without a hearing or explanation. The trainee argued that he was entitled to a hearing because his one year probationary period started upon appointment as a trainee and the probationary period had expired before he was terminated. The trial court held that the probationary period started upon permanent appointment. The officer appealed to the Supreme Court, Appellate Division, Second Department. The appellate division court noted that a temporary employee cannot become permanent and begin serving a probationary term without first qualifying for the position. Because the remaining portions of the police officer examination were not given until after the officer was selected by the village as a candidate for the permanent position, his probationary term did not start until permanent appointment to police officer. Therefore, the officer's termination was during his probationary period. A hearing or explanation for his termination was not required. *Garypie v. Inc. Village of Sag Harbor*, 551 N.Y.S.2d 570 (A.D.2d Dep't 1990).

A tenured Alabama school teacher was notified that the board intended to cancel his employment contract. Hearings were conducted in which the board terminated his contract. The State Tenure Commission affirmed the board's decision and the teacher sued in an Alabama trial court. The trial court upheld the commission's decision, and the teacher appealed to the Court of Civil Appeals of Alabama. The appellate court noted that under Ala. Code (1975), § 16-24-9 (1987 Repl. Vol.), an employment contract with a tenured teacher may only be cancelled if the board of education gives notice in writing to the teacher, stating in detail the reasons for the cancellation. In this case, the only reasons given by the board were incompetency, neglect of duty and other just cause. There was no detailed statement of why the board came to its conclusion. The appellate court held that the reasons given by the board were not sufficiently detailed to comply with the statutory notice requirements. The appellate court reversed and remanded the trial court decision. *Gardner v. Alabama State Tenure Commission*, 553 So.2d 606 (Ala.Civ.App.1989).

The New York City Board of Education's Bureau of Pupil Transportation received anonymous phone calls that a school bus driver for handicapped students had fondled himself while on the job. Several other complaints about the bus driver's conduct were made by bus attendants. The Bureau of Pupil Transportation decided to conduct a hearing. It sent a notice of hearing to A.C.J. Transportation Corp., the private contractor who supplied bus service, and requested that a copy be given to the bus driver. However, A.C.J. failed to do so. All the bus driver received was a handwritten note from his supervisor to appear at the hearing. He appeared at the hearing with a union representative. Bureau officials allowed the bus driver to present letters attesting to his good character. Shortly thereafter A.C.J. fired him. The bus driver then sued, alleging that the lack of proper notice violated his due process rights. The U.S. Court of Appeals, Second Circuit, agreed that the bus driver had been deprived of due process, but it refused to award the driver damages for lost salary. The court of appeals remanded the case for a determination of whether the bus driver would have been fired even if proper notice had been given. *Stein v. Bd. of Educ. of City of New York*, 792 F.2d 13 (2d Cir.1986).

Two National Weather Service employees submitted fraudulent travel vouchers with the agency for travel reimbursement. Another employee had been asked by them if he wanted to join their carpool, which he did, but he suspected they were submitting false reports. When he found some evidence of this, he informed their supervisor, fearing he would be implicated if he kept silent. The supervisor assumed there had been an error and talked with the two employees, suggesting the error and requesting they resubmit their vouchers. They declined. He then reported the matter to his supervisor, who contacted them, informed them he had evidence that their vouchers were wrong, and advised that they change them. Again, they declined. He proposed their removal, and they then obtained counsel and met with him again. He found that their vouchers were fraudulent and dismissed them. They appealed unsuccessfully to the Merit Systems Protection Board (MSPB), and further appealed to the U.S. Court of Appeals.

The appellate court held that, at the pretermination stage, it was not a violation for the same person to both propose dismissal and be the decisionmaker in that regard. The law presumes that a supervisor will be capable of changing his mind on hearing the employee's side of the case. Here, the employees had been given a chance to recalculate and resubmit their vouchers, and had retained an attorney for the pretermination reply to the charges. Following their termination, they had been given full evidentiary hearings. The court affirmed the MSPB's decision to uphold their dismissals. *De Sarno v. Department of Commerce,* 761 F.2d 657 (1985).

Two Alabama firemen, permanent fulltime employees, joined a police and firefighters' strike, and were subsequently arrested for several offenses. The charges were dismissed and the strike ended. Even though the strike had been illegal, the strikers went back to work with the understanding that none of them would be disciplined for striking. Only those who had committed criminal offenses would be disciplined. Later, the fire chief notified the two men that their employment was terminated, subject to a pretermination hearing. A hearing was commenced at which their dismissal was upheld, but the prosecutor at the hearing was also the advisor for the committee. Further, prior to the hearing, one of the committee members stated that he would vote whichever way the mayor voted. The firefighters successfully appealed to an Alabama trial court, and the city then appealed to the Supreme Court of Alabama.

The supreme court first recognized that since the strike had been illegal, the city could have immediately discharged the strikers, but having chosen not to do so, it reinstated their property rights when it allowed them to return to work. The court then held that the fact that the prosecutor was also the advisor to the hearing committee presented an image of unfairness. More importantly though, it found the committee member's statement that he would vote with the mayor to be an even more serious violation of due process. Because the hearing was not conducted before an impartial tribunal, the court determined that the firefighters had not received adequate due process. The court affirmed the trial court's decision, and granted backpay and reinstatement to the firefighters. *City of Huntsville v. Biles*, 489 So.2d 509 (Ala.1986).

An Arkansas firefighter was arrested and charged with manufacture and possession of a controlled substance after state police searched his house and found marijuana. Shortly after his arrest, the fire chief notified him in writing that a pretermination hearing would be held in four days. At the hearing, the firefighter asked for a continuance because his attorney was unable to be present. His request was denied and the fire chief terminated his employment. The civil service commission upheld that decision, and the firefighter appealed to an Arkansas trial court. Prior to his appeal, all criminal charges were dropped because the search warrant was invalid. Nevertheless, the trial court considered evidence of the firefighter's possession of marijuana in its affirmance of the commission's decision. He further appealed to the Court of Appeals of Arkansas.

On appeal, the court held that evidence illegally seized in a criminal proceeding, though inadmissible for criminal prosecution, was admissible in this type of civil proceeding. It also ruled that the fire chief had not been required to grant the continuance in the pretermination hearing. The court determined that the deterrent purpose and effect of excluding unlawful police conduct was only necessary in criminal proceedings, not civil actions. The city's interest in accurate information was sufficient to allow such evidence to be included. The court affirmed the trial court's decision, and upheld the firefighter's termination. *Miller v. City of Little Rock*, 743 S.W.2d 9 (Ark.App.1988).

Please see Chapter One of this Volume for additional cases involving employee search and seizure.

Prior to being hired as a North Carolina police officer, a man admitted to an investigatory officer that he had used marijuana and other narcotics on a "teenage experimental" basis. This did not prevent his certification as an officer. Five years later, the North Carolina Criminal Justice Education and Training Standards Commission discovered this information and, without a hearing, revoked the officer's license. The officer contested the revocation by filing a lawsuit in state court. He alleged that he should be entitled to a hearing, and that the commission's decision was arbitrary and capricious. The court ruled in favor of the officer, and the commission appealed to the Court of Appeals of North Carolina.

A North Carolina statue prescribes an opportunity for hearing "prior to any agency action in a contested case" which could affect an employee's rights. The court ruled that the license revocation had the effect of a termination, and that the officer was entitled to notice and a hearing. The record showed that the commission had notice of the officer's action for six years prior to the discipline. The commission argued that it was unaware of the prior conduct, but the court felt that it should have been aware; the commission had possession of or access to all necessary documents. The court noted the passage of time since the conduct, the officer's exemplary service, and the fact that the officer had volunteered the information. It then found the commission's action to be arbitrary and capricious. The appeals court affirmed the trail court's reversal of the commission's decision. The officer was reinstated. *Scroggs v. Cr. Just. Ed. & Tr. Standards*, 400 S.E.2d 742 (N.C.App.1991).

A Louisiana firefighter entered a clinic to overcome a drug addiction problem. While there, he received a letter notifying him of his dismissal from the department. He appealed to the civil service commission, asserting that he was being discharged solely because of his drug addiction, and that he was fully recovered. The commission found that his dismissal arose only partly from his addiction, and that his whole record had been taken into account, including the 200 absences from work he had incurred in the prior four years. However, the Court of Appeal of Louisiana reversed that decision because he had not been given a pretermination hearing, and it reinstated him. After returning to work, he was ordered by telephone to his superintendent's office, where he was informed that a pretermination administrative hearing would be held immediately. After the hearing, he was again terminated, and the commission again upheld that decision. He once more appealed to the Court of Appeal of Louisiana.

The appellate court held that the firefighter had not received sufficient notice of his hearing. Not only was he not given a written notice of the hearing, he was not even told that the hearing would be conducted until just before it started. The court again held that the department had failed to satisfy the firefighter's due process rights, and reversed the commission's decision. *Brumfield v. Department of Fire*, 523 So.2d 876 (La.App.4th Cir.1988).

A full-time firefighter worked for the city of Bartlesville, Oklahoma and was an active member of the local firefighters union. He, along with other union members, met with the fire chiefs of two neighboring cities. They requested that the fire chiefs keep their fire departments from responding to any calls for mutual aid from Bartlesville until all off-duty Bartlesville firemen were called back to work for overtime wages. Bartlesville's fire chief felt that this conduct endangered the safety of Bartlesville citizens. Upon learning of the firefighter's involvement with the request to the other departments the fire chief discharged him. Pursuant to a collective bargaining agreement, the union filed a grievance on behalf of the firefighter, and the matter went to arbitration. The arbitrator ruled in favor of the firefighter, holding that he had been dismissed without "just cause" as required under his employment contract. The arbitrator ordered the firefighter's reinstatement with full backpay and benefits. The firefighter then sued in a federal district court alleging that city officials had deprived him of his property interest without due process of law, because they did not give him a pretermination hearing. The district court refused to grant the city officials' motion for summary judgment on the firefighter's due process claim. The city officials appealed the district court's order denying their summary judgment motion to the U.S. Court of Appeals, Tenth Circuit.

The appellate court noted that a pretermination hearing is an initial check to determine whether there are reasonable grounds to believe that the charges against the employee are true. It is intended to supplement the more detailed posttermination hearing. The appellate court held that the pretermination procedure given to the firefighter did not violate his due process rights. He was given notice and an opportunity to respond, the essential requirements of due process, when his fire chief asked him if he had asked the other fire departments not to sign a mutual aid agreement. This was adequate to put him on notice, and he had an opportunity to respond at that time but declined to do so. The appellate court reversed and remanded the case with instructions that the district court enter summary judgment for the city officials on the due process claim. *Powell v. Mikulecky,* 891 F.2d 1454 (10th Cir.1989).

A Texas police chief composed a letter imposing an indefinite suspension on a police officer charged with violating Civil Service rules concerning intoxication while off duty and conduct unbecoming an officer. The officer appealed the suspension to the Civil Service Commission which entered a written order upholding the indefinite suspension imposed by the police chief. The commission's order stated that "the commission, having heard all testimonies from both parties, and having considered the letter of indefinite suspension filed by the police chief" upheld the indefinite suspension. The officer then appealed the Civil Service Commission's decision to a Texas trial court which set aside and vacated the commission's order. The city appealed to the Court of Appeals of Texas. The court noted that the Firemen's and Policemen's Civil Service Act stated than an officer may not be suspended or dismissed by the commission except for violation of the Civil Service rules and after a finding by the commission of the truth of the specific charges against the officer. The court noted that the commission's order failed to state the finding of truth of the specific charges against the officer. The court therefore upheld the trial court's decision and reinstated the officer. *City of Laredo v. Rodriguez,* 791 S.W.2d 567 (Texas.App.-San Antonio 1990).

Five Indiana firefighters were demoted by the city fire chief without prior notice or a hearing. Their demotions were approved by the city's board of public works and safety, again without prior notice. The Board's president sent the firefighters letters offering them post-demotion hearings, but the firefighters instead sued in an Indiana trial court. The court ruled for them, and the city appealed to the Court of Appeals of Indiana.

ing. The court held that it need not consider whether the firefighters had protectable liberty interests which had been deprived because state law guaranteed a contractual property right to the firefighters. The appellate court affirmed the trial court's decision, reinstating the firefighters and awarding them back pay. *City of Terre Haute v. Brighton*, 450 N.E.2d 1039 (Ind.App.4th Dist.1983).

A Minnesota man worked for a city's board of water commissioners as a driver-operator for fifteen years. In 1986, another employee was discovered selling stolen tires to other coworkers. The other employee had been doing so for four years. That man informed the police that he had sold a large number of tires to the driver-operator. The police subsequently seized thirty-four stolen tires from the driver-operator's garage. He pleaded guilty to the charge of receiving stolen property, and was put on probation. His department conducted its own separate investigation into the matter, and sent him a letter advising him that he had been terminated, effective one week later, and that he had until then to meet with his supervisor to discuss the matter. After the meeting, his supervisor could "affirm, modify or withdraw" his discharge. He did not meet with his supervisor, and was discharged. Subsequently, a full administrative hearing was conducted, and his termination was upheld. He appealed to a Minnesota trial court, which ruled for the city, and he then appealed to the Court of Appeals of Minnesota.

The appellate court held that the employee's pretermination rights had been satisfied because he had received notice and an opportunity to respond. However, the court recommended that, in the future, notices should discuss proposed actions only, and not imply that charges had been reviewed and found proven. This would eliminate any inference by the employee that such a meeting would be a waste of his time. The court also ruled that the commission's decision had been supported by the evidence, since the employee had admitted receiving stolen property. The court affirmed the trial court's decision and upheld the employee's dismissal. *Conlin v. City of St. Paul,* 418 N.W.2d 741 (Minn.App.1988).

A Missouri man, employed by the division of liquor control, was indicted by a grand jury on charges arising from gambling and bribery. He was suspended without pay and, while the criminal action was still pending against him, he received oral notice of a pretermination hearing and of the charges against him. He initially refused to answer the charges against him at the pretermination hearing, but after assurances that no information would be turned over to his criminal prosecutors, and after consulting with his attorney, he did answer the charges. Subsequently, he was dismissed and received a full posttermination hearing. He appealed unsuccessfully to a Missouri trial court, and further appealed to the Missouri Court of Appeals.

The appellate court held that the employee's consultation with his attorney at the pretermination hearing was sufficient to satisfy his due process rights. Also, it noted that since he had received a full posttermination hearing, he had been afforded a sufficient pretermination hearing because he had been given notice and a chance to respond to the charges. This was all that was required if a full posttermination hearing was going to be conducted. Finally, the court held that the evidence was sufficient to support the dismissal, and accordingly, it affirmed the trial court's decision. *Williams v. State*, 740 S.W.2d 297 (Mo.App.1987).

A Florida man, employed by a city utility department, was required to work a certain amount of "standby time." Essentially, he was required to be "on call" during certain nonbusiness hours. This was required of all the department's employees. One particular evening, the man was unavailable to respond to a call when he had been scheduled to be on standby. When confronted with that, he stated that he had other obligations and that he would be unable to work standby for the rest of the week. His supervisor informed him that unless he agreed to work standby, he would be terminated. He still declined to do so, and subsequently received oral notice of his discharge. He went to see the city manager, who met with his supervisor and upheld the termination. The man received written notice. He then sued the city in a federal district court, asserting that he had been deprived of due process. The court held for the city, and he appealed to the U.S. Court of Appeals, Eleventh Circuit.

The appellate court held that the employee had not been deprived of substantive due process because the city's reasons for discharging him were proper. The court then looked to procedural due process and determined that the meeting with his supervisor and the city manager had afforded the man a sufficient pretermination procedure. However, the court decided that he had been entitled to a formal posttermination hearing, of which he had been deprived. Even if he had no quarrel with the facts surrounding his termination, he might wish to show that his dismissal was too severe a punishment for his offense. Also, the court deemed it necessary to allow him to confront his chief accuser in the presence of a decisionmaker. The court reversed the trial court's decision on this issue, but affirmed on the others. It remanded the case to the trial court for a complete determination. *Kelly v. Smith*, 764 F.2d 1412 (11th Cir.1985).

A Louisiana woman was employed by the Department of Health and Human Resources (DHHR) as an account clerk. The DHHR informed the employee by two letters that her employment was terminated because she had abandoned her position. The employee appealed to the state Civil Service Commission (CSC). The hearing referee upheld the termination, finding just cause for her dismissal. The employee appealed the referee's decision to the CSC which denied her application for review. She then appealed to the Court of Appeal of Louisiana which upheld the referee's decision. The Louisiana Supreme Court set aside the judgment and remanded the case to the court of appeal for reconsideration. The court of appeal found that the termination letters did not notify her that she had a right to respond either orally or in writing to the dismissal charges. The court of appeal reversed the CSC's decision and remanded the case for further proceedings. The employee then requested a hearing. A hearing was held in which the CSC refused to reinstate the employee and awarded her backpay for the period between the termination date and the posttermination hearing. The employee appealed to the Court of Appeal of Louisiana.

The court of appeal held that the employee had never been legally terminated. The DHHR had failed to institute pretermination proceedings after the employee's initial termination was set aside. The employee's due process rights had been denied and she was entitled to her salary until she was lawfully removed or suspended for cause. The court noted that the fact that the employee had a posttermination hearing did not make her termination constitutional. The employee had retained her status as a civil service employee. The court of appeal reversed the CSC decision and reinstated the employee with pay until lawfully terminated. *Maurello v. DHHR, Office of Mgmt. & Fin.*, 546 So.2d 545 (La.App.1st Cir.1989).

An Alaska career police officer drove a woman home and allegedly engaged in sexual activity with her while on duty. After receiving a complaint against the officer, the city undertook an investigation. It accumulated a substantial amount of evidence against the officer, then interviewed him. He denied the allegations and voluntarily submitted to a polygraph test, which he failed. The police chief, the officer and the officer's shop steward met and the officer was given a further opportunity to explain any of the gathered evidence. He merely repeated his blanket denial. The police chief dismissed him at the end of the meeting. When the officer's labor association did not press his claim, he sued for reinstatement and backpay in an Alaska trial court. The court ruled for the city, but offered the officer a full posttermination evidentiary hearing. He refused, and appealed to the Supreme Court of Alaska.

The supreme court stated that the officer had been entitled to a formal evidentiary posttermination hearing within a reasonable time because minimum pretermination procedures had been followed. However, here the trial court had offered the officer a hearing on his claim of termination without just cause, and he had refused it. Since he had refused a posttermination hearing, the court decided he could not assert that his due process rights had been violated. The court affirmed the trial court's decision, and denied relief to the officer. *Storrs v. Municipality of Anchorage*, 721 P.2d 1146 (Alaska 1986).

An Arizona employee of the state department of economic security was terminated by letter of dismissal in 1982. He appealed to the state personnel board and a posttermination hearing was conducted, where his dismissal was upheld. He further appealed to an Arizona trial court, again unsuccessfully. The following year, he moved for a new hearing, asserting that one of the witnesses at his posttermination hearing committed perjury. A hearing was conducted on this issue and it was found to be without merit. He also argued that the recent U.S. Supreme Court holding in *Cleveland Board of Education v. Loudermill*, 470 U.S. 532 (1985), see above, entitled him to a pretermination hearing which had not been held. His motion for another new hearing was denied, and he appealed to the Court of Appeals of Arizona.

The appellate court refused to retroactively apply *Loudermill* in this case because the employee had not raised his constitutional right to a pretermination hearing earlier, which he had been required to do. The court stated that *Loudermill* applied only to cases pending on appeal and not to new trials or hearings. It held that no valid purpose would be served by holding another hearing. His discharge had been valid and the court upheld it. The court affirmed the trial court's decision. *Brubaker v. Arizona Dep't of Economic Security*, 754 P.2d 304 (Ariz.App.1987).

A New York City Transit Authority civil service employee was charged with manslaughter for the stabbing death of his wife. He was acquitted by reason of mental disease or defect and committed to the state mental health commissioner's custody. He was incarcerated in a mental hospital for over three years. As a civil service employee, he was entitled to a due process hearing before discharge. However, when the transit authority called the hearing, the employee was in custody and release was impossible. After the employee was released from custody, he sued the transit authority in a New York trial court, which ruled in his favor and granted reinstatement to his former position. The authority appealed to a New York appellate division court which affirmed the trial court's decision. The authority then appealed to the New York Court of Appeals.

The Court of Appeals noted that the authority had a legitimate interest in promptly resolving the employee's employment status. When the hearing was held, the employee had been unable to carry out his duties for almost two years. Further delays would have been unreasonable and burdensome. The hearing officer had correctly conducted the hearing in the employee's absence when it was clear that he would be unable to attend in the near future. Since the hearing was based on the same issues involved in his commitment proceedings and his conduct had been fully explored at that time, the employee had been given full opportunity to challenge the underlying charges against him. The court reversed the lower courts' decisions, ruling in favor of the transit authority. *Rao v. Gunn*, 532 N.E.2d 1275 (N.Y.1988).

An employee of the Florida Department of Natural Resources (DNR) took three consecutive days off work without an authorized leave of absence.

The DNR subsequently took the position that he had abandoned his job and resigned. He was not given a pretermination hearing, but the DNR did provide him with a full posttermination evidentiary hearing. At this hearing, his termination was approved. He appealed to the District Court of Appeal of Florida.

The appellate court agreed with the employee's assertion that he had been deprived of due process rights because he had not been given a pretermination hearing, but upheld his discharge. It stated that since he was eventually given a full and complete posttermination hearing, which properly resulted in a final order to terminate, his dismissal would be upheld. The court noted, however, that if the employee had suffered damages as a result of this "deprivation of due process," he might be able to recover them in a subsequent lawsuit. The court affirmed the DNR's termination of the employee. *Simmons v. Dep't of Natural Resources*, 513 So.2d 723 (Fla.App.1st Dist.1987).

An Ohio custodian for the Cleveland Public Library had an altercation with his supervisor. The supervisor reported to the head supervisor that he had been physically assaulted. Further, he stated that he had instructed the custodian to report to the head supervisor's office, but the custodian had refused and left the premises. The head supervisor then met with the director of the library, and a decision was made to terminate the custodian's employment. They wrote a letter to him, discharging him from his position, even though a personnel manual required that there be a hearing prior to termination. The custodian sued the library and the supervisors in the U.S. District Court, Ohio, alleging that his federal civil rights had been violated. The supervisors argued that their unease at keeping the custodian on the worksite was sufficient to excuse their failure to provide the custodian a hearing.

The district court determined that the custodian, as a permanent employee, had been deprived of a property interest without due process because of the lack of a pretermination hearing. The court noted that the U.S. Supreme Court, in *Cleveland Board of Education v. Loudermill*, 470 U.S. 532 (1985), above, had provided the necessary solution to employers in this type of situation: suspend the employee with pay. Because the library had failed to do this and simply discharged the custodian, the court ordered that he be reinstated with pay until a pretermination hearing could be held. *Irizarry v. Cleveland Public Library*, 727 F.Supp. 357 (N.D.Ohio 1989).

III. SUSPENSION

In general, the rules for public employee suspensions are indistinguishable from the principles applied in termination cases. If a termination hearing would be required, then a suspension hearing will also be necessary. A suspension is usually considered by courts to be a depri-

vation of a property interest provided that the employment contract, or the nature of the employment, creates a mutual expectation of continued employment.

The U.S. Fish and Wildlife Service (FWS) hired a man as an administrative officer for a youth conservation camp. His position was to last for the duration of the program. Prior to that time, however, the FWS advised him that it intended to dismiss him for, among other things, his unauthorized use of a government vehicle. After he replied to the charges, the FWS dismissed him, but failed to advise him of his right to a formal hearing. Over a year later, the FWS concluded that it should only have suspended him for thirty days, and offered him backpay from the time the suspension would have ended to the time when the program had ended. He elected to sue in the claims court, asserting that the suspension was unwarranted. The claims court stated that the Civil Service Reform Act (CSRA) comprised the exclusive catalog of remedies. The employee successfully appealed to a federal district court, and the court of appeals denied the government's request for a rehearing. The case came before the U.S. Supreme Court.

The Supreme Court held that the claims court had been correct in denying the employee a review of the personnel action taken against him. The Court stated that the CSRA had deliberately excluded employees in the nonpreference, "excepted service" category from judicial review for a suspension action. It ruled that the employee's action could only be heard by either the Merit Systems Protection Board or the FWS itself. The Court reversed the lower court's decision, and denied judicial review to the employee. *U.S. v. Fausto,* 484 U.S. 439, 108 S.Ct. 668, 98 L.Ed.2d 830 (1988).

Several Florida police officers received suspensions for unrelated offenses. The county code required that the officers be given hearings within sixty days to appeal the suspensions. The earliest hearing was scheduled for twelve months later. Because of the delay in the hearings, the officers sued in a Florida trial court, seeking compensation for lost wages and deletion of the suspensions from their records. The trial court complied, and the county appealed that decision to the District Court of Appeal of Florida.

The county argued that the suspensions did not curtail property rights because they were not discharges. Further, it argued that even if the officers were deprived of a property interest, the trial court had fashioned an improper remedy. The appellate court found that the officers had a property interest in uninterrupted employment without regard to suspensions, discharges or demotions. It stated that the county's failure to conduct prompt hearings was a denial of due process rights. However, the court agreed that the trial court had erred in deleting the suspensions and awarding backpay.

The appellate court stated that if the officers could show they had been damaged by the delay in the hearings, they would be entitled to recover for that harm. However, to qualify for backpay and a rescission of the suspensions, the officers would have to go through the hearings to determine if the suspensions were justified. If they were, no backpay could be awarded, and the suspensions would stand. The appellate court affirmed the trial court's decision that the officers had been deprived of a property right, but reversed with respect to the award of backpay and the deletion of the suspensions from the record. *Metropolitan Dade County v. Sokolowski*, 439 So.2d 932 (Fla.App.3d Dist.1983).

A Florida county suspended one of its officers for two days without pay. The reasons given for the suspension were incompetence, inefficiency and violation of departmental rules. The officer appealed his suspension, and although the county code required a hearing within sixty days, it was not conducted for over two years. At the hearing, the officer asked that the suspension be dismissed because of the delay, but the hearing officer refused. No documents were missing and all the witnesses remembered the incidents which gave rise to the suspension. The officer's suspension was upheld. He then appealed to a Florida court, asserting that the delay was a due process violation which required reversal of his suspension. The court agreed and the county appealed to the District Court of Appeal of Florida.

The appellate court noted that the officer had not been adversely affected by the delay in time between the suspension and the hearing. Because it did not affect his ability to prove that the disciplinary action taken against him was unjustified, he did not suffer damages. The court agreed that there had been a deprivation of due process, but because the officer had not suffered any harm because of that deprivation, he was only entitled to nominal damages. The court reversed the lower court's decision, and granted the officer damages not to exceed one dollar. *Metropolitan Dade County v. Caputi*, 466 So.2d 1087 (Fla.App.3d Dist.1985).

A Wyoming police officer, during a routine spotlight check of a warehouse, ran into a fixed post with his patrol car. Considerable damage to the car resulted. Subsequently, the officer was suspended for four ten-hour days by his supervisors. However, neither of the two supervisors who suspended him was a department head, even though the personnel policy provided that only department heads could issue suspensions. The officer appealed his suspension to a trial court, which ruled that it did not have jurisdiction to hear the case. The officer further appealed to the Supreme Court of Wyoming.

The supreme court held that the district court did have the authority to review the suspension. Although Wyoming law did not clearly provide for reviewability by the courts in suspension cases, the court found that such power was in the best interests of the state. The supreme court reversed and remanded the case to the trial court for a review of the suspension. *Keslar v. Police Civil Serv. Comm'n*, 665 P.2d 937 (1983).

A police officer for the Louisiana State University Medical Center, a civil service employee, called his supervisor to report that he was taking sick leave for a day. The officer's supervisor was then informed by the manager of the resident hall where the officer was assigned that the officer might also call in sick the next day because the officer had something to do. When the officer called in sick the next day, his supervisor set up surveillance of his house. His supervisor was in an unmarked car, parked legally a short distance from his house. The supervisor saw him leave his residence twice on the day he called in sick. A meeting was held between the officer and his superiors, in which he was suspended for five days for violating the university's sick leave rule. The rule required an employee on sick leave to notify his supervisor if he had to leave his residence while on sick leave. The officer appealed his suspension, and a hearing was held before a civil service referee. The referee upheld the suspension, and the officer appealed to the civil service commission. The commission reversed the referee's decision and remanded it to make a determination of whether he was aware, or should have been aware, of his obligation to call in if he had to leave his residence while on sick leave. After the second hearing, the referee determined that he was aware of the sick leave rule, because the rule was in a procedure book that he was required to read and become familiar with. The suspension was upheld, and the commission adopted the referee's decision. The officer appealed to the Court of Appeal of Louisiana, First Circuit.

On appeal, the officer argued that the evidence uncovered during the surveillance of his house should have been excluded because it violated his Fourth Amendment protection of unreasonable search or invasion of privacy. The appellate court held that the surveillance of his house from a public street was neither a search nor an invasion of privacy. Any observation from a place where one has a right to be is not a search within the meaning of the Fourth Amendment. The appellate court affirmed the decision of the commission. *Claverie v. LSU Medical Center,* 553 So.2d 482 (La.App.1st Cir.1989).

Section 112 of the Los Angeles city charter provides that a city employee has the right to have the disciplinary measures given by his or her supervisor reviewed by the state Board of Civil Service Commissioners. However, § 112 also requires that any alteration in the disciplinary measure recommended by the board be consented to by the disciplinary officer who imposed the penalty, thus limiting the board's ability to reduce the penalty.

Section 112 was challenged by two city employees who sought review by the board of penalties levied against them. In the first case, a director for the department of parks and recreation received a 10-day suspension from his supervisor for mishandling money. A hearing examiner recommended the suspension be reduced to a warning. The department of parks and recreation objected to this recommendation. The board unanimously agreed with the hearing officer's recommendation, but the employee's supervisor refused to reduce the suspension. As a result, the board had to affirm the suspension. The employee then asked a California trial court to declare § 112 unconstitutional. The trial court declared the provision unconstitutional, reasoning that the top governmental official's ability to override the board amounted to a violation of due process for all city workers.

In the second case, a city employee had been discharged for violating his employment contract by allegedly engaging in activities constituting a conflict of interest. The employee filed suit alleging that the board had suspended review of disciplinary action because its hearing procedure was unconstitutional, as determined in the director's case. The employee asked that his employment be reinstated until a full due process hearing could be held. The trial court granted his request. The city then appealed both cases to the California Court of Appeal.

The court of appeal concluded that the city employees possessed property rights in their continued employment because § 112 provided that they could not be suspended or terminated without written cause. However, it reversed the trial court's decisions and held that § 112's provisions for review of disciplinary actions did not violate either state or federal due process guarantees. The court stated that the ultimate decision-maker neither exhibited animosity towards the employee, nor was it financially interested in the employee's termination. The court concluded that there was no evidence to indicate that the department officials were biased. The court reversed the trial court's decisions and held that § 112 is constitutional. *Burrell v. City of Los Angeles,* 257 Cal.Rptr. 427 (Cal.App.2d Dist.1989).

A Chicago school principal counseled and then gave remedial warnings to a tenured teacher at his school concerning classroom problems. During a fifty-day remediation period following the warning, the principal observed the teacher thirty times and took notes. He then wrote to the district superintendent that the teacher had failed to correct her teaching deficiencies. The school board began dismissal proceedings based on the principal's observations. A hearing was arranged. However, as attorneys for the board prepared for the hearing, the principal withdrew his cooperation. He denied having any memory of observing the teacher. He then notified the attorneys that he could not testify without having his memory refreshed.

The board determined that it could not proceed against the teacher without the principal's cooperation and dropped the dismissal charges. The superintendent sought to suspend the principal for thirty school days for insubordination. At his suspension hearing, the hearing officer recommended a suspension. A board member remarked that the principal was an "amnesia principal." The principal sued the school board in an Illinois trial court, alleging due process violations, "retaliatory suspension" and defamation. The court dismissed the action and the principal appealed to the Appellate Court of Illinois. The court ruled that the school board acted lawfully and had sufficiently notified the principal. There was no due process violation, and the principal's "retaliatory suspension" claim did not exist under Illinois law. The principal was unable to prove school board maliciousness, which was required to prove defamation. The lower court's dismissal was affirmed. *Stutzman v. Chicago Bd. of Educ.*, 525 N.E.2d 903 (Ill.App.1st Dist.1988).

A Pennsylvania teacher was hired in October, 1972. He worked from this date until the end of 1983 when he was suspended because he had less seniority than another teacher who was retained as a guidance counselor. The counselor was hired in September, 1972. During the 1973-74 school year funding was delayed and the counselor worked half-time for a month. The teacher sued the school district in a Pennsylvania trial court asking to be reinstated since the counselor's parttime service constituted a leave of absence which reduced the counselor's seniority. The trial court ordered the teacher to be reinstated. The school district appealed to the Commonwealth Court of Pennsylvania. On appeal, the court held that the teacher's parttime service did not constitute a leave of absence which would reduce seniority. *School Dist. of Duquesne v. Sturm,* 547 A.2d 891 (Pa.Cmwlth.1988).

A tenured Minnesota county employee was suspended from his job without pay during the pendency of his campaign for elective office. The county board of commissioners had a personnel policy which called for a mandatory leave of absence without pay for any appointed county employee who ran for elective office. The suspended employee sued the county for violation of his due process rights under the Fourteenth Amendment to the U.S. Constitution. The court ruled for the county and the employee appealed to the Minnesota Court of Appeals. The court of appeals reversed, holding that the county's personnel policy did not afford the employee sufficient procedural due process. The county appealed to the Minnesota Supreme Court.

The supreme court reinstated the judgment of the trial court, holding that the employee had a "property interest" in his continued employment, which was protected by the due process clause. The temporary leave of absence without pay was sufficient to constitute "deprivation" of the property interest in his job. However, the court noted that the government may constitutionally suspend or discharge any government employee who seeks elective office. This policy ensures that government employees serve the public and not a political party and promotes efficiency and integrity in the workplace. The procedures adopted by the county board of commissioners to determine whether the employee was a candidate for elective office were sufficient to meet constitutional standards of procedural due process without need of a hearing before being placed on mandatory leave of absence. *Martin v. Itasca County*, 448 N.W.2d 368 (Minn.1989).

IV. EMPLOYMENT ABANDONMENT AND AUTOMATIC RESIGNATION

When employees abandon their positions, they will usually be held to have automatically resigned. An abandonment is frequently defined by state statute to be an absence without leave for five consecutive days. So long as the employee has intended an abandonment, the automatic resignation will be upheld. However, if the absence was a result of a misunderstanding or was taken in good faith, courts will be reluctant to enforce an automatic resignation.

After twenty-eight years with the Florida Department of Health and Rehabilitative Services, a Florida public assistance specialist severely injured his back while working. As a result, he was out of work for one year and received workers' compensation benefits. When he was able to return to his job, he often lost time from work due to frequent back pain. At a counseling session, his supervisor informed him that if he had back problems he should wait until he saw the doctor before calling in to explain his status. The specialist called the office to report his absence one day but did not call in to explain the absence until seven days later, at which time he was informed that his unexplained absence was considered a voluntary abandonment of his position. When the specialist received notice of separation, he filed an appeal before the Public Employees Relation Commission (PERC) and the Department of Administration (DOA). The PERC dismissed the appeal, denying jurisdiction. The DOA hearing officer determined that since the specialist was absent without authorized leave, he voluntarily abandoned his position. The specialist appealed to the Court of Appeal of Florida.

On appeal, the court noted that the PERC has exclusive jurisdiction over dismissals. Since voluntary abandonment was similar to dismissal, the court determined that jurisdiction was properly with the PERC. The court reversed the hearing officer's decision to dismiss the specialist, noting that a state employee need only show that he had a reasonable basis for his failure to seek authorization, which he did by indicating that his supervisor had not expected him to call in until he saw his doctor. *Tomlinson v. Department of Health and Rehabilitative Services*, 558 So.2d 62 (Fla.App.2d Dist.1990).

A man was employed as a telecommunications specialist by the state of California. After an argument with his supervisor, the employee fainted and eventually began receiving temporary disability benefits. The benefits were later stopped as per medical advice, but the employee did not return to work. The supervisor contacted the employee, who assured him that the termination of benefits was a mistake and that he would look into it. The supervisor tried to contact the employee fifteen days later, but was unsuccessful. The supervisor then terminated the employee under the automatic resignation provision of the California absence without leave (AWOL) statute. The employee argued that the AWOL statute was unconstitutional because it deprived him of a property interest in employment without the procedural safeguards mandated by the due process clause. Unsuccessful challenges were heard by the California Superior Court and the Court of Appeal, and the suit reached the California Supreme Court.

The court held that the statute was unconstitutional. The issue then became whether procedural safeguards should accompany its use, and if so, what safeguards were required. The employee argued that the effect of the statute was the same as termination for cause. Therefore, it should require notice and an opportunity to respond before severance, as well as a postseverance hearing. The state argued that the employee had voluntarily resigned by his absence, and that no procedural safeguards were necessary. The court distinguished the AWOL statute from termination for cause because severance under AWOL produced no stigma. The AWOL statute was also distinguished from voluntary resignation because it is not self-executing; it requires state discretion and factual determinations. The court held that procedural safeguards were needed only to avoid unwarranted severance, and mandated both preseverance notice and an opportunity to respond. It reasoned that only these safeguards were necessary because of the uncomplicated factual determinations made by the state. A postseverance hearing was unnecessary. The court ruled that under these standards the man had been treated fairly, and that this case did not warrant a reversal of the dismissal. *Coleman v. Dep't of Personnel Admin.*, 278 Cal.Rptr. 346 (Cal.1991).

A California man, employed as a counselor with the state department of education, reported to school late in three different years due to extended summer vacations. Each time this occurred, he notified the school by postcard that he would be late, and the school accepted the postcards without comment. A year after the last incident, he got married and notified several supervisors that he would probably be late again, due to an extended honeymoon. Though they did not have the authority to grant leaves of absence, they accepted his statement. Again he sent a postcard to the school, informing it that he would be late in arriving. However, when he returned, he was informed that his employment had been automatically terminated because of a state law which provided for automatic resignation on five days absence without leave. He appealed to the state personnel board and was reinstated over seven months later, but was denied back pay for the period between his "resignation" and reinstatement. He appealed unsuccessfully to a California trial court, and further appealed to the California Court of Appeal, First District.

The court of appeal held that the employee never intended to resign his position, and because he had informed the authorities of his intention to return to school late, to hold that he had resigned was a violation of his due process rights. The school had not said anything when he had sent postcards in three previous years, so the court ruled that it could not now assert that it had not received sufficient notice or that he had been absent without leave. The court reversed the trial court's decision, and granted backpay to the employee. *Zike v. State Personnel Board*, 193 Cal.Rptr. 766 (Cal.App.1st Dist.1983).

A city of Seattle employee missed significant amounts of work due to alcoholism. His supervisor referred him to a counseling program. However, the employee was unaccountably absent for a number of days on three separate occasions. Following two suspensions and warnings, the employee was again absent without notice and the city terminated his employment. The termination was based solely upon excessive absenteeism. The employee was eventually taken to a detoxification program by his family; however, the city refused to keep his position open while he underwent treatment. The employee filed a wrongful discharge complaint against the city with the city's civil service commission. The commission ruled that there was just cause for termination. The employee then sued the city in a Washington trial court for failure to reasonably accommodate his alcoholism handicap. The court ruled in the city's favor and this decision was affirmed by the Washington Court of Appeals. The employee appealed to the Washington Supreme Court.

The court noted that Washington's civil rights statute did not define handicap. Whether a person was handicapped within the meaning of the statute was a question to be determined by a jury. The definition of handicapped was for the state legislature to determine. The court noted that the U.S. Congress had amended the Rehabilitation Act in 1986 to exclude alcoholics from handicapped status where their performance could constitute a direct threat to other persons or property. The trial court could reasonably have found that keeping his job position open would have been burdensome and the termination was affirmed. *Phillips v. City of Seattle*, 766 P.2d 1099 (Wash.1989).

A Georgia man was employed by the Georgia Department of Revenue as a tax field agent. The employee was hospitalized and did not report to work for several days. After he was discharged from the hospital he received a letter from the department stating that his absence from work was deemed an abandonment of his position. State officials told him that he had no appeal rights. The employee then brought a civil rights action against the department in federal district court, alleging his termination violated the Fourteenth Amendment, Title VII, and 42 U.S.C. § 1985. After a one day bench trial, the court granted the employee partial relief, namely a hearing before the state personnel board. The employee appealed to the U.S. Court of Appeals, Eleventh Circuit.

The court of appeals held that the employee had a constitutionally protected property interest in continued employment and that the department had deprived him of that interest without due process. The employee had not waived his right to a hearing following his termination by failing to immediately appeal that ruling. The employee had never received any notice of his right to obtain review and had been told by state officials that he had no appeal rights. The court of appeals affirmed the district court's decision. *Brown v. Georgia Dep't of Revenue*, 881 F.2d 1018 (11th Cir.1989).

A New York man was a permanent-status employee of the State Division of Equalization and Assessment. The employee submitted his resignation to the division's administrative officer, stating that his resignation became effective in two weeks. Approximately one week later the employee attempted to withdraw his resignation. The administrative officer refused the request and noted that the resignation had been accepted on the day it was submitted. The employee again demanded reinstatement. A year after receiving no response, he filed a lawsuit in a New York trial court, challenging the refusal to permit withdrawal of the resignation as arbitrary and unconstitutional. The court dismissed the petition as untimely, as it was governed by a four-month statute of limitations. The employee appealed to the New York Supreme Court, Appellate Division.

The appellate division court held that the four-month limitation period began to run on the effective date of the employee's resignation. The lawsuit, which was commenced one year later, was clearly untimely. The employee's statement demand did not extend the limitation period. The court further found that the employee's due process rights had not been violated because the employee had voluntarily resigned and did not retain any constitutionally protected property interest in continued employment. The supreme court affirmed the trial court's decision. *Smith v. Kunkel*, 544 N.Y.S.2d 240 (A.D.3d Dep't 1989).

An Alabama tenured teacher was elected to the position of county superintendent for five years and then sought a teaching position at her old school. The school denied her a position stating that she had abandoned her teaching contract when she was elected superintendent. The woman first petitioned the State Tenure Commission which affirmed the termination. She then appealed to an Alabama trial court which reversed the commission's decision. The school further appealed to the Alabama court of Appeals.

The court of appeals stated that the woman did not abandon her contract or neglect her duties. The woman ran for and was elected to the position of county superintendent, which was a logical promotion for a teacher. The school must give notice and a hearing to tenured teachers upon dismissal, which the school did not do in this instance. Further, the court stated that the tenure laws were designed to protect teachers from arbitrary dismissals such as this one. The court of appeals affirmed the trial court's decision. *Alabama State Tenure Comm'n v. Weaver*, 559 So.2d 176 (Ala.Civ.App.1989).

A Pennsylvania teacher failed to report for work on the first day of school. She had notified the administration that she would be unable to report because of illness and she requested a medical leave of absence. The leave was denied. After her nonappearance the school district terminated her without a prior hearing. The Commonwealth Court of Pennsylvania rejected her contention that her dismissal was improper, pointing out that after the dismissal a hearing was held at her request and the termination was upheld. The court noted that while the teacher perhaps was unable to report for work because of medical reasons, she was not, as a matter of right, entitled to a medical leave of absence. Whether to grant such a leave was within the discretion of the school board. The teacher's failure to report for work amounted to an abandonment of her contract and the board was justified in terminating her employment. *Kearns v. Lower Merion School Dist.*, 346 A.2d 875 (Pa.Cmnwlth.1975).

The Supreme Court of Nevada held that the termination of an elementary school principal for insubordination was arbitrary and capricious. Years prior to the principal's dismissal his son had left on a two year mission. At that time the principal made a commitment to his son that at the conclusion of his mission, the principal would join him in Europe and accompany him home. The principal planned to use ten of his forty accumulated leave days for the trip. Before his scheduled departure, the school district changed its leave policy by limiting administrators' use of earned leave to no more than five school days per year, or two days in succession, except in cases of "emergency." The principal's request for leave was denied, but he completed the trip as planned. Upon returning he was presented with a notice of suspension and intention of the district to initiate dismissal proceedings. The principal then brought suit against the school district. The district argued that under the definition of "insubordination," which was "a willful disregard of express or implied directions, or such a defiant attitude as to be equivalent thereto," the dismissal was valid. The Supreme Court of Nevada noted that the school district did not claim that the students or the school were detrimentally affected by the principal's absence, and that his unexcused absence could be characterized as "an error of judgment resulting in no harm to his employers." The court found that the penalty was excessive. Accordingly, the court reversed the principal's dismissal. *Rust v. Clark County School Dist.*, 683 P.2d 23 (Nev.1984).

V. MISCONDUCT

When an employee is guilty of misconduct, the public employer is given greater leeway in terminating the employee. Although no due process rights are generally given up, the employer may be allowed a broader range of discretionary conduct in discharging such an employee.

A. Misconduct While On Duty

An officer for the Kansas Highway Patrol and Capitol Area Security Patrol was observed behaving "different[ly]" while at work. His eyes were watery and bloodshot, and his speech was louder than usual. At noon, the man was tested by breathalyzer to have a blood-alcohol content of .173%. The officer admitted that he had stayed up late while drinking the night before. The officer was then dismissed. His dismissal was upheld by the Kansas Civil Service Board and a trial court, and an appeal reached the Court of Appeals of Kansas. The issue was whether the officer could be dismissed for being intoxicated on the job, despite a failure to show that his condition impaired his ability to perform. An earlier Kansas case involving termination required showing a relationship between the employee's action and the impairment of service. However, a Kansas statute was later passed which allowed termination for "personal conduct detrimental to state service." This specifically included being under the influence of alcohol or drugs while on duty. The statute did not include a specification of whether the alcohol must impair the employee's service. The appellate court determined the legislative intent to be a creation of a *per se* cause of dismissal for intoxication. It expressed that this reading would be in harmony with other statutes and regulations. The dismissal was upheld. *Sanstra v. Kansas Highway Patrol*, 804 P.2d 1009 (Kan.App.1991).

A prostitute revealed that two Phoenix vice officers had had sexual relations with her and another prostitute. An investigation revealed the sexual relations had occurred while the officers were on-duty and involved money paid from the city to the prostitutes who were to act as informants. The city discharged the officers for violating a departmental general order. The officers appealed to the Phoenix civil service board, which reinstated the officers without back pay for the time they were suspended. The officers sued the city board for back pay and injunctive relief, claiming constitutional violations. The district court found that the basis for the city rule regulating behavior was based upon an Arizona statute prohibiting adultery. The court held that there was no proof that the officers had violated the statute, and that therefore there could be no basis for violation of the city rule. The city department order prohibited conduct unbecoming of an officer.

The city civil service board then ruled that even without a statutory violation, the board would still have imposed suspensions without pay for conduct unbecoming an officer and contrary to department general orders. The officers appealed to the U.S. Court of Appeals, Ninth Circuit, claiming that they were being punished for private sexual activity. On appeal, the city argued that the activities had arisen from the city police department's organizational methods. The court noted that the U.S. Constitution does not explicitly protect privacy rights, and to the extent that personal privacy rights have been recognized they tended to be linked to family and marital rights. In this case, the officers had engaged in extramarital sex while on the job, necessarily affecting their job performance. The sexual activity had also implicated a conflict of interest and the possibilities of blackmail and of diminishing the department's reputation and morale. It was significant that the officers' behavior was open and widely known among city and county employees. The city had a legitimate interest in maintaining the moral integrity of its employees and board regulations governing police behavior were appropriate. Though the regulations were vague they were intended to protect a legitimate departmental interest and had been based on city board organization. The regulations were presumptively valid and the court affirmed summary judgment for the civil service board. *Fugate v. Phoenix Civil Service Bd.,* 791 F.2d 736 (9th Cir.1986).

A California police officer was accused of discharging a weapon in violation of departmental rules, and received a written reprimand following a disciplinary hearing with a lieutenant. The officer was then allowed to appeal the reprimand to the police chief. A hearing was held in which the officer was represented by counsel and was allowed to present arguments on his behalf. The chief upheld the reprimand, and the officer unsuccessfully appealed to a state trial court. The officer then appealed to the California Court of Appeal. On appeal, the officer contended that his due process rights were violated. The officer took the position that he should be afforded certain prediscipline due process rights, and that the chief's hearing filled that role. The officer further argued that he should be allowed a postdiscipline appeal. However, the court disagreed that the officer must be granted prediscipline due process rights. The court distinguished a written reprimand from situations where due process rights are mandated, such as: demotions, suspensions without pay, or dismissals. The court held that the appeal to the chief satisfied statutory requirements. The judgement was affirmed. *Stanton v. City of West Sacramento*, 277 Cal.Rptr. 478 (Cal.App.3d Dist. 1991).

A West Virginia man, employed by the department of finance and administration, attained the position of postmaster within the department. He had a clean record with the department. At one point, the purchasing division of the department sought bids for the financing of the purchase of an airplane. Two registered letters were delivered to the post office in the department on the morning of the bid closing date, but were somehow returned to the federal post office. The postmaster testified that he had instructed an employee to deliver the letters, that he had later checked the table where they had been placed and found them gone, and that he assumed they had been delivered. He was dismissed for his failure to make timely delivery of the letters, and the civil service commission upheld the dismissal. He appealed to the Supreme Court of Appeals of West Virginia.

The appellate court first stated that the dismissal of a permanent civil service employee must ultimately rest on a substantial ground of misconduct. Further, it recognized that an employee in a supervisory position has a duty to exercise reasonable care to keep himself informed of the work performance of his employees. However, the court stated that public employees are generally not liable for the negligent acts or omissions of their subordinates unless they participate in the acts or otherwise sanction them. Here, the court decided that there was insufficient evidence to show that good cause existed for the dismissal. The court reversed the civil service commission's decision, and reinstated the employee. *Oakes v. West Virginia Dep't of Finance and Administration*, 264 S.E.2d 151 (W.Va.1980).

The West Virginia Department of Veterans' Affairs terminated an audit clerk at a state veterans' home, claiming that she was negligent for failing to detect embezzlement of $290,000 by an employee under the clerk's supervision. The clerk did not participate in the embezzlement, and evidence indicated that the clerk had no prior history of disciplinary proceedings or reprimands. Her department was responsible for manually billing and servicing patient accounts and she had requested additional employees and a computerized system in the past. The clerk appealed her dismissal to the state civil service commission. During a hearing conducted by the commission, the clerk presented evidence of her excellent work evaluations and her requests for additional staff. She claimed that the dismissal was motivated by a personality conflict with her superior. The commission determined that the clerk was negligent in her work performance and determined that good cause existed for her termination. The clerk appealed to the Supreme Court of Appeals of West Virginia.

The court noted that West Virginia statutes permit termination of civil service employees only for good cause, which is defined as misconduct of a substantial nature having a direct effect on the public interest. Good cause was only present when the employee's conduct showed a gross disregard for professional responsibilities or the public safety. In this case, the clerk's sole error was her reliance upon the dishonest employee. The commission had failed to consider the clerk's previous good work record and working conditions at the veterans' home. Concluding that there was insufficient evidence to establish good cause for her termination, the court reversed and remanded the commission's decision. *Drown v. West Virginia Civil Service Comm.*, 375 S.E.2d 775 (W.V.1988).

An Ohio librarian for the Veterans Administration requested an intra-agency transfer to Kentucky. Several months before his move, he completed and submitted an intra-agency transfer request form (form 3918) listing his dependents as his wife and daughter. He had, however, been separated from his wife and daughter for a number of years. He was in fact living with a woman and his other daughter. The form 3918 requested authorization for travel to Lexington in his car, for subsistence expenses for himself and his dependents, and for moving expenses associated with this transfer. The agency authorized up to $12,000 for the expenses of the move. Although the librarian was entitled to the money, the government asserted that it was defrauded because he did not list the proper daughter as his dependent. The librarian asserted that he did not list his daughter because he wanted to protect his second "family" from embarrassment and to maintain his privacy regarding his personal life. The employee was removed from his job by the Veterans Administration. He sought review at the Merit Systems Protection Board's regional office which reversed the agency's decision. The agency petitioned for review of the Merit Systems Protection Board decision to a federal district court which upheld the removal and the employee appealed to the U.S. Court of Appeals, Federal Circuit.

The court noted that the Veterans Administration must prove that the librarian intended to defraud the government. Since the librarian's misrepresentation did not support the inference of an intent to defraud, the court determined that the misrepresentation was not material. The librarian did not attempt to receive a greater monetary benefit form the government than he would have been entitled to had he supplied accurate information. The court reversed the trial court's decision and reinstated the librarian. *Bradley v. Veterans Administration*, 900 F.2d 233 (Fed.Cir.1990).

An Illinois city's fire department's emergency medical services committee determined that employees who were not yet state certified paramedics should be given training at area hospitals. The chief of the fire department ordered two firefighters to take an entrance examination in order to attend paramedic training sessions. When the two firefighters sat for the entrance examination they were very disruptive. They told the nurses administering the test that the fire chief was "stupid" to make them attend paramedic school and stated they both had strong preferences not to attend the training program. The hospital refused to admit either of the firefighters due to their negative attitudes. The

Fire Department Board concluded that the behavior and statements of the firefighters demonstrated that neither wished to become paramedics or attend the classes. Thus, they deliberately thwarted or sabotaged compliance with the chief's order. The board imposed ten-day suspensions plus fines in the amount of $3,500 against one of the firefighters and $1,500 against the other. The firefighters then appealed to an Illinois trial court. It affirmed the suspension but reduced the fines to $500 and $200. The officers appealed to the Illinois Court. The appellate court stated that the firefighters' comments and actions towards the nurses administering the test reflected a negative attitude. Thus, the firefighters' behavior thwarted departmental efforts to increase the number of paramedics and improve service to the community. The appellate court affirmed the trial court's decision and held that the suspensions and fines were appropriate forms of discipline. *Kadzielawski v. Fire and Police Comm'rs*, 551 N.E.2d 331 (Ill.App.1st Dist.1990).

Two New York police officers were involved in a vehicle chase which ended in an accident. The officers made false statements to their superiors at the accident scene and at an official department interview regarding the incident. There was testimony from eyewitnesses which conflicted with the officers' version. The hearing officer weighed the evidence and chose to believe the eyewitness testimony. The hearing officer imposed a thirty day suspension including forfeiture of pay, benefits and service time lost as a consequence of the suspension. The officers then instituted an Article 78 proceeding in a New York trial court. The trial court transferred the case to the Supreme Court, Appellate Division. The supreme court, appellate division, may review the hearing officer's decision but may not review the evidentiary finding of facts. Therefore, the court may only review the imposition of the thirty day suspension. The court determined that the suspension and loss of benefits was not so disproportionate to the offense as to shock one's sense of fairness. Therefore, it upheld the hearing officer's decision. *Freeman v. Ward*, 556 N.Y.S.2d 563 (A.D.1st Dep't 1990).

A Colorado woman was fired from her position as postmaster when undelivered bulk business mail was found in a trash dumpster. Although each postal customer had received a copy of the mail, the woman failed to follow correct procedure on excess mail which was incorrectly addressed. Some of the incorrect procedures at the post office began before her appointment, and others involved new regulations which were distributed during the busy Christmas season. For these reasons, an appeal to an administrative law judge (ALJ) resulted in a recommendation of demotion to the woman's last held nonsupervisory position instead of termination. This decision was upheld by the Merit Systems Protection Board (MSPB). The woman sought reinstatement and appealed to the Colorado Court of Appeals. On appeal, the woman sought reversal of the earlier ruling because of a refusal by the ALJ to admit and consider performance reviews in the misconduct hearing. The court fully examined the earlier decision and upheld the demotion because the woman's misconduct was not wilful. However, the court found that because the woman did not raise the issue of performance evaluations on her earlier appeal to the MSPB, she was precluded from appealing on that issue now. The determination that demotion was the correct penalty was affirmed. *Boley v. U.S. Postal Service*, 917 F.2d 19 (Fed.Cir.1990).

A custodian was responsible for cleaning an Illinois school library and was entrusted with a set of keys for this purpose. The assistant superintendent of schools noticed that the library Xerox machine was producing unusually low revenue. In an effort to detect the culprit the principal dusted $25 worth of dimes with a powder that would be visible only under a "black light" and placed them in the coin box. The assistant superintendent later confronted the custodian and stated that he had seen him take the coins. He requested that the custodian place his hands and his coins under a black light to determine whether the coins had been taken from the Xerox machine. The custodian refused and was sent home and told not to appear for work until he met with the assistant superintendent to discuss the matter further. Two days later the assistant superintendent informed the custodian that unless he resigned he would recommend to the school board that the custodian be dismissed for theft. The custodian resigned. He brought suit in U.S. district court alleging that his constitutional rights had been violated. However, the district court ruled against the custodian and held that the assistant superintendent had properly requested that he submit to a black light test. The Fifth Amendment privilege against self-incrimination applies only to criminal proceedings, not employment proceedings. The court noted that at no time did any school official threaten to institute criminal charges against the custodian. Because the matter was not a criminal proceeding the court held that the custodian was entitled to no Fifth Amendment privilege. His resignation was properly obtained. *People v. Bd. of Educ.*, 606 F.Supp. 385 (N.D.Ill.1985).

A Washington school district terminated a bus driver's employment for deficient and unsafe conduct and failure to correct performance deficiencies. The discharge notice mentioned four unrelated incidents including driving with an underinflated tire, leaving the bus running and unattended in a loading zone, and driving at excessive speeds. The final reason for the discharge was the driver's failure to be in the immediate area while students were boarding on two occasions shortly before the discharge. The other incidents occurred in previous school years. The driver filed a grievance which was denied by the school board, but the Court of Appeals of Washington ruled in his favor. The court stated that it was error for past incidents to be considered because of their dissimilarity and remoteness and because those deficiencies had apparently been remedied. The driver should have been given the opportunity to remedy the deficiencies occurring immediately before his termination. The driver's behavior was inappropriate but discharge was not justified. *Butler v. Lamont School Dist. No. 246*, 745 P.2d 1308 (Wash.App.1987).

A University of Florida police officer was discovered allegedly under the influence of alcohol during work hours on four separate occasions from 1983 through 1985. On each occasion the police officer was advised of the state policy on alcoholism, but the police officer responded that he had no drinking problem. Following the fourth incident, he was informed that he would be terminated for reporting to work under the influence of alcohol. The police officer appealed this termination. The Florida District Court of Appeal noted that when public relations or work conditions are adversely affected by a problem drinker's behavior, the employee should be placed on compulsory leave before being discharged. It then held that the police officer's termination could not be overturned. *Univ. of Florida v. Mossburg*, 503 So.2d 404 (Fla.App.1st Dist.1987).

A teacher employed by the Chicago public school system allegedly solicited a student to kill his principal and two assistant principals. Criminal proceedings brought against the teacher resulted in a verdict of not guilty. When the Chicago school board sought to dismiss him for conduct unbecoming a teacher, the hearing officer determined that the board had not proven its case by "clear and convincing evidence," and accordingly he ordered that the complaint against the teacher be dismissed. The school board appealed. The board contended that the less stringent "preponderance of the evidence" standard should govern the case. Disagreeing, the Appellate Court of Illinois upheld the hearing officer's decision. The rule in Illinois states that in civil proceedings where criminal charges are the basis for dismissal, the charges must be proven by clear and convincing evidence. *Kimbrough v. Bd. of Educ.*, 481 N.E.2d 67 (Ill.App.1st Dist.1985).

Two police officers were investigating the setting off of a school's burglar alarm system when they discovered the school's head janitor asleep on a shop table. The custodian was subsequently found guilty of misconduct in the performance of his duties and discharged. The New York Supreme Court, Appellate Division, found that the police officers' testimony established sufficient evidence that the man had been asleep while on duty and was therefore guilty of misconduct. It also found that the penalty of dismissal was not "shockingly disproportionate" to the offense. The custodian's dismissal was affirmed. *Smith v. Bd. of Educ.*, 510 N.Y.S.2d 29 (A.D.3d Dept.1986).

A New York community college maintenance supervisor was terminated for sexually harassing two female employees under his supervision. He was terminated pursuant to a hearing in which a hearing officer sustained seven charges and recommended demotion. The supervisor contended that termination was excessive, disproportionate to the offense and unsupported by evidence. He appealed to a New York appellate division court, which affirmed the termination. The court cited previous New York decisions which held that sexual harassment was "among the most offensive and demeaning torments an employee can undergo." The record substantiated termination with ample evidence of unwanted touching, kissing and sexually oriented conversations objected to by female employees. *Crookston v. Brown*, 528 N.Y.S.2d 908 (A.D.3d Dep't 1988).

A Philadelphia school district terminated an employee who was chronically late for work. The employee claimed that his chronic lateness was the result of mental disability and that the school had discriminated against him. His psychologist testified that the lateness was a personality disorder which he could not control. The court, however, held that the school district did not have a duty to compensate for a personality disorder. The court held that the employee was not disabled and that his claim was without merit. *Philadelphia School Dist. v. Friedman*, 507 A.2d 882 (Pa.Cmwlth.1986).

A custodian at a Michigan public school received eight reprimands. One of the reprimands was for leaving work two and one-half hours early. When he left work early again he was suspended pending a hearing. After the hearing the man was discharged based upon the second offense of leaving work early and his unsatisfactory work record. The Michigan Court of Appeals found sufficient evidence in the record to support the determination that the incidents, considered collectively, constituted misconduct under Michigan law. The man's termination was therefore justified. *Watson v. Holt Public Schools*, 407 N.W.2d 623 (Mich.App.1987).

A tenured elementary school teacher was accused of touching several female students on their buttocks, legs, shoulders and chests. The Education Board of Chicago suspended him without pay pending a hearing. A hearing officer held that the teacher had improperly touched the students but reinstated him because the board, prior to suspension, failed to give notice to the teacher. The hearing officer concluded that the charge of unprofessional physical contact was not proven by the board and therefore the conduct was not irremediable. The teacher's suspension was reversed and he was ordered reinstated with full back pay. The board appealed to an Illinois trial court which reversed the hearing officer's decision. The teacher appealed to the Appellate Court of Illinois.

The appellate court held that the teacher's improper touching did constitute "unprofessional physical contact" sufficient to warrant dismissal. A tenured teacher, before being dismissed, must be given written warnings if the alleged conduct is deemed remediable. However, in this case, the teacher's improper touching of female students was irremediable and written warnings prior to the teacher's discharge were unnecessary. The appellate court affirmed the trial court's decision. *Board of Educ. of Chicago v. Box*, 547 N.E.2d 627 (Ill.App.1st Dist.1989).

In 1978, Congress enacted the Civil Service Reform Act (CSRA), which precluded judicial review of many federal administrative personnel decisions. A major exception was CSRA Chapter 75 which created a class of covered employees including those in the competitive service, and preference eligible postal employees, such as veterans. A Virginia postal operations manager was accused of sexually harassing six employees under his supervision. The employees submitted a formal complaint, leading to an investigation and charges of sexual harassment, unethical conduct and unsatisfactory performance. The postmaster terminated the manager's employment. After exhausting his administrative remedies, the manager sued the postal service in a federal district court.

The court granted the service's motion to dismiss the complaint for lack of jurisdiction. The manager appealed to the U.S. Court of Appeals, Fourth Circuit. The appeals court noted that the CSRA barred judicial review of federal administrative personnel actions which were not within the narrow exceptions of Chapter 75. Because the manager was neither preference eligible nor in the competitive service, he did not fit the exceptions. The employee was without recourse in federal courts to challenge the postmaster's decision and the court affirmed the district court's decision. *Yokum v. U.S. Postal Serv.*, 877 F.2d 276 (4th Cir.1989).

An Alabama police captain was injured in an auto accident while on duty. His examining physician placed him on light duty and he returned to work. The next day, however, the captain placed himself on injury-with-pay status without notifying his superior officer. Approximately one week later, a doctor told him he could return to work with certain restrictions. The captain then participated in several softball games. After the games he complained to his superior officer that he was having back problems and requested more time off to see a doctor. However, the captain did not see his doctor but instead participated in a softball tournament. He again placed himself on injury-with-pay status without approval from his superior officer. The police department terminated the captain's employment and he appealed to the county personnel board. The personnel board conducted a public hearing and affirmed the dismissal. The captain appealed to an

Alabama trial court which also affirmed the termination. The captain then appealed to the Alabama Court of Civil Appeals.

The court of civil appeals determined that the matter depended upon the weight and credibility of the evidence. In this case, the evidence was sufficient to support the court's determination. Medical testimony indicated that the captain suffered no significant injury. Because there was no showing that the board's termination action was arbitrary its determination was affirmed. *Rouse v. City of Birmingham*, 535 So.2d 167 (Ala.Civ.App.1988).

A long-time Library of Congress employee habitually disappeared from work without permission. Frequently he worked a halfday, left for lunch and did not return. The employee admitted that he often failed to return because he was drinking. On a few occasions he returned to work intoxicated. His supervisors did not confront him with the possibility that he was an alcoholic, nor did the employee raise the issue. However, his supervisors repeatedly referred him to health services and encouraged him to seek assistance. When the library terminated the employee, he protested the action through the library's review procedure. An arbitrator affirmed the dismissal. The employee then sued the library in the U.S. District Court for the District of Columbia, claiming that the library violated the Rehabilitation Act, the Comprehensive Alcohol Abuse and Alcoholism Prevention, Treatment and Rehabilitation Act and Office of Personnel Management and library regulations. The court dismissed the lawsuit and the employee appealed to the U.S. Court of Appeals, District of Columbia Circuit.

On appeal, the employee argued that the Rehabilitation Act applied to Library of Congress employees. The appeals court noted that although the act had been extended in part to library employees, the section relied upon by the employee was still limited to executive branch and postal employees. The Alcohol Abuse Act prohibited federal agencies from failing to select employee applicants or fire current employees for prior alcoholism, but left the agencies free to discharge alcoholic employees who were not performing their jobs satisfactorily. Because the employee was fired for recurring misconduct the library did not violate the act. The court also rejected the employee's argument that the library had violated administrative regulations when it failed to give him a choice between accepting treatment or other punishment. The appeals court affirmed the district court's dismissal of the lawsuit. *Judd v. Billington*, 863 F.2d 103 (D.C.Cir.1988).

B. Misconduct While Off Duty

An off-duty Ohio police officer, who had been disciplined on many occasions, became involved in efforts taken by her sister to recover a stolen purse. Because of this incident, the officer was later charged with conduct unbecoming an officer. During a subsequent internal affairs investigation, the officer refused to answer questions. A guarantee was then given that the information would not be used in later criminal proceedings. The officer still refused to answer questions. The sheriff then terminated the officer. After five unsuccessful appeals for reinstatement, the case reached the Supreme Court of Ohio. The court faced two issues: can off-duty "vigilante activity" constitute conduct unbecoming an officer, and could the officer be forced to answer questions in light of her Fifth Amendment rights and the guarantee given? On the first issue, the court observed that police officers are held to a higher standard of conduct than the public, even when off-duty. The actions taken by the officer were found to bring disrepute on her department. The court upheld the dismissal based upon off-duty misconduct. Can a public employee be forced to answer possibly incriminating questions when she is guaranteed that her testimony will be protected from use in a criminal trial? The court ruled that the guarantee given removed the officer's option of refusing to answer. Although the officer could possibly lose her job by answering, this was not found to be protected by the Fifth Amendment. The court's justification for the infringement was based on the importance of effective internal investigations to a police department. The supreme court upheld the dismissal of the officer. *Jones v. Franklin County Sheriff*, 555 N.E.2d 940 (Ohio 1990).

A public school janitor in Pennsylvania was arrested at school and charged with a drug offense. However, the arrest had nothing to do with his conduct while on the job; instead the police had previously searched his apartment and found amphetamines and other drugs. As a result of the drug charges the janitor was fired. The Commonwealth Court of Pennsylvania upheld his dismissal, ruling that "improper conduct" leading to dismissal need not occur on school property. It was also irrelevant whether his job performance was affected. The only relevant inquiry, stated the court, was whether the possession of methamphetamines constituted improper conduct. Finding that it did, the court upheld his dismissal. *School Dist. Philadelphia v. Puljer*, 500 A.2d 905 (Pa.Comwlth.1985).

A police officer was discovered negotiating the sale of unregistered weapons to an unlicensed individual when other officers entered the bathroom of a bar. The police commissioner of the city of New York held a termination hearing for the accused officer. The officer was found guilty of wrongful possession and attempted sale of a weapon, among other charges, and was terminated. The officer attempted an appeal through the courts. The trial court transferred the case to the Supreme court, Appellate Division of New York. The terminated officer sought review based on allegations that the arresting officers had been intoxicated. The court examined the evidence produced at the pretermination hearing. The decision of a hearing officer would be overturned only when clearly erroneous or when injustice would result. The commissioner's decision was supported by enough relevant proof so that a reasonable mind could come to the same conclusion. Weighing the credibility of the witnesses was done by the commissioner and was not the role of the appellate court. The commissioner's decision was upheld. *Romanelli v. Ward*, 549 N.Y.S.2d 722 (A.D.1990).

A Louisiana prison guard was a classified employee with the Department of Public Safety and Corrections (DPSC). It was discovered that he had "spring-loaded" a twelve gauge shotgun into the fort of a tree in front of his house. The prison warden sent a letter to the officer stating precisely the day, time, violation and time at which the officer was arrested for the felony. The letter was to inform him that he was suspended. However, the state dismissed the charges against the officer but still held him suspended. The officer appealed to the State Civil Serivce Commission which reinstated him with pay effective prospectively. After several administrative hearings the commission still reinstated the officer since there was no finding that state criminal law was ever violated. The DPSC appealed the commission's decision to the Court of Appeal of Louisiana.

The court of appeal stated that cause for termination included conduct which would be prejudicial to public service or detrimental to its efficient operation. Further, conduct which constitutes a violation of a criminal statute may constitute cause. The court of appeal decided that the commission correctly observed that an acquittal on a criminal charge does not preclude a civil service disciplinary action on the same set of facts. For these reasons, the decision of the commission was reversed and the action was remanded to the commission for findings on whether a criminal statute was violated by the officer. *Dep't of Pub. Safety and Corr. v. Hooker*, 558 So.2d 676 (La.App.1st Cir.1990).

Over the span of eight hours, two Montana city police officers attended a number of bars. A citizen turned in a complaint about their activities, which arose from a conversation which they had engaged in that evening, while the officers were off-duty. The officers then contacted a third officer for a ride home. The city police commission brought misconduct charges against the officers and suspended them without pay. Montana statutes permit police commission decisions to be modified or vetoed by the mayor or city manager. The city manager modified the decision and immediately terminated the employment of the three officers. The officers petitioned a Montana trial court for review. The court affirmed the decision, and the officers appealed again to the Montana Supreme Court.

The supreme court ruled that the terminations were supported by substantial evidence. Evidence that the two officers were intoxicated was overwhelming, and because they denied intoxication, the commission's finding of dishonesty was supported by the record. Although the third officer was less culpable than the two who had gone to the bar, his dishonesty before the commission was sufficient to warrant termination. There were no grounds for reversal on any of the officers' complaints that the commission had made procedural errors. The city's finding of dishonesty was beyond the jurisdiction of Montana courts. *Gentry v. City of Helena*, 773 P.2d 309 (Mont.1989).

An off-duty New Jersey police chief consumed three drinks. He then was involved in an automobile accident and suffered serious injuries. Two fellow officers arrived shortly after but did not administer a breathalyzer test. The doctors requested a blood sample and the chief refused. A blood sample was taken about three hours later. The alcohol concentration was extrapolated to show that the concentration at the time of the accident was above the level for intoxication. The chief was charged with driving while intoxicated. A municipal court acquitted the chief of the DWI charge. The township committee decided to file a four count complaint against the chief. The complaint charged him with: operating a vehicle under the influence in violation of established township policy, violating the rules and regulations of the police department by engaging in conduct contrary to good order and discipline, and violating the rules and regulations of the department by acting under the influence of alcohol. The committee determined that the chief had been under the influence of alcohol, in violation of departmental regulations. The chief appealed the township's determination. On appeal, the law division found the chief guilty only of violating departmental regulations by acting contrary to good order and discipline. The law division also ruled that the penalty demoting the chief to patrolman was appropriate. The chief appealed to the New Jersey Court of Appeal. The appellate division reversed the law division's decision and dismissed all charges against the chief. The township appealed to the Supreme Court of New Jersey.

On appeal, the court noted that the issue was whether the departmental regulation could be construed more broadly than the statutory DWI offense. The court noted that the finding of intoxication, in violation of department rules and regulations, could be determined on less-stringent criteria than necessary to establish a statutory violation. The charges brought against the chief were not based solely on the statutory offense. The decision of the appellate division was therefore reversed in part and affirmed in part by the supreme court. *In Re Phillips*, 569 A.2d 807 (N.J.1990).

A North Dakota employee worked for the state highway department for eight years as an equipment operator. In addition, he repaired automobiles during his off-duty time as a personal business. Department policies required that outside employment not interfere with an employee's performance and that the job be done outside assigned working hours. It also prohibited the use of state vehicles for personal purposes. Departmental policy, of which the man was aware, provided sanctions for violation of the policies which included dismissal. The department received a report that the employee had used a state vehicle for personal purposes, and its investigation discovered that he had twice used a state vehicle to pick up automobile parts for his personal use. The department suspended him for three days. Later, the department learned of another incident that had occurred prior to the suspension which also involved the employee's use of a state vehicle for personal purposes. The department terminated the employee and he appealed to the state personnel board which upheld the dismissal. He appealed to a North Dakota trial court. When the court ruled for the state, he appealed to the Supreme Court of North Dakota. The supreme court found that there was substantial evidence to confirm the department's charges against the employee. Although the employee had not been entitled to a full evidentiary pretermination hearing, he had received a full post-termination hearing to satisfy his due process rights. Finally, the court noted that the department could discipline the man for a violation which occurred prior to the earlier disciplinary action because the department had no knowledge of the incident when it suspended him. The court affirmed the trial court's decision, upholding the employee's termination. *Berdahl v. North Dakota State Personnel Bd.*, 447 N.W.2d 300 (N.D.1989).

After a Wisconsin police officer struck his girlfriend in public, the police chief suspended the officer with pay until a disciplinary hearing could be held. The disciplinary committee recommended that the police officer be terminated for conduct unbecoming an officer. The officer failed to file an appeal with the committee and instead sued the committee in a Wisconsin trial court. The trial court affirmed the termination and the officer appealed to the Court of Appeals of Wisconsin. The appellate court was limited to two questions on review; whether the committee kept within its jurisdiction and whether it proceeded on a correct theory of law. The officer contended that the committee members were biased because they were appointed by the police chief, who filed the charges. The court noted that a decisionmaker is always presumed to be impartial. The mere fact that members of the disciplinary committee had been appointed by the police chief was not, without more, sufficient to overcome the presumption of the committee's impartiality. Next, the officer contended that he was penalized twice for the same incident, which was against regulations. The court, however, determined that the officer's suspension with pay was not a disciplinary action within the meaning of the statute because he was not "proved guilty." The court affirmed the termination. *Reedy v. Law Enf. Disciplinary Committee*, 457 N.W.2d 505 (Wis.1990).

A West Virginia man, employed by the department of corrections, either sold or gave a shotgun and a revolver to a felon less than twenty-four hours after the felon's release from prison. The felon had been convicted three times for armed robbery or attempted armed robbery. Shortly after the felon received the guns, he was arrested in a state of intoxication. The prison warden suspended the employee pending an investigation into the charge that the employee had sold guns to the felon. A week later, the warden dismissed the employee, and the employee appealed to the state civil service commission. The commission agreed with the state that the employee had sold the guns to the felon, but reduced the dismissal to a three-month suspension. The state department of corrections appealed to the Supreme Court of Appeals of West Virginia.

The appellate court noted that although dismissal would be inappropriate if the employee's violation had been merely a technical one, in this case the violation was of a much more serious nature.The court stated that the employee's conduct was potentially damaging to the rights and interests of the public, and it made no difference that the violation occurred while the employee was off-duty. If further stated that the employee's conduct showed a gross disregard for his professional responsibilities and for the public safety. The court found that the potential danger to the public of an armed, intoxicated repeat felon was sufficient reason to discharge the employee. The court reversed the civil service commission's order, and upheld the employee's dismissal. *West Virginia Dep't of Corrections v. LeMasters,* 313 S.E.2d 436 (W.Va.1984).

A Montana police officer pursued an interest in hypnosis. After extensive study, he began a private hypnosis business in his home during his off-duty hours. Rumors of sexual advances to certain treated women triggered an investigation, where it was learned that he had gained their confidence and trust by using his status as a police officer, then attempted to seduce them. The police commission conducted a hearing and discharged him. He appealed unsuccessfully to a Montana trial court, and further appealed to the Supreme Court of Montana.

The supreme court recognized that the officer had certain privacy rights while off-duty, and that he had not been charged with any criminal sexual conduct. However, it ruled that there was substantial evidence to show that his conduct was reprehensible and repugnant, and constituted conduct unbecoming an officer. Here, the officer advertised his business and traded on his position as an officer to gain customers' trust, then breached that trust through wholly unexpected practices. The court found that the officer's privacy rights did not extend to this type of off-duty conduct. The court affirmed the trial court's decision, upholding the officer's dismissal. *Matter of Raynes*, 698 P.2d 856 (Mont.1985).

A prison employee put white sheets over his body and walked through the prison causing the inmates to think of the Ku Klux Klan. His supervisor acted as a prosecutor in a later disciplinary hearing, and it resulted in a thirty day suspension for the employee. He then threatened the supervisor and harassed him by driving on his lawn, racing a car's engine outside of his house, spinning car tires in his driveway, and sitting in a parked car outside his house. This harassment led to a petty disorderly persons offense conviction, and a forfeiture of his rights to continued public employment. This forfeiture was appealed and upheld by a merit board and an appellate court, and the case reached the Supreme Court of New Jersey. The employe argued that he could not be found to have forfeited his right to employment for off-duty and off work premises conduct. The court disagreed. Its decision balanced the seriousness of the crime and the qualifications required of the employee against the employee's right to continued employment. The court found that the infraction "cast a shadow over the employee as to make his ... continued service appear incompatible with the traits of trustworthiness, honesty, and obedience to law and order." The record supported the determination of forfeiture, and the decision was upheld. *Moore v. Youth Correctional Institute*, 574 A.2d 983 (N.J.1990).

VI. LAYOFFS AND FINANCIAL REASONS

Generally, if public employers need to lay off employees for financial reasons, the employees will not be afforded the same due process rights they would receive in terminations or suspensions for other causes.

A city employee was appointed administrator for the human affairs office for a four year term. After only two years in office, the mayor verbally notified the employee of his dismissal due to the city's financial crisis. There were no performance or disciplinary reasons for the dismissal. Nine months after his dismissal, the employee instituted an action seeking both damages and reinstatement to his former position. The trial court dismissed the action. He then appealed to the Supreme Court of Connecticut. On appeal, the issue was whether the mayor's implied authority to dismiss city personnel for financial reasons superseded the city employee's right to serve his full four year term as administrator for human affairs. The city employee had to establish that he had a clear legal right to the office and that the city had no discretion with respect to the dismissal. The court found that the employee's appointment for a four year term would ordinarily entitle him to serve the entire term, but it also found that the mayor's responsibility to manage the city's finances afforded him the implied power to dismiss city personnel for serious fiscal reasons. Since the mayor had the discretion to remove the plaintiff under circumstances of financial stringency, the employee's dismissal was appropriate. The supreme court affirmed the trial court's decision to dismiss the action. *Hennessey v. Bridgeport*, 569 A.2d 1122 (Conn.1990).

When Kentucky's new governor assumed office in 1979, he undertook an analysis of the budget in an effort to reduce expenditures. Because of the constitutional mandate requiring a balanced budget, he ordered a review of all departmental operations in an effort to meet the mandate. Subsequently, 254 layoff plans were implemented affecting 1,800 state merit system employees. Forty-two of the laid-off employees then sued the state, asserting that they had been deprived of certain constitutional rights. The federal trial court dismissed their claims, and they appealed to the U.S. Court of Appeals, Sixth Circuit.

The appellate court noted that the state's supervisory personnel had not acted in a way that would have violated the employees' constitutional rights. There was no constitutional violation in this case. Layoffs were not "discharges" within the meaning of Kentucky law and the layoffs did not adversely stigmatize the employees so as to affect their reputation in the community. The court affirmed the trial court's decision and dismissed the employees' claims. *Riggs v. Commonwealth of Kentucky*, 734 F.2d 262 (1984).

In 1981, the Governor of Missouri ordered a reduction in expenditures. As a result, 900 employees of the department of mental health were laid off. Two nonprobationary employees filed appeals with the Personnel Advisory Board (PAB), contending that they were victims of personal animosity by their supervisor. PAB dismissed their appeals, stating that so long as the prescribed procedures had been followed, it had no authority to review layoffs caused by a shortage of funds. The employees successfully appealed to a Missouri trial court, and the department then appealed to the Missouri Court of Appeals.

The appellate court noted that judicial review was allowed only when all administrative remedies had been exhausted and the employees had been aggrieved by final decisions in contested cases. A contested case is one where a prior hearing must be held. In this case, no prior hearing had been necessary. In fact, to provide prelayoff hearings to 900 employees would have delayed the layoffs to the point that the danger which the layoffs sought to prevent would become a reality. Because the state interest was so strong, and because the proper procedures had been followed, the court refused to grant relief to the employees. The court reversed the trial court's decision. *Walker v. Personnel Advisory Bd. of State*, 670 S.W.2d 1 (Mo.App.1984).

The Department of Housing and Urban Development (HUD) issued a reduction in force (RIF) notice, informing employees that it was doing so to resolve "workload and skills imbalances." Fifty-four individuals affected by the RIF appealed this decision to the Merit Systems Protection Board (MSPB), contending that HUD's action was not authorized by federal law. The law allowed RIFs when there was a lack of work, shortage of funds, reorganization, reclassification, or the exercise of reemployment rights.

The MSPB ruled in favor of HUD, and the individuals appealed to the U.S. Court of Appeals.

The appellate court agreed with the MSPB that federal law did not require HUD to use only the specific terms in the regulation. "Workload and skills imbalances" were the equivalent of a reorganization of the agency and therefore fit into the federal law guidelines of when a RIF action could be taken. The court held that HUD did not need to use the "magic words" in the regulation. It only needed to present reasons that fell within the scope of the regulation. The court affirmed the MSPB's decision, and allowed the RIF. *Bacon v. Dep't of Housing and Urban Development*, 757 F.2d 265 (1985).

A Connecticut city determined that it was in a financial crisis. Accordingly, the city's mayor created a "layoff plan", which was then implemented. Several classified, nonprobationary employees who were laid off according to the plan, appealed to the civil service commission. It ordered their reinstatement, but the city and the mayor refused to comply. The employees then sued in a Connecticut trial court, seeking reinstatement, and the court ruled for the city. They appealed to the Supreme Court of Connecticut.

The supreme court held that the city and the mayor had acted within their authority when they ordered the layoffs to get through a genuine fiscal crisis.

Further, the court stated that the commission had no jurisdiction over such financially motivated layoffs. When the city must terminate an employee because of financial distress, the employee has no constitutional right to a hearing. Had the layoffs been motivated by something else, the court ruled that the commission would have had review power. The court affirmed the trial court's decision, upholding the layoffs. *Perretta v. City of New Britain*, 440 A.2d 823 (Conn.1981).

A "fourth-class" city in Missouri hired two police officers after they had undergone certain training and educational requirements. Shortly thereafter, the mayor laid them off in an effort to cut the city's costs during the winter months. The officers sued the city and the mayor in a Missouri trial court, asserting that they had been unlawfully discharged without a hearing. The trial court agreed, and ordered that they be given a hearing on any dismissal action. The city and mayor then appealed to the Supreme Court of Missouri.

On appeal, the court noted that appointed officers or employees of "fourth-class" cities were essentially at-will employees. The court stated that the officers did not have a legal or contractual right to continued employment. Also, it found that no false or defamatory statements had been made concerning the officers. Finally, the court held that even though the officers had been required to undergo certain training and education because the city was located in a "first-class" county, they did not gain any extra rights by virtue of the city's location. The court reversed the trial court's decision, and denied the officers a hearing. *Amaan v. City of Eureka*, 615 S.W.2d 414 (Mo.banc 1981).

An Alaska man worked for the state department of commerce and economic development. He was a member of the Alaska Public Employees' Association (APEA) and was subject to the collective bargaining agreement (CBA). In 1984, he attended a workshop and while there denigrated to some extent the chances for success of a state-owned mine. After his remarks had been published in a local newspaper, his supervisor asked him if the article was accurate. He admitted that it was, and when asked to resign, he refused. Subsequently, he was dismissed. He filed a grievance with the APEA, and upon review, was reinstated. Later, the state budget included insufficient funds for the department, and his position was absent from the budget. He sued in an Alaska trial court, unsuccessfully, and then appealed to the Supreme Court of Alaska.

The supreme court held that the employee's sole remedies lay with the CBA unless and until the legislature decided to change the law. Because the CBA provided a comprehensive scheme for redressing employee grievances, the court chose not to step in and contest those procedures. The court acknowledged that instances might occur where an employee would be less well off with the CBA than otherwise, but in most cases it would benefit employees. The court affirmed the trial court's decision. *Walt v. State*, 751 P.2d 1345 (Alaska 1988).

An Arkansas school district terminated a custodian's employment contract after the superintendent became concerned that the district would end the year with a deficit. Arkansas statutes provide that teachers' employment contracts may be terminated if a school district is threatened by a financial shortfall. When the custodian appealed his termination the Arkansas Supreme Court ruled that the school district had breached his employment contract. The court reasoned that once the school district entered into a written contract with the custodian, it was obligated to abide by the contract's terms. Neither the custodian's employment contract nor any statute provided that the custodian's employment contract could be terminated because of an impending financial shortfall. *Calico Rock School Dist. v. Speak*, 736 S.W.2d 10 (Ark.1987).

Due to declining enrollment an Alabama school board voted to reduce a lunchroom worker's hours from thirty-five to thirty hours per week. The worker requested a hearing under the State's Fair Dismissal Act but the school board denied the request stating that its action was neither a "termination" nor a "transfer" within the meaning of the Act. After a trial court upheld the school board decision, the worker appealed to the Alabama Supreme Court which observed that the trial court did not address the principle that a public employee with a "legitimate claim of entitlement to continued employment must be given an opportunity to prove the legitimacy of his claim." The board's reduction of the worker's hours was a partial determination, and the trial court's decision was reversed. *Ledbetter v. Jackson County Bd. of Educ.*, 508 So.2d 244 (Ala.1987).

A Florida civil service employee was promoted from city finance manager to assistant finance director. The new position was not a civil service job and the city provided no written contract. She was later advised that as a result of budget cutbacks, her position as assistant finance director had been abolished. She was informed that she could receive severance benefits only if she resigned as assistant finance director and executed a release. She resigned and executed the release without any advice as to her rights or the legal effect of her resignation upon her civil service position. She was also advised that the position of finance manager had been abolished. Before she was terminated, however, an employee with less seniority serving as the city's finance manager was employed to perform the functional equivalent of the finance manager position. The terminated employee sued the city in a Florida circuit court seeking reinstatement and backpay. The court ordered reinstatement and backpay and the city petitioned the District Court of Appeal of Florida, Third District.

The court held that the release signed by the former employee was invalid because the city had failed to inform her of her alternatives. It ordered her reinstated. The court noted that the employee's due process rights were violated when the city failed to inform her of her right to obtain another civil service position. She had been misled by the city and did not knowingly relinquish her civil service rights. The court further noted that where a civil service employee has been denied due process, the circuit court has the authority to order reinstatement. The district court affirmed the decision for the employee. *City of Miami v. Meynarez*, 546 So.2d 771 (Fla.App.3d Dist. 1989).

A Missouri city hospital contracted with four doctors as physicians-in-training on a year to year basis. They moved to the city, discontinued their search for a residency at other hospitals and began work. The city then decided to terminate the program because of financial distress, and it did not renew their contracts. Nevertheless, they stayed on at the hospital without pay, working there until they completed their residency. They then appealed to the civil service commission, seeking back pay and damages. Because they were not permanent employees, the commission stated that it could not hear their appeal. They accordingly appealed to a Missouri trial court, which held for the city, and they further appealed to the Missouri Court of Appeals.

The appellate court held that the doctors did not have protected property or liberty interests in continued employment. Further, because the program had been ended for financial reasons, the doctors were not entitled to termination hearings. Finally, the court held that the evidence of budgetary constraints and legitimate reasons for terminating the program were sufficient to support the city's position. The court affirmed the trial court's decision, and disallowed back pay to the doctors. *Kennedy v. City of St. Louis*, 749 S.W.2d 427 (Mo.App.1988).

The Michigan legislature amended its workers' compensation act, establishing an autonomous board of magistrates within the state department of labor to replace workers' compensation hearing referees. The displaced referees claimed that the elimination of their civil service positions by the state legislature was unconstitutional. They sued the state in a Michigan trial court for an order to prohibit the governor from executing the amendments. The referees claimed that the legislature had enacted the law as a partisan and discriminatory measure to award their jobs to political appointees. The court found the statute unconstitutional. A direct appeal to the Michigan Supreme Court was approved, and the supreme court reversed the trial court's decision. On remand, the trial court granted the state's summary judgment motion, finding that the supreme court had summarily disposed of the substance of the referees' claim. The court also ruled against the referees' claim that the legislative act was a bill of attainder. The referees then appealed to the Michigan Court of Appeals.

The appeals court ruled that the trial court had correctly dismissed the bad faith and equal protection claims, as they had been previously addressed by the supreme court. The trial court had properly dismissed the referees' breach of contract complaints because they were civil servants without express or implied employment contracts. Finally, the legislative action was not a bill of attainder. While the referees may have had legitimate employment expectations, the act did not deprive them of their civil service status. The appeals court affirmed the trial court's decision for the state. *Matulewicz v. Governor of Michigan*, 435 N.W.2d 785 (Mich.App.1989).

VII. RETALIATORY DISCHARGE AND POLITICAL PATRONAGE

In general, retaliatory discharges are not allowed by the courts. However, political patronage dismissals may be upheld provided that the employees dismissed are in policymaking positions where complete loyalty is needed. If the employees are not in such positions though, the courts will not allow patronage dismissals.

The government of Illinois instituted a hiring freeze for every agency under his control, which prohibited state officials from hiring any employee, from filling any vacancies, or from creating any new positions. Exceptions were granted through the governor's personnel office with a majority going to those employees affiliated with the Republican Party. Five state employees brought suit in a federal district court alleging that they suffered discrimination with respect to promotions, transfers and recalls because they had not been supporters of the state's Republican Party. The district court dismissed the complaint. The employees appealed to the U.S. Court of Appeals, Seventh Circuit, which reversed in part and affirmed in part, noting that only those employment decisions that have the effect of a dismissal violate the First Amendment. The employees further appealed to the U.S. Supreme Court.

On appeal, the Republican Party argued that since the employment decisions were not punitive and did not adversely affect the terms of employment, they did not violate the First Amendment. In a five to four decision, the majority determined that employees who did not compromise their beliefs tended to lose increases in pay and job satisfaction attendant to promotions, transfers and recalls. The Court noted that these are significant penalties and are imposed in retaliation for the exercise of rights guaranteed by the First Amendment. The majority, therefore, determined that promotions, transfers and recalls based on political affiliation were an impermissible infringement on the First Amendment rights of public employees. The Court established the constitutional principle "that party membership is not a permissible factor in the dispensation of government jobs, except those jobs for the performance of which party affiliation is an appropriate requirement." *Rutan v. Republican Party of Illinois*, 110 S.Ct. 2729, 111 L.Ed.2d 52 (1990).

An Illinois man was appointed to a city's electrical department as its director. He served in the position for twelve years until his discharge by a new mayor. During the election campaign, the director was involved in extensive negotiations with a power company to provide electrical power to the city at a substantial cost savings over the city's previous supplier. The mayoral candidate allegedly approached the director and asked that he "slow down" the negotiations so that the incumbent would not receive the political benefit from the successful conclusion of the negotiations. The director refused. When the candidate was eventually elected, he then supposedly asked some city vendors for political contributions to eliminate his debt. The vendors asked the director if they needed to make the contributions to continue doing business with the city, and the director told them they did not need to do so. Later, the mayor also instructed the director not to inform the city aldermen of certain power supply issues. When the director asked the mayor for a clarification as to what his job was, because of the restrictions put on it by the mayor, the mayor terminated his employment. The director sued in an Illinois trial court, alleging that he had been discharged in retaliation for his refusal to cooperate with the mayor's questionable and possibly illegal activities. The trial court dismissed his claim, and he appealed to the Appellate Court of Illinois.

The appellate court held that the director had stated sufficient facts to show that his discharge had been retaliatory. Further, the director's dismissal may have been a tortious interference with an employment relationship. The court found a public policy existed which might have been violated by the discharge, so the dismissal had been improper. The court reversed the trial court's decision, and remanded the case for trial. *Fellhauer v. City of Geneva*, 546 N.E.2d 791 (Ill.App.2d Dist.1989).

A man had dedicated a twenty year professional career with the state of New York toward the advancement of employment opportunities for handicapped persons. He was then promoted to a statewide position, and consistently received high evaluations. During an audit, the man discovered improprieties in payments to private corporations -- some of which had close personal ties to the man's supervisors. The man contacted the FBI. He then began to receive poor work evaluations. The FBI decided, after an investigation, that the case should not be prosecuted. The man was then demoted. He filed suit against his superiors in a federal district court alleging that he had been demoted in retaliation for exercising his free speech rights. A jury found for the employee, and called for both compensatory and punitive damages. The trial judge overruled the allowance of punitive damages, and both parties appealed to the U.S. Court of Appeals, Second Circuit. The appeals court found that the man's conduct amounted to speech on a matter of public concern and was, therefore, entitled to protection. The court also agreed that the employee had been discharged for exercising his rights. A burden then falls on the employer to show that the employer's interest in efficiency outweighs the interest of the employee to speak. Because of the importance of the employee's speech, which concerned the potential for fraud, theft, or misallocation of public funds, The employer did not satisfy this burden. The supervisors then argued that they should be entitled to qualified immunity. The court felt that the supervisors knew or should have known that their actions would violate the employee's clearly established rights, and disallowed the immunity defense. The threshold of proof required for an allowance of compensatory or punitive damages is the same, and the trial court erred in this respect. Awards of punitive damages are discretionary and the jury should have been allowed to award them. The court remanded the case for trial on the amount of punitive damages that should be awarded. *Vasbinder v. Ambach*, 926 F.2d 1333 (2d Cir.1991).

An Illinois woman worked for a city's mass transit district for over three years. She sustained an injury in the course of her employment, and filed for workers' compensation benefits. Less than four months later, while she was still receiving benefits and unable to return to work, the district terminated her employment. She sued the district in an Illinois trial court, asserting that she had been discharged in retaliation for her filing for workers' compensation benefits. The district asked the trial court to dismiss the claim, but the court refused. The district then appealed to the appellate court, unsuccessfully, and further appealed to the Supreme Court of Illinois.

The district argued that it could not be liable for retaliatory discharge because, as a public entity, it was immune from punitive damages. The supreme court agreed that the district was immune from punitive damages claims, but stated that the employee could still bring an action for retaliatory discharge against the district. She simply could not recover punitive damages, and was limited to those damages which would directly compensate her for any injuries she received. The court affirmed the appellate court's decision, and rejected the district's motion for dismissal. *Boyles v. Greater Peoria Mass Transit District,* 499 N.E.2d 435 (Ill.1986).

A New York school district fired two bus drivers for attending a Public Employment Relations Board (PERB) hearing during working hours. The drivers requested a hearing before the state PERB. The board determined that the school district had committed an improper labor practice when it terminated the drivers. It ordered them reinstated with back pay. The district appealed to the New York Supreme Court, Appellate Division. The court held that the drivers' attendance at the meeting was a protected activity and that the district's termination of the drivers was in retaliation for their attendance. Because the district failed to demonstrate that the terminations were prompted by legitimate business concerns, the court affirmed the PERB's finding that the district had committed an improper labor practice. *Bd. of Educ. of the Deer Park Union Free School Dist. v. New York State Public Employment Relations Bd.*, 561 N.Y.S.2d 810 (A.D.2d Dep't 1990).

The municipality of Anchorage fired an employee for complaining to the state and the mayor of Anchorage about unsafe working conditions which resulted in employee injuries. The Alaska Department of Labor (DOL) determined that the municipality terminated the employee in violation of Alaska's "whistleblower protection" statute and sued. The employee brought his own action against the municipality for wrongful discharge in an Alaska trial court. The court dismissed the case and the employee appealed to the Supreme Court of Alaska which vacated the decision and remanded the case to the trial court. On remand, the trial court ruled that the "whistleblower protection" statute provides the exclusive statutory remedy available to the employee for retaliatory discharge for safety complaints. The employee appealed to the Supreme Court of Alaska.

The supreme court held that Alaska's "whistleblower protection" statute does not create an exclusive cause of action for retaliatory discharge for safety complaints. Therefore, the employee may bring his own cause of action under common law for breach of contract. The supreme court reversed the trial court's decision. *Reed v. Municipality of Anchorage*, 782 P.2d 1155 (Alaska 1989).

A social worker was employed by the Louisiana state mental health hospital for the criminally insane. The Assistant Secretary of the state Department of Health and Human Resources (DHHR) claimed that the social worker had spread unsubstantiated rumors, had failed to adequately protect the confidential records of patients and had failed to report his supervisor's illegal activity. The secretary allegedly told the social worker that a termination and investigation were necessary because his conduct had been so disruptive and inflammatory that he had endangered the safety of all individuals at the facility. The secretary then sent the social worker a letter which detailed the reasons for his termination. The social worker sued immediate supervisors, the secretary and the DHHR's deputy secretary in a federal district court. After the district court found for the government officials, the social worker appealed to the U.S. Court of Appeals, Fifth Circuit. He maintained that the termination was in retaliation for exercising his First Amendment rights, and was without procedural due process. The court weighed the employee's First Amendment rights against the hospital's interest in promoting the efficiency of its public service. It ruled that the statements made to the patients and staff members were too disruptive to be protected speech. The court found that even if the statements had been substantial factors in the termination, the social worker nevertheless would have been terminated because of his disruptive behavior. In addition, the court held that the officials were entitled to qualified immunity because no right had been violated. The status of state employees' pretermination procedural rights was uncertain. The court of appeals affirmed the lower court's decision, finding that the social worker's First Amendment rights had not been violated. *Price v. Brittain*, 874 F.2d 252 (5th Cir.1989).

After a Michigan city prosecutor took office, he failed to renew the contracts of several assistant prosecutors. The assistant prosecutors brought an action in a federal district court alleging that the prosecuting attorney failed to reappoint them based on political affiliation. The prosecuting attorney moved for summary judgement. The court noted that political affiliation could not be used as a factor in an employment decision unless party affiliation was an appropriate requirement for the effective performance of the office involved. The court noted that in this case the public prosecutor's position involved policymaking responsibilities and, therefore, political affiliation was an appropriate requirement for the decision not to renew the contracts of the assistant prosecutors. The court granted summary judgement to the prosecuting attorney. *Monks v. Marlinga*, 732 F.Supp. 749 (E.D.Mich.1990).

A Puerto Rican city's Civil Defense Director of the Municipality (director) was removed from office by order of the Mayor. The director sought reinstatement under 42 U.S.C. § 1983, alleging that the decision to remove him was politically motivated. The mayor moved for summary judgment, on the ground that the director's job was confidential and that political affiliation was an appropriate requirement, in a federal district court. If the position's function was such that party affiliation was an appropriate requirement then the termination would be upheld. The director's position indicated that he would act on behalf of the mayor in the mayor's absence. Therefore, the position was confidential in nature and political affiliation was an appropriate requirement. The court granted summary judgement to the mayor. *Lopez Carrillo v. Soto Ayala*, 737 F.Supp. 150 (D.Puerto Rico 1990).

A Kansas City police sergeant learned that a childhood friend was the treasurer of a campaign fund for a congressional candidate. The officer made a contribution to this fund, without knowledge that a statute prohibited political contributions. Specifically, the statute prohibited department employees from "giving anything of value" to political campaigns. The officer's chief of police learned of the contribution and began proceedings which eventually led to the sergeant's termination. The sergeant claimed that the local statute was preempted by the Federal Election Campaign Act Amendments of 1974, and that it violated his free speech and equal protection rights. The U.S. Court of Appeals held against the officer on the first two claims, and later also found against the officer on the equal protection issue. The U.S. Supreme Court denied review. The officer then filed a state claim asserting that the local statute was penal in nature and thus did not allow termination without a showing of intent. The case reached the Missouri Court of Appeals. The court explained that the statute was a civil statute, which was penal in nature. A civil penal statute does not have all the requirements of a criminal statute, such as intent. The statute was designed to allow law enforcement officials to be free from political pressure. It must be enforced in "unblinking fashion." The termination of the officer was upheld. *Reeder v. Bd. of Commissioners of Kansas City*, 800 S.W.2d 5 (Mo.App.1990).

A municipal police chief wished to have a certain candidate elected county sheriff. The chief organized a meeting between himself, the press, his favored candidates, and a local family, This interview resulted in the local media charging the opposing candidate with accepting bribes. The meeting took place while the chief was on duty and utilized a department automobile. Further, the chief expressed his political views and distributed tickets to a fund raising banquet while on duty and in uniform. The chief was later dismissed by the city council for violating police personnel manual regulations prohibiting an on-duty officer from becoming actively involved in, or expressing opinions on, political issues. The officer appealed his dismissal to the Missouri Court of Appeals. The chief's first argument was that the decision was arbitrary. The court found that the evidence supported the council's decision. The chief then argued that the regulations and ordinances were vague and unconstitutionally overbroad. The court explained that police officers have long been subject to political restrictions in order to assure the public that police protection is free from political pressure. The statute is clear in allowing political expression only when off-duty and in civilian attire. The court found the statute to be both narrowly drawn and constitutionally applied. The police chief's termination was upheld. *State Ex Rel. Trautman v. City of Farmington*, 799 S.W.2d 638 (Mo.App.1990).

Several Illinois noncivil service employees, who had been appointed to their positions by a Republican sheriff, were discharged when the new Democratic sheriff was elected. It had been the practice of newly elected sheriffs to replace noncivil service employees from the opposing party with members of their own party upon assuming office. This time, however, the discharged employees sued in a federal trial court to prevent the terminations. The court ruled against them, and they successfully appealed. The incoming sheriff then appealed to the U.S. Supreme Court.

The Supreme Court noted that patronage dismissals were acceptable if they targeted policymaking employees. However, where nonpolicymaking employees were concerned, it was not acceptable for an incoming party to terminate all those employees who had supported the opposing side. It held that the practice of patronage imposed an unacceptable restraint on freedom of speech in most cases because to maintain their jobs, employees were required to switch their political affiliations or lose their jobs.

The Court further noted that not only would efficiency not be lost by keeping employees from the opposing party, it might actually be promoted by denying wholesale replacement of large numbers of public employees each time political offices changed hands. Finally, the Court determined that the democratic process would not be threatened by the denial of patronage dismissals and hirings. Political parties had existed prior to active patronage and would continue to exist with this diminished patronage power. The Court affirmed the court of appeals' decision, disallowing the patronage dismissals. *Elrod v. Burns*, 427 U.S. 347, 96 S.Ct. 2673, 49 L.Ed.2d 547 (1976).

Four Rhode Island town solicitors, who had been appointed by a Democratic town council, were dismissed from their positions when a Republican town council was elected. They challenged their dismissals because they were politically motivated, and sued the town manager, who had dismissed them, and also sued the town, seeking reinstatement. The trial court held that they had no protection from political dismissals, and they appealed to the Supreme Court of Rhode Island.

On appeal, they argued that their civil rights had been violated by the dismissals, which were in violation of 42 U.S.C. § 1983. The court disagreed, finding that the employees' relationship with the town council required trust and loyalty, and that party affiliation was a permissible way to ensure that the necessary trust and loyalty existed. The political nature of the employees' positions and the fact that the town charter stated that they held their positions "at the pleasure of" the town manager indicated that they had no property interests in future employment. They were simply at-will employees. The court affirmed the trial court's decision, and disallowed reinstatement to the solicitors. *Montaquila v. St. Cyr*, 433 A.2d 206 (R.I.1981).

An Indiana county commissioner appointed his campaign manager to a political patronage position. Although he received annual compensation of $18,700, the campaign manager described himself as "a political hack employed in a make-work position doing virtually nothing in an unnecessary job." The manager never filled out a time sheet and did not know who his immediate supervisor was. The commissioner was defeated in a subsequent election, and the newly-elected commissioner fired the manager from his make-work job in order to replace him with his son. Meanwhile, the manager and defeated commissioner were successfully prosecuted and incarcerated for tax evasion. The manager nonetheless sued the new commissioner under § 1983 for reinstatement and backpay. He alleged that his firing violated the First Amendment. A federal magistrate dismissed the lawsuit, and the manager appealed to the U.S. Court of Appeals, Seventh Circuit.

The appeals court refused to apply previous U.S. Supreme Court cases that limited public employers from terminating employees on political grounds. In reaching its decision, the court considered the interest of taxpayers and the public. In addition, Indiana had a statute making "ghost employment" of this nature illegal. The political appointee was not expected to do any work and his dismissal did not violate the First Amendment. The court affirmed dismissal of the lawsuit. *Byron v. Clay*, 867 F.2d 1049 (7th Cir.1989).

VIII. NATIONAL SECURITY

When national security is at stake, the federal government has fewer restraints when it comes to discharging employees. However, the government employer may not use national security as a pretext for eliminating all employees whose lifestyles do not meet with their employer's approval.

The Navy hired a veteran's-preference civilian employee to work at its refit facility, which works on the Trident submarine. All employee positions at the facility are classified as sensitive. While waiting for a security clearance, the employee performed only limited duties. His security clearance was denied after he had been at the facility for more than a year because the Navy discovered that he had several felony convictions. He was dismissed for cause after administrative proceedings were held, and he appealed. He argued that because he had been removed for cause and not for national security reasons, he had not been afforded sufficient procedural protections. The U.S. Court of Appeals agreed, and the Navy appealed to the U.S. Supreme Court.

The Supreme Court held that the employee received sufficient procedural due process. It stated that the employee had been dismissed for cause because he did not have the necessary security clearance. The decision not to issue a security clearance was not reviewable in this case, where national security granted broad discretion to the Navy to determine who should have access to classified information. The Court held that since a security clearance was a requirement for employment at the facility, the clearance-denied employee had been dismissed for just cause. The Court reversed the court of appeals' decision. *Department of Navy v. Egan*, 484 U.S. 518, 108 S.Ct. 818, 98 L.Ed.2d 918 (1988).

A NASA employee was observed picking up a man, driving around the block, and dropping the man off again. It was learned that he had invited the man to his apartment for a drink. The NASA security chief interrogated the employee and proposed his dismissal. Although the employee denied he was homosexual, NASA concluded that he was. It terminated the employee after administrative hearings because of his "immoral conduct." He appealed to a U.S. district court, unsuccessfully, and further appealed to the U.S. Court of Appeals, District of Columbia Circuit.

On appeal, the court found that the employee's "homosexual advance" could not have been reasonably held to be a sufficient justification for dismissal. He was a "competent employee" doing "very good" work. Even if he was homosexual, no national security problem would arise which could justify his dismissal. The court held that NASA had terminated the employee out of embarrassment, and not out of a motivation to promote the efficiency of the service. The court reversed the trial court's decision, and reinstated the employee. *Norton v. Macy*, 417 F.2d 1161 (1969).

The National Security Agency (NSA) terminated the employment of a cryptographic technician for engaging in homosexual relationships with foreign nationals. He had been employed for sixteen years by the NSA. The NSA proposed terminating the employee according to its personnel regulations. The termination letter noted that the employee's "indiscrimi-

concluded that the employee's access to classified material was inconsistent with national security. After a hearing the employee's security clearance was revoked and because this was a condition to NSA employment, his termination became final. The employee then requested a hearing before the Secretary of Defense, claiming that the 1959 NSA Act did not authorize termination without a hearing before the defense secretary. The secretary's response was that the removal was for cause under the NSA's regulations and did not require the secretary's authority.

The employee sued the secretary in the U.S. District Court for the District of Columbia, claiming that the act did not delegate authority to remove employees to the NSA's director. The district court granted the secretary's motion for summary judgment. The U.S. Court of Appeals, District of Columbia Circuit reversed the district court's decision ruling that the act applied. The defense secretary appealed to the U.S. Supreme Court.

The Supreme Court noted that the NSA Act authorized the defense secretary or his designee to establish positions and make necessary appointments to carry out the function of the agency. The authority to appoint also implied a power to remove. The act was not the exclusive means to remove NSA employees for national security reasons. The alternative selected by the NSA director was a correct procedure for removal because of permissive language in the act. The secretary had broad discretion to terminate employees consistent with national security, just as discretion was present in the selection of NSA employees. The termination procedure selected by the NSA director provided a hearing equivalent to that provided under the NSA Act. The U.S. Supreme Court reversed and remanded the case for a determination of the employee's remaining claims that the NSA violated its own regulations in removing him and that his constitutional rights had been violated. *Carlucci v. Doe*, 488 U.S. 93, 109 S.Ct. 407, 102 L.Ed.2d 395 (1988).

On remand, the court of appeals stated that the NSA neither violated nor misapplied its regulations. The case turned on whether the employee was terminated for cause, in which case Chapter 370 of the NSA regulations would apply, or terminated for national security reasons, in which case Chapter 371 would apply. The court stated that the employee was terminated for cause, not national security, as indicated by the fact that the NSA took fifteen months to terminate the employee after first giving notice. The court also stated that since a federal employee has no right to a security clearance, the employee could not argue that the NSA deprived him of a property interest without due process. The employee was denied no protectable liberty interest since the NSA's actions were not stigmatizing. *Doe v. Cheney*, 885 F.2d 898 (D.C.Cir.1989).

A homosexual California man was employed by a government contractor. The employee filed an application with the contractor for a security clearance to work on a classified project for the Department of Defense.

The employee stated on his application that he was a member of a gay organization. The contractor never submitted the employee's application because it believed the government forbade submittal of applications revealing "evidence of homosexuality". The employee failed to receive a clearance and was unable to learn of the reason. He sued the contractor and the department in a federal district court, claiming that the decision to not submit his application deprived him of his constitutional rights. The district court dismissed the action against the department, ruling that the employee's claims were moot. Alternatively, it found that the action could not be litigated without disclosing state and military secrets. The employee appealed to the U.S. Court of Appeals, Ninth Circuit.

The court of appeals held that the state privilege to protect military and state secrets could provide an adequate ground for upholding the dismissal independent of the mootness issue. The government had properly asserted the military and state secrets privilege in its motion to dismiss as an alternative ground for dismissal. The entire action was barred because further litigation would inevitably lead to disclosure of privileged information. The court of appeals affirmed the district court's decision. *Weston v. Lockheed Missiles & Space Co.*, 881 F.2d 814 (9th Cir.1989).

IX. OTHER CASES

An Oklahoma city's sheriff deposited his resignation with the county clerk four days before it was to become effective. Prior to the effective date, the sheriff changed his mind and contacted the county clerk to withdraw his resignation. The resignation was not withdrawn, however, and the board of county commissioners (board) announced that a vacancy existed. The sheriff filed a declaratory judgement action in an Oklahoma trial court against the board, seeking a judgement that the office of sheriff was not vacant. The trial court entered judgement for the board and the sheriff appealed to the Court of Appeals of Oklahoma. Oklahoma law states that resignations may be made by a written a statement in the office of the county clerk and shall take effect at the time affixed upon the resignation. To withdraw the resignation, an elected county officer must submit a written statement of cancellation before the date affixed to the resignation. The sheriff failed to provide evidence of a written withdrawal. Therefore, the written resignation became effective on the date affixed to the resignation. The court affirmed the trial court's decision. *Mickle v. Latimer Cty*, 793 P.2d 308 (Okl.App.1990).

An Illinois man worked for the Chicago Department of Health. The city required that its employees reside in the city. The man lived outside the city until he was questioned about his noncompliance with the residency requirements. At that point, he tried to convince his wife to move back to the city, but she refused. Eventually, they separated, and he moved into an apartment in the city. The separation was amicable and the man visited his children on weekends at his wife's residence. He also visited them occasionally on weekdays. The city conducted a random surveillance of the man at both addresses, seeing him leave his wife's residence seven times over a seven month period. In four surveillances of his address over the same seven month period, he was not seen leaving his apartment at all. The city's personnel board conducted a hearing and determined that he had failed to comply with the residency requirements of the city. It dismissed him. He appealed unsuccessfully to an Illinois trial court, and further appealed to the Appellate Court of Illinois.

On appeal, the court held that there was insufficient evidence to show that he intended to or did live outside the city of Chicago. There was no evidence that anyone else inhabited his apartment. Further, just because the man was only separated from his wife, and not divorced, did not mean he was living at her residence. The court stated that the failure to see him in four surveillances over a seven month period simply was not sufficient evidence to show that he had violated the residency requirements of Chicago. The court reversed the trial court's decision, and reinstated the employee. *Raczkowski v. City of Chicago,* 491 N.E.2d 1309 (Ill.App.1st Dist.1986).

An employee of a Mississippi state mental retardation center was assigned to supervise residents. One resident created a disturbance and ran off. The employee's supervisor then relieved him so that he could retrieve the resident, which he did. A second employee later discovered that the resident had been injured. A subsequent investigation produced no leads, and the employee and the supervisor were asked to submit to a polygraph examination. They refused. A warning of termination failed to persuade them, and both the employee and the supervisor were terminated. The dismissals were upheld by the Employees Appeal Board and a county circuit court, and then reached the Mississippi Supreme Court. The employees first contended that a dismissal based on a refusal to take a polygraph exam was unreasonable. The first step in the court's analysis resulted in a finding that the request for the exam was reasonable. It next examined the parties' duties. The center had a duty to investigate any injury to a resident, and employees of the center had a duty to cooperate. The court agreed with a list of both in-state and foreign jurisdiction decisions which have upheld dismissal of public employees based on a refusal to take a polygraph exam. The second argument by the employees was that the exam procedure violated their due process rights. However, the employees had signed preemployment statements authorizing polygraph exams. The employees were also advised of the limited scope of the exam, and were granted a guarantee that the results would not be used in later criminal proceedings. The dismissals were upheld. *Jackson v. Hudspeth Mental Ret. Center*, 573 So.2d 750 (Miss.1990).

A Colorado university hired two men as food service workers. At the time they were hired, both men wore beards. No mention was made to them of a "no-beard" policy as a condition of their employment. Two years later, the university hired a food service manager who decided to implement a hair restraint policy which included a "no-beard" rule. The policy had been in existence previously, but had not been enforced by past management. The two men's supervisor gave them written and oral notice of this new policy. After they refused to shave, they were suspended for one week and advised that they could return to work if they changed their minds. When they returned to work with their beards intact, again stating their resolve not to shave, they were given written and oral notice of their discharges. A hearing officer upheld their terminations and the state personnel board agreed with the hearing officer. They appealed to a Colorado trial court unsuccessfully, and further appealed to the Supreme Court of Colorado.

The supreme court held that a legitimate health-related policy had been imposed on all the workers within their job classification. It stated that the university did not act arbitrarily in enforcing its hair restraint policy. Further, it noted that the employees' right to wear beards was not a "fundamental right" such that it could not be overridden by their employer's substantial interest in providing a sanitary food service. Since the policy was an effective way of bringing about safe, clean working conditions and sanitary meals, the court ruled it to be valid. The court affirmed the trial court's decision. *Chiappe v. State Personnel Board*, 622 P.2d 527 (Colo.1981).

A police officer with over twenty years experience was suspected of having sexual contact with young boys. Although there were rumors, there was no direct proof of any contact. The sheriff sought to have the officer submit to a psychological examination. The officer was told that refusal to be examined would result in suspension. The officer sought an administrative hearing. After exhausting administrative remedies, the officer appealed to a Minnesota trial court. The trial court ruled arbitration was necessary, as called for in the officer's contract, but only with regard to the selection of a psychologist. The demand for an examination was upheld. The officer appealed further to the Minnesota Court of Appeals. The court of appeals was forced to choose between the necessity for grievance procedures on conditions of employment, and a public employer's privilege to determine managerial policy. The examination here was to be applied to the individual officer only, in contrast to a managerial policy which would be applied to all employees. Therefore, the court found subjection to a psychological examination to be a condition of employment, and thus subject to arbitration under the officer's contract. The court of appeals affirmed and modified the trial court's decision. *Hill v. City of Winona*, 454 N.W.2d 659 (Minn.App.1990).

In 1977, the New Jersey Supreme Court administrative office issued a bulletin prohibiting marriages between municipal court clerks and police officers in the same municipality. Those who were married prior to the date the bulletin was issued were prohibited from dealing with matters involving their spouses. Those who married after the issuance date faced demotion or termination. In 1988, a woman who served as a municipal court clerk married a police detective in the same municipality. The couple sued in federal court seeking an injunction forbidding the state from enforcing the regulation and a declaration that the regulation violated the Fourteenth Amendment's Equal Protection Clause by creating a classification that prohibits certain family relationships between court clerks and police officers while allowing others. They also claimed that the regulation infringed on their constitutionally protected rights of privacy, family association and marriage. The state claimed that the regulation was intended to serve the goal of preserving the integrity of the courts.

A federal district court in New Jersey stated that while the state's goal was laudable, any regulation which had a chilling effect on legitimate marriages must be narrowly tailored. The regulation in this case was not narrowly tailored to the goal and did not utilize the least restrictive means available. The court also held that the regulation violated the Equal Protection Clause since some familial relationships, such as brother and sister, in which the possibility for abuse was as great were allowed, while spousal relationships were not. The court granted the permanent injunction. *Hughes v. Lipscher*, 720 F.Supp. 454 (D.N.J.1989).

The Pennsylvania Department of Transportation revoked the driving privileges of a school bus driver who had worked for eighteen years at a public school district. The license revocation occurred nearly two years after the driver was diagnosed as a diabetic and found incompetent to drive a school bus under a Pennsylvania statute. The driver appealed to a Pennsylvania trial court, which ruled that the transportation department's action violated § 504 of the Rehabilitation Act of 1973, 29 U.S.C. § 794. The court reinstated the driver's driving privileges, but also ordered the district to perform a blood prick test on the driver each day she was scheduled to drive and to suspend her immediately if her condition was not under control. The district was also ordered to supply copies of blood tests to the transportation department. The department appealed to the Pennsylvania Commonwealth Court.

The commonwealth court considered the trial court's decision in view of the U.S. Supreme Court's decision in *School Bd. of Nassau County v. Arline*, 107 S.Ct. 1123 (1987). The *Arline* case held that in Rehabilitation Act cases, courts were to evaluate the condition of the individual handicapped person who was otherwise qualified to perform the job duties. In each case, the inquiry must be into whether the employee was able to perform the job duties. In this case, the driver's diabetes had been under control since her release from the hospital. Because the school district and transportation department would not suffer a great burden by accommodating the school bus driver, the trial court had properly reinstated her. The transportation department's argument that a diabetic presented a risk to the safety of bus passengers was speculative. Because the transportation department was solely authorized to make department rules and regulations, the commonwealth court affirmed the driver's reinstatement, but not the extra testing requirements. *Comm. of Pennsylvania v. Tinsley*, 564 A.2d 286 (Pa.Cmwlth.1989).

A tenured Missouri teacher taught English and media classes at his high school. His students submitted news stories, cartoons, and advertisements to be included in a publication for a class assignment. The teacher edited the articles, then typed and printed the paper and distributed it to the class. The teacher critiqued the material to the class, indicating that much of the material was objectionable. He did not retrieve all copies of the publication and some copies achieved a general circulation within the school and the community. The district superintendent charged the teacher with immoral conduct and following a hearing, terminated the teacher's contract. The teacher then appealed to a Missouri trial court.

During the appeal, the teacher filed a claim for unemployment benefits with the Labor and Industrial Relations Commission. The commission refused to grant compensation to the teacher, since the teacher had intentionally and substantially disregarded the employer's interest by preparing and distributing the material. The teacher did not seek judicial review of the commission's position and it became final. The school board then filed a motion to dismiss the lawsuit against it, arguing that since the commission had already determined the teacher's misconduct, the factual issues should not be relitigated. The circuit court dismissed the case, and the teacher appealed to the Missouri Court of Appeals, Eastern District.

The court of appeals recognized that a prior adjudication of a factual issue by an administrative tribunal could be invoked to prevent subsequent relitigation in a judicial proceeding. However, the court stated that the commission's decision was not a prior adjudication. The action pending in the circuit court against the board of education predated the action of the commission. Furthermore, the issue decided in the prior proceeding was not identical to the issue in the present action. The issue here was whether the teacher's actions constituted immoral conduct, whereas the commission had found the teacher extremely negligent. The court of appeal reversed the circuit court's dismissal and remanded the case for further proceedings. *Gerig v. Bd. of Educ. of Cent. School Dist.*, 767 S.W.2d 586 (Mo.App.1988).

A county correctional institute filled five newly created Correctional Team Leader positions through a process which was ruled to be unfair. Applicants were tested, and the top scoring applicants were interviewed.

However, the interviews consisted of only one interview panel, not three panels as required by the personnel system. The panel consisted solely of members of the sheriffs department, and each applicant was known personally to the interviewers. Several unsuccessful applicants challenged the selections and eventually the county was ordered to retest and reinterview all applicants. One of the previously successful applicants, a veteran, retested but did not receive an interview as a top-scoring applicant. The veteran then contended that his removal was in violation of the Veterans Preference Act. The Commissioner of Veterans Affairs ordered reinstatement with backpay, but was reversed by an appellate court. The issue then reached the Minnesota Supreme Court. The Minnesota Veterans Preference Act allows termination of a veteran only for incompetency, misconduct, or where the position was abolished in good faith. The court noted that none of these conditions were present, but noted that the applicability of the Act was the issue in this case. Previous cases have demonstrated that some terminations or removals are not within the purview of the act. The court felt that the appointment process in this instance so seriously violated the county's personnel system that the veteran never validly held the position. The Veterans Preference Act, therefore, did not apply and the county did not have to reinstate the veteran. *Ochocki v. Dakota County Sheriff's Dep't*, 464 N.W.2d 496 (Minn.1991).

A South Dakota city hired a Korean War veteran as a custodian and employed him for about six years. He became hospitalized and unable to work and was terminated by the city under its extended sick leave policy. A South Dakota statute required notice and a hearing to public employees who were members of preferred classes, including veterans, in order to remove them from their positions. The city replaced the veteran with a non-veteran without holding an incompetency hearing or providing notice. The veteran sued the city for wrongful discharge. However, he did not make a claim under the veteran's preference statute. The court reinstated the veteran to his former position and awarded him damages from the date he commenced the action until his reinstatement. However, no damages were awarded for the approximately two years between his termination and the institution of his lawsuit. The damages were reduced by income received by the veteran from other employment.

The veteran appealed to the Supreme Court of South Dakota, claiming that he should have been awarded damages from the date of his dismissal. The court ruled that although the veteran's delay in bringing his lawsuit was not unreasonable, he was not entitled to damages which he could have prevented by filing his suit promptly. The Supreme Court affirmed the trial court's decision. *Brown v. City of Yankton*, 434 N.W.2d 376 (S.D.1989).

The Tennessee Valley Authority (TVA) hired an Alabama man as a cement mason. He was a veteran, a preference eligible employee and a competitive level employee. In 1985, he and eighteen other cement masons in his competitive level were separated from the TVA by a reduction-in-force action. The mason challenged his separation by filing an Equal Employment Opportunity Commission complaint against the TVA, alleging that he had been discriminated against on the basis of race and age. The agency denied his complaint and the mason appealed to the Merit Systems Protection Board (MSPB), asserting that the TVA had discriminated against him and had illegally failed to recognize and honor his reemployment rights under the Veterans' Preference Act. The MSPB denied the appeal. The mason then abandoned his discrimination claims, and appealed the veterans preference complaint to the U.S. Court of Appeals, Federal Circuit. The appellate court determined that the MSPB was without power to review the case. Since it could find nothing in the law which authorized the MSPB to hear an appeal on reemployment rights, the court did not feel it had authority over the case either. The court determined that preference eligibles of the employee's status were unable to seek redress of violations of their reemployment rights by appealing to the MSPB. The appellate court dismissed the case. *Noble v. Tennessee Valley Authority*, 892 F.2d 1013 (Fed.Cir.1989).

CHAPTER THREE
FREEDOM OF EXPRESSION

I. MATTERS OF PUBLIC CONCERN

In a series of cases spanning over two decades, the U.S. Supreme Court has set out the principles which govern a public employee's right to First Amendment protection. *Pickering v. Bd. of Education*, 391 U.S. 563, (1968), established that an employee's interest as a citizen in commenting upon matters of public concern must outweigh the interest of the government in promoting the efficiency of the public services it performs in order for the employee's speech to be protected by the First Amendment. The Court held in *Connick v. Myers*, 461 U.S. 138, (1983), that a public employee's speech upon matters of purely personal interest is not afforded constitutional protection. Further, under *Rankin v. McPherson*, 483 U.S. 378, (1987), whether an employee's speech addresses a matter of public concern must be determined by the content, form, and context of a given statement as revealed by the entire record. Whether speech is protected is a question of law to be determined by the court.

A. Protected Speech

An Illinois school district fired a high school teacher for sending a letter to the editor of the local newspaper. The letter criticized the board and district superintendent for their handling of school funding methods. Voters in the district voted down a tax rate increase to fund a bond issue for two new schools. The local teachers organization and the district superintendent published articles in support of a second tax increase proposal. District voters then rejected a second tax rate increase proposal. The teacher's letter came as a response to the superintendent and teacher organization articles and the second electoral defeat of the tax rate increase. The letter particularly criticized the board's handling of the bond issue and allocation of funding between school educational and athletic programs. The teacher also charged the superintendent with attempting to stifle opposing views on the subject. The board then held a hearing at which it charged the teacher with publishing a defamatory letter. After deeming the teacher's statements to be false, the board fired the teacher. An Illinois court affirmed the board's action, finding substantial evidence that publication of the letter was detrimental to the district's interest. The Illinois Supreme Court affirmed the dismissal, ruling that the teacher's speech was unprotected by the First Amendment because his teaching position required him to refrain from statements about school operations.

The U.S. Supreme Court found no support for the state supreme court's view that public employment subjected the teacher to deprivation of his constitutional rights. The state's interest in regulating employee speech was to be balanced with individual rights. The Court outlined a general analysis for evaluating public employee speech, ruling that employees were entitled to constitutional protection to comment on matters of public concern. The public interest in free speech and debate on matters of public concern was so great that it barred public officials from recovering damages for defamatory statements unless they were made with reckless disregard for their truth. Because there was no evidence presented that the letter damaged any board member's professional reputation, the teacher's comments were not detrimental to the school system, but only constituted a difference of opinion. Since there was no proof of reckless disregard for the truth by the teacher and the matter concerned the public interest, the board could not constitutionally terminate his employment. The Court reversed and remanded the state court decision. *Pickering v. Board of Education*, 391 U.S. 563, 88 S.Ct. 1731, 20 L.Ed.2d 811 (1968).

An untenured teacher was not rehired after a number of incidents which led the school board to conclude that he lacked tactfulness in handling professional matters. Included in these incidents was a shouting match with a school cafeteria employee over the amount of spaghetti served the teacher, an argument with another teacher which resulted in a face-slapping and obscene gestures made by the teacher to two girls when the girls failed to obey his directives, and a telephone call placed by the teacher to a local radio station in which the teacher aired his opinions about a new school dress code. After the board decided not to reemploy the teacher, he asked for and received a list of the reasons for the board's decision. The board stated its reason for not rehiring in a general manner but also specifically cited the obscene gesture and radio station incidents. The teacher sued for reinstatement on the grounds that his discussion with the radio station was protected by the First Amendment and that to refuse reemployment on the basis of his exercise of a constitutionally protected right was a violation of his free speech rights. A U.S. district court and later a court of appeals agreed and ordered reinstatement with back pay. The school board appealed to the U.S. Supreme Court.

The Court first rejected the school board's argument that the Eleventh Amendment barred private lawsuits against local political subdivisions such as a school district. City and county governments were not "states" within the meaning of the Eleventh Amendment. However, the Court overturned the court of appeals and district court decisions, holding that apart from the actions for which the teacher might claim First Amendment protection, the board could have chosen not to rehire him on the basis of several other incidents. The radio station incident, while clearly implicating a protected right, was not the substantial reason for nonrenewal. The board could have reached the same decision had the teacher not engaged in constitutionally protected conduct. A marginal employee should not be able to prevent dismissal by engaging in constitutionally protected activity and then hiding under a constitutional shield as protection from all other actions which were not constitutionally protected. The lower courts were instructed to determine whether the board's decision could have been reached absent the constitutionally protected activity of phoning the radio station, and, if such a decision could have been reached, whether remedial action to correct the constitutional violation would be necessary. *Mount Healthy City School District v. Doyle*, 429 U.S. 274, 97 S.Ct. 568, 50 L.Ed.2d 471 (1977).

A Mississippi junior high school English teacher was discharged by her school district for allegedly not cooperating with administration officials over school policy. The teacher then intervened in a federal district court action ordering the school district to desegregate. She sought reinstatement, arguing that the school district had violated her First and Fourteenth Amendment rights to free speech by firing her in retaliation for vocally opposing the school district's segregative policies. Before the federal district court, the school district contended that it had dismissed the teacher for justifiable reasons. It pointed to several earlier encounters between the teacher and school officials, in which the teacher had allegedly made petty and unreasonable demands in a rude manner. However, the district court concluded that the teacher had been discharged for exercising her free speech rights. The teacher had legitimately been speaking out against school policies that she thought were racially discriminatory. Thus, the dismissal violated the First Amendment. The U.S. Court of Appeals, Fifth Circuit, reversed. It concluded that because the teacher had privately expressed her concerns with the school principal, the speech was not protected under the First Amendment. It stated that public employees do not have a right to privately express their views to a higher authority. The U.S. Supreme Court granted certiorari.

The Court rejected as clearly erroneous the court of appeals' conclusion that public employee speech in private situations was unprotected by the

First Amendment. The Court's previous decisions in *Pickering v. Board of Education* and *Mt. Healthy City Board of Education v. Doyle,* above, did not stand for the proposition that public employee expression in private was without constitutional protection. Those cases had involved public employees making public criticism of school policies. However, protection of speech was not dependent on the public character of the speech. The principal, by opening his door to the teacher, had not been an "unwilling recipient" of the teacher's views. The court refused to adopt the view that the First Amendment makes a distinction between private and public speech by public employees. The Court vacated the court of appeals' decision and remanded the case. *Givhan v. Western Line Consolidated School District,* 439 U.S. 410, 99 S.Ct. 693, 58 L.Ed.2d 619 (1978).

An assistant district attorney in New Orleans had the responsibility of trying criminal cases. When the district attorney proposed to transfer the assistant to prosecute cases in a different section of the criminal court, she opposed the transfer. She then expressed her views on the matter to several of her superiors. Shortly thereafter, she prepared and distributed a questionnaire to other assistant district attorneys in the office concerning the office's transfer policy, morale, the level of confidence in superiors, and whether the employees felt pressured to work for political campaigns, among other things. The district attorney then fired her for refusing the transfer and for the act of insubordination in distributing the questionnaire. The assistant sued in federal court, alleging that she had been discharged in violation of her First Amendment rights. The district court agreed and she was reinstated with back pay and attorney's fees. The U.S. Court of Appeals, Fifth Circuit, affirmed and the U.S. Supreme Court granted review.

The court stated that in order to determine a public employee's rights of free speech, the balancing test of *Pickering v. Bd. of Educ.* (see above) must be utilized. The interests of the employee as a citizen in commenting upon matters of public concern must outweigh the interest of the state, as employer, in promoting efficiency in the workplace. As a threshold matter, the Court stated that when a public employee speaks not as a citizen upon matters of public concern, but instead as an employee upon matters of only personal interest, a federal court is not the appropriate forum in which to review the wisdom of a personnel decision taken by a public agency in reaction to that speech. Here, except for the assistant's question regarding pressure to work in political campaigns, the questions were not matters of public concern. The state also need not prove substantial disruption of the office in order to justify dismissal when the First Amendment right is limited. In this case, the district attorney's action was reasonable if he thought that the speech in question would disrupt the office, undermine his authority and destroy working relationships in the office. *Connick v. Myers,* 461 U.S. 138, 103 S.Ct.1684, 75 L.Ed.2d 708 (1983).

A data entry employee in a Texas county constable's office was discharged for a remark to a coworker, after hearing of an attempt on President Reagan's life. "If they go for him again, I hope they get him." The statement was overheard by another employee who reported it to the constable. The constable questioned the employee about the remark and then fired her. The employee brought suit in a federal district court alleging that the constable had violated her First Amendment rights by firing her. The district court held for the constable, ruling that the employee's speech was unprotected. The U.S. Court of Appeals, Fifth Circuit, vacated the holding and remanded on the ground that substantial issues of material fact remained regarding the context in which the statements had been made. On remand, the district court once again held for the constable. The court of appeals reversed, holding that the employee's remark had addressed a matter of public concern. The Supreme Court granted certiorari and affirmed the court of appeals' decision.

The Court stated that the content, form, and context of the employee's statement supported the conclusion that her speech was on a matter of public concern. Although a statement which amounted to a threat to kill the President would not be protected by the First Amendment, the court stated that the employee's speech, in this instance, could not be characterized as a threat. The Court also stated that the employee's relatively low position in the office and the lack of evidence that her statement interfered with the efficient functioning of the office undermined the argument that the state had an interest outweighing the employee's First Amendment rights. *Rankin v. McPherson*, 483 U.S. 378, 107 S.Ct. 2891, 97 L.Ed.2d 315 (1987).

A Virginia physical education teacher was given poor ratings in job performance after he wrote a satirical response to a letter in a student newspaper claiming that there was sexual bias in the physical education department. Prior to publication, the school's principal and faculty advisor read the letter and voiced no objections. Following publication, however, the principal informed the teacher that there were serious problems with the letter. After receiving poor ratings, the teacher filed a grievance according to the appropriate regulations. Although a deputy superintendent of schools supported the teacher, the school board denied the grievance. The teacher then sued in federal district court. The district court held for the school and the teacher appealed to the U.S. Court of Appeals, Fourth Circuit.

The court of appeals stated that the totality of circumstances indicated that the teacher's letter addressed a matter of public concern. The letter was written in response to another letter which had raised a serious issue. The fact that it was taken literally, despite the teacher's satiric intent, was immaterial. The court stated that the public expression of ideas may not be prohibited merely because the ideas are offensive to some listeners. *Seemuller v. Fairfax County School Board*, 878 F.2d 1578 (4th Cir.1989).

A Texas man was elected to a four-year term as a justice of the peace. The justice discovered that many persons appealing traffic convictions had their cases dismissed or had their fines sharply reduced. The benefit of this tendency was limited, however, to persons who contacted local "in the know" attorneys. The justice explained this situation in an "open letter," which was eventually circulated in the local press, and predicted an increased workload for the appeals court. The Texas Commission on Judicial Conduct (commission) later issued a public reprimand of the justice criticizing his conduct. The justice filed a 42 U.S.C. §1983 claim asserting a restriction of free speech rights and requesting partial expungement of the reprimand. He also sought attorney's fees. A federal district court granted summary judgment to the commission, and the justice appealed.

The appeals court first needed to determine if the justice had spoken on a matter of legitimate public concern. It was found that he had. The court must then balance the justice's interest in free speech with the commission's interest in promoting efficiency of its services. The commission argued that it would have reprimanded the justice even without his writing the letter. The court ruled that the letter had at least partially motivated the reprimand. The next argument was that the harm done to the commission's interest outweighed the justice's interest. However, the court found that it did not. Finally, since the reprimand concerned additional issues, the commission argued that expungement would place the justice in a better position than he would have been absent his letter. The court found that partial expungement would not place the justice in a better position. The justice sought expungement of only that portion of the reprimand addressing the letter. The court reversed the finding of the district court, ordered partial expungement and awarded attorney's fees. *Scott v. Flowers*, 910 F.2d 201 (5th Cir.1990).

A Washington man was hired by the General Services Division of the Department of Public Utilities and was assigned to work in a garage. Two years later a new supervisor was hired. The new supervisor set deadlines for tasks to be done, since the garage employee was behind in his work. The garage employee failed a number of times to meet the deadlines for the completion of the projects. Some employees began discussing among themselves complaints they had against the new supervisor. Eventually, they asked the garage employee to prepare a complaint against the new supervisor. Although the document stated that a majority of the employees supported the complaint, only the garage employee signed it. The garage employee sent the complaint to the board of directors of the Department of Public Utilities. In a meeting of management officials they determined the complaint to be without merit.

Because of difficulties between the supervisor and the garage employee, management officials decided to reassign him to the gatehouse outside the garage, where he would be away from the supervisor's area of responsibility. Although the garage employee requested a return to his old job, management refused. The garage employee then filed suit in the district court against the city. The jury returned a verdict in his favor, but he received only a portion of the damages requested. Both parties appealed to the Supreme Court of Washington.

To determine if a public employer has violated the employee's right to free speech the court must employ a four step inquiry. First, the public employee must establish that his speech deals with a matter of public concern. Second, he must prove that his interest in commenting on matters of public concern is greater than the employer's interest in promoting the efficiency of the services it performs. Third, he must demonstrate that his speech was a substantial and motivating factor in the adverse employment decision. And finally, if the public employee is able to prove these three elements, the burden then shifts to the employer to prove that it would have reached the same decision even in the absence of the employee's conduct. The court noted that the complaint involved matters of public concern only in its most limited sense, and concluded that the public employee's interest was slight. The supreme court reversed the decision and held in favor of the city. *Binkrey v. City of Tacoma*, 787 P.2d 1366 (Wash.1990).

A firefighter for a Texas city spoke to the news media concerning a house fire in which one firefighter died and another was injured. In his discussions with the press, he criticized the staffing policies of the city. In response, the firefighter was suspended for thirty days without pay, demoted, and put on probation for six months. In support of the suspension, the city quoted fire department regulations which read: "Refrain from furnishing information relative to department policy, practices, or business affairs except as authorized by the Chief of the department." The firefighter sued seeking injunctive relief, attorney's fees and damages for violation of his First Amendment rights. A federal district court denied the firefighter all relief. The firefighter appealed to the U.S. Court of Appeals, Fifth Circuit.

The court of appeals noted that the firefighter's speech was a matter of public concern. The court stated that the public, naturally, cared deeply about the ability of its fire department to respond quickly to a fire. The court also noted that the interest of the firefighter in speaking out was very high, while the city's interest, in comparison, was minimal. As such, the court remanded the case to the district court for trial on the issue of a proper remedy. *Moore v. City of Kilgore*, 877 F.2d 364 (5th Cir.1989).

The chief of police for a Pennsylvania township was fired by township supervisors when he allegedly refused to withdraw certain citations which he and his subordinates had issued. The chief not only refused to withdraw the citations, but he informed a local television station of the supervisors' demands. The chief sued in federal court alleging that his firing was in retaliation for his exercise of his free speech rights. He also alleged that he was defamed by false statements made by the supervisors at the meeting at which he was fired. The supervisors asserted that the chief had been fired for insubordination and assaulting another officer. They also denied the chief's allegations of wrongdoing. The federal district court dismissed the case on the ground that the chief's speech was not protected by the First Amendment. The court also dismissed the defamation claim because under Pennsylvania law the supervisors possessed official immunity. The chief then appealed to the U.S. Court of Appeals, Third Circuit.

The court of appeals stated that a state may not discharge a public employee based upon the exercise of the employee's constitutionally protected interest in freedom of expression. However, a state has an interest as an employer in regulating the speech of its employees in order to operate its enterprise effectively. Under *Pickering v. Bd. of Educ.*, the court must balance these interests to determine whether an action taken in response to an employee's exercise of free speech rights is legitimate. The court stated that the chief's allegations of corruption by government officials were of the utmost public concern. The chief's interest in speaking out on the alleged supervisors' corruption outweighed the supervisors' need to oust a disruptive employee. The court stated that if, on remand, the district court found the chief's allegations to be true and the chief was fired in retaliation for these remarks, the district court should find for the chief on the First Amendment claim. The court, however, affirmed the district court's dismissal of the defamation claim based on state common law immunity. *O'Donnell v. Yanchulis*, 875 F.2d (3d Cir.1989).

A registered nurse at a Louisiana correctional center reported numerous violations of nursing practices to her supervisor. The supervisor took no action. She then reported the incidents to the center's warden and assistant warden. The warden refused to investigate and threatened to transfer the assistant warden if he attempted to investigate. The nurse's supervisor reprimanded her in response to her report. The nurse then spoke with an administrator in the state department of corrections about nursing practices. She also provided documentation to prove her allegations. The administrator conducted an investigation at the center and found the allegations to be well founded. The violations continued, however, and the nurse spoke with the warden again. He stated that he would fire her if she went to the media or the state board of nursing. The nurse then contacted the state board of nursing. In support of her allegations, she sent inmate records to the board. The board charged the nurse's supervisor with violations of the Louisiana Nursing Practice Act. The nurse was then fired for violating department rules by sending inmate records to the state board of nursing without the inmates' consent. The Louisiana Civil Service Commission, however, ordered the nurse to be reinstated and all references to termination to be expunged from her record. The nurse then sued the correction center's officials in federal court under 42 U.S.C. § 1983, alleging violations of her First and

Fourteenth Amendment rights, and state law claims for retaliatory discharge and intentional infliction of physical, emotional and mental injuries. The court held that the nurse was entitled to lost wages, attorney's fees and punitive damages. The officials then appealed to the U.S. Court of Appeals, Fifth Circuit.

The court of appeals stated that the nurse's speech was certainly a matter of public concern. Although the nurse's whistleblowing caused tension and difficulties at the center, when weighed against the exposure of unethical medical practices, the state's interest in preventing this disruption was a minimal interest. The court stated that it would be absurd to hold that the First Amendment authorized corrupt officials to punish subordinates who blow the whistle because the office is somewhat disrupted. The court finally held that the officials were not entitled to qualified immunity, since reasonable officials would have known that firing the nurse in these circumstances would violate her constitutional rights. *Frazier v. King*, 873 F.2d 820 (5th Cir.1989).

An associate mathematics professor had a long history of bad relations with the president of his university. The professor had published letters containing personal criticism of the president and attacks on the president's management style. The professor's criticism culminated in a lawsuit by the professor aimed at forcing disclosure of university employment practices. The professor later applied for promotion to full professorship but this was denied. The professor sued the president, the university, and other administrators, claiming that he had been denied the promotion because he had exercised his right to free speech and had sued the university. The district court dismissed the free speech claim and found that the professor would have been turned down even if he had not participated in the original lawsuit. The professor appealed to the United States Court of Appeals, Eleventh Circuit. The court of appeals held that the district court's dismissal of the professor's free speech claim was improper because the professor's criticisms of both university expenditures and the president's management style were issues of public concern. The court of appeals vacated the decision of the district court and remanded the case for further proceedings. *Kurtz v. Vickrey*, 855 F.2d 723 (11th Cir.1988).

A Texas newspaper received a letter that the local police department was keeping a file on two of the paper's columnists. The letter came from an anonymous sergeant in the police department. The letter also described a department cover-up of an officer's cocaine possession and the improper use of firearms by unqualified personnel in carrying out an illegal search. The chief of police learned of the letter and began an investigation to determine its source. During the investigation, the focus was on four officers, who answered prepared questions. It was determined that one particular officer did not write the anonymous letter and did not know who did. This officer, as well as the others, then complained to a statewide officers' organization about their treatment during the investigation. The organization's staff attorney wrote to the chief of police and requested that no further interrogation be carried on without his presence. The attorney's letter also requested an investigation of the conduct revealed by the anonymous letter. Copies of the letter were also sent to city officials and the newspaper. After receiving the attorney's letter the chief initiated a second investigation, purportedly to inquire about the possible existence of the secret police files. The chief questioned the officer who had been cleared by the earlier investigation. The officer refused to answer without an attorney present. As a result, he was fired for insubordination. The Civil Service Trial Board reduced his termination to a thirty day suspension without pay. When he returned to work, the investigation was still in progress. He still refused to answer written questions without an opportunity to contact his lawyer. He was again terminated for insubordination. The officer sued the department and the chief of police in federal court, alleging that the department had required him to conduct illegal investigations and then fired him for making that information public by way of his attorney's letter. The chief of police sought immunity, but the district court refused. The chief appealed the denial of immunity to the U.S. Court of Appeals, Fifth Circuit.

The court of appeals stated that the chief could only be entitled to qualified immunity if the right violated was not clearly established at the time of discharge. The court stated that it was clearly established at the time that a public employee's speech revealing improper conduct is protected by the First Amendment. The district court properly refused to dismiss the case and stated that if, on remand, the district court determined that the termination was motivated by the officer's protected expression, it should rule for the officer. *Brawner v. City of Richardson*, 855 F.2d 187 (5th Cir.1988).

A Virginia state corrections officer was suspended, transferred, and eventually fired for criticizing the warden's policies at a correctional facility at which he worked. There was a dispute between the officer and the warden as to the manner in which the officer voiced his criticism. The officer stated that his views were expressed privately with coworkers. The warden believed they were shouted within the hearing of prisoners. The officer filed a grievance and was successful in regaining employment at the facility, but not at his former level. The officer sued the facility administrators and then resigned, claiming that his transfer, suspension and discharge violated his First Amendment rights. The trial court dismissed the claim and the officer appealed to the U.S. Court of Appeals, Fourth Circuit.

The court noted that in order for the officer's speech to have been protected it must have been upon a matter of public concern, rather than upon a matter of purely private concern. Even if the speech is upon a matter of legitimate public concern, it is not protected if the public employer's interest in the effective operation of its enterprise outweighs the employee's interest in free expression of that particular idea. The court held that the officer's criticism of the warden's policies was of legitimate public concern, and the fact that it was voiced only to coworkers did not lessen the conclusion. Having determined that the officer's speech was a matter of public concern, the court of appeals remanded the case to the district court for trial. At trial, the court was to balance the officer's interest against the interests of the prison officials. *Jackson v. Bair*, 851 F.2d 714 (4th Cir.1988).

An assistant attorney general in the New York State Department of Law was concerned about the way in which his department was handling a dispute with the Internal Revenue Service. The department had overseen the distribution of a settlement between a private corporation and its workers. A dispute developed with the IRS over whether the department was liable for withholding the employees' taxes on the disbursements. Until a decision was reached, the attorney's superiors had decided not to distribute the funds to the workers. The department also refused to disclose the reason for its failure to disburse the funds. The attorney was convinced that the department was mishandling the issue and behaving unethically. He wrote a memo to his superiors informing them that he was considering resignation if some appropriate action regarding the matter was not taken. The attorney was immediately fired. He submitted a grievance alleging ethical misconduct on the part of his supervisors and then sued the department in federal court. The supervisors asked for qualified immunity because the law regarding employees' First Amendment rights was not clearly established at the time. The district court refused to allow immunity and the supervisors appealed to the U.S. Court of Appeals, Second Circuit.

The court of appeals stated that the attorney's concern that the strategy formulated by department officials was illegal and unethical did touch upon matters of public concern, and that this dimension of his speech should have been apparent to reasonably informed superiors. However, the court noted that executive officials enjoy immunity from liability for damages if their actions do not violate clearly established statutory or constitutional rights. In this case, it would not have been clear to the supervisors that the attorney's interest in expressing his opinion outweighed the department's interest in running an efficient organization. The court therefore granted the supervisors immunity from the attorney's claim of money damages and remanded the case for a determination of his claim for reinstatement. *Giacalone v. Abrams*, 850 F.2d 79 (2d Cir.1988).

A detective with the rank of lieutenant in a New Jersey county prosecutor's office spoke out against a plan to reorganize the way in which promotions were handled for the office's detectives. After the plan was implemented, nineteen employees were promoted according to the new procedure. The detective had attempted to be transferred according to the new procedure, but was unsuccessful. He was then transferred to a nonsupervisory position. The detective wrote a letter to the Civil Service Commission complaining that the new procedures were in violation of the Civil Service Regulations. The commission's initial determination was unfavorable to the detective. He appealed that determination to an appellate division of the commission. On this appeal, he made clear that he was not claiming entitlement to a promotion, but rather that the way in which the new procedures were handled violated the rights of all civil servants. Following an unsuccessful appeal, the detective sued in a New Jersey state court, which ultimately ruled against him. He then sued the prosecutor in federal court for engaging in retaliatory actions from the time he began to protest the new procedures. These retaliatory actions included his transfer to a nonsupervisory position, a suspension without pay for failing to keep accurate records, a $100 fine for using office stationery to write his complaints to the Civil Service Commission, orders to turn in his gun and submit to a psychiatric exam for his "attitude" problems, numerous written reprimands for, for example, failing to say "good morning" to the prosecutor, sending a memo directly to the prosecutor rather than through the chain of command, asking an assistant prosecutor about his case during office hours, and not being available during work hours. The detective alleged that such retaliatory actions violated his First and Fourteenth Amendment rights and also gave rise to the state law tort of wrongful retaliation and intentional infliction of emotional distress. The federal district court dismissed the case and the detective appealed to the U.S. Court of Appeals, Third Circuit.

The court of appeals stated that a public employee's criticism of the internal operations of his or her place of public employment is a matter of public concern. The fact that the detective had a personal stake in the outcome was immaterial. The court stated that it was then necessary to determine whether the detective's speech caused such interference with the effective functioning of the prosecutor's office as to justify the actions taken in response. Although the court of appeals remanded the question of the amount of interference the detective's speech had with the office's operation to the district court for a determination, it suggested that the arguments made by the prosecutor's office seemed weak. The court also held that while the detective could sustain a claim for wrongful retaliation on remand, the standard for proving a claim for intentional infliction of emotional distress is much higher. Thus, that portion of the case was properly dismissed. *Zamboni v. Stamler*, 847 F.2d 73 (3d Cir.1988).

A North Carolina school board held a public meeting to solicit comments on a high school principal's tenure. A teacher at the high school spoke out in favor of renewing the principal's contract at the public meeting. The teacher also allowed his students to discuss the matter in his social studies class and circulated a petition in support of the principal in class. The school board refused to renew the principal's contract. In school board elections two of the incumbents voting against the principal's reappointment were defeated, altering the antiprincipal majority. The teacher was reassigned by the "lame duck" school board to a junior high school approximately forty miles from his home. The action was justified by the board members on the ground that the teacher's conduct had been "divisive and disruptive." The teacher filed suit against the school board in federal district court complaining of various civil rights violations under the U.S. Constitution. The district court granted summary judgment to the school district.

The U.S. Court of Appeals, Fourth Circuit, reversed and remanded the case. The court stated that the teacher's speech related to matters of great public concern and were therefore protected by the Constitution. The court noted that the teacher was probably not motivated by self interest and the matter did not essentially involve a private matter between employer and employee. The issue of the principal's employment was open for discussion in a public forum, and this type of speech should not be chilled. The court stated that teachers have an important voice in decisions regarding employment of school officials and that the public had a need to know their opinions. The vital concerns of both the teacher and the community outweighed the school board's interest in this matter. *Piver v. Pender County Bd. of Educ.*, 835 F.2d 1076 (4th Cir.1987).

A postal service employee in Michigan was fired after he wrote an article encouraging union membership in a union newsletter. In the article he revealed that he had read the contents of some third-class mail he had been sorting. He also revealed the content of that mailing in this article. A postal supervisor questioned the employee about the article. The employee stated that he had fabricated the portion of the article in which he described reading the mail, and promised to print a retraction. The employee printed a retraction, but was discharged for engaging in "conduct prejudicial to the Postal Service." The employee and his union filed a grievance, claiming that the employee was being discharged without cause, in violation of the collective bargaining agreement between the union and the postal service. An arbitrator upheld the dismissal, stating that it was immaterial whether the employee had actually read the mail or not. Since he had made a public expression that he had read the mail while on the job, the effect was to seriously erode the public's confidence in the postal service. On appeal, a federal district court held that under the balancing test of *Pickering v. Bd. of Educ.*, the employee's article constituted speech on a matter of public concern and the mail-reading story was simply a harmless fiction. Since there was no showing of any actual harm to the postal service, the court held that the employee's First Amendment rights outweighed the government's interests. The postal service then appealed to the U.S. Court of Appeals, District of Columbia Circuit.

The court stated that although public employees enjoy First Amendment protection, that protection is lessened since the government has a significant interest in regulating the speech of its employees in order to perform its public services effectively. The court stated that the mail-reading issue needed to be addressed in its context. Since it was part of a larger article addressing a matter of public concern and since there was no evidence that any harm resulted from the employee's story, the court ordered the employee to be reinstated and held that he was entitled to full back pay. *APWV v. Postal Service*, 830 F.2d 294 (D.C. Cir.1987).

Federal law provides subsidiaries to states which declare the goal of providing a "free appropriate public education for all handicapped children." Concerned about the delay in implementing such a program in Arkansas, a group of public school teachers addressed a letter to the state department of education. The letter resulted in an investigation which uncovered a failure to follow established procedures. The school district then allegedly engaged in a series of retaliatory actions in response. The teachers sued stating that such retaliation violated their First Amendment rights. A federal district court entered judgment in favor of the teachers and the school district appealed to the U.S. Court of Appeals, Ninth Circuit.

The court of appeals upheld the decision. The teachers were not asserting private grievances, but rather voicing concerns similar to those raised in *Pickering v. Bd. of Educ.* (see above). The court also stated that sufficient evidence existed to link the retaliation to the teachers' expression of their protected views. *Southside Public Schools v. Hill*, 827 F.2d 270 (8th Cir.1987).

A member of an Illinois city's Civil Service Commission wrote a letter to a local newspaper complaining about the amount of attention minority problems had been given by the city, and stating that the "founding families" had needs too. Two days after the letter was published, the commissioner was fired. He sued under 42 U.S.C. § 1983, charging that the firing deprived him of his First Amendment free speech rights, and due process of law. A federal district court dismissed the complaint, and the commissioner appealed to the U.S. Court of Appeals, Seventh Circuit.

The court of appeals stated that the case was dismissed prematurely because the letter was on a matter of public concern and the fact that it could be considered offensive did not deprive it of its protected status. No evidence was presented showing that the comments hampered the commissioner's ability to perform on the commission. The court also stated that the trial court had dismissed the due process claim solely on the grounds that the mayor's interest in protecting the civil service commission from legal troubles outweighed the commissioner's interest in speaking publicly. The court stated that this improperly merged the First Amendment and due process claims together. The court reversed and remanded the case for trial. *Jungels v. Pierce*, 825 F.2d 1127 (7th Cir.1987).

After a high school teacher/assistant coach complained to school board members concerning mileage allowances and liability insurance for assistant coaches, the school superintendent informed him that according to school district policy, all communication to the school board must take place through the superintendent. The teacher continued to make his complaints directly to the school board members and as a result the principal and superintendent placed negative letters of evaluation in the teacher's personnel file, transferred him to an elementary school and removed him as assistant coach. He then sued the school district claiming damages for emotional distress, community humiliation and loss of professional reputation, and damages were awarded. The U.S. Court of Appeals, Seventh Circuit, held that the teacher's First Amendment rights to freedom of speech had been violated by the school district. It stated that issues such as mileage allowances and liability insurance for coaches were matters of general public interest and that the teacher had a constitutional right to speak directly to school board members concerning such matters. Since the teacher had been disciplined for exercising his constitutional rights, the award of damages was proper. *Knapp v. Whitaker*, 757 F.2d 827 (7th Cir.1985).

Teachers in Oklahoma brought a First Amendment challenge to a state statute prohibiting teachers from engaging in "public homosexual activity." Specifically, the statute prevented teachers from advocating, soliciting, encouraging or promoting public or private homosexual activity in a manner that creates a substantial risk that such conduct will come to the attention of school children. The U.S. Court of Appeals, Tenth Circuit, held that the statute was overbroad and that it had a deterrent effect on legitimate expression. Under the statute, any public statement that could come to the attention of school children, their parents, or school employees could result in a teacher's dismissal. The court declared those portions of the statute referring to the advocacy of public or private homosexual activity unconstitutional. *Nat'l Gay Task Force v. Bd. of Educ.*, 729 F.2d 1270 (10th Cir.1984).

Controversy arose in Alabama when a teacher informed his school board about some practices of an unnamed principal which he deemed to be dangerous to students. Prior to this the teacher had given the news media a press release informing them of the nature of his meeting with the school board. The board accused him of going to the press after the meeting despite a board request to remain silent on the matter. The board then put a letter in the teacher's file which labeled him as unethical and unprofessional. The U.S. Court of Appeals, Fifth Circuit, ruled for the teacher citing a U.S. Supreme Court decision which recognized that teachers are the members of the community most likely to have informed and definite opinions on issues of public importance concerning operations of schools and that it is essential that they be able to speak out freely without fear of retaliation. Absent proof of false statements knowingly or recklessly made, a teacher's exercise of his right to speak on issues of public importance may not furnish the basis for his dismissal from public employment. *Swilley v. Alexander*, 629 F.2d 1018 (5th Cir.1980).

B. Unprotected Speech

An Oklahoma school nurse became concerned about the school system's medication policy. She expressed her concern to the school system and outside government agencies. She also voiced her concerns to other school district nurses, which caused them to fear that they might lose their jobs and nursing licenses. The school system requested that she voice her grievances through the school district's formal complaint procedures. She used the procedure and a school board hearing was held to discuss the district's medication policy. At this hearing she testified that the nurses were "indiscriminately" administering drugs to students. Evidence at the hearing demonstrated that this accusation was false. After the hearing, the school board met again and decided not to renew her contract. The board held a hearing to review its decision not to renew her contract and upheld its original decision, holding that she had created a disruptive atmosphere among the health services staff. She then sued the school district in a federal district court, alleging that her First Amendment rights were violated when her contract was not renewed because of her outspokenness against the district's medication policy. The jury returned a verdict for her, but the district court granted a judgment notwithstanding the verdict for the school district. The district court held that her speech was not constitutionally protected under the balancing test established by the U.S. Supreme Court in *Pickering v. Bd. of Educ.* (see above) because it had disrupted the school system. She appealed to the U.S. Court of Appeals, Tenth Circuit.

The appellate court applied the Supreme Court's *Pickering* test to determine whether the speech was constitutionally protected. First, the speech must touch a matter of public concern. Second, the employee's interest must be balanced against that of the employer, but only after the employer has established its interest "in promoting the efficiency of the public services it performs through its employees." The appellate court held that the nurse's speech sufficiently touched on a matter of public concern. However, it was disruptive to the school district's health service program, and her interest in the speech was outweighed by the school district's interest in promoting the efficiency of its public services. The appellate court affirmed the district court decision. *Johnsen v. Indep. School Dist.*, 891 F.2d 1485 (10th Cir.1989).

An Illinois deputy sheriff was a close friend of the sheriff when he began working for him. Also, for the first nine years, the two men were brothers-in-law. In 1982, the sheriff and the deputy's sister were divorced and personal relations between the two men soured at this time. In the mid-1980's, the deputy sheriff and other members of the department became upset over what they viewed as favoritism being shown by the sheriff toward one of his female employees, The deputy began to study the work habits and compensation of the female employee. He took this information to the county's state attorney. The attorney contacted the office of the Illinois Attorney General. The deputy's charges were investigated by the Illinois Department of Criminal Investigation which determined that there was no basis for criminal prosecution on the allegations and the investigation was closed. The sheriff then terminated the deputy's employment. The deputy brought an action in a federal district court asserting that his First Amendment rights had been violated. The district court granted the sheriff's motion for summary judgment, and the deputy appealed to the U.S. Court of Appeals, Seventh Circuit.

The court noted that the deputy did not relinquish his First Amendment rights when he joined the department, but that he implicitly agreed that his rights would be balanced against the sheriff's interest in running an efficient department. The court noted that the issue was whether the deputy's statements involved matters of public concern so that the sheriff's discharge decision would be subject to judicial review under the First Amendment. The deputy's complaints would not qualify for First Amendment protection under the public concern test. It was apparent that the matter arose in a personal complaint by the deputy. The deputy was motivated by self-interest to win better working conditions for himself. Therefore, the court held that the discharge did not violate the First Amendment. *Breuer v. Hart*, 909 F.2d 1035 (7th Cir.1990).

A Colorado police officer wrote a letter to the city council complaining of command level personnel mismanagement in the police department. He also complained of not being selected for training school or for promotions. The officer was later denied a promotion to the rank of captain. Upon retirement, the officer sued the city and its acting and former chiefs of police in a federal district court alleging that he was denied the promotion to captain because he had exercised his First Amendment rights. The city officials moved for summary judgment claiming qualified immunity on the basis that the officer's letter was unprotected speech under the First Amendment. The district court denied the motion and the city officials appealed to the U.S. Court of Appeals, Tenth Circuit.

The court of appeals held that the letter was not entitled to First Amendment protection. The court noted that the officer's letter did not relate to a topic of political, social or other community concern. The letter had complained that internal politicking and favoritism governed transfers, training and personnel relationships within the department. The officer also complained of the department's failure to select him for training school or to promote him. The court found that the officer's letter alleged mismanagement and inequities, not misconduct. The officer's principal purpose in writing the letter was to air his frustrations at having failed to receive a promotion, which was not protected speech under the First Amendment. The court of appeals reversed and remanded the district court's decision. *McEvoy v. Shoemaker*, 882 F.2d 463 (10th Cir.1989).

A social worker at a Louisiana state mental hospital was fired after he had directly contacted federal law enforcement officials about alleged illegal activities at the hospital and had spread rumors among the hospital's criminally insane patients that he was working for the government and that the hospital administration had ordered the murder of a patient. The worker characterized his actions as whistleblowing, while the hospital officials characterized it as disruptive rumor mongering. The worker sued the officials in federal court, but the federal district court held for the officials. The worker then appealed to the U.S. Court of Appeals, Fifth Circuit.

The court of appeals noted that the courts recognize a strong interest in protecting public employees who have the courage to blow the whistle on wrong-doings in public institutions. Under the balancing test of *Pickering v. Bd. of Educ.*, the court stated that the worker's direct communication with federal law enforcement officials was protected speech; however, the spreading of rumors among a body of criminally insane patients was not protected under that same test. The court found that the worker's direct communication was not the reason he had been fired. Instead the evidence showed that it was for his unprotected rumor mongering. *Price v. Brittain*, 874 F.2d 252 (5th Cir.1989).

An attorney for the District of Columbia Child Support Section had a case transferred to him which involved the monthly child support settlement of a District of Columbia official. The parents had reached the settlement and the attorney was instructed to "sign off." The attorney became concerned that political pressure had been exercised to force the settlement, and that the attorney for the official had performed unethically. After a refusal to sign off on the settlement, the attorney was criticized and later his contract was not renewed. The attorney filed a lawsuit in a federal district court claiming that his constitutional rights had been denied. Specifically, the attorney argued violations of the First Amendment and the due process clause.

To prove that free speech rights were violated, it must first be shown that the attorney was speaking on a matter of public concern. The court then must balance the interest of the attorney to speak on the matter with the interest of the employer in promoting efficient service. However, the court found that defying a superior's order to sign off on a settlement reached by the parents was not a matter of public concern and therefore not protected speech. The attorney's concern about the opposing counsel's ethics were not communicated to any third person and were thus not speech. The court also found that the attorney did not have a protectable property interest in employment, and was not entitled to a hearing or reinstatement. His contract spelled out his term and went unchallenged until this lawsuit. Discussions of permanent employment did not alter the attorney's employment status. The court granted summary judgment to the District of Columbia. *Mulhall v. Dist. of Columbia,* 747 F.Supp. 15 (D.D.C.1990).

Six police officers employed on a Michigan city's emergency response team sent a letter to the local police chief complaining about factionalized conditions on the team. In the letter, they resigned from the team, but not from the police force. Copies of the letter were sent to the mayor, city council, and two members of the police department of a nearby municipality. The police chief accepted their resignations, and brought charges against the officers for "publicly criticizing orders given by a superior officer," and for "giving information to any person concerning the business of the police department, which is detrimental to the police department." One officer contested the charges, but was unsuccessful. Letters of reprimand were placed in their personnel files for one year. Four of the officers then sued in federal court for abridgement of their First Amendment rights. The district court held for the city and the officers appealed to the U.S. Court of Appeals, Sixth Circuit.

The court of appeals stated that under the balancing test of *Pickering v. Bd. of Educ.* and *Connick v. Myers*, there were no constitutional violations. The officers' concerns in the letter were of limited public interest. What sort of factions existed, and which side the chief supported were not matters of public interest. The court stated that even if these were matters of public interest, the city's interest in discouraging public dissension within its ranks would outweigh the officers' need to voice their opinions publicly about such matters. As such, the court affirmed the judgment for the city. *Brown v. City of Trenton*, 870 F.2d 318 (6th Cir.1989).

An Ohio woman accepted a position as a part-time police officer in her village. When a full-time officer retired, she applied for the position. The police chief told her that he intended to hire another applicant, a male, for the position. He stated that a knee injury which the officer had previously suffered might keep her from being able to perform her duties full-time. The officer filed a claim with the Ohio Civil Rights Commission alleging that she had been discriminated against based on her sex and her knee injury, which she claimed was a handicap. Later, the male applicant told the police chief that he had accepted another job and could not accept the full-time police officer position. The chief then offered the fulltime position to the female officer. The mayor and city council agreed to appoint the officer to the full-time position. However, the officer was quoted in an interview with a newspaper as saying that she planned to continue the sex discrimination claim to let people know "what's happening in the police department." As a result, the full-time appointment was withdrawn and the officer was immediately fired. The officer sued the village and its officials in federal court and was successful at the trial court level. The village and officials appealed to the U.S. Court of Appeals, Sixth Circuit. On appeal, the village officials argued that the officer's statements in the newspaper were not protected by the First Amendment since they did not concern a matter of public interest. They also argued that the newspaper interview did not play a motivating role in the officer's termination and that the department's interest in maintaining discipline outweighed the officer's First Amendment rights. The court of appeals held that the statements did involve a matter of public concern since they addressed the matter of sex and handicap discrimination. There was ample evidence to support the jury's finding that the interest was a substantial motivating factor in her dismissal. The court also stated that the officer's First Amendment rights outweighed the employer's interest in maintaining discipline. The court of appeals sustained the trial court's ruling for the officer. *Matulin v. Village of Lodi*, 862 F.2d 609 (6th Cir.1988).

Two school police officers, one male and one female, drove in a van to the home of a third person. When the two arrived, she went into the house while he remained outside. While he waited, city police officers approached the van and, having spotted cigarette rolling papers in the van, searched the van. The search uncovered an envelope containing marijuana. The male officer claimed that the package was not his. He also claimed that he told the officers that he did not know whether the package belonged to the female officer. The police officers claimed, however, that he had told them that the marijuana belonged to the female officer. He was arrested, she was not. Criminal charges against the male officer were dropped, and the female officer was fired after a department of education investigation led it to believe that the marijuana was hers. The female officer filed sex discrimination charges against the department board on the disparate treatment she had received. The male officer was questioned in connection with the case and told an investigator that he did not know whether the marijuana belonged to the female officer. He was then fired "for lying" to the investigator. The male officer then sued the city claiming that he had been fired for speaking out on an issue of public concern, sex discrimination, and that this firing violated his First Amendment rights. A federal district court ruled that the male officer's statement was a matter of public concern and that the department had failed to prove that it was disruptive or impaired the department's work in any way. The city then appealed to the U.S. Court of Appeals, Fourth Circuit.

The court of appeals noted that the male officer was fired for stating that he did not know whether the quantity of marijuana found in his van belonged to a coworker. The court stated that this was not a matter of public concern and was made solely to further the interests of the two terminated officers. The court stated that the district court had improperly elevated context over content. The court reversed the district court's judgement. *Arvinger v. Mayor and City Council of Baltimore*, 862 F.2d 75 (4th Cir.1988).

A tenured faculty member at the University of the District of Columbia (UDC) was appointed to the position of athletic director in order to "bring the UDC Athletic Department into full compliance with [NCAA] and UDC Guidelines." During his employment as athletic director, the employee publicly voiced his concerns about violations of athletic rules and guidelines at UDC. Eventually, the employee was forced to resign as athletic director. The university president admitted that the employee was terminated because of pressure from the UDC's board of trustees and not because of deficient performance. The employee sued claiming that statements he had made criticizing the university played a substantial role in his firing and that they should have been protected by the First Amendment. The trial court dismissed the employee's claim and he appealed to the U.S. Court of Appeals, District of Columbia Circuit.

The court stated that in order to support a claim for First Amendment violations, a public employee must have been speaking on a matter of public concern, and the interests of the employee must outweigh the government's interest in promoting an efficient work place. In addition, the speech must be a substantial or motivating factor in the employee's discharge and the government must not be able to show that it would have reached the same decision even absent the protected conduct. In this case, the court held that the athletic director's speech was clearly on a matter of public concern. However, the court held that the government's interest in requiring loyalty from its athletic director outweighed the employee's interest in speaking out on matters of public concern. The employee's position was related to a policy area and his duties were such as to identify him as a prominent policy level official. The UDC had a significant interest in ensuring that its athletic director be perceived to be compatible with the president and board of trustees. The court held that the employee could be dismissed for expressing views on matters within the core of his responsibilities which reflected a policy disagreement with his superiors. *Hall v. Ford*, 856 F.2d 255 (D.C.Cir.1988).

An Illinois man served as the intramural athletic coordinator for the Community College of Lake County (CLC) in its athletic department. Following a personal dispute with another employee and the college president, the coordinator filed a grievance against the president with the board of regents alleging a number of violations of CLC policy and civil law. The coordinator was then dismissed from his position as athletic coordinator. The CLC said that the coordinator's termination was part of a legitimate reorganization of his department. The coordinator was the only employee terminated by the reorganization. He claimed that his termination was in retaliation for exercising his First Amendment rights in speaking out against the alleged misconduct of CLC's president. The coordinator alleged that his criticism was a matter of public concern and, therefore, was protected by the First Amendment. The district court dismissed the case and the coordinator appealed to the United States Court of Appeals, Seventh Circuit. The court of appeals stated that the criticism in question "could only serve to undermine [the president's] ability to maintain discipline and harmony among CLC's workforce" and only "touched upon a single matter of public concern among persistent personal disputes" and was not protected by the First Amendment. The trial court's decision was affirmed and the case dismissed. *Berg v. Hunter*, 854 F.2d 238 (7th Cir.1988).

The female human relations coordinator of a Wisconsin school district alleged that her supervisor sexually harassed her by attempting to kiss her, making propositions to meet after work, and by suggestive remarks or conduct. The woman complained to school district officials in an oral and informal fashion because she did not want to make a public issue of the allegations. The woman was then stripped of some duties and transferred to a new office at a school where she was the only administrative staff person. She believed that this "reassignment" was actually a demotion. The woman sued the school district and school officials claiming that she had been retaliated against for making the informal complaints of sexual harassment. She alleged that this violated her First Amendment rights to free speech.

The U.S. Court of Appeals, Seventh Circuit, noted that public employees cannot be punished for speaking on matters of public concern. It also noted that the purpose of speech by a public employee must be considered in deciding whether the speech is on a matter of public concern. Because the woman in this case wanted her grievance to be resolved internally to avoid public controversy, the court determined that she was not speaking out as a citizen concerned with problems facing the school district. She was instead speaking as an employee attempting to resolve her own private dilemma. The court concluded that the woman's private complaints of sexual harassment were not constitutionally protected. The court ruled in favor of the school district and its officials. *Callaway v. Hafeman*, 832 F.2d 414 (7th Cir.1987).

A tenured high school psychology teacher refused to perform hall supervision duties on the ground that it would constitute "a negation of his classroom teaching that students are responsible for their own behavior." The school board unanimously voted to dismiss the teacher for insubordination, and the teacher appealed. He argued before the Colorado Court of Appeals that his dismissal violated his constitutional right to speak on issues of public concern. The court noted that a school board is not required to "tolerate action it reasonably believes would disrupt the school and undermine its authority," and that the teacher's refusal to perform hall supervision duties therefore was not protected. The court affirmed his dismissal. *Lockhart v. Bd. of Educ.*, 735 P.2d 913 (Colo. App.1986).

In a meeting with his principal, a Florida teacher expressed his opinions against allowing physical education teachers who lacked social studies certification to fill vacancies in the social studies department. After this meeting, the teacher discovered that he would no longer be teaching American history and political science to juniors and seniors between 6:45 a.m. and 2:15 p.m. Instead, he was assigned to teach elective courses to freshmen and sophomores from 9:45 to 5:15 p.m. The teacher brought suit and the U.S. Court of Appeals, Eleventh Circuit, ruled that the teacher's comments had not been made about matters of public concern, but had instead been directed to internal school policies and personal employment matters. The teacher, therefore, could not protest the retaliatory schedule change on constitutional grounds. *Ferrara v. Mills*, 781 F.2d 1508 (11th Cir.1986).

In a Texas case a nontenured teacher had been employed by her school district for three years. In the teacher's most recent evaluation the principal gave her a generally satisfactory rating but noted that her attitude was unsatisfactory. She met with her principal for an evaluation conference but he did not explain his negative comments to her satisfaction. The teacher then wrote a letter to the principal expressing her dissatisfaction with the negative evaluation and requesting further clarifications. When she received no response she filed a formal grievance challenging her evaluation. The school district refused to arbitrate the grievance and stated that dissatisfaction with the substance of a principal's evaluation could not be grieved. The teacher was informed that her contract would not be renewed. She brought suit in U.S. district court contending that she had been dismissed in retaliation for exercising her right to free speech and her right to petition the government for redress of grievances. The U.S. Court of Appeals, Fifth Circuit, held that because the complaint to her principal concerned only private employment matters they were not protected by the First Amendment. *Day v. South Park Indep. School Dist.*, 768 F.2d 696 (5th Cir.1985).

C. Libel and Slander

Whereas a public employee's comments upon matters of public concern are afforded constitutional protection, in general, no such protection is afforded to comments which are libelous or slanderous. The distinction here is that constitutionally protected speech is not a personal attack, whereas defaming speech is. One exception to this general rule is that public figures or officials may not recover damages for defamatory statements relating to official conduct, unless the statements were maliciously made.

A controversy developed on the Duke University campus around a machine known as the Thermotron RF-8, which is used for deep heating cancerous tumors. The machine was loaned to the university by a Japanese manufacturer on the condition that a particular professor in the radiology department at Duke supervise and control its use. A doctor at Duke decided to take control of the project, but the professor refused. The dispute escalated to the point that the doctor prevented the professor from gaining access to the machine. The professor secretly gained access and removed vital parts of the machine and rendered it inoperative. During this dispute the doctor told a colleague that the professor was "a liar, deceitful, absolutely useless, and does not have a Ph.D., and was a fraud." The professor sued the doctor for slander. A North Carolina trial court agreed with the professor and awarded him damages. The doctor appealed to the Court of Appeals of North Carolina. The court of appeals held that the statements concerning the professor's academic credentials were allegations which impeached the professor and his profession. The court stated "[a]s a member of Duke university's faculty and as a research scientist, plaintiff depended on his academic degree in his work." Therefore, the statements were slanderous. The court of appeals affirmed the trial court's decision and damage award. *Raymond U v. Drake Univ.*, 371 S.E.2d 701 (N.C.App.1988).

A Pennsylvania high school vice-principal received a poor written evaluation from the school's principal. At a public hearing, a school board member stated that the vice-principal was "grossly insubordinate, if not incompetent." Another school board member stated "you're the cause of all this," to the vice-principal's wife. The vice-principal and his wife sued the district, school officials and board members in a Pennsylvania trial court for defamation. The court held for the officials. The vice-principal and his wife appealed to the Pennsylvania Commonwealth Court. The court ruled that the actions taken by the officials were within the scope of their duties. However, the board member's comment regarding the vice-principal's wife might serve as the basis for a defamation lawsuit. The case was remanded to the trial court. *Malia v. Monchak*, 543 A.2d 184 (Pa.Cmwlth.1988).

A Colorado junior high school assistant basketball coach was confronted by the head basketball coach at the school, and told to resign since a rumor had been circulating that the assistant coach had been implicated in child molesting. Rather than be fired, the assistant coach resigned. He then sued the head coach and the school district for defamation. A Colorado district court dismissed the case and the assistant coach appealed. The court of appeals noted that the assistant coach had been convicted fourteen years earlier for sexual abuse. The court held that the truth of the head coach's statements precluded the defamation action. *Lindemuth v. Jefferson County Sch. Dist.*, 765 P.2d 1057 (Colo.App.1988).

II. UNION AND POLITICAL ACTIVITY

The extent to which public employees may engage in the free exercise of speech regarding union or political activities varies depending upon the governmental entity for which the employees work, the context of the speech, and the importance of such speech.

A. Union Activities

Although limitations exist on a public employee's right to engage in political activities, it is well established that public employees have a First Amendment right to form and engage in union activities. Although labor relations are discussed, for the most part, in other chapters, free speech issues often arise in the union context.

The Immigration and Naturalization Service (INS) requires that its inspectors wear official INS uniforms. The INS Administrative Manual and Officers' Handbook prescribes the official uniform: a light blue shirt bearing the INS insignia on the sleeve, dark blue pants, black shoes, black socks, a belt, a tie, and a tie tack. The tie tack and belt buckle design were not prescribed. All uniforms must be "complete in all details and devoid of all ornaments which are not part of the uniform." Despite this regulation, some inspectors wore other adornments, including a San Diego Padres button and an Olympic pin. Two inspectors, who had worn union paraphernalia on their uniforms were asked to remove it. The union sued, claiming that the removal of the union ornaments was an unfair labor practice and that 5 U.S.C. § 7102, which gives employees the "right to form, join or assist any labor organization" gave the inspectors the right to wear union advertising on their official uniforms. The Federal Labor Relations Authority (FLRA) concluded that the INS had committed an unfair labor practice by prohibiting the inspectors from wearing union insignia and the INS appealed to the U.S. Court of Appeals, Ninth Circuit.

The court of appeals noted that cases in the private sector had denied uniformed employees the right to wear union insignia on their uniforms. The court concluded that § 7102's legislative history does not support the idea that federal employees enjoy greater rights to assist their unions than private sector employees. The court continued that even if § 7102 did grant such a right, the INS right to require a uniform under § 7106 would allow the INS to forbid the employees from wearing union insignia. The court also rejected the idea that allowing a Padres button and an Olympic pin, but forbidding union insignia was viewpoint discrimination. There was no evidence the inspector's supervisor noticed the violations. Moreover, rare transgressions from an otherwise consistently enforced rule do not establish viewpoint discrimination. *INS v. FLRA*, 855 F.2d 1454 (9th Cir.1988).

A city charter contained a provision which forbade any city official from "recognizing" a collective bargaining agent or representative of city employees. On numerous occasions, in private meetings with city officials, representatives from the Fraternal Order of Police (FOP) were told that they would be met with as individuals, but not as FOP representatives. The representatives were never denied a right to speak at city council meetings or at any other meeting which was open to the public. FOP filed suit in a federal district court and alleged that the charter provision, and its application, violated its freedom of speech and protection rights. The district granted judgment for the city, and FOP appealed to the U.S. Court of Appeals, Fourth Circuit.

The court noted that the First Amendment guarantees free speech, but does not guarantee a right to collective bargaining. FOP argued that the charter provision went beyond forbidding collective bargaining and actually restricted the rights to free speech of its representatives. The court focused on the key word in the provision, recognize, and construed it to have a meaning as it ordinarily does in labor law; recognized means that an employer is obligated to bargain with a certain representative. The court ruled that the city may legally prohibit this type of recognition, and that the provision was not per se unlawful. The court then focused on the equal protection issue and turned to the application of the provision outside of the bargaining context. No incident complained of consisted of a restriction of the right to speak or advocate to the public. The only restriction mentioned involved private meetings with public officials. The court quoted the U.S. Supreme Court: "public officials at all levels of government daily make policy decisions only on the advice they decide they need and choose to hear." The FOP had no right to privately address city officials, and thus had no right which was burdened. Its equal protection claim was unsuccessful. The decision of the trial court was affirmed. *Fraternal Order of Police v. Mayor and City Council of Ocean City, Maryland*, 916 F.2d 919 (4th Cir.1990).

Idaho State University (ISU) hired a faculty member to serve as an instructor and to chair the history department. He was initially employed under a series of one year contracts. He was reappointed to a three year term as the history department chairman but remained untenured. The faculty member became president of the ISU chapter of the American Federation of Teachers. The faculty member then became involved in a dispute with university officials. The dispute involved a petition for waiver of a required class by a student who was a son-in-law of the dean emeritus. The faculty member refused to permit the waiver contending the student should not receive special treatment. The university officials supported the student. The faculty member wrote a letter to ISU's president asking for review of the matter but ISU then suspended him. The following year, ISU provided a one year "terminal contract" to the faculty member, one day after he criticized ISU policies in the local press. The faculty member sued ISU in an Idaho trial court claiming that his speech and conduct were protected by the First Amendment. The trial court awarded the faculty member $100,000 in compensatory damages but refused to order his reinstatement or award him reasonable attorney's fees. ISU officials appealed to the Idaho Supreme Court which held that the faculty member's union activities (but not the disputed waiver) were constitutionally protected speech. His letter to the president concerned general school policies and was entitled to First Amendment protection. The court remanded the case to the trial court for a determination on the faculty member's demand for reinstatement, attorney's fees and reconsideration of the compensatory damage award. *Hale v. Walsh*, 747 P.2d 1288 (Idaho App.1987).

Nonunion employees (nonmembers) brought suit against a union and a school district challenging the method by which the union collected the "fair share fee." A fair share fee is collected by the union from nonmembers who benefit from the union's bargaining. It is designed to cover the nonmembers' share of the bargaining activities, while not forcing them to pay for political or ideological efforts. The local union bargained for a new contract and sent nonmembers notice of the method for collection and computation of the fair share fee. The nonmembers challenged the union and the school district in a federal district court. The union moved for summary judgment, and the school district moved for dismissal.

The union claimed that it had followed the correct procedures. The school district asserted that it should not be forced to administrate the fair share fee. The nonmembers objected to the notice given and the disclosure of the information regarding the computation of the fees. The first part of the nonmembers' complaint alleged that the estimated and actual expenses of the union were unaudited. Although the union employed an accountant, he did not verify the breakdown between chargeable and nonchargeable expenses. The court then found that the notice given to nonmembers did not give them enough information to make their decision about challenging the fair share fee. The court looked at the school district's argument that it had no duty to ensure that the correct procedures were followed. Courts have consistently found otherwise. A public employer does have responsibility to oversee the procedure and guarantee the nonmembers' constitutional rights. The district court ruled against dismissal of the school district, and against summary judgment for the union. *Mitchell v. Los Angeles Unif. School Dist.*, 739 F.Supp. 511 (C.D.Cal.1990).

A representative of the Baltimore City Teachers' Association gave leaflets to teachers as they arrived for work. The teachers at the school were represented by the Baltimore Teacher's Union. When the representative refused to leave he was arrested. After he was tried and acquitted on a charge of trespass on school premises, he filed a lawsuit against the school board and the school's principal alleging that his First Amendment right to free speech had been violated. A U.S. district court ruled in favor of the school board and principal, and the representative appealed. The U.S. Court of Appeals, Fourth Circuit, decided that the school parking lot was not a forum for public communication. The court ruled that constitutionally protected activity on school grounds was limited to "activity which is related to the educational purposes of public school property." Because the representative's activities were not related to the education of students, his removal from school grounds was reasonable. *Grattan v. Bd. of School Comm'rs*, 805 F.2d 1160 (4th Cir.1986).

Two fifth grade teachers at an Arkansas elementary school filed three written grievances with their school district's superintendent. Although in the past the teachers always received satisfactory evaluations, the following spring they were rated as being in need of improvement. The superintendent recommended that their contracts not be renewed and the school board unanimously agreed. When the teachers sued for reinstatement, the U.S. Court of Appeals, Eighth Circuit, ruled that the teachers' grievances were unprotected because they addressed supervisory and funding matters which had been approved through proper faculty and administrative processes. "[G]overnment as an employer has a legitimate interest in achieving compliance with decisions that, while once open for discussion, have been made through proper channels." The case was remanded for a determination of whether the union activity of one of the teachers had been a factor in her dismissal. *Roberts v. Van Buren Pub. Schools*, 773 F.2d 949 (8th Cir.1985).

While participating in a picket line in front of his school, a Missouri teacher referred to two of the school's assistant principals as "scabs." When his school board later attempted to transfer him to another school within the district, the teacher argued that to transfer him was a form of punishment for exercising his constitutional right to free speech. The Supreme Court of Missouri disagreed and held that the reason for the transfer was not punishment for the exercise of free speech, but rather that the remark, considering the circumstances, demonstrated disrespect for superiors. *Austin v. Mehlville R-9 School Dist.*, 564 S.W.2d 884 (Mo.1978).

A Missouri school board voted not to renew the contracts of three of its probationary teachers. The teachers had publicly advocated higher teacher salaries and affiliation with the Missouri NEA. They contended that their contracts were not renewed in retaliation for these activities in violation of their First Amendment rights to free speech and association. After a three-day trial, the jury returned a verdict in favor of the teachers for $7,500 in damages and the lower court judge ordered reinstatement of the teachers. On appeal, the U.S. Court of Appeals, Eighth Circuit, agreed that despite the probationary or nontenured status of these teachers, the school board could not constitutionally refuse to renew their contracts in retaliation for the exercise of their First Amendment rights. The court remanded the question of damages to the lower court with respect to allowing both back pay and adequate attorney fees to be included in the award. *Greminger v. Seaborne*, 584 F.2d 275 (8th Cir.1978).

B. Political Activities

The Hatch Act, U.S.C. § 7321-27, prohibits all employees of the executive branch or any individual employed by the government of the District of Columbia from using the employee's official authority or influence for the purpose of interfering with or affecting the outcome of an election or taking an active part in political campaigns or political management. The employee retains the right to vote as the employee chooses and to express an opinion on political matters. The political prohibitions of the Hatch Act do not apply to educational or research institutions in the District of Columbia, or to any employee paid from the appropriation for the office of the President. It also does not apply to the department head or assistant head of any executive or military department, or to employees appointed by the President with the advice and consent of the Senate or the mayor of the District of Columbia and other District of Columbia officials. Any employee who violates the political activity prohibition may be removed. However, the act allows employees to engage in nonpartisan political activity.

The constitutionality of the Hatch Act has been brought before the Supreme Court twice and upheld on both occasions. In *U.S. Civil Service Commission v. Nat'l Ass'n of Letter Carriers*, 413 U.S. 548, 93 S.Ct. 2880, 37 L.Ed.2d 796 (1973), the court held that the prohibition against employees assuming an active role in political campaigning or management was neither overbroad nor unconstitutionally vague. In *United Public Workers of America v. Mitchell*, 330 U.S. 75, 67 S.Ct. 556, 91 L.Ed. 754 (1947) the Court stated that it was within Congress' power to regulate the political conduct of federal employees.

The *Nat'l Ass'n of Letter Carriers* case also held that the act forbids such activities as organizing political clubs or parties, participating in political fund-raising, becoming a partisan candidate for elected office, managing the campaign of a partisan candidate, initiating a nominating petition for a partisan candidate or serving at a party convention. The Merit System Protection Board will determine whether an employee's action violates the Hatch Act.

The Hatch Act does not apply to most state and local employees, but many states regulate the political activities of their employees by statute,

A group of Republicans who were noncivil service employees of an Illinois sheriff's office brought a class action suit alleging that they were discharged, or threatened with discharge, because they were not affiliated with or sponsored by the Democratic Party. Finding that the group had failed to show irreparable injury, the district court denied their motion for a preliminary injunction and ultimately dismissed their claim for failure to state a claim upon which relief could be granted. The U.S. Court of Appeals, Seventh Circuit, reversed this decision and the U.S. Supreme Court granted review.

The Supreme Court stated that the practice of patronage dismissals violates the First and Fourteenth Amendments. Patronage dismissals severely restrict political belief and association and government may not force a public employee to relinquish his right to political association as the price of holding a public job. Though First Amendment rights are not absolute, they may be curtailed only by interests of vital importance, the burden of proving the existence of which rests on the government. The inefficiency of wholesale replacement of public employees on a change of administration belies the argument that employees not of the same political persuasion will not be motivated to work effectively. *Elrod v. Burns*, 427 U.S. 347, 96 S.Ct. 2673, 49 L.Ed.2d 547 (1976).

Two union presidents were on extended leave, without pay, from the Postal Service in order to serve as union officers. Both unions circulated monthly newsletters, to which both presidents contributed regularly. In their columns, they generally expressed support for the candidacy of Walter Mondale for president and opposed incumbent President Reagan. They also criticized the Reagan administration on issues of interest to postal employees. They encouraged union members to vote for Walter Mondale and contribute to the unions' political action funds. The presidents were eventually suspended for sixty days for violating the Hatch Act. The Merit Systems Protection Board stated that the articles contained more then mere opinion and exhorted others to vote in a particular way. The presidents appealed their suspensions to the U.S. Court of Appeals, Second Circuit.

The court of appeals stated that in order to violate the Hatch Act the presidents would have to have acted in tandem with the Democratic Party and not merely toward the same goal independently. Neither president had any connection to the Democratic Party and both operated independently. The court said that following *Mitchell* and *Letter Carriers* (see above), the presidents' First Amendment rights to publicly express their opinions on political subjects was greater than the government's interest. *Biller v. U.S. Merit System Protection Board*, 863 F.2d 1079 (2d.Cir.1988).

A Louisiana sheriff prohibited all sheriff's office personnel from campaigning for any candidate other than himself in an upcoming sheriff election. A deputy sheriff served as a cook at a meeting of potential supporters of the sheriff's political rival. A few days later, he and his family attended the local Catfish Festival. The deputy's wife and son wore campaign buttons, shirts, and hats in support of the sheriff's opponent. The deputy was reprimanded, but privately told the sheriff that although he would abide by the rules, he would vote for the sheriff's opponent. A week later the deputy stopped by the opponent's office, as did many deputies and the sheriff himself since the opponent provided free coffee and doughnuts. The sheriff heard from a third party that a campaign meeting occurred while the deputy was present. Although the deputy denied this, he was terminated. The deputy sued the sheriff alleging that the termination violated his First Amendment rights. The jury found for the deputy and the court stated that the political activity policy as applied to the deputy, bore no relationship to any legitimate interest of the employer. The sheriff then appealed to the U.S. Court of Appeals, Fifth Circuit.

On appeal, the sheriff argued that he could not be personally liable for violations in his capacity as a public official which did not violate clearly established statutory or constitutional rights of which a reasonable person would have known. The sheriff also argued that the department's political activity policy was constitutional. The court of appeals agreed that the sheriff was entitled to personal immunity. The law at the time was insufficiently clear that a reasonable sheriff would have known that the policy violated the deputy's First Amendment rights. The court of appeals, however, held that the deputy's speech was protected by the First Amendment. A person's choice of candidates in an election is a matter of public concern, and there was no evidence that the sheriff's office was in any way impaired by the deputy's activities. *Matherne v. Wilson*, 851 F.2d 752 (5th Cir.1988).

In a Mississippi case, a superintendent fired several teaching assistants who had been active in a recall petition drive directed at members of the school district's board of education. They filed a lawsuit claiming they had been fired due to their political activity. A school district administrator was subpoenaed to give testimony describing the school district's employment decision-making process in the teaching assistants' lawsuit. Her testimony was helpful to the teaching assistants, whose lawsuit was successful. At the next school board meeting the superintendent proposed that the administrator be transferred to a newly created position. The administrator was moved from her office into the kitchen of a home economics classroom in a junior high school. She was given no job description. A contract she signed for the next year contained a substantial pay cut. The administrator sued the superintendent and school board alleging retaliation for her testimony. A U.S. district court agreed that the testimony was protected by the First Amendment and that the superintendent had retaliated against her. However, it held that because the administrator had accepted the new position voluntarily by signing a contract at the lower pay level, reinstatement and back pay could not be awarded. The administrator appealed. The U.S. Court of

Appeals, Fifth Circuit, ruled that the administrator's acceptance of the new contract did not preclude an award of back pay. The administrator was entitled to reinstatement to her old position even though a replacement had been hired. *Reeves v. Claiborne County Bd. of Educ.*, 828 F.2d 1096 (5th Cir.1987).

C. Loyalty Oaths

The Arkansas legislature established a statute which required every teacher employed by a state supported school or college to file an annual affidavit listing every organization to which he or she had belonged in the past five years. Arkansas had no real tenure system and teachers were not considered within the civil service system. Teachers were hired on a year-to-year basis, but were automatically renewed if the teacher was not notified within ten days after the end of the school year. A teacher who had worked for an Arkansas school system for twenty-five years was told he would have to file such an affidavit before the start of the next school year. After he failed to do so, his contract for the next year was not renewed. The teacher was a member of the National Association for the Advancement of Colored People (NAACP). The teacher then filed a class action lawsuit against the school district in a federal district court. The court found that the teacher was not a member of the Communist Party, nor of any organization advocating the violent overthrow of the government. It upheld the statute, finding that the information requested by the school district was relevant. The Supreme Court of Arkansas had previously upheld the statute's constitutionality in a case brought in the state court system by other teachers. The U.S. Supreme Court agreed to hear both cases and consolidated them for a hearing.

Both groups challenging the act argued that it deprived teachers of their rights to personal, associational and academic liberty as protected by the Fourteenth Amendment's Due Process Clause. The Court noted that the state certainly had a right to investigate teachers, since education of youth was a vital public interest. It stated that the requirement of the affidavit was reasonably related to the state's interest. However, the Court held that requiring teachers to name all their associations was an interference of teacher free speech and association rights. The constant pressure upon teachers to watch what they said and wrote, and to report their personal associations, clearly interfered with their free speech rights. The knowledge that they could be disciplined or discharged without an opportunity to explain their associations, could lead teachers to curtail all inquiry and thought. Nowhere was this effect more devastating that in education. "Scholarship cannot flourish in an atmosphere of suspicion and distrust." The Court ruled that because fundamental rights were involved, governmental screening of teachers was required to be narrowly tailored to the state's ends. Because the statute went beyond what was necessary to meet the state's inquiry into the fitness of its teachers, the Court ruled it unconstitutional. *Shelton v. Tucker*, 364 U.S. 479, 81 S.Ct. 247, 5 L.Ed.2d 231 (1960).

Florida law required all state employees to submit a written oath, certifying that he or she had never lent counsel, advised, aided or supported the Communist party. A failure to submit such an oath resulted in an employee's immediate termination. A teacher who had taught in the same Florida school district for nine years was dismissed when he refused to sign the oath. The teacher sought a declaration that the statute was unconstitutional and an injunction to prevent its enforcement. He argued that the statute was an ex post facto law and a bill of attainder. A Florida trial court refused to grant an injunction, and the Florida Supreme Court affirmed this decision.

After determining that the case was based on federal law and was properly a matter in which it had jurisdiction, the U.S. Supreme Court struck the statute down as a violation of the Fourteenth Amendment's Due Process Clause. The statute was too vague to pass constitutional standards. It compelled state employees to take the oath or face immediate dismissal. Because the statute lacked objective standards, no employee could truthfully take the oath. Statutes which made persons of average intelligence guess at their possible meanings and applications violated the Due Process Clause because they did not constitute true rules or standards. The Court reversed the Florida court decision, ruling for the teacher. *Cramp v. Board of Public Instruction of Orange County*, 368 U.S. 278, 82 S.Ct. 275, 7 L.Ed.2d 285 (1961).

Faculty members at the University of Washington brought a class action suit to declare two state statutes unconstitutional. One statute required all state employees to take loyalty oaths, and the other required all teachers to take an oath as a condition of employment. Both oaths dealt with employee loyalty to the federal Constitution and to the government. The public employee statute applied to all public employees and defined a "subversive person" as one who conspired to overthrow the government. The Communist Party was also named as a subversive organization. Persons designated as subversives or Communist Party members were ineligible for public employment. The university board of regents sent a memorandum to all its instructors, requiring them to take the oath. A federal district court held that the public employee act was constitutional. It abstained from ruling on the teachers' act pending consideration by the state courts. The teachers appealed to the U.S. Supreme Court.

Before the Court, the teachers argued that the statutes were vague and overbroad, and violated the Fourteenth Amendment's Due Process Clause. The Court reversed the appeals court's decision, holding that both statutes were too unspecific to provide sufficient notice of what conduct was prohibited. This constituted a denial of the teachers' due process rights. The university could not require its teachers to take an oath which applied to some vague behavior in the future, especially since there were First Amendment freedom of speech and association claims at stake. Finally, the court of appeals should have decided the constitutionality of the teachers' act to avoid piecemeal legislation and to avoid possible inhibition of First Amendment rights. *Baggett v. Bullitt*, 377 U.S. 360, 84 S. Ct. 1316, 12 L.Ed.2d 377 (1963).

An Arizona teacher who was a Quaker refused to take an oath required of all public employees under Arizona law. The oath swore that the employees would support both the Arizona and the federal constitutions as well as state laws. The legislation also stated that anyone who took the oath and supported the Communist Party or the violent overthrow of government would be discharged from employment and charged with perjury. The teacher sued for declaratory relief in the Arizona courts, having decided she could not take the oath in good conscience because she did not know what it meant. The case eventually reached the Arizona Supreme Court, which upheld the constitutionality of the oath and potential sanctions under the statute. The U.S. Supreme Court vacated the court's decision and remanded the case for reconsideration in light of its then-recent decision in *Baggett v. Bullitt*, above. On reconsideration, the Arizona Supreme Court again upheld the oath, distinguishing the case from *Baggett*. The U.S. Supreme Court granted certiorari.

The Court began by noting that political groups may have both legal and illegal aims and that there should not be a blanket prohibition on all groups that might have both legal and illegal goals. Such a prohibition would threaten legitimate political expression and association. The Court held that mere association with a group cannot be prohibited without a showing of "specific intent" to carry out the group's illegal purpose. It went on to say that the Arizona statute was constitutionally deficient because it was not confined to those employees with a "specific intent" to do something illegal. The statute infringed employee rights to free association by not punishing specific behavior that yielded a clear and present danger to government. The statute was struck down as unconstitutional. *Elfbrandt v. Russell*, 384 U.S. 11, 86 S.Ct. 1238, 16 L.Ed.2d 321 (1965).

A group of faculty members were employed by the privately owned University of Buffalo in New York. They continued their employment when the university merged into a state operated university. Because they became public employees, the faculty members were required to comply with a state plan that disqualified subversive persons from public employment. Four professors refused to sign a certificate that they were not Communists and that if they ever had been, they had notified the state university's president. One instructor was dismissed immediately for refusing to sign the certificate. Two more continued to teach until their contracts ran out. Another employee who worked in the library refused to answer under oath whether he had ever been a Communist Party member and was dismissed. The group sought injunctive and declaratory relief in a federal district court. The district court held the state requirements were constitutional. The U.S. Supreme Court agreed to hear the case.

The Court first recounted its decision in *Adler v. Board of Education.* It refused to follow the *Adler* rationale, stating that "pertinent constitutional doctrines have since rejected the premises upon which that conclusion rested." It also noted that shortly before the trial of this case, the certificate signing requirement had been rescinded. However, this did not render the group's claims moot. The Court then examined the statute which allowed the removal of public school teachers for "treasonable or seditious" utterances or acts. The Court held that such words were too vague to allow teachers to know the difference between seditious and nonseditious utterances or acts. In addition, another section of the statute allowed dismissal of any person who "by word of mouth or writing willfully and deliberately advocates, advises or teaches the doctrine" of the violent overthrow of government. The Court struck it down as too vague and sweeping, stating that it may allow dismissal of an employee who merely believes in such doctrine, without actually advocating it. Because of such vague provisions, teachers would not know exactly what is prohibited and would stay away from all utterances or acts that may constitute treachery or sedition. Thus, teachers' free speech association rights would be inhibited. Although the state has a legitimate interest in screening teachers, it must do so only in a manner that does not stifle fundamental personal rights. The Court expressed the nation's deep commitment to academic freedom and the free flow of ideas. States may only legislate within a narrow specificity directly related to their interests. Finally, the Court struck down New York's scheme as unconstitutionally vague. The Court went on to attack the *Adler* premise, that public employment may be conditioned upon the surrender of constitutional rights. In rejecting this premise, the Court struck down the scheme's provision that proscribed mere membership in a communist organization as grounds for dismissal without any showing of specific intent to further an organization's aims. Such a provision is unconstitutionally overbroad and thus infringes on rights. The Court reversed the district court's decision. *Keyishian v. Board of Regents*, 385 U.S. 589, 87 S.Ct. 675, 17 L.Ed.2d 629 (1967).

A teacher was offered a position with the University of Maryland. However, he refused to take a loyalty oath required by the university for its employees. The oath required the employee to swear that he was not engaged in any attempt to overthrow the government by force or violence. The oath was authored by the state attorney general and approved by the university board of regents under a state statute which authorized state agencies to establish procedures to determine whether a prospective employee was a subversive person under the act. The act defines a subversive person as someone who attempts or advocates the overthrow, destruction or alteration of the government by revolution, force or violence, or someone who is a member of such an organization. The teacher filed suit in a federal district court, challenging the oath's constitutionality. The board of regents argued that it had the authority to establish the oath under the legislative act. The board also argued that the act should be construed as a bar only to those who seek to overthrow or destroy the government by force or violence. A severability clause contained in the statute purported to allow the Supreme Court to strike down parts of the statute, while leaving its constitutional parts intact. The district court dismissed the teacher's challenge. The U.S. Supreme Court granted certiorari.

The Court first decided that the oath's constitutionality had to be considered in conjunction with the state statute allowing the university board of regents to establish the oath. In addition, free speech rights were implicated because the First Amendment protects controversial as well as conventional dialogue. The Court held that the authorizing statute was too vague and overboard. It falsely assumed that someone belonging to a subversive group also supported the violent overthrow of the government. The statute also put continuous surveillance on teachers by imposing a perjury threat. Such a concept was hostile to academic freedom, limiting the free flow of ideas in places of learning. The Court ruled that the line between permissible and impermissible conduct must be clearly drawn. Because the statute failed to clearly define prohibited behavior, the Court reversed the district court's decision. *Whitehill v. Elkins*, 389 U.S. 54, 88 S.Ct. 184, 19 L.Ed.2d 228 (1967).

III. PERSONAL APPEARANCE AND DRESS CODES

In general, the government may regulate the appearance of its employees provided that such regulation is not arbitrary and is rationally related to a governmental purpose.

A New York county police department had a regulation which established hair-grooming standards for male members of the police force. The regulations were directed at the style and length of hair, sideburns, mustaches, beards and goatees. The local patrolmen's benevolent association sued the county under 42 U.S.C. § 1983, claiming that the regulation violated the freedom of expression under the First Amendment and the due process and equal protection rights under the Fourteenth Amendment. The district court and court of appeals held for the association, and the U.S. Supreme Court granted review.

The Supreme Court noted that the association sought the protection of the Fourteenth Amendment, not for members of the citizens at large, but for employees of the police department. The Court stated that this was highly significant because the state has a wider latitude in imposing restrictive regulations on its employees than it does in regulating its citizens at large. The association would have to have shown no rational connection between the regulation and the promotion of safety of persons and property. Since the desire to make police officers readily recognizable to the public and to foster the "esprit de corps" that uniform garb and appearance may inculcate within the police force is sufficiently related to the department's goals, the regulation was not unconstitutional. *Kelley v. Johnson*, 425 U.S. 238, 96 S.Ct. 1440, 47 L.Ed.2d 708 (1976).

The Arkansas Department of Parks and Tourism, Park Division, issued a regulation requiring park superintendents, rangers, and naturalists to keep their hair cut above collar-length. A naturalist at one state park wore his hair longer than allowed. He was given an oral and written warning of the violation and told he would be fired if he did not cut his hair. Division regulations provided for an administrative hearing for employees about to be fired, but the naturalist's hearing was scheduled after his termination date. The naturalist sued the division director alleging that the regulation violated his constitutional right to govern his appearance, was promulgated as the result of a personal vendetta by division personnel, and deprived him of a property interest without due process. After a hearing, a federal district court found that the regulation violated the naturalist's constitutional right to govern his own appearance. The division appealed to the U.S. Court of Appeals, Eighth Circuit.

The court stated that *Kelley v. Johnson* (see above) established that the constitutional right of a state employee to govern his appearance can be limited by the state if the state has a rational, nonarbitrary reason for such a limit. The court stated that the naturalist's duties made him something of an "authority figure." The court also believed that the state's stated goals in having the regulations, public recognizability, deterrence of park violations, and "esprit de corps," were all legitimate. The court of appeals reversed and remanded the case for adjudication of the due process claims. *Lowman v. Davies*, 704 F.2d 1044 (8th Cir.1983).

Following a classroom evaluation, a teacher was directed to visit a dentist to improve the condition and appearance of his teeth and visit a physician for help in losing weight. The teacher objected and the New York Commissioner of Education ruled that the school district lacked authority to compel him to visit the dentist or the physician, except to have a physical examination. The teacher then filed a lawsuit against the school district's superintendent alleging that his constitutional rights had been violated. A New York appellate court observed that the school district never took any action to compel the teacher to comply with the directives. The court determined that even if the teacher had a constitutional liberty interest in his appearance, that interest had not been burdened by the school district. The school district had not violated the teacher's constitutional rights. His case was dismissed. *Mermer v. Constantine*, 520 N.Y.S.2d 265 (A.D.3d Dept.1987).

The U.S. Court of Appeals, Second Circuit, upheld a Connecticut school district's dress code for teachers. A teacher had objected to the requirement that he wear a shirt and tie with his sport jacket rather than a turtleneck sweater or open neck sport shirt with his jacket as he desired. He contended that the dress code requirement was an unconstitutional abridgement of his rights to free speech under the First Amendment and to liberty under the Due Process Clause of the Fourteenth Amendment. In rejecting these contentions the court held that the speech involved was "symbolic speech" rather than pure speech and as such was not entitled to the same degree of protection from regulation as pure speech would be. The court said that the dress code was a rational means of promoting the board's goals of respect for authority, traditional values and discipline in the classroom. With respect to the Fourteenth Amendment claim, the court held that the teacher had failed to carry the burden of demonstrating that the dress code was so irrational that it could be branded as arbitrary. Thus, the regulation was upheld. *East Hartford Educ. Ass'n v. Bd. of Educ.*, 562 F.2d 838 (2d Cir.1977).

A Texas math teacher was suspended by his school district superintendent for failing to shave off a beard before the commencement of classes as ordered by the superintendent. The school district trustees voted to terminate this teacher, but the termination was overturned by the State Board of Education. On appeal, the Court of Civil Appeals of Texas held that since no dress code nor rule regarding beards for faculty was even in existence at the time the superintendent ordered this teacher to shave off his beard, the state board was justified in finding that this teacher's contract was wrongfully terminated. The court also awarded back pay to the teacher. *Ball v. Kerrville Indep. School Dist.*, 529 S.W.2d 792 (Tex.App.1975).

CHAPTER FOUR
GOVERNMENTAL IMMUNITY AND TORT LIABILITY

I. ABSOLUTE IMMUNITY

The preeminent case concerning whether a government employee is entitled to absolute immunity is *Harlow v. Fitzgerald* where the U.S. Supreme Court defined who is entitled to the defense and who is entitled to only qualified immunity. Very few public employees are entitled to absolute immunity as a defense.

A management analyst, with the U.S. Department of the Air Force, appeared before a joint congressional committee and testified to cost overruns, which embarrassed his superiors. The department then conducted a reorganization and reduction in force to promote economic efficiency of the armed forces, and the analyst's position was eliminated. He then sued two White House aides in a federal district court, asserting that he had been unlawfully discharged in retaliation for his public statements. The White House aides asked the court to dismiss the suit because they were entitled to absolute immunity, but the court refused. They appealed unsuccessfully to the court of appeals, and further appealed to the U.S. Supreme Court.

The Supreme Court stated that absolute immunity existed for the President, legislators and judges, in their judicial functions, and to certain officials in the executive branch. However, for most executive officials, the Court recognized only a qualified immunity. These officials required some protection to shield them from undue interference with their duties, but they could also be held liable for constitutional violations of citizens' rights. The Court held that in order to be entitled to absolute immunity a presidential aide would first have to show that his job included functions so sensitive that absolute immunity was essential. Because the aides had not shown that their jobs were of such a sensitive nature, the Court determined that they were not entitled to absolute immunity. It did find, however, that they were entitled to qualified immunity provided that their actions did not violate clearly established statutory or constitutional rights of which a reasonable person would have known. The Court vacated the court of appeals decision, and remanded the case to the district court for a determination as to whether the aides' conduct fell within the immune category. *Harlow v. Fitzgerald*, 457 U.S. 800, 102 S.Ct. 2727, 73 L.Ed.2d 396 (1982).

In 1970, the Attorney General of the United States authorized a warrantless wiretap for the purpose of gathering intelligence about activities of a radical group which had made tentative plans to threaten the nation's security. After the wiretaps, the U.S. Supreme Court ruled that warrantless wiretaps were not constitutional in cases involving domestic threats. After this ruling, the man who had been wiretapped sued the attorney general in a federal district court, asserting that the surveillance he had been subjected to violated the Fourth Amendment. The attorney general sought to dismiss on immunity grounds, and the man who had been wiretapped sought a declaration that the attorney general was not immune. The district court ruled against the attorney general, who then appealed to the U.S. Court of Appeals, Third Circuit. The court of appeals held that he was not entitled to absolute immunity and that he could not appeal the qualified immunity ruling until a final order had been made. The attorney general then appealed to the U.S. Supreme Court.

The Supreme Court held that even though he was a cabinet officer, the attorney general was not absolutely immune from a suit for damages. However, the Court held that he was entitled to qualified immunity for his authorization of the wiretap because his action was not a violation of clearly established law. Even though the Court had held warrantless wiretaps to be illegal and unconstitutional, it had not done so until after the attorney general had authorized the wiretap. *Mitchell v. Forsyth*, 472 U.S. 511, 105 S.Ct. 2806, 86 L.Ed.2d 411 (1985).

Police in Rhode Island conducted a court-authorized wiretap of a house and determined that marijuana had been used there. Accordingly, an officer drew up felony complaints against several persons, charging them with possession of marijuana. He presented the complaints to a state judge who signed the warrants, and the officer arrested the suspects. However, the charges were dropped when the grand jury did not return an indictment. The arrestees then sued the officer in a federal district court, asserting violations of their constitutional rights. The court ruled for the officer on immunity grounds and they appealed successfully to the U.S. Court of Appeals, First Circuit. The officer petitioned the U.S. Supreme Court for review, which it granted.

On appeal, the Court ruled that the officer was not entitled to absolute immunity just because he submitted the warrants to a neutral magistrate. It found that he could only assert qualified immunity as a defense. This required that he knew probable cause existed or reasonably believed probable cause existed before seeking the warrants. His act in applying for the arrest warrant was not automatically reasonable because he believed certain facts were true and relied on the judge's determination of whether to issue the warrants. If a reasonably well-trained officer would have known probable cause did not exist, the Court held that seeking the warrants would be unreasonable. The Court affirmed the court of appeals' decision and remanded the case for a determination on that issue. *Malley v. Briggs*, 475 U.S. 335, 106 S.Ct. 1092, 89 L.Ed.2d 271 (1986).

An agency of a California county received a telephone call charging parents with suspected child abuse. That evening, two police officers and two officials of the Child Protection Services Division arrived at the parents' residence and advised the parents that they had come to investigate a report of child abuse. The officials took each of the children into the bathroom of their home where they searched their bodies for signs of child abuse. When the examination revealed no signs of abuse, the officials informed the parents that the report had been unfounded. The parents filed a complaint in a California trial court, alleging negligent infliction of emotional distress, battery, and false imprisonment. The trial court determined that the government was immune from tort liability and the parents appealed to the Court of Appeal. The Child Abuse and Neglect Reporting Act (CANRA) requires childcare custodians, health practitioners and employees of child protection agencies to report suspected incidents of child abuse discovered within the scope of their employment. It gives unqualified immunity to childcare custodians and employees of child protection agencies who report suspected child abuse. CANRA serves to encourage and regulate the reporting of suspected child abuse. The court noted that the act does not apply to actions taken by the officials who merely receive reports of abuse. Under the State Health and Welfare Code, county employees cannot be held liable for performance of their duty to investigate child abuse in emergency situations by taking action such as examining a child for signs of abuse or preparing the appropriate report. This immunity also extends to the police officer the department reasonably enlisted to assist in the investigation. The immunity, however, did not extend past the decision to investigate. The court of appeal reversed the trial court's decision to grant governmental immunity for the allegedly tortious act of making the investigation. *Newton v. County of Napa*, 266 Cal.Rptr. 682 (Cal.App.1st Dist.1990).

An Alabama university police officer detained a medical student he had found in a building's storeroom. The building was several blocks from the medical school's facilities, but the student had keys to the building and stated that he had unrestricted permission to use the room for studying. The officer found some evidence that the student was living in the storeroom, which may have given the officer some reason to detain the student. The student subsequently sued the officer in an Alabama trial court, alleging false arrest and imprisonment and a violation of his Fourth and Fourteenth Amendment rights. The officer asserted that he had sovereign immunity, but the trial court disagreed. A jury awarded the student $50 in damages, but no attorney's fees, and both parties appealed to the Court of Civil Appeals of Alabama.

The appellate court determined that the officer was not entitled to sovereign immunity because the suit against him was not also against the state. Here, the student had simply asserted that the officer unlawfully arrested and imprisoned him. Although the officer may have been acting within the scope of his authority, the court found that no valid public policy was served by immunizing a public employee from liability when his tortious conduct resulted in personal injury to another. The court affirmed the trial court's decision in this regard, but reversed and remanded the case on the attorney's fees questions. It stated that attorney's fees could be disallowed only in special circumstances when such an award would be unjust. *Parker v. Downing,* 547 So.2d 1180 (Ala.Civ.App.1988).

An Alabama woman, employed by a state university as a learning center aide, placed a three-year-old child on a piece of playground equipment. The child fell, severely and possible permanently injuring his jaw. His mother sued the university, its president and the employee in an Alabama trial court, arguing that they were negligent in the care of her son. The trial court granted a summary judgment for all the defendants because of sovereign immunity, and the Supreme Court of Alabama affirmed that decision. The child's mother then applied for a rehearing from the supreme court.

On rehearing, the supreme court held that the suit against the employee was not within the scope of the state's sovereign immunity. Any state interest was too far removed from the alleged negligent conduct of the aide for the state's immunity to cover her. Even without this, however, the employee could still invoke immunity if she was engaged in a discretionary act, did not exceed the privilege granted her in the performance of her duties, or was not negligent in the performance of her job. Here, the court determined that the employee's actions did not fall within this definition and, accordingly, it denied immunity to her. The court stated that no public policy would be served by granting her immunity if she had tortiously injured another. The court reversed the previous ruling on the employee's immunity, but affirmed on the state's claim of immunity. *DeStafney v. University of Alabama,* 413 So.2d 391 (Ala.1982).

A handgun, purported to have been destroyed in a Missouri city's police department's property room, turned up in the possession of a felon. This prompted an investigation, and the eventual dismissal of the police chief by the city manager. The police chief was not given any reason for the discharge, and was only given a written notice that the dismissal was made according to the city charter. He then sued the city, the city manager and the city council members in a federal district court under 42 U.S.C. §1983,The district court ruled for the defendants, and the chief appealed unsuccessfully to the U.S. Court of Appeals, Eighth Circuit. He then further appealed to the U.S. Supreme Court.

The Supreme Court held that § 1983 actions were not barred by a city's claim of immunity. It further held that the city's officers could not assert that they had acted in good faith as a defense to a § 1983 action. A city has no discretion to violate the Constitution. When it does violate the Constitution, it cannot claim that it was exercising its own judgment or discretion and in that way avoid liability. Since it was the liability of the city itself that was at issue, there was little, if any, injustice in subjecting the city's officials to liability. Such liability would not deter an official's willingness to execute his office effectively because, so long as he conducted himself in good faith, the damages would be chargeable to the populace as a whole, and not to him. *Owen v. City of Independence*, 445 U.S. 622, 100 S.Ct. 1398, 63 L.Ed.2d 673 (1980).

A California woman claimed she was raped, and her testimony brought a conviction. However, during the time that a preliminary hearing was being held on the case, the police investigated an incident wherein she had voluntarily entered a vehicle to smoke marijuana and was allegedly raped and beaten. This information, which cast doubt on her testimony, was not brought forward until after the defendant had been convicted. Upon its release, his conviction was overturned, and he sued the prosecutor and investigating officer in a California trial court, asserting tort law claims for malicious prosecution and negligence and violations of his civil rights. The court dismissed his claims, and he appealed to the Court of Appeal, First District.

The court of appeal held that the officer and prosecutor were immune from liability for the state claims of malicious prosecution and negligence because the legislature had determined such was necessary to promote fearless and effective law enforcement. Further, the court ruled that the prosecutor was immune from the federal civil rights claim, but the officer was not. The prosecutor was in an office of public trust and had to make many discretionary decisions about the state's case. However, the officer's role was more investigatory in nature, and courts had not extended absolute immunity to officers. Unless the officer's activities were actually part of the judicial proceeding, he was not entitled to immunity, and in this case his questioned activities had not been part of that process. The court affirmed all aspects of the trial court's decision, except that it refused to grant immunity to the officer on the civil rights claims. *Randle v. City and County of San Francisco*, 230 Cal.Rptr. 901 (Cal.App.1st Dist.1986).

A twenty-three-year-old Rhode Island Hmong suffered a seizure while sleeping. He had apparently been in good health prior to his attack. An ambulance rushed him to the hospital, but the hospital staff could not revive him. Three days later, he died without ever having regained consciousness. His doctors could not determine the cause of his seizure or death, and accordingly contacted the state medical examiners' office as required by law. The body was shipped there and the chief medical examiner then performed an autopsy on the body without the permission or knowledge of the parents. This also failed to uncover a cause of death. The parents then sued the medical examiner in the U.S. District Court, D. Rhode Island.

They asserted that their religious beliefs prohibited any mutilation of the body, including autopsies and removal of organs during an autopsy. They alleged that the medical examiner's actions violated their constitutional rights. The medical examiner moved to dismiss, arguing that § 1983 actions could not be maintained against state officials acting in their official capacities because such suits are really against the state and the state is not a "person" under § 1983. The court agreed with the medical examiner that such a suit could not be brought against him, but stated that the parents could sue directly under the Constitution to enforce their rights. Here, the medical examiner had violated their First Amendment rights and performed the autopsy when he should have known that to do so would violate the parents' religious beliefs. Further, the examiner had not shown sufficiently grave circumstances to justify the autopsy. The court thus denied the medical examiner's motion to dismiss and held him liable for damages in performing the unauthorized autopsy. *You Vang Yang v. Sturner*, 728 F.Supp. 845 (D.R.I.1990).

The New Mexico police found a sixty-year-old Navajo Indian's body in an alley. In the course of their investigation, they discovered that the man had had cash and a bottle of whiskey with him the day before. His wallet was missing and he had several bruises and scratches on his face when they found him. The body was sent to Albuquerque for an autopsy without the consent of the man's relatives, and after the autopsy had been performed, the relatives sued the state and the state medical investigator in a New Mexico trial court. They asserted that the medical investigator had been negligent in performing the autopsy and that his acts violated their Navajo religious beliefs. The trial court dismissed the case, and the relatives appealed to the Court of Appeals of New Mexico.

The court of appeals first held that the state should be dismissed from the case because no claim had been made that the state did anything wrong or had any responsibility for the alleged harm suffered by the relatives. The court then determined that the medical investigator had been acting in the scope and course of his employment and therefore was immune from liability for his decision to perform the autopsy on negligence grounds. However, the court determined that the relatives could bring suit against the investigator on their claim that his actions had injured their free exercise of religion. The court reversed the trial court's decision to dismiss this claim, and remanded the case to the trial court for a determination on this issue. However, the court affirmed the trial court's decision to dismiss the other claims. *Begay v. State*, 723 P.2d 252 (N.M.App.1985).

A videotape rental store in Utah rented an allegedly pornographic tape to a minor, triggering an investigation of the store's owners. The county attorney met with them and advised them of their duty to comply with Utah law. The police continued monitoring the video store, and subsequently, two minors, acting as police informants, rented allegedly pornographic tapes from an employee of the store. The police charged the two owners with aiding and abetting the distribution of harmful materials to minors, but the judge dismissed the charges at a preliminary hearing because the two owners had not been properly charged. The owners then sued the officer who had served them, the county attorney and the police chief in a federal district court under 42 U.S.C. § 1983. The district court ruled that the county attorney had absolute immunity from prosecution, but denied the officer's and police chief's claims of immunity. All parties appealed to the U.S. Court of Appeals, Tenth Circuit.

The court of appeals held that the police chief and the officer were entitled to qualified immunity because they had acted in good faith by relying on the county attorney's advice. The court further held that the county attorney was absolutely immune from liability for his prosecutorial actions, but ruled that certain statements which the attorney had made to the media were not prosecutorial and thus allowed him only qualified immunity for his statements. The court remanded the qualified immunity issue of the attorney to the trial court for a full determination. The court reversed the district court's decision with respect to the officers, and affirmed in part the decision on the attorney's immunity. *England v. Hendricks*, 880 F.2d 281 (10th Cir.1989).

A high school football coach resigned in August, 1983. In September of that year a student at the school died while participating in a football game. It was discovered that a required physical examination had not been performed on the student, nor had parental consent been obtained for his participation. The superintendent of schools placed a reprimand in the coach's personnel file stating that he had failed to observe required rules and regulations. The letter made no mention of responsibility for the student's death. The superintendent also stated at a press conference that she would officially reprimand each member of the coaching staff who had not followed the required procedures. The coach filed a lawsuit against the city and the superintendent alleging that the reprimand and the press statement were defamatory. After a New York trial court dismissed the coach's lawsuit, he appealed. The New York Supreme Court, Appellate Division, ruled that with respect to the reprimand, the superintendent was protected by absolute immunity because she had acted within the scope of her duty. The superintendent was protected by a qualified privilege for her statements to the press because of her "interest in providing the public with information as to what steps were being taken to prevent a reoccurrence of the tragic incident." The coach failed to overcome his qualified privilege because he failed to prove that the superintendent was motivated by malice. The dismissal was affirmed. *Santavicca v. City of Yonkers*, 518 N.Y.S.2d 29 (A.D.2d Dept.1987).

As a New York woman entered her parked car, she was assaulted and pulled into it by a man who then sped off. Two witnesses heard the woman's screams and followed the car until they lost sight of it. While trying to relocate the car, the witnesses came upon a police officer. They told the officer what they had observed and gave a description of the abductor, the car and its license plate number. The officer advised the witnesses that he would "call it in." The witnesses made no further reports to the police. The officer never reported the incident and took no further action. Meanwhile, the abductor drove the woman to another town where he repeatedly raped and assaulted her. The woman sued the city and the police officer in a New York trial court. She alleged that the officer was negligent in failing to provide assistance and that the city was vicariously liable for the officer's conduct. The city moved for dismissal, contending that the woman had not demonstrated the existence of a "special relationship" between herself and the municipality. The court held for the woman and the city appealed to the Supreme Court, Appellate Division. The appellate division court reversed and the woman appealed to the Court of Appeals of New York.

The court of appeals held that the city and police officer were immune from liability. The court noted that in order to impose liability upon the municipality, there must be proof of a "special relationship" between the person and the municipality. A special relationship is created when a municipality involuntarily undertakes to act on behalf of a particular citizen who detrimentally relies on the promise of protection. The court found that the officer did not affirmatively undertake to protect the woman. The woman had not detrimentally relied on the municipality's assurances of protection. The court noted that the officer had simply failed to provide police protection to the general public, which was within the scope of governmental immunity. The court of appeals affirmed the appellate division court's decision. *Kircher v. City of Jamestown*, 544 N.Y.S.2d 995 (Ct.App.1989).

II. QUALIFIED IMMUNITY

***Gomez v. Toledo*, below, changed the course of civil suits brought against public employees by no longer requiring the plaintiff to plead and prove that the employee was acting in bad faith. Instead, the**

employee had to show that the conduct in question was reasonable given all the circumstances. This made it easier for public employees to be sued in their official capacities. Another leading case in the area of qualified immunity is *Anderson v. Creighton*, below, where the standard of reasonable conduct required was clarified by the Supreme Court.

A Puerto Rican police officer submitted a sworn statement to his supervisor, asserting that two other agents had offered false evidence in a criminal case they were investigating. As a result of the officer's statement, he was transferred to the police academy, where he was given no investigative authority. The departmental supervisor subsequently found that all the officer's allegations were true. When the "false evidence criminal case" came to trial, the officer was called to testify as a defense witness, which he did. As a result of his testimony, the officer was suspended by his supervisor, who then discharged him without a hearing. The officer appealed to an administrative commission, which reinstated him. He then sued his supervisor in a federal district court under 42 U.S.C. § 1983, contending his due process rights had been violated, and that his reputation in the community had been damaged. The district court dismissed the case because the supervisor was entitled to qualified immunity for acts done in good faith within the scope of his official duties, and the officer had failed to state in his pleading that the supervisor had acted in bad faith. The officer appealed unsuccessfully to the U.S. Court of Appeals, First Circuit, and further appealed to the U.S. Supreme Court.

The Supreme Court held that the qualified immunity defense depends on facts which are "peculiarly within the knowledge and control" of the public official making the defense. The official must act sincerely and with a belief that he is doing the right thing by his action. Since the officer could not know if his supervisor was so acting, the Court determined that the burden was on the supervisor to plead that "his conduct was justified by an objectively reasonable belief that it was lawful." The Court reversed the appellate court's decision. *Gomez v. Toledo*, 446 U.S. 635, 100 S.Ct. 1920, 64 L.Ed.2d 572 (1980).

An FBI agent conducted a warrantless search, with other law enforcement officers, of a Minnesota family's home. He believed a suspected bank robber might be found there, but the suspect was not there. The family then sued the FBI agent in a Minnesota trial court and the agent removed the case to a federal court and sought a summary judgment on qualified immunity grounds. The court granted the summary judgment and, on appeal, the U.S. Court of Appeals, Eighth Circuit, reversed. It then held that unresolved factual questions existed regarding the agent's probable cause, and further held that the right which the agent had violated (to be protected from warrantless searches) had been clearly established. The agent further appealed to the U.S. Supreme Court.

The Supreme Court held that the agent was entitled to summary judgment on qualified immunity grounds if he could establish that a reasonable officer would have believed the search comported with the Fourth Amendement, even though it did not. Further, the Court ruled that the right which the agent had violated was not a clearly established right if probable cause and exigent circumstances existed. Moreover, the Court determined that it was not inappropriate to give qualified immunity to government officials who had acted reasonably. Even if the agent violated the Fourth Amendment, the violation was not necessarily unreasonable just because it was unconstitutional. The court vacated the court of appeals' decision and remanded the case for a determination as to whether the agent's actions had been reasonable. *Anderson v. Creighton*, 483 U.S. 635, 107 S.Ct. 3034, 97 L.Ed.2d 523 (1987).

County officials in Wisconsin became aware that a young boy was probably being abused. However, they did not feel they had enough evidence to retain the boy in the custody of the juvenile court. Instead, they made recommendations to his divorced father to seek counselling and to enroll the boy in a preschool program. Over the next year, the boy was admitted to the emergency room of a local hospital on two separate occasions. His caseworker also noticed suspicious injuries on the boy's head when she visited the boy at home. Even though all this information was recorded and presumably made known to the county officials, they continued to take no action. Subsequently, the boy was admitted to the emergency room again, this time in a coma. Emergency brain surgery revealed a series of traumatic injuries inflicted over a long period of time. The boy suffered severe and probably permanent brain damage. His father was convicted of child abuse. His mother then sued the county officials, claiming that they had deprived her son of his liberty interest in bodily integrity in violation of his Fourteenth Amendment rights. The federal district court granted summary judgment to the county officials, and the U.S. Court of Appeals, Seventh Circuit, affirmed.

On further appeal, the U.S. Supreme Court ruled that a state's failure to protect an individual against private violence generally does not constitute a Fourteenth Amendment violation. The Court also held that the county officials' knowledge of the boy's danger and their willingness to protect him did not establish a "special relationship" so as to create an affirmative duty to protect the boy. The county officials did not create the danger to the boy, nor did they do anything to make him more vulnerable to harm. Accordingly, the officials had not committed any constitutional violation, and the grant of summary judgment was affirmed. *DeShaney v. Winnebago County DSS*, 489 U.S. 189, 109 S.Ct. 998, 103 L.Ed.2d 249 (1989).

Maryland police officers twice appeared at an apartment complex responding to complaints of screaming and other disruptive behavior. On their second visit, a brief investigation was conducted. The officers then seized a black woman who lived alone and forced her to undergo an emergency psychiatric evaluation. The officers alleged they believed the woman possessed multiple personalities and that she was at risk of harm to herself. It was later conclusively determined that the noise had come from another apartment. The woman also produced a witness who testified that he explained the correct source of the noise to the police, and that the police gained an admission from the true source of the disturbance before seizing the innocent woman. The woman claimed that the police action was motivated by racial animus, and filed a civil rights claim alleging deprivation of her rights. The officers then moved for summary judgment on qualified immunity grounds. A federal district court denied the officers' motion, and an appeal was filed with the U.S. Court of Appeals, Fourth Circuit.

Qualified immunity protects government officials with discretionary duties so long as their actions are reasonable in light of clearly established law. It is designed to allow officials to do their jobs effectively without constant fear of monetary liability for a mistake. In the officers' motion for summary judgment, all factual disputes were to be construed in a light most favorable to the woman. The officers contended that their action was reasonable because the standard for determining when to seize a person suspected of having a mental disturbance is unclear. The court ruled that all seizures are subject to the same probable cause requirements as are criminal seizures. Construing all facts most favorably for the woman, a genuine issue of fact existed over whether the officers' actions were reasonable. The appeals court affirmed the denial of the officers' motion for summary judgment. *Gooden v. Howard County, MD*, 917 F.2d 1355 (4th Cir.1990).

A Michigan police officer, responding to a radio call, saw two men carrying items of personal property out of a house. When the men saw the police car, they dropped the items and began to run. The officer chased one of the men and yelled, "Halt, police," three different times. When the man kept running, and the officer felt he could not otherwise catch the man, he fired one shot and hit the man in the neck. Subsequently, the man sued the officer in a Michigan trial court, asserting that the officer had used excessive force in violation of the Fourteenth Amendment. He also sued the city, but the trial court directed a verdict for the city on grounds of immunity. The officer asserted that he too was entitled to qualified immunity, but the court rejected his argument and the jury awarded the man $472,000 in damages. The officer appealed unsuccessfully to the court of appeals and further appealed to the Supreme Court of Michigan.

The supreme court followed the U.S. Supreme Court decision in *Harlow v. Fitzgerald*, 457 U.S. 800 (1982), which stated that "a government official performing discretionary functions is entitled to immunity" when his conduct "does not violate clearly established statutory or constitutional rights of which a reasonable person would have known." Here, the jury found that the officer knew or should have known that his act was not lawful, and the officer had not shown that extraordinary circumstances existed to justify his conduct. The court thus upheld the jury's verdict, and denied qualified immunity to the officer. *Guider v. Smith*, 431 N.W.2d 810 (Mich.1988).

A nine-year-old girl was repeatedly raped and assaulted while locked in a maintenance shed by a New York City playground employee. The employee was hired pursuant to the Work Relief Employment Plan (WREP). WREP was brought about by the New York legislature in 1971. It required hiring people currently on welfare, including convicts, and allowing them to work and receive training. Also included in WREP were safeguards which included criminal record checks which could affect the placement of the employee. It was later discovered that this employee possessed a lengthy criminal record which included rape, but that no city employee ordered new placement for the convict after receiving this information. The victim sued the city for negligence. After several earlier trials, the case reached the Court of Appeals of New York.

The issue was whether the city could be held liable for an employee hired under WREP. Government immunity shields a municipality and its employees from liability for conduct which is found to be a reasonable exercise of discretion. The court found this immunity inapplicable because of the absence of any discretionary action. The safeguards required in WREP had eventually produced the criminal record which should have precluded this employee from these duties. No city employee took the results and made a discretionary decision as required by statute. The court ruled that the strong public policy toward reformation of convicts did not outweigh the need to comply with statutory guidelines in this foreseeably dangerous situation. An award of damages was affirmed. *Haddock v. City of New York*, 553 N.E.2d 987 (N.Y.1990).

Two Illinois police officers were directed to investigate the rape of a twelve-year-old girl. The rape victim had identified her attacker as a bus driver. The victim's mother gave the officers the bus driver's badge number and location. The bus driver's supervisor indicated where and when the bus driver would be driving by an intersection and the officers met him there. They asked the bus driver his name but did not check his badge number. The bus driver was handcuffed and pushed into the back of the marked police car, where he hit his head on the door or roof of the car. At the police station the police officers realized they had arrested the wrong bus driver. They then released him. The bus driver sought treatment for his injuries, but suffered no permanent physical injuries related to his mistaken arrest.

He brought a civil rights suit against the arresting officers in a federal district court.

The bus driver claimed that the police officers violated his Fourth and Fourteenth Amendment rights to be free from unreasonable searches and seizures. The police officers, however, stated that their actions were proper because they had probable cause to arrest the bus driver. When police officers have probable cause to believe that a person has committed a felony, they may make a warrantless arrest in a public place. A sexual assault of a twelve-year-old girl had taken place so there was a need for prompt action on the part of the police. Based on this need and the reliability of the information available to them, the officers had probable cause to arrest the bus driver when they stopped him at the intersection. They were under no duty to further check details such as his badge number. Qualified immunity is an affirmative defense that shields government officials who perform discretionary functions from liability for civil damages if their conduct does not violate clearly established constitutional rights of which a reasonable person would have known. Under the standard governing excessive force cases in effect at the time the bus driver was arrested, the officers did not violate any of the bus driver's clearly established rights. First, as a matter of law, his injury was not severe. Neither were the actions taken by the officers grossly disproportionate to the need for action under the circumstances. Thus, the court determined that the police officers were entitled to qualified immunity for their actions taken following the bus driver's arrest. *Boyd v. Angarone*, 729 F.Supp. 1194 (N.D.Ill.1990).

A company owned a lounge in Florida which had an approved occupancy load of 191 persons, exclusive of employees. The company was apparently in violation of the occupany load by allowing a total of 235 persons to occupy its premises, and the city police and fire departments served a cease and desist order on the company after an inspection. The company sued the city and various city employees in a Florida trial court, asserting violations of its civil rights under 42 U.S.C. §§ 1983 and 1985, and tortious interference with a business relationship. The trial court dismissed the company's claims, and it appealed to the District Court of Appeal of Florida.

The court of appeal held that the tortious interference claim was rightfully dismissed because the company was merely alleging interference with its relationship with the community. An interference claim can only be brought when certain specific customers' or prospective customers' relationships have been interfered with. The claim does not extend to the community at large. Also, the court upheld the dismissal of the § 1985 claim because it could find no conspiracy by the city employees to deprive the company of any equal protection of the law, or to discriminate against the company. Next, the court reversed the dismissal of the § 1983 claims against the city and its employees because a factual question existed as to whether they had committed wrongful acts against the company in violation of its due process and equal protection rights. If they had, they would not be immune from liability unless they had acted in good faith and with a reasonable belief that the law they were enforcing was constitutional. The court affirmed the trial court's decision in part and reversed in part. *Southern Alliance Corp. v. City of Winter Haven*, 505 So.2d 489 (Fla.App.2d Dist.1987).

A New Jersey family services caseworker requested that the police department investigate the questionable scalding of a three-year-old child. The officer assigned to the case interviewed the man who lived with the child's mother. He stated that the burns had resulted from a broken bathroom sink pipe, and agreed to take a polygraph examination. However, he failed to appear for the test. The officer then met with a county prosecutor and, acting on the prosecutor's advice, filed a criminal complaint against the man and arrested him. Later, the doctor who had treated the child stated that the burns appeared to be accidental. The officer then dismissed the charges against the man who then sued the city and the officer under 42 U.S.C. § 1983, alleging that he had been arrested without probable cause. The jury agreed, but the New Jersey trial judge overruled their decision and ruled for the officer. On appeal, the appellate division reversed, and the case was further appealed to the Supreme Court of New Jersey.

The supreme court held that the officer could defend against the § 1983 action if she could establish that she acted with probable cause or, even if probable cause did not exist, that a reasonable officer could have believed that probable cause existed. Further, the court held that in this case the investigation focused on a three-year-old, the officer reviewed the case with a county prosecutor, confirmed the family services report and scheduled a polygraph test for the suspect. She had acted like a well-trained police officer, and could have reasonably believed she had probable cause to arrest. The court reversed the appellate division's decision, and reinstated the trial court's dismissal of the complaint notwithstanding the jury's verdict. *Kirk v. City of Newark*, 536 A.2d 229 (N.J.1988).

An employee of a Kansas "second-class" city's department of public safety sent a letter of criticism to the city commission, allegedly at the request of a city commissioner. He was subsequently suspended without pay for ten days by the city's director of public safety, and sued both the city and the director in a Kansas trial court. He alleged violations of his property interest in employment and his free speech rights. The court ruled against the employee, and he appealed to the Court of Appeals of Kansas.

The court of appeals first noted that the employee did not have a property interest in continued employment. He held his position at the will of the city manager, and thus could not argue that he had been deprived of an expectation of further employment. However, the court held that it was possible the employee had been wrongfully suspended in violation of his free speech rights. Although his right to speak freely was not absolute, part of his statment had been a matter of public interest, so it was up to the court to determine whether the employee's interest outweighed the state's. Further, the director had been held immune from liability by the lower court because he did not know his actions violated clearly established standards. The court disagreed with this holding, and ruled that the correct standard for determining the director's liability was whether a reasonable person in his position should have known that the suspension might be violative of the employee's free speech rights. The court affirmed the dismissal of the property interest claim, but reversed the trial court's decision on the free speech claim, and remanded the case to the trial court for a determination of that issue. *Riddle v. City of Ottawa*, 754 P.2d 465 (Kan.App.1988).

In 1982, the Ku Klux Klan held a march in Washington, D.C. Local and national media captured on film an assault of a man by police officers. He was subsequently arrested for burglary and convicted of a lesser offense. He sued the police department and various officers for malicious prosecution, abuse of process and violation of his Fifth Amendment rights. He sought to use the film footage as evidence of the officers' ill-will toward him. The officers moved to dismiss on immunity grounds, but the federal district court judge denied the motion. They then appealed to the U.S. Court of Appeals, D.C. Circuit.

The appellate court held that the officers should have been granted absolute immunity on the tort claims against them because no allegations had been made that they conspired to unlawfully prosecute the man. With respect to the Fifth Amendment claim, the court held that the officers were entitled to qualified immunity and unless their intent, motive or purpose was unconstitutional, they were immune from suit for their actions. However, it concluded that the suit against the officers should not be dismissed until the man had had a last chance to show that the officers had not acted in good faith. The court vacated and remanded the case to the district court to allow the man an opportunity to show improper motive. *Martin v. D.C. Metropolitan Police Dep't*, 812 F.2d 1425 (D.C.Cir.1987).

A Michigan attorney and his partner were in the business of promoting tax shelters and leased non-existent ethanol equipment to investors. He became concerned that his partner would testify against him and allegedly arranged to have his partner murdered. After several failed attempts on the partner's life, the hired killer was arrested and convicted. He then testified against the attorney, who was convicted of conspiracy to commit interstate murder-for-hire. Through an administrative mistake, the attorney was placed in the same penitentiary as the witness who had testified against him. The attorney talked to the witness who stated that the prosecutors had intimidated him into falsely testifying against the attorney. The prosecutors then discovered that the two men were in the same facility and informed the case manager that they should be separated at once. The attorney was placed in administrative segregation and then transferred to another institution. He sued the prosecutors in the U.S. District Court, E.D. Michigan, asserting that they had violated his civil rights. The court dismissed the claims against the prosecutors, holding that the false testimony claim was barred by the prosecutors' absolute immunity. Further, the prosecutors' actions in informing the case manager had been reasonable and according to prison policy. Thus, the prosecutors were entitled to qualified immunity for this discretionary action. The court dismissed the claims against the prosecutors. *Leibowitz v. U.S. Dep't of Justice*, 729 F.Supp. 556 (E.D.Mich.1989).

A Wisconsin couple came under investigation by the Fish and Wildlife Service (FWS) and the Internal Revenue Service (IRS) because of purported violations of fish and game laws and tax evasion. An agent for the IRS learned of an impending FWS search of the couple's house and asked if he and another IRS agent could accompany the search team. They were allowed to do so with the understanding that they not take an active part in the search. However, during the search, they copied information from various documents. Later, the couple pled guilty to criminal tax evasion. They then sued the agents in a federal district court, asserting that the agents had unreasonably seized information during the search. The agents moved unsuccessfully to dismiss on immunity grounds, and appealed to the U.S. Court of Appeals, Seventh Circuit.

The appellate court ruled that the agents were not entitled to qualified immunity for their actions in illegally seizing the information at the couple's home. It rejected the agents' argument that no seizure had been made because nothing tangible had been removed from the home. Information taken is an interference with the owners' possessory interest in it. The court thus held that the taking of information was clearly a seizure and clearly violated the couple's Fourth Amendment rights against unreasonable searches and seizures. It affirmed the district court's decision and held that the agents were not entitled to qualified immunity. *LeClair v. Hart*, 800 F.2d 692 (7th Cir.1986).

A Connecticut police officer came upon a scene where another officer had just shot a teenage boy. He asked the other officer what had happened, left the scene for a moment, and when he returned, he noticed a knife lying next to the body which he hadn't seen before. He suspected it was planted, but was not questioned by anyone in the department about it. Subsequently, federal officials conducted an investigation in which he cooperated. He was then harassed and his car and house were vandalized because of his testimony before a grand jury. The other officer was finally acquitted and the police superintendent then suspended the officer who had cooperated with the federal authorities. However, the board of police commissioners ordered him reinstated with full back pay and seniority. Harassment continued against the officer and he received seven changes in duty assignments. He then sued the superintendent under 42 U.S.C. § 1983, asserting deprivations of property and liberty interests without due process, and retaliation for his free speech protected testimony. The superintendent moved for dismissal on immunity grounds, which a federal district judge denied, and he appealed to the U.S. Court of Appeals, Second Circuit.

The appellate court held that the superintendent was entitled to qualified immunity on the due process claims, but disallowed immunity on the free speech retaliation claim. Since the prohibition against retaliation for free speech had been clearly established for a long time, the court held that the supervisor should have known that retaliation was wrongful. The court affirmed the district court's decision to deny immunity on the free speech claim but reversed and allowed immunity on the due process claim. *Dobosz v. Walsh*, 892 F.2d 1135 (2d Cir.1989).

A Michigan youth unsuccessfully attempted to steal a car located in a bakery's parking lot. A bakery employee observed the youth's actions and called an off-duty police officer to the scene. The officer approached the car and identified himself as a police officer, showing the youth his badge and gun. He told the youth to leave the car, which the youth first refused to do. He then got out, however, ran to a nearby fence and began to climb it. The officer chased him, grabbed him from behind and as he did so, the gun accidentally discharged, firing a fatal shot into the youth's back. The youth's mother sued the city and officer in a Michigan trial court, and the case was removed to a federal district court. She asserted violations of 42 U.S.C. § 1983, arguing that the officer's actions constituted an unreasonable seizure violation of the Fourth Amendment. The court ruled for the city and the jury ruled for the officer, and she appealed to the U.S. Court of Appeals, Sixth Circuit.

The court of appeals held that the city's policy was not to allow force in all felony cases, but just those where resistance to arrest was dangerous and obstinate. It thus agreed that the city was not liable for damages. The court then looked to the officer's actions and determined that his decision to draw his gun was reasonable because it was dark and he did not know whether the youth was armed. He had also had very little time to holster his gun because the youth ran off so quickly. If he had stopped and done so, the youth might have escaped. Therefore, although the results were tragic, the officer's actions were not unreasonable. The court affirmed the district court's ruling. *Pleasant v. Zamieski*, 895 F.2d 272 (6th Cir.1990).

A Michigan university student was observed driving erratically along a campus road. A campus police officer stopped the student and noticed that he appeared to be intoxicated. She gave him two sobriety tests and took him into custody when the tests showed he was intoxicated. She radioed for permission to take the student to the county jail, but was instructed to take him to the university's holding cell for processing. She placed him in the holding cell without removing the student's belt or socks and did not check up on him for about thirty-five minutes. When she did, she discovered that he had made a noose from his belt and socks, and had hung himself. The student's estate then sued the officer for negligence, and under 42 U.S.C. § 1983, in a Michigan trial court. The jury returned a verdict for the student's estate, and the officer appealed to the Court of Appeals of Michigan.

She argued, on appeal, that her actions were entitled to governmental immunity, but the court of appeals disagreed. Had her acts been discretionary, or involved significant decision-making, and been performed in good faith within the scope of her employment, the court would have granted her immunity. However, the court determined that her actions had been ministerial, or involving the execution of a decision and entailed only minor decisionmaking. The court thus determined that she was not entitled to governmental immunity, and affirmed the trial court's decision. *Hickey v. Zezulka*, 443 N.W.2d 180 (Mich.App.1989).

An assistant U.S. attorney and several employees of the Department of Health and Human Services received information which led them to believe a Medicaid fraud was being perpetrated by several patients involved with two neighborhood health centers. They conducted searches and seizures of the health centers. Subsequently, the health centers and some of the patients sued the employees, alleging violations of their privacy rights and discrimination under 42 U.S.C. § 1983. The defendant employees asked for summary judgment on qualified immunity grounds. A federal district court denied their motions and they appealed to the U.S. Court of Appeals, Tenth Circuit.

The court of appeals held that, with respect to the privacy claims, the employees were entitled to qualified immunity because their searches and seizures were reasonable. The employees had been told that a valid search warrant would be obtained and they were entitled to rely on that statement. However, on the discrimination claims, the court ruled that the case should be remanded to the district court for a proper determination as to whether the employees acted with an improper motive. If they had, they would not be entitled to the qualified immunity defense. The court reversed the district court's decision. *Pueblo Neighborhood Health Centers, Inc. v. Losavio*, 847 F.2d 642 (10th Cir.1988).

A Michigan inmate escaped from confinement and committed an armed robbery in Ohio. He was subsequently apprehended in Michigan on other charges and waived extradition to Ohio in exchange for dismissal of the Michigan charges. On that day, the Michigan Department of Corrections filed a detainer against him because he was an escaped inmate. However, he served his time and was released because the detainer had not been sent to the Ohio authorities. He was later arrested and released again. Finally, over five years after the detainer had been issued, he was stopped for a traffic offense in Ohio and detained without bond because the detainer had then been forwarded to Ohio. He sued the director of the department under 42 U.S.C. § 1983 in a federal district court, alleging that the detainer was unlawful and deprived him of his liberty without due process. The director asserted that he was entitled to qualified immunity, and asked for a dismissal which the district court refused to grant, and he appealed to the U.S. Court of Appeals, Sixth Circuit.

The court of appeals held that issues of fact existed which barred dismissal of the claim. It stated that the director had only asserted that he was acting in good faith, without offering any support for his contention. However, the court also recognized that the inmate had not shown that the director had violated clearly established law, and that the director should have clearly understood that he was under an affirmative duty to refrain from such conduct. The court vacated the district court's decision and remanded the case for a determination of what the clearly established law was at the time of the director's action, so that it could be determined whether he was entitled to qualified immunity. *Dominque v. Telb*, 831 F.2d 673 (6th Cir.1987).

Three complaints were made against a Texas attorney by various parties, and the state bar association invited him to provide a written response to the complaints. He failed to do so, and the bar association eventually filed a lawsuit against him. He then sued the bar association and two of its employees in a federal district court, asserting that the employees had acted in bad faith and in violation of his due process rights. The district court granted summary judgment for the defendants, and the attorney appealed to the U.S. Court of Appeals, Fifth Circuit.

The court of appeals held that the state bar was a state agency and thus could not be sued by the attorney for damages. Further, it noted that the two employees had acted in good faith and within the scope of their employment. The court recognized that broad immunity must be given to members of bar grievance committees and their staff because of the importance of the disciplinary process to the judiciary. The court thus affirmed the district court's decision, and held the two employees to be entitled to good faith qualified immunity. *Bishop v. State Bar of Texas*, 791 F.2d 435 (5th Cir.1986).

An Alabama employee of the state driver license division applied for and received a transfer to the highway patrol division as a trooper. He was told that there was a residency requirement and agreed to abide by it upon his transfer. However, he could not find a home for his family, so he rented a room within the required area while his family continued to live outside the jurisdiction. Subsequently, he received a written memorandum which he interpreted as allowing him to live outside the jurisdiction because it allowed for some officers to live outside the area. He moved back with his family for three years until notified that he had read the memorandum differently than the department and that he was still required to live within the jurisdiction. He then sued the director of the department of public safety and the division chief in an Alabama trial court for unequal application of the residency requirement policy, asking for monetary damages, and the court awarded them. The director and division chief appealed to the Court of Civil Appeals of Alabama.

The appellate court held that he was not barred by the statute of limitations even though he had waited three years, because he did not realize different interpretations were being given to the memorandum until he had moved back with his family for three years. Also, the director and division chief were not allowed to now assert the defense of qualified immunity because they had waited until after the trial to do so. It thus came too late. The court affirmed the trial court's decision, and upheld the award of monetary damages to the trooper. *Prescott v. Pritchett*, 509 So.2d 222 (Ala.Civ.App.1986).

A Virginia high school student was injured while playing tackle football without any protective equipment during a physical education class. The student claimed that the instructor knew or should have known of the danger posed to the participants. The student sued the instructor to recover for the injury and medical expenses. The instructor claimed that he was immune from suit because he was acting for the school. The trial court dismissed the lawsuit, and the student appealed to the Virginia Supreme Court. The supreme court reasoned that an employee of a governmental body "shared the benefits of sovereign immunity where his activities involved the exercise of judgment and discretion." The court also noted that holding teachers liable while performing such functions would discourage others from becoming teachers and also make orderly administration of school systems more difficult. The supreme court affirmed the trial court's dismissal of the case. *Lentz v. Morris,* 372 S.E.2d 608 (Va.1988).

Three incidents involving school officials, students and a parent led to the firing of a South Dakota teacher. The first incident involved a conference where the teacher met with the principal and a parent. The teacher claimed that the principal and the parent acted together when the parent poked, shoved and threatened the teacher. The second incident involved a teacher evaluation conference in which the teacher alleged that the school superintendent falsely imprisoned him in an office until the teacher signed the evaluation form. The third incident involved an implication by the superintendent to a group of students that the teacher was interested only in drawing a paycheck. The teacher sued his school district and school officials alleging intentional infliction of emotional distress, battery and false imprisonment. A state circuit court ruled for the school district and officials, stating that both were immune from liability since the officials were acting within the scope of their employment during the incidents. On appeal by the teacher, the South Dakota Supreme Court held that the circuit court was wrong in ruling for the school officials. The principal would lose his immunity if the teacher could prove that the principal acted in concert with the parent. The supreme court agreed with the state circuit court that the school district was not liable for any of the incidents, but it remanded the case to the circuit court to determine whether the school officals were liable. *Bego v. Gordon*, 407 N.W.2d 801 (S.D.1987).

A California woman reported that she believed her two children had been sexually abused by her next-door-neighbor. When the report was confirmed, the neighbor was arrested. The police also questioned the neighbor's five-year-old son and took him into protective custody. Although the son denied being abused, two county social workers arranged for temporary protective detention and refused to release him to his mother until a dependency hearing was held five days later. The couple then sued the social workers under 42 U.S.C. § 1983, claiming that seizure of their son and holding him until the hearing violated their civil rights. A federal district court refused to grant the social workers' request for qualified immunity. The workers appealed to the U.S. Court of Appeals, Ninth Circuit.

The court stated that government officials performing discretionary duties enjoyed qualified immunity from civil liability as long as their conduct did not clearly violate constitutional rights of which reasonable persons would be aware. The court rejected the couple's argument that they had a protected liberty interest in the integrity and unity of their family which would require the social workers to obtain a warrant to deprive them of custody. Rather, the case should be analyzed in terms of the reasonable belief by the social workers that the son was being held in protective custody under established law and the information which they possessed. In this case, there was no attempt by the social workers to permanently sever the parent-child relationship. Because of the evidence of child abuse the court stated that the social workers had not violated established law by holding the son in temporary protective custody. The social workers were entitled to qualified immunity and the court reversed and remanded the case to the district court with instructions to dismiss the case. *Baker v. Racansky*, 887 F.2d 183 (9th Cir.1989).

A Michigan man was arrested for driving while intoxicated. The man allegedly cried and remarked to the arresting officers that he wished he were dead. The officers placed the man in a cell with horizontal bars. A television monitor in the cell which was used to watch the prisoners was inoperative. After the officers refused to give the man a cigarette, he threatened to kill himself. A short while later, the man was found dead, hanging by his shirt from a bar in the cell. The man's family then sued the officers and their supervisors, alleging violation of the man's constitutional rights under 42 U.S.C. § 1983. After a federal district court found that the officers had violated the man's Fourteenth Amendment rights not to be punished while in pretrial detention and to be free from unsafe confinement, the officers appealed to the U.S Court of Appeals, Sixth Circuit.

The officers contended that they were entitled to qualified immunity from the lawsuit. The man's family maintained that by ignoring the man's suicide threats and placing him in a horizontal bar cell, the officers had not exercised professional judgment in determining whether confinement conditions were safe. The court of appeals held that the officers were entitled to qualified immunity because no right existed at the time which would have required the officers to screen prisoners for suicidal tendencies. It noted that there is a distinction between the right to medical care for someone requesting it and the right to physical security. Since there was no such right, a reasonable officer could not have known that he or she was violating a prisoner's constitutional rights. The court also held that the supervisors were immune because they could not have trained the officers to meet a duty that did not exist. *Danese v. Asman*, 875 F.2d 1239 (6th Cir.1989).

III. GOVERNMENTAL LIABILITY

The government and public employees can be liable in tort the same as private individuals. There are often limits put on government liability and attorney's fees are often provided to the successful party. However, a litigant must often pursue various administrative remedies before attempting to use the courts.

A group of involuntarily confined Missouri patients sued state hospital officials in a federal district court, asserting that they had been mistreated and that the conditions at the hospital violated the Constitution. They also asserted that they had been placed in the hospital without due process. The district court ruled that there were constitutional violations in several areas, but that several more complaints were not violative. After this limited success, the group filed a request for attorney's fees. The district court granted that request, and the court of appeals affirmed. Appeal was taken to the U.S. Supreme Court.

The Supreme Court noted that when a party is unsuccessful on a claim unrelated to the successful claims, the hours spent on that claim should be excluded from the amount of reasonable attorney's fees. However, if the unsuccessful and successful claims are related, the attorney's fee should not be reduced simply because the court did not rule on each contention raised. In this case, the Court found that only limited success had been achieved against the state officials. Accordingly, it ordered that only those fees which were reasonable in relation to the results obtained should be awarded. The

Supreme Court reversed the appellate court's decision, and remanded the case for a determination of what the attorney's fees should be. *Hensley v. Eckerhart,* 461 U.S. 424, 103 S.Ct. 1933, 76 L.Ed.2d 40 (1983).

An Illinois city held a lakefront festival on the shores of Lake Michigan. A twelve-year-old citizen attended and was strolling with a friend on the breakwater. At the tip of the breakwater, the boy fell into the water and sank. Immediately his friend ran for help. Within ten minutes of the boy's fall into the water, two lifeguards, two firefighters and one police officer were on the scene with equipment to effect a rescue. In addition, two nearby scuba diving civilians offered the assistance of themselves, their boat and equipment. Before any rescue attempt could begin, however, a county deputy sheriff arrived in a marine patrol boat. The city and county had previously entered into an intergovernmental agreement that required the county to provide all police services in the entities' concurrent jurisdiction on Lake Michigan. Under its authority, the county had instituted a policy that directed all members of the sheriff's department to prevent civilians from attempting to rescue a person in danger of drowning in the lake. Because of this policy, the deputy ordered all persons on the scene to cease their rescue efforts. Twenty minutes after the arrival of the initial rescuers, and thirty minutes after the boy had fallen in, the officially authorized divers retrieved the boy's body. The parents filed an action in a federal district court against the city, the county and the deputy alleging that their son's civil rights had been violated.

The court assumed for the purposes of its decision that the child would have survived had the deputy not stopped the initial rescue attempts. The city and the county were being sued here for the policies that led to the prevention of the child's rescue. The court dismissed the claims against the city and county, and entered summary judgment in favor of the deputy. The mother appealed to the U.S. Court of Appeals, Seventh Circuit. The court determined that the city would not be held liable but that the county's policy of preventing unauthorized rescues deprived the victim of his right to life. The case was remanded to the trial court for a ruling on the civil rights violations. *Ross v. U.S.*, 910 F.2d 1422 (7th Cir.1990).

A twenty-one-year-old Texas man was involved in an automobile accident while he was out celebrating his birthday. When the police arrived and asked questions, the man was uncooperative. The police officers arrested him for public drunkenness and took him to the city jail. While booking the man, the arresting officer asked him a series of medical questions, pursuant to the police officers' handbook. The man was belligerent and uncooperative and the arresting officer took him to his jail cell at 3:10 a.m. At 4:00 a.m. the man was found dead after having hanged himself. The man's mother filed suit against the city in a federal district court alleging violations of 42 U.S.C. §1983. The court granted summary judgment to the city and the mother appealed to the U.S. Court of Appeals, Fifth Circuit.

On appeal, the mother argued first, that the officers failed to make hourly cell checks called for by the department's handbook, and second, that the department had provided inadequate training to police officers in the medical/psychological screening of detainees. The court determined that since the man was found dead within the hour, an hourly cell check would not have prevented his suicide. It also determined that the failure to adequately train police officers may rise to the level of constitutional deprivation only if the detainees' rights include an absolute right to a psychological screening. The court ruled that there was no right because such a right would require the skills of an experienced medical professional. The court of appeals affirmed the district court's decision. *Burns v. City of Galveston, Texas*, 905 F.2d 100 (5th Cir.1990)

An Illinois man worked as a journeyman electrician for the city of Chicago. The electrician drove his car to a terminal lunchroom, which required him to leave an airport on an access road and re-enter the airport. After returning from lunch, he was confronted by his supervisor, who accused him of violating a work order that forbade leaving the airport. The supervisor then ordered the electrician to sign out and go home. When the electrician refused, the supervisor called the Chicago police and asked them to arrest the electrician for disorderly conduct. The supervisor stated to the police that the electrician was suspended from his job, and that his presence on the job was causing a safety hazard. The Chicago police officers spoke to the deputy commissioner of the department who also requested that the electrician be arrested. He then sued his supervisor, the deputy commissioner, and the city of Chicago under 42 U.S.C. § 1983. He claimed that the defendants were at all times acting in their official capacities and under color of law and that the defendants wilfully and maliciously violated his constitutional rights by procuring his arrest. The district court granted all three defendants' motions to dismiss. The electrician appealed to the U.S. Court of Appeals, Seventh Circuit.

Since the individual defendants were sued in their official capacities, the suit was construed as a suit against the muncipality itself. There were two separate issues presented by the parties. First, the court had to define whether the complaint alleged activity taken under color of state law. It if concluded that the action was taken under color of state law, it then needed to decide whether the complaint alleged that the defendants' action was taken pursuant to a policy that would justify the imposition of liability on the municipality. The court determined that the complaint sufficiently alleged action taken under color of state law. Since the defendants failed to show that the deputy commissioner was not the final policy making authority with respect to the decision, the court also concluded that the municipality could be held liable under § 1983 of the Civil Rights Act. The court of appeals reversed the district court's decision to dismiss the complaint and remanded for further proceedings. *Yeksigan v. Nappi*, 900 F.2d 101 (7th Cir.1990).

Several involuntarily committed patients at a Maryland state hospital were violently beaten on several occasions by an aide. As they were all profoundly retarded, a nonprofit advocacy agency was appointed to handle their cases. They sued the aide in a Maryland trial court, alleging due process violations, violation of the state health code, and assault and battery. The court dismissed the first two claims because the patients could recover under the assault and battery claim. The jury awarded the patients only one dollar in compensatory and one dollar in punitive damages, and the patients appealed to the Court of Special Appeals of Maryland.

The court of appeals held that the due process claim should not have been dismissed because it provided for attorney's fees to the prevailing party. However, apart from that aspect, there was no difference between recovery under the due process claim and the assault and battery claim because the patients could receive no greater damages under the due process claim than they had already received. Because the court found that the jury's verdict was not clearly wrong, it refused to overturn it. The court affirmed the verdicts, but remanded the case for a determination of attorney's fees consistent with the patients' successful verdicts on their due process claims. *Shapiro v. Chapman*, 520 A.2d 1330 (Md.App.1987).

An Indiana woman applied for and received a teaching position at a juvenile detention center. She had significant educational and employment experience. Her supervisor, a trial court judge who ran the center, employed a strict dress code to maintain a professional image and keep the public's confidence in the center and its employees high. The employee received reprimands for failing to conform to the dress code, and eventually was terminated for insubordination. Further, she was denied a teaching position at another county facility, and the job was given to an inexperienced male. She sued the county and the judge in a federal district court, asserting sex discrimination in her discharge. She also had filed a complaint with the Equal Employment Opportunity Commission (EEOC) approximately seven months after learning that the man had been hired in place of her, asserting discrimination. The district court ruled for the county and judge, and the teacher appealed to the U.S. Court of Appeals, Seventh Circuit.

The court of appeals determined that she had been fired because of her violations of the dress code and not because she was a woman. It found that she had failed to show a disparate impact on women of the dress code requirements because other women working at the facility had not been adversely affected by the policies. Further, it noted that her EEOC complaint had been filed too late and was therefore barred by the statute of limitations. The court affirmed the district court's decision. *Wislocki-Goin v. Mears*, 831 F.2d 1374 (7th Cir.1987).

A firefighter in Alabama was called to fight a grassfire on a day when the temperature was over ninety degrees. The man was required by municipal policy to wear "full turnout gear." This included heavy clothing such as a helmet, coat, gloves, pants and boots. The firefighter suffered a heatstroke and was found dead at the scene of the fire. The firefighter's widow claimed that the municipality was negligent in formulating the requirement of wearing full turnout gear. She filed suit in an Alabama trial court and won a judgment of $384,000. The city appealed to the Alabama Supreme Court.

The judgment of the trial court will be overturned only if found clearly wrong based on a review of the evidence. The officer in charge at the time of the death testified that he "used the guidelines" to fight the fire. This meant wearing full turnout gear at all fires. Further, it was commonly believed that a firefighter who was injured while not in full gear would not receive injured with pay status. The fire chief testified that a training manual from the International Fire Service Training Association warns of both fatigue and exhaustion which may result from wearing full gear. The coroner testified that wearing full turnout gear would cause a problem with the body's heat elimination system, which would increase the potential for heat stroke. The city argued that the firefighter was contributorily negligent, and had assumed the risk. The court disagreed, and found that the evidence supported the judgment. The decision was affirmed. *City of Birmingham v. Hale*, 574 So.2d 784 (Ala.1991).

An IRS agent examined the tax returns of a Pennsylvania man and determined that $247,000 was owed to the government. Believing that the man had liquidated his real estate holdings and given the proceeds to the woman he was living with, the agent sought to apply assessments against the woman. He received permission to do so, and after completing the assessments, another IRS officer filed liens against the woman's farm and bank accounts. However, he failed to obtain the approval of the IRS regional counsel as required by the service's manual. Because of this, the liens and assessments were abated. The woman then sued the two agents in a federal district court, asserting violations of her Fourth and Fifth Amendment rights. The court awarded her damages, and the agents appealed to the U.S. Court of Appeals, Third Circuit.

The court of appeals held that even though the agents had violated the internal policy of the IRS, they were not liable to the woman because she could not have relied on their noncompliance with the policy. Since she had already received a remedy of reversal of the IRS's actions, she had been sufficiently compensated for their noncompliance with service policy. Further, the court held that the seizure of her property did not violate a privacy interest under the Fourth Amendment. The court reversed the district court's decision and held that the agents were not liable for damages. *Lojeski v. Boandl*, 788 F.2d 196 (3d Cir.1986).

An Ohio doctor, employed by a state university hospital, sued hospital officials in an Ohio trial court, asserting federal civil rights and tort claims against them. Among the charges were slander, conspiracy to restrain trade, deprivation of certain property rights and conspiracy to monopolize surgery services at the hospital. The trial court dismissed the claims and, on appeal, the court of appeals affirmed in part and reversed in part, by dismissing only some of the claims. Both parties further appealed to the Supreme Court of Ohio.

The supreme court held that the hospital officials were not immune from individual liability because, if the allegations against them were true, their acts were not performed within the scope of their employment or responsibilities, which would give them immunity. Further, the court ruled that if the allegations were true, the officials could be found to have acted in bad faith, and therefore would not qualify for limited immunity. However, the court did determine that there was insufficient evidence to support the claim of civil rights violations and deprivation of property rights. Accordingly, the court affirmed the appellate court's decision in part and reversed in part. It allowed the dismissal of the civil rights claim, but disallowed the dismissal of the tort claims. *Cooperman v. University Surgical Associates, Inc.*, 513 N.E.2d 288 (Ohio 1987).

Residents of a South Dakota Indian reservation sued various military personnel and federal officials in a federal district court for damages arising from the residents' seizure and confinement within the village of Wounded Knee. They asserted that the seizure was in violation of federal law and the Constitution. The district court dismissed their suit, and they appealed to the U.S. Court of Appeals, Eighth Circuit. The court of appeals first recognized that a qualified immunity defense might be available to the federal officials, but decided it was unnecessary to look at that issue yet because the lawsuit had not reached that stage. It then held that even if the seizure was allowed by the Constitution, if it violated federal law, it could be considered a violation of the Constitution. The court reversed the district court's decision, and remanded the case for a complete determination on whether the seizure violated the law and the Constitution, and on whether the officials were immune from liability for their acts. *Bissonette v. Haig*, 800 F.2d 812 (8th Cir.1986).

A woman sightseer, visiting the Charleston Navy Yard which houses the U.S.S. Constitution and its museum, was injured while alighting from a sightseeing bus. She sued the bus operator, its driver and the U.S. government in federal district court. She alleged that the government had prior knowledge of the highly dangerous and defective conditions, namely, an unsafe foothold, which had caused the injury. She settled and voluntarily dismissed her claims against the operator and driver. The district court dismissed her claim against the government and she appealed to the U.S. Court of Appeals, First Circuit.

The court of appeals held that the district court should not have dismissed the case against the government. Although it would be difficult for her to prove the unsafe conditions had recklessly been allowed to exist, the court felt she should have a chance to prove it. Further, the court noted that the other defendants might be able to cross-claim against the government because its case was no longer dismissed. Finally, the court noted that if the government was receiving economic benefits from the museum, it would have as much liability as a private person would in a tort action. The court reversed and remanded the district court's decision. *DiMella v. Gray Lines of Boston, Inc.*, 836 F.2d 718 (lst Cir.1988).

The doctrine of governmental immunity was not allowed as a defense in a case where two high school football players were overcome by heat prostration. The Michigan Court of Appeals ruled that the school district, the school principal, and the superintendent were not liable under the doctrine but that the individual teacher/coaches could be held liable since the negligence imputed to them arose from their own personal conduct and not their conduct as funtionaries of the school district. *Lovitt v. Concord School Dist.*, 228 N.W.2d 479 (Mich.App.1975).

A high school basketball coach directed the team's student manager to post players' names on the score board. The student asked if he could use a scaffold that was available, but the coach told him to use a ladder. The coach then tested the ladder for steadiness before the student used it. While on the ladder the student, who was an epileptic, blacked out. He fell to the gymnasium floor and was seriously injured. The student sued the local board of education for personal injuries he suffered in the fall. He alleged that the board of education was negligent because he was not provided with proper equipment (the scaffold) with which he could safely climb to the scoreboard. A state district court jury returned a verdict in favor of the student, but the judge entered a decision in favor of the board of education notwithstanding the jury verdict. On appeal, the Appellate Court of Illinois noted that damages could be awarded if the student was injured because the board of education failed to provide proper equipment. The court decided that since the scaffold was available when the injury occurred, the board of education had not failed to "furnish" it. The scaffold was not used because the student was directed to use a ladder by the coach. Because the coach's action did not exhibit a reckless disregard for the student's safety, no damages could be awarded on the basis of his negligence either. The state district court judge's decision notwithstanding the jury verdict was affirmed. *Braun v. Bd. of Educ.*, 502 N.E.2d 1076 (Ill.App.5th Dist.1986).

An employee for the city of Cleveland worked at a local recreation center. She was injured when a co-worker struck her on the head with a board. She sued the city in an Ohio trial court, claiming that its decision not to install a security system at the recreation center caused her injuries. The city filed a motion for summary judgment stating that its decision not to install a security system was an executive and planning function for which it could not be held liable. The trial court granted the city's motion for summary judgment, and she appealed to the Court of Appeals of Ohio.

The appellate court held that the city's decision not to install a security system was a basic policy decision which involved executive and planning functions. As such, the city could not be held liable for tort claims. Further, the court stated that the co-worker's intentional act of assaulting her could not be imputed to the city in order to hold the city liable under the "intentional torts" exception to the city's immunity. The appellate court affirmed the trial court decision. *Fisher v. City of Cleveland*, 547 N.E.2d 1226 (Ohio App.1988).

Emergency Medical Service (EMS) technicians delayed in responding to an emergency call and failed to give proper care once they arrived at the scene. As a result, a Detroit man died. His estate sued the city and individual EMS personnel. The trial court granted summary judgment for the city and EMS personnel. The court held that they were immune from liability under a Michigan law which protected emergency service personnel from liability unless their acts or omissions were the result of gross negligence or wilful misconduct. The estate appealed to the Court of Appeals of Michigan.

The appellate court held that the city and EMS acts did not constitute gross negligence or wilful misconduct, and they were immune from liability under Michigan law. Further, the court stated that there was no implied contract created by telephoning EMS for assistance. The city and the EMS owed a preexisting duty to provide emergency medical services to anybody in need, without regard to their ability to pay. Thus, no implied contract was created. The appellate court affirmed the trial court decision. *Mallory v. City of Detroit*, 449 N.W.2d 115 (Mich.App.1989).

A gunman who was out on parole shot three police officers while they were investigating an armed robbery. All three officers were injured, one fatally. The surviving officers and representatives of the deceased officer sued the New York state board of parole for wrongful death and negligence. The officers claimed that the parole board was negligent in not having filed a detention warrant against the gunman for parole violation based upon two prior felony arrests. The New York Court of Claims granted summary judgment to the parole board. The officers appealed to the Supreme Court, Appellate Division.

The supreme court noted that it is a common-law rule that officers cannot recover for service-related injuries against a public entity employing those whose negligence caused the injuries. Recovery by officers for injuries sustained during their work, for which they have been trained and compensated by the public, is against public policy. Further, public entities are immune from liability in negligence arising out of performing governmental functions. However, if a special relationship was established between the officers and the parole board which created a special duty to protect the officers, and the officers relied on that duty, the parole board would not be immune from liability. In this case, the court held that the officers did not establish a special relationship with the state parole board. Thus, the board was immune from liability to the officers for negligence. *Ruotolo v. State*, 549 N.Y.S.2d 22 (A.D.1st Dep't 1990).

A Maryland man experienced headaches, fever, nausea, stiff neck and other symptoms. Two private health care facility doctors examined him and diagnosed his condition as a virus and instructed him to return home. The man's condition continued to deteriorate and he was admitted to the hospital. The doctors finally consulted a specialist who immediately diagnosed Rocky Mountain spotted fever. The man died twenty-four hours later. The man's wife brought a medical malpractice lawsuit against the doctors before the Maryland Health Claims Arbitration Board. During the lawsuit, the government informed the wife that the doctors were employed by the United States Public Health Service while working in the private facility. The board dismissed the wife's lawsuit, nearly two-and-a-half years after the state proceedings had been initiated. The Board ruled that the doctors were federal employees and could not be sued in state court. Almost two years later, the wife filed a Federal Tort Claims Act (FTCA) medical negligence claim with the United States Department of Health and Human Services. The department denied her claim, contending that it was barred under the two-year FTCA statute of limitation. The wife sued the department in a federal district court. The court dismissed the lawsuit noting that the wife's claim had accrued on the date of her husband's death and was barred under the statute of limitations. The wife appealed to the U.S. Court of Appeals, Fourth Circuit.

The court of appeals held that the FTCA claim did not accrue until the wife first learned that her husband's doctors were federal employees. The wife had filed the FTCA claim within two years from the time she discovered that the doctors were federal employees. The court of appeals reversed the district court's decision and remanded the case for further proceedings. *Gould v. U.S. Dep't of Health and Human Servs.*, 884 F.2d 785 (4th Cir.1989).

An Ohio man was stranded by his friends twenty miles from his home after he had been drinking while celebrating his birthday. The man was picked up by two police officers after they saw him stumbling down the street. They drove him to a friend's house. Later that night, the man appeared at the front desk of the city's police department and requested a ride home. The desk sergeant offered to telephone a taxicab, but the man maintained he could place the call himself and went into the station's lobby. After a few moments, the desk sergeant checked the lobby but the man had left the station. The man later died after he was struck by a car on the interstate. The man's estate sued the city in an Ohio trial court, alleging that the man's death was proximately caused by city police officers' negligent failure to detain him when he was clearly intoxicated. After the trial court dismissed the case, the estate appealed to the Ohio Court of Appeals.

On appeal, the city maintained that the officers did not have custody of the man while at the police station, and therefore they were under no duty to act. The estate argued that the city had a duty to arrest and detain the man since he was visibly intoxicated. The court of appeals upheld the trial court's decision, ruling that the decision to arrest a person for disorderly conduct while he or she is intoxicated is discretionary. Since the record showed that the man was intoxicated but not harmful to himself or others, the exercise of professional judgment by the officers had not been abused. The court also ruled that the city had no duty to detain the man because the officers had no knowledge or reason to anticipate the man walking along the interstate. The court dismissed the case. *Knapp v. Gurish*, 541 N.E.2d 121 (Ohio App.1989).

A Georgia private school held a festival. A volunteer parent contacted the Atlanta police department for help. A sergeant sent three off-duty officers who wore their police uniforms and drove police motorcycles. The school paid the officers $15 per hour. The volunteer described the areas of coverage to one of the officers. The car of one of the persons leaving the festival was struck by another car as it left school grounds. The drivers contended that the officer caused the accident by giving negligent traffic instructions. The injured driver of the other vehicle sued the school, claiming that it had employed the officer and was therefore responsible, and that the school had failed to hire sufficient traffic control officers or to properly control traffic. The driver sued the school in a Georgia trial court, which held that the officer was an independent contractor, and that the school was not liable for his alleged negligence. The driver appealed to the Georgia Court of Appeals.

The appeals court ruled that employer liability cases involving police officers required consideration of whether the officer was performing a public duty at the time of the alleged negligence. In this case, the officer was performing a police function because he was directing traffic on a public thoroughfare. Thus his possible negligence could not be imputed to the school. The trial court had correctly granted summary judgment for the school, and the appeals court affirmed its decision. *Beck v. Paideia School*, 381 S.E.2d 132 (Ga.App.1989).

A Pennsylvania police officer attempted to stop a drunk driver. When the officer turned on his siren and lights, the driver sped away with the officer in pursuit. The driver crashed into several telephone poles, and his passenger was injured. The passenger then sued the officer and his department in a Pennsylvania trial court. He alleged that the officer's negligent or reckless conduct caused his injury even though the police vehicle did come into contact with the driver's vehicle. After the trial court dismissed the case, the passenger appealed to the Commonwealth Court of Pennsylvania.

The passenger argued that his negligence and recklessness allegations against the officer stated a cause of action which is included in the vehicle liability exception to governmental immunity. The court agreed with the passenger, holding that when negligence is alleged, a cognizable claim within the vehicle liablity exception is stated. It held that a trial was necessary to determine whether governmental immunity applied, and reversed and remanded the case. *Baker v. Hawks*, 560 A.2d 939 (Pa.Cmwlth.1989).

A man filed a civil rights complaint in a federal district court against an Illinois city and the police officers who arrested him. He alleged that the officers had used excessive force during his arrest and that the city had allowed these violations. When the city sought defense from its primary general liability insurer, the general insurer refused to defend either the officers or the city. The city then obtained defense from its excess insurance carrier, which settled the lawsuit. The excess insurer then sought a declaration in a federal district court that the city's general liability insurer had to reimburse it for expenses incurred in defending the police officers and city. The district court found that the general liability insurer was not obligated to defend because there was no potential liability under its policy. The excess insurer then appealed to the U.S. Court of Appeals, Seventh Circuit.

On appeal, the excess insurer pointed to an endorsement in the general liability insurance policy which covered employees acting within the scope of their employment. The general liability insurer maintained that the policy endorsement excluded any claim arising out of the wilful misconduct of a policeman. The court of appeals affirmed the district court's decision, concluding that the arrestee's injuries had been expected or intended by the officers. The arrestee's complaint alleged that the officers had repeatedly hit him during the arrest. The officers should have reasonably anticipated the detainee's injuries, and coverage under the general insurer's policy was therefore excluded. The court held that the general liability insurer also had no duty to reimburse the excess insurer for the city's defense. Since the arrestee's complaint alleged that the city had been reckless, his injuries were expected and therefore excluded by the policy. The court upheld the district court's decision, finding that the general insurer was under no duty to reimburse the excess insurer. *Calvert Ins. Co. v. Western Ins. Co.*, 874 F.2d 396 (7th Cir.1989).

Workers on the playground of a private school knotted the bottom of a playrope in order to keep it from fraying. The rope subsequently frayed above the knot, and a five-year-old child was hanged to death. A lawsuit resulted, which was settled between the parents and the school. The school contended that it was entitled to indemnification from the county and its inspector (county) because the inspector had failed to discover this safety hazard. The settlement stipulated that any claims by the parents against the county would be subrogated to the school. The school then initiated a legal action against the county. A Maryland trial court granted summary judgment for the county, and an appeal was heard by the Court of Special Appeals of Maryland.

To be successful on a negligence claim the school would need to prove three elements: that the county owed a duty of care to the injured party, that the county breached that duty, and that injury resulted from that breach. Did the county owe a duty to the child, the observance of which would have averted the injury? The school first alleged a duty was created by a Maryland statute which provides that the county shall "ensure proper care, protection and supervision of children." The court refused to infer a duty to inspect for all possible hazards from this statute. To do so would in effect make the county into a liability insurer of children's safety. The court then sought to determine if the county owed a duty to the child on any other theories. The general rule is that a county will owe no duty to an individual without a "special relationship." An affirmative action may give rise to a special relationship to a specific child, but not to children in general. Further, regulation or inspection of an industry or business does not give rise to a special relationship. Any cause of action resulting from regulation and inspection must be expressly provided by statute. The court explained that the legislature creates policies for the regulation and inspection of almost all industries and concerns. Allowing the regulations to create an implied special relationship would result in the state owing a duty to ensure the safety of "virtually every citizen or visitor." The summary judgment granted to the county by the trial court was affirmed. *Willow Tree v. P.G. County*, 584 A.2d 157 (Md.App.1991).

A man discovered an unconscious woman and phoned 911. A basic life support unit responded even though an advanced life support unit was available, and could have been immediately dispatched. Upon assessment of the woman, an immediate request for the advanced unit was made. A second request was later transmitted, and the advanced unit was finally dispatched. The woman died. Her representative filed a lawsuit against the city which in essence asserted that the city's emergency medical personnel acted negligently and that the care was neither timely nor adequate. Summary judgment was granted to the city, and the woman's representative appealed to the District of Columbia Court of Appeals.

The issues of this case focused on the applicability of the public duty doctrine. This doctrine shields public employees with discretionary duties from liability for their actions. Despite arguments to the contrary, the court found that the doctrine does apply to emergency ambulatory personnel. Their duties were found to be discretionary. Under the public duty doctrine, a city owes no duty to provide ambulatory services to a citizen unless a "special relationship" is established. This relationship is normally limited to persons that have been placed by the city in a position where they are unable to care for themselves, such as prisoners. The individual attention and care given to the woman in this case did not create a special relationship. Nor did the charging of a fee. Without a special relationship, the city did not owe, and could not have breached, a duty to the woman. Summary judgment for the city was upheld. *Heinz v. District of Columbia*, 580 A.2d 133 (D.C.App.1990).

IV. EMPLOYEE LIABILITY

The sheriff for the Louisiana parish of Orleans deputized all cooks in the sheriff's office so that they could receive a state supplement in pay. The cooks underwent deputy training, which in this case included eight hours of instruction with firearms. While off-duty, one of the cooks accidentally shot a man in the head. The man suffered serious injuries, and he and his family brought a claim of negligence against the cook, the sheriff, and the parish. A trial court awarded $785,000 to the man and his family. The defendants appealed to the Court of Appeal of Louisiana, Fourth Circuit.

The court began its review by affirming the judgment amount, and the findings against the deputy. It then focused on the sheriff's liability. The man and his family argued that the sheriff was negligent, first, by deputizing the cook and second, in failing to adequately train him. The cook's eight hours of firearm instruction were shown to be less than the standard thirty hours, and it was also shown that the cook had not been given an examination as per standards. Through expert testimony the cook was found to lack the requisite knowledge on firearm mechanics and safety. Further, the court felt that the cook should have been excluded by minimum hiring standards. Specifically, he did not have a high school diploma, and failed the intelligence test that he was given. The cook acquired the gun and the right to carry it only after being deputized. The court felt that the sheriff's deputization of the cook, and failure to adequately train him, "contributed mightily" to the shooting. The court held that the sheriff breached his duty to ensure the public of sufficient training of deputized personnel. The trial court's decision was affirmed. *Roberts v. Benoit*, 574 So.2d 1256 (La.App.4th Cir.1991).

During a city council meeting, a city resident walked in and asked to talk to one of the councilmen and started shooting. The police chief was unarmed at the request of the mayor. He then ran out to his car to get his shotgun. Since his keys remained in the council chambers, he was unable to retrieve the shotgun, and went back in without it to help subdue the crazed man. The man was eventually subdued but the mayor was killed and two council members were injured. The injured council members brought a personal injury action against the police chief in an Iowa trial court. The trial court granted summary judgment to the police chief because he did not owe a duty of care to the council members. The council members appealed to the Supreme Court of Iowa.

The council members contended that the police chief owed them a duty to protect them because a special relationship existed between the chief and the members. The court determined that a special relationship giving rise to a duty of care must be premised on the foreseeability of harm to the injured person. It noted that the chief could not have reasonably foreseen the possibility of the violent shooting spree and taken precautions against it. Nor did the police chief undertake to protect the council members. He was only at the meeting to provide information. The supreme court affirmed the trial court's decision and dismissed the case. *Sankey v. Richenberg*, 456 N.W.2d 206 (Iowa 1990).

A Virginia man was arrested and imprisoned for possession of a concealed weapon. He indicated to the arresting officr that he would kill the officer because he had already killed. Prison officials accidentally released the man before his time was up. A few weeks later, the convict was again arrested and was released from jail by prison officials after only four hours because they failed to check prison records. While out of confinement, the convict robbed and murdered a night auditor at a hotel. The night auditor's wife then sued prison officials for negligent release. The trial court concluded that the prison officials owed no special duty to the night auditor. The widow of the night auditor appealed to the Supreme Court of Virginia.

Generally, a person owes no duty to control the conduct of third persons in order to prevent harm to another unless a special relationship exists between the actor and the third person or a special relationship exists between the actor and the victim. In negligence claims against a public official, a distinction must be drawn between a public duty owed by the official to the citizenry at large and a special duty owed to a specific identifiable person or class of persons. The court found that the night auditor was not an identifiable person, or a member of an identifiable class of persons, to whom the prison officials owed a duty distinguished from the duty they owed to the citizenry at large. The night auditor simply was a member of the general public. The Supreme Court of Virginia affirmed the trial court's decision to dismiss the actions against the prison officials. *Marshall v. Winston*, 389 S.E.2d 902 (Va.1990).

A night manager of a Puerto Rican fast food restaurant was robbed at gunpoint. He phoned the police and several officers drove up to the restaurant while the robber was still inside. The robber then grabbed the manager and held him hostage. He told the police that he would kill the manager if the police did not let him go. He then ran into the street and commandeered a passing car, taking over the driver's position with the manager on his lap. When the car moved slightly, the pursuing officers fired and one bullet hit the manager in the jaw, severely injuring him. The manager then brought a suit for damages in a federal district court alleging that the police actions violated various constitutional provisions. A jury found that the three officers violated his Fourth Amendment right to be free from unreasonable seizure and awarded him damages. The officers appealed to the U.S. Court of Appeals, First Circuit.

The Fourth Amendment to the U.S. Constitution protects individuals against unreasonable searches and seizures. The issue was whether the officers' shooting in a hostage situation could be termed a seizure that would be implicated by the Fourth Amendment. The court noted that the U.S. Supreme Court has determined that unless the restraint of liberty at issue resulted from an attempt to gain control of the individual there is no Fourth Amendment seizure. A police officer's deliberate decision to shoot at a car containing a robber and a hostage for the purpose of stopping the robber's flight does not result in the sort of wilful detention of the hostage that the Fourth Amendment was designed to govern. The court reversed the district court's decision. *Landol-Rivera v. Cruz Cosme*, 906 F.2d 791 (1st Cir.1990).

CHAPTER FIVE
DISCRIMINATION

I. AGE DISCRIMINATION

The Age Discrimination in Employment Act, 29 U.S.C. §§ 621 <u>et seq.</u> (ADEA) is one of the major federal antidiscrimination statutes under which aggrieved public employees have sued their employers. The act broadly prohibits discrimination based upon age, unless there are job-related reasons for not hiring a person. This can generally be only where the age restriction is reasonably related to an essential business operation and there is a factual basis for the age limit such as inability to perform job duties.

A sixty-three-year-old man was accepted into a training program with the Internal Revenue Service (IRS). On April 26, 1987, the man was informed that his performance was not satisfactory. He requested a demotion and transfer so that he could avoid termination. The man felt that he had been a victim of age discrimination, and in September of 1987, attempted to gain relief through the Department of the Treasury. He also notified the IRS of an intent to sue if the matter was not resolved to his satisfaction. The appeal to the Department of the Treasury was dismissed because the man had not acted within 30 days of the employer's action. The man then appealed to the Equal Employment Opportunity Commission (EEOC) which upheld the dismissal. In May, 1988, a lawsuit was filed in a federal district court. Again the man's claim was dismissed. The court held that the man could either proceed directly to federal court within 180 days of the employer's action and notify the EEOC within thirty days of bringing suit, or attempt to gain relief through the appropriate agency and bring suit only after an exhaustion of administrative remedies. The suit was brought more than 180 days after the employer's action, and an untimely claim does not constitute an exhaustion of administrative remedies. The man then appealed to the U.S. Court of Appeals, Fifth Circuit. That court held that the man was not required to bring suit within 180 days of the employer's action. He only needed to serve notice within that time. However, the dismissal was upheld because the man's notice to the EEOC was not within thirty days of his filing suit in a federal court. The case then reached the U.S. Supreme Court.

The Supreme Court ruled that the requirement of notice to the EEOC was incorrectly applied. Section 15(d) of 29 U.S.C. § 633a(d) allows a federal employee to proceed directly to federal court by serving notice of the alleged unlawful practice to the employer within 180 days, and requires only that the employee notify the EEOC (of the employee's intent to sue) not less than thirty days from when the suit is brought. The man had met this requirement. He had served notice to his employer within 180 days, and had filed suit more than thirty days after notifying the EEOC. The case was reversed and remanded for trial. *Stevens v. Dep't of the Treasury*, 111 S.Ct. 1562, 114 L.Ed.2d 1(1991).

A California man was hired in 1976 as a deputy city attorney. He held this position, as a trial deputy, until he was terminated in 1987 at age sixty-two. The man asserted that the dismissal was because of his age. He then filed an age discrimination suit with a federal district court which dismissed his claim based on a lack of jurisdiction. An appeal was filed with the U.S. Court of Appeals, Ninth Circuit.

The issue before the court was whether the discharge was in violation of the Age Discrimination in Employment Act (ADEA). As a deputy city attorney, the man held the position "at the pleasure of" the elected city attorney. This employment status is provided by the California Code. Therefore, the man was not subject to the civil service laws as are other city employees. Although the "personal staff exception" had not been previously recognized in ADEA cases, it had been recognized in Title VII cases. The purpose for the two acts is identical, and the two acts must be construed consistently by the courts. Because the act did not apply to the man, the federal court had no power to hear the case. The appeals court upheld the district court's decision and dismissed the claim. *Monce v. City of San Diego*, 895 F.2d 560 (9th Cir.1990).

Two Nebraska public employees were employed by the Department of Public Institutions (DPI), a state agency. The legislature targeted this particular department for reduction of about $58,000 in fiscal year 1987-1988. The director of DPI responded with a proposal to meet that mandate. He proposed reducing the custodial staff and the elimination of a fulltime program specialist. This enabled DPI to meet the legislative targets. The supervisor, however, decided to terminate the employment of a fifty-nine year-old and a sixty-nine year-old employee of the department. The men were the two oldest nonclerical DPI employees working in the central office. The employees then commenced an age discrimination suit against the state. A jury found that the state had violated the ADEA when it fired the two men. The state appealed to the U.S. Court of Appeals, Eighth Circuit.

The appellate court noted that its task was simply to decide whether the record supported the ultimate finding of discrimination. The court's review of the record determined that there was sufficient evidence to support the finding of discrimination. The court noted that each of the employees was the oldest in the department and they were the only employees laid off. There was an inference that they were singled out and terminated. Significantly, the process that led to the firing of the employees took little more than one week. The court thought that a decision leading to the termination of two competent senior employees would be supported by more in depth investigation. This lack of an investigation may have supported the jury's inference that the supervisor's motives were not legitimate. The court affirmed the district court's decision. *Rademaker v. State of Nebraska*, 906 F.2d 1309 (8th Cir.1990).

An Arkansas man was the Director of International Agriculture Programs at a state university. The man had his seventieth birthday after the school adopted a written policy that all employees were automatically retired at the age of seventy, effective at the end of the fiscal year in which the employee attained the age of seventy. The university entered into a contract with the man after his seventieth birthday so that his contract would be extended for a year. At the end of that one year the school sent the man a notice that his contract would not be extended any further and the man filed a claim in a federal district court alleging that the university discriminated against him solely on the basis of age and, thus, that the university had violated the Age Discrimination in Employment Act (ADEA). The district court granted summary judgment to the university finding that the man did not have a valid claim and the man appealed to the U.S. Court of Appeals, Eighth Circuit.

The man argued on appeal that he was discriminated against because he was still able to adequately perform his job. However, the court of appeals stated that the man was not protected under ADEA because the statute

age seventy the act did not require employers to retain public employees, even if they competently performed their duties. Further, the court stated that even if the man was protected by the ADEA, he could not establish discrimination. The man's contract had expired and he had reapplied for the position along with ten other people. However, the school only interviewed and offered the job to one person. Thus, the man could not distinguish himself as being discriminated against. The court of appeals affirmed the trial court's decision that the man did not have a valid claim. *Evans v. Pugh*, 902 F.2d 689 (8th Cir.1990).

Shortly before his thirty-fifth birthday, a postal worker applied for the position of postal inspector. The postal service has a maximum age limit of thirty-five years for that position. Because the worker was ineligible to be appointed or placed on a register for the position before he reached the maximum age limit, he was denied the position. The worker noted that the postal service had given waivers to persons who were over the maximum age limit in the past, and filed suit complaining of discrimination. A federal district court judge granted summary judgment to the postal service, and the worker appealed to the U.S. Court of Appeals, Eleventh Circuit.

The worker claimed, on appeal, that the postal service's maximum age limitation violated the Age Discrimination in Employment Act (ADEA). In the alternative, he claimed that the postal service discriminated against him by refusing to promote him while promoting other persons in or above his age group to the desired position. The foremost issue in this case was whether the postal service was in violation of the ADEA. The postal service contended that federal agencies are allowed to set maximum limits notwithstanding the requirements of the ADEA, and the appellate court agreed. The court found that to rule otherwise would ignore congress' intent to secure a "young and vigorous" workforce. On the issue of age discrimination, the worker would be required to show that age was a determining factor in the denials of the age limit waiver. The parties did not dispute that the maximum age limit had been waived for certain people in the past. However, in each of these instances there were non-discriminatory reasons for the waiver. In any event, there was no evidence presented that the reason for denial of the waiver was based upon the worker's age. In fact, there were older persons for whom the waiver had been granted. Therefore, the court upheld the summary judgment for the postal service. *Patterson v. U.S. Postal Service*, 901 F.2d 927 (11th Cir.1990).

A Massachusetts law required automatic retirement at the age of fifty for its uniformed state police officers. An officer who was automatically retired sued the state board of retirement in a federal district court, asserting that the law denied him equal protection. Four months before his retirement, he had passed a rigorous examination and he stated that his mental and physical health still rendered him capable of performing the duties of a uniformed officer. The district court agreed with the officer that compulsory retirement at age fifty was irrational and violated equal protection. The board then was granted leave to appeal the case to the U.S. Supreme Court.

The Court first determined that the proper standard to use in deciding whether the law violated equal protection was the "rational basis" standard. So long as the law was rationally related to a legitimate state interest, the Court would uphold it as valid because officers over fifty are not a "suspect class" of persons requiring heightened judicial scrutiny. It then noted that the Massachusetts law was rationally related to a legitimate state interest because physical ability generally declines with age. Further, the state's needs in protecting the public outweighed the interests of the few officers who were still capable of performing their duties after age fifty. Although the state could have chosen a more individualized means to determine fitness than an arbitrary cut-off at age fifty, its law did not violate equal protection merely because it was not perfect. The Court reversed the district court's decision and upheld the mandatory retirement law. *Massachusetts Board of Retirement v. Murgia*, 427 U.S. 307, 96 S.Ct. 2562, 49 L.Ed.2d 520 (1976).

The U.S. Congress enacted a mandatory retirement age of sixty for participants in the foreign service retirement system. Employees covered by the civil service retirement system were not required to retire until age seventy. A group of past and present foreign service employees sued in a federal district court, challenging the constitutionality of the classification requiring earlier retirement, and a special three-judge court was convened to hear the case. It held that the law was violative of equal protection and that no distinction should be made between civil service and foreign service employees. The government then sought review from the U.S. Supreme Court.

The Supreme Court noted that so long as there was a rational basis for the law, it would be upheld, because foreign service personnel over age sixty were not members of a suspect class of people who required strict judicial scrutiny. The Court then determined that an earlier mandatory retirement furthered a legitimate governmental interest in two ways. First, it created incentives to morale and performance by assuring more predictable promotions. Second, it removed from service those who were sufficiently old that they might be less able to face the rigors of overseas duty. Even if the decision by Congress may not have been wise, Congress had chosen a rational means to achieve a legitimate end. The Court refused to find the law unconstitutional and reversed the district court's decision. *Vance v. Bradley*, 440 U.S. 93, 99 S.Ct. 939, 59 L.Ed.2d 171 (1979).

California law provides increased incentives to judges who retire at or before age seventy. The law grants extra pay to a judge who elects to retire early and also provides increased benefits to spouses who survive such retiring judges. Various state judges sued the state controller and the public employee's retirement system, challenging the constitutionality of the law. The trial judge held for the state and the judges appealed to the Court of Appeal, First District.

On appeal, the court noted that the law was rationally related to the legitimate interest of preventing a superannuated judiciary. Being a judge was not a fundamental right which required strict scrutiny of the law infringing on that right. The court found that early retirement increased the opportunity for others to attain such positions. Further, it noted that even if judges should be individually evaluated to better ensure judicial competence, the retirement statute could not be held unconstitutional solely on that ground. The court did acknowledge, however, that the system did seem to reflect a questionable age stereotype by imposing an economic penalty on judges who remained in office past age seventy. Yet, even with the imperfections, the law could be justified as achieving a legitimate state interest. The court affirmed the trial court's decision. *Rittenband v. Cory*, 205 Cal.Rptr. 576 (Cal.App.1st Dist.1984).

In October of 1983, the mayor of Baltimore directed all department and bureau heads to recommend budget cuts in their respective agencies so as to achieve a five percent budget reduction for the upcoming year. The real estate department head then recommended that two positions be eliminated, both held by employees in their sixties, and a new position be created. Eventually, the mayor and city council approved this plan and the two employees were let go. They sued in a federal district court claiming age discrimination under 29 U.S.C §§ 621 et seq., the Age Discrimination in Employment Act, and wrongful discharge under state law. The district court granted summary judgment for the city on legislative immunity grounds, and the employees appealed to the U.S. Court of Appeals, Fourth Circuit. The appeals court held that the overall budgetary process had been properly characterized as legislative by the lower court. Since legislative conduct is immune from liability, the summary judgment had been properly granted. The court affirmed the district court's decision. *Baker v. Mayor and City Council of Baltimore*, 894 F.2d 679 (4th Cir.1990).

A forty-two-year-old Puerto Rican woman worked as a producer, writer and performer of the arts and culture segment of the nightly news program on public television. She had worked in public television and radio for fifteen years, most of that time in radio. Her work performance was rated excellent and there had been no complaints regarding job performance. However, without prior notice, and with no opportunity to inform her audience, she was removed from the program and reassigned to radio programming and later to radio broadcasting. She sued the station and station manager in a federal district court under 42 U.S.C. § 1983, claiming she had been discriminated against on the basis of age and sex. A jury found no sex discrimination, but did award her damages for age discrimination. The station and manager then appealed to the U.S. Court of Appeals, First Circuit.

The appeals court first noted that it was not yet fully clear whether Congress intended the Age Discrimination in Employment Act to be the sole remedy in age discrimination claims. If so, the employee would not be allowed to prevail on the § 1983 claim. However, the court then held that there was a rational basis for the decision to replace the employee and that her transfer was not a deprivation of a constitutionally protected right. Here, the public station sought to increase its viewership by bringing in "new and young faces," and this was a rational belief even if it was not accurate. The court then reversed the district court's ruling, and disallowed recovery to the employee. *Izquierdo Prieto v. Mercado Rosa*, 894 F.2d 467 (1st Cir.1990).

A forty-five-year-old police officer, employed with the Baltimore City Police Department, was informed that he was going to be transferred to another division within the department. Although he received the same pay upon his transfer, he felt that the new position was of lesser status. He sued the department in a federal district court under 42 U.S.C. §§ 1983 and 1985, asserting that he had been discriminated against on the basis of age. The department contended that he had been transferred because of his harsh demeanor with local merchants and visitors, and his poor attitude. The district court granted summary judgment to the department, finding that the officer did not have a property interest in a specific position within the department. The officer appealed to the U.S. Court of Appeals, Fourth Circuit.

The court of appeals held that the officer should have used the Age Discrimination in Employment Act (ADEA) rather than §§ 1983 or 1985 because Congress had intended the ADEA to provide the exclusive remedy for age discrimination claims within the officer's age group. Here, the court felt the officer had brought his claims under §§ 1983 and 1985 just to avoid the administrative procedures required by the ADEA. Accordingly, the court affirmed the district court's decision, but for different reasons. *Zombro v. Baltimore City Police Dep't*, 868 F.2d 1364 (4th Cir.1989).

An Indiana woman was sworn in as a police officer after she reached the age of thirty-six. Indiana law provided that a person may not be sworn in as an officer after the age of thirty-five unless the person was a member of the police officers' and firefighters' pension and disability fund (pension fund). Although the woman had worked with a marshall's department previously, she had not been a member of the pension fund. The city then terminated her employment because she was too old to meet the statutory requirement. She sued the city for reinstatement in an Indiana trial court which ruled for the city. She then appealed to the Court of Appeals of Indiana.

The court of appeals held that the Indiana statute did not violate the equal protection clause of the Constitution. The city had demonstrated rational reasons for putting an age limitation into the law. The court further held that age was not a suspect class to which increased judicial scrutiny applied. Moreover, she was not entitled to protection under the Age Discrimination in Employment Act because she was not between the ages of forty and seventy. Because the court found a legitimate state interest in the law, it upheld the law's constitutionality even though some inequality resulted. The court affirmed the trial court's decision, and denied reinstatement to the officer. *Sobieralski v. City of South Bend*, 479 N.E.2d 98 (Ind.App.4th Dist. 1985).

An Ohio attorney worked for the Veterans Administration (VA) for several years. A vacancy occurred in the office of assistant district counsel and she applied for it. She was sixty-one-years-old at the time. A younger man was promoted to the position over her, and she then sued the VA in a federal district court, asserting Title VII violations and a violation of the Age Discrimination in Employment Act. The district court held that no discrimination had occurred, and the employee appealed to the U.S. Court of Appeals, Sixth Circuit.

The appellate court found that although both attorneys had been well-qualified for the promotion, the younger man's attitude and work habits had apparently given him the edge in the final decision to promote. Just because the unsuccessful applicant was a sixty-one-year-old female did not necessarily mean she had been discriminated against. She had not offered sufficient proof of discriminatory animus on the part of the VA. The court thus affirmed the district court's decision. *Sims v. Cleland*, 813 F.2d 790 (6th Cir.1987).

Six warehouse employees of the New Mexico Veterans Administration (VA), aged forty-seven through fifty-four, sought promotion to the position of warehouse foreman. However, a twenty-seven-year-old male was selected for the job. They then sued the Administrator of the VA, asserting that they had considerably more experience than the younger man. They alleged violations of the Age Discrimination in Employment Act (ADEA), but the federal district court judge determined that the younger man's selection had been legitimate. They then appealed to the U.S. Court of Appeals, Tenth Circuit.

On appeal, they argued that the VA knew that the younger man had given a particular response during a supposedly anonymous rating test, and that the VA then inflated his score on that question to assure he would get the job. The court of appeals disagreed with this analysis. It recognized that a subjective standard had been used in the final selection process, but held that it was permissible for an employer to use discretion in choosing between equally qualified candidates. The employer simply could not use unlawful criteria in making its decision. The court found that no discrimination had been shown by the employees, and affirmed the district court's decision. *Lujan v. Walters*, 813 F.2d 1051 (10th Cir.1987).

The Age Discrimination in Employment Act of 1967 prohibits age-based discrimination by public and private employers, subject to some exceptions. One of the exceptions permits employers to maintain bona fide employee benefit plans which are not enacted as a subterfuge to evade the act. A California county's retirement plan was created in 1947, and predated the ADEA. A modification of the plan in 1975 resulted in a new formula for computing service and disability retirement benefits. Under the formula, workers who retired at a later age were granted lesser benefits than workers with the same amount of service who retired at an earlier age. The county conceded that there were no economic or cost considerations to justify the formula change. A retired county employee claimed that this formula change was a discriminatory subterfuge and demanded increased benefits. The county denied his request and the retiree sued the county in a federal district court claiming age discrimination in violation of the ADEA. The court ruled for the county, finding the retirement plan exempt from ADEA scrutiny. The retiree then appealed to the U.S. Court of Appeals, Ninth Circuit.

The court noted that to prove that a plan modification is a subterfuge, the employee must show that the employer's intent in making the modification related to hiring and firing, wages and salaries, or other nonfringe-benefit terms and conditions of employment. The court of appeals held that the county's concession that there were no economic or cost considerations to justify the change in formula did not establish that the modification was a subterfuge to evade the ADEA. The retiree failed to show that the change in benefits formula demonstrated an intent to discriminate in any nonfringe-benefits area. The exception for bona fide benefits plans exempted the county's retirement plan from ADEA scrutiny. The court of appeals affirmed the district court's decision. *Robinson v. County of Fresno*, 882 F.2d 444 (9th Cir.1989).

A forty-nine-year-old attorney worked for the Miami City Attorney's office. She was within the protected age group of the Age Discrimination in Employment Act (ADEA). After nine years of employment, a newly-appointed supervising attorney undertook reorganization of the staff, compelling some employees to resign. The attorney was openly critical of the supervisor's reforms and eventually refused to speak to him without a witness. The supervisor hired a thirty-two-year-old attorney to work on the same projects which the attorney was handling, but assured her that he was not replacing her. The attorney interpreted some of the supervisor's criticisms as harassment aimed at getting her to retire. After the attorney made some critical remarks at a fund raiser, the supervisor gave her a choice of being fired or being allowed to retire, considering her comments an act of insubordination. The supervisor then hired a forty-six-year-old woman to fill the attorney's position. The attorney unsuccessfully sued the city, seeking an order to prevent her replacement. She then filed a civil rights lawsuit against the city and the supervisor under the ADEA and Title VII for age, sex and religious discrimination. The court dismissed most of the attorney's claims, but ruled in favor of her age discrimination claim. The city appealed to the U.S. Court of Appeals, Eleventh Circuit.

The court found no direct evidence of discrimination and stated that only the most blatant, intentional remarks constituted direct evidence of age discrimination. Here, statements made by the supervisor which the attorney relied upon had been directed toward another employee and were insufficient evidence of discrimination. Although the attorney had made out a prima facie case of discrimination, the district court should have granted the city's motion for summary judgment. While a prima facie case created a rebuttable presumption of discrimination, it did not automatically entitle an aggrieved employee to go before a jury. The appeals court reversed and remanded the district court's decision. *Carter v. City of Miami*, 870 F.2d 578 (11th Cir.1989).

A tenured New York guidance counselor received a negative evaluation after seventeen years of employment with his school district. He was fifty-seven at the time. He filed an age discrimination complaint with the New York Division of Human Rights (DHR) and the EEOC. Two months after filing the complaint, the school district fired him for incompetence and neglect of duty. The counselor added retaliatory discharge to his complaint. The parties agreed to an $18,957.25 settlement in return for the counselor's withdrawal of the age discrimination complaint and his resignation. The counselor attempted to rescind the settlement by letter on the same day, but deposited the settlement check upon receiving it and withdrew his DHR and EEOC charges. The counselor then accepted employment with another school district, which discharged him at the end of his first day of work. The counselor filed an amended charge with the DHR and EEOC, stating that the first employer caused the second discharge by supplying negative information in retaliation.

The counselor avoided DHR and EEOC procedures by filing the matter in a federal district court nineteen days after filing his amended complaint. The federal ADEA requires aggrieved parties to wait sixty days before filing charges in a federal court. The court granted the district's motion to dismiss the matter and, on appeal, the U.S. Court of Appeals, Second Circuit, affirmed the dismissal. It said that federal courts have no jurisdiction over matters which do not go through the sixty-day waiting period and such suits are barred. However, the district court should have stayed the matter rather than dismissing it. The court reversed the district court's dismissal and remanded with directions to stay the matter for sixty days. *Dalessandro v. Monk*, 864 F.2d 6 (2d Cir.1988).

A group of Massachusetts individuals brought a complaint based on the Age Discrimination in Employment Act (ADEA) to the Equal Employment Opportunity Commission (EEOC). The complaint alleged that the Massa-massachusetts Registry of Motor Vehicles discriminated against older persons by refusing to accept applicants over age thirty-five for examiner positions. The EEOC sued the Commonwealth of Massachusetts on behalf of the individuals. The commonwealth defended its action on the basis of a Massachusetts statute which permitted discrimination against individuals according to age for employment as law enforcement officers. The district court agreed with the commonwealth and ruled that examiners were law enforcement officers. The EEOC appealed to the U.S. Court of Appeals, First Circuit.

The appeals court found that the district court had correctly ruled that the motor vehicle examiners were law enforcement officers. There was evidence that examiners wore uniforms, carried weapons, had the power to make inspections and investigations, and had the power to arrest. However, the case was remanded to the district court for further consideration. This was because the alleged discrimination occurred prior to 1986, which was the effective date of an ADEA amendment which concerned the outcome of the case. *EEOC v. Comm. of Massachusetts*, 864 F.2d 933 (1st Cir. 1988).

A Kentucky statute established fifty-five as the mandatory retirement age for all state police department officers. The Age Discrimination in Employment Act (ADEA) 29 U.S.C. § 623 forbids age based employment discrimination. An exception to the ADEA permits discrimination where the age limit is a bona fide occupational qualification (BFOQ). A recent amendment to the ADEA permits mandatory retirement for police, fire fighters and other government employees until 1993. However, causes of action arising before January 1, 1987, were unaffected by the amendment.

The Equal Employment Opportunity Commission (EEOC) sued the Kentucky State Police Department in a federal district court, claiming that the statute violated the ADEA. The court ruled for the police department and the EEOC appealed to the U.S. Court of Appeals, Sixth Circuit. Although the record indicated that police officers were required to have substantial cardiovascular fitness and aerobic capacity, the department had no regular fitness testing program for its officers. The department also permitted officers to remain on the job despite known heart problems. While aerobic capacity was related to age, lifestyle also had an impact on fitness. The appeals court ruled that mandatory retirement upon attaining age fifty-five was arbitrary and that age by itself did not indicate ability to perform the particular job. The ADEA required employers to establish that job qualifications were reasonably necessary to the business and that the employer was compelled to rely on age as an indicator for job qualifications. The police department had not demonstrated that the fifty-five-year age limit was a BFOQ. The appeals court reversed the district court's decision. *EEOC v. Kentucky State Police Dep't*, 860 F.2d 665 (6th Cir.1988).

Two school bus drivers in Alabama were forced to retire when they reached age sixty-five. They filed a lawsuit challenging the mandatory retirement policy of their county board of education asserting that the policy violated the ADEA. The board then requested a ruling that it was impossible or highly impractical to test older employees on an individual basis for safety. The U.S. Court of Appeals, Eleventh Circuit, pointed out that to disprove a violation of the Act, an employer must show 1) the existence of a job qualification "reasonably necessary to the essence of [its] business, and 2) that it is compelled to rely on age as a proxy for an individual determination of that job qualification. The court ruled that the board had met the first part of this test by asserting that the ability of school bus drivers to drive safely is reasonably necessary to their responsibilities. It ruled, however, that because expert testimony given to the lower court was in conflict, a question of fact existed on the feasibility of individually testing people age sixty-five and older for safety. The court determined that the case should proceed to trial in the lower court. *Childers v. Morgan County Bd. of Educ.*, 817 F.2d 1556 (11th Cir.1987).

An employee with seven years of experience at the Ohio Department of Transportation filed a reverse sex discrimination charge against the department which was resolved amicably. Five years later, an administrative assistant took a temporary leave of absence and the employee was temporarily promoted to that position. The promotion was rescinded three days later, but the position became a permanent vacancy when the former administrative assistant decided not to return from his leave of absence. The employee unsuccessfully sought the position and then sued the department and its officials in a federal district court under the Age Discrimination in Employment Act and 42 U.S.C. §§ 1983 and 1985. He alleged that another person was appointed to the job as a political patronage maneuver and that the department was retaliating against him for filing the earlier discrimination charge. This claim was based on the argument that his right to file a discrimination charge was protected by the First Amendment. The court granted summary judgment for the department on the §§ 1983 and 1985 claims. The age discrimination claim was then dismissed by stipulation, and the employee appealed the other claims to the U.S. Court of Appeals, Sixth Circuit.

According to the court, neither a state nor its officials acting in their official capacities are "persons" under § 1983. The court also rejected the employee's First Amendment retaliation charge because it was not a matter of public concern. It ruled that the employee was not a member of a class which historically had been entitled to discrimination protection, and affirmed the district court's judgment. *Rice v. Ohio Dep't of Transp.*, 887 F.2d 716 (6th Cir.1989).

II. HANDICAP DISCRIMINATION

The Rehabilitation Act of 1973 prohibits public employers from refusing to hire otherwise qualified persons because of their handicaps. So long as the prospective employee will be able to perform the "essential functions" of the job with only reasonable accommodation by the employer, the handicapped employee will be considered qualified for the position.

A. Rehabilitation Act

The U.S. Supreme Court ruled that tuberculosis and other contagious diseases are to be considered handicaps under § 504 of the Rehabilitation Act. The law defines a handicapped individual as "any person who (i) has a physical or mental impairment which substantially limits one or more of such person's major life activities, (ii) has a record of such impairment or (iii) is regarded as having such an impairment." It defines "physical impairment" as disorders affecting, among other things, the respiratory system and defines "major life activities" as "functions such as caring for one's self and working." The case involved a Florida elementary school teacher who was discharged because of the continued recurrence of tuberculosis. The teacher sued the school board under § 504 but a U.S. district court dismissed her claims. The U.S. Court of Appeals, Eleventh Circuit, reversed the district court's decision and held that persons with contagious diseases fall within § 504's coverage. The school board appealed to the U.S. Supreme Court.

The Supreme Court ruled that tuberculosis was a handicap under § 504 because it affected the respiratory system and affected her ability to work (a major life activity). The school board contended that in defining a handicapped individual under § 504, the contagious effects of a disease can be distinguished from the disease's physical affects. However, the Court reasoned that the teacher's contagion and her physical impairment both resulted from the same condition: tuberculosis. It would be unfair to allow an employer to distinguish between a disease's potential effect on others and its effect on the afflicted employee in order to justify discriminatory treatment. Allowing discrimination based on the contagious effects of a physical impairment would be inconsistent with the underlying purpose of § 504. According to the court, that purpose is to ensure that handicapped persons are not denied jobs because of prejudice or ignorance. It noted that society's myths and fears about disability and disease are as handicapping as the physical impairment, and concluded that contagion cannot remove a person from § 504 coverage. The Supreme Court remanded the case to the district court to determine whether the teacher was "otherwise qualified" for her job and whether the school board could reasonably accommodate her as an employee. *School Board of Nassau County v. Arline*, 480 U.S. 273, 107 S.Ct. 1123, 94 L.Ed.2d 307 (1987).

On remand, the Florida federal district court held that the teacher was "otherwise qualified" to teach. The teacher posed no threat of tuberculosis to her students in 1978. The court observed that at the time she was on medication, medical tests indicated a limited number of negative cultures. Her family members tested negative and she had limited contact with students. The court ordered her reinstatement or a front-pay award of $768,724 representing her earnings until retirement. *Arline v. School Bd. of Nassau County*, 692 F.Supp. 1286 (M.D.Fla.1988).

A man with Parkinson's disease was hired as a construction inspector for a Texas municipality. The position required substantial physical activity. The city later received reports that the inspector would occasionally stumble or fall while performing inspections. The inspector visited a neurologist at the request of the city, and was eventually evaluated by two others. Based on the doctors' reports, the city terminated the inspector because it felt he was a safety risk to himself or others. The inspector filed suit and alleged that his termination was in violation of the Rehabilitation Act of 1973. A federal district court granted summary judgment to the city, and the inspector appealed to the U.S. Court of Appeals, Fifth Circuit.

The Rehabilitation Act of 1973 applies to programs which receive federal funding, and prohibits discrimination against handicapped individuals. It also mandates that an employer make any reasonable accommodations of an otherwise qualified handicapped individual which do not place an undue burden on the employer. The inspector argued that that he was otherwise qualified because he could perform his job without endangering others, and that the city should not be able to terminate him based on a danger to himself. The court disagreed and stated that the inspector's health was a legitimate concern of the city. The inspector next alleged that his handicap should have been accommodated. The city showed that it attempted accommodation in three different ways, none of which proved feasible. The inspector argued that other work was available, including parttime work. The court ruled that the city was not required to offer alternative positions. The inspector was shown to be unfit for his job, whether full or part-time. The court of appeals upheld the dismissal of all claims. *Chiari v. City of League City*, 920 F.2d 311 (5th Cir.1991).

In 1973, a Pennsylvania university implemented work rules allowing disciplinary action after the eleventh absence and termination after the sixteenth absence. An x-ray attendant was employed with the university. The x-ray technician sustained an eye injury while at work in 1976, and received workers' compensation benefits. The x-ray technician had a long record of absenteeism and had previously received disciplinary action. In the 1987-1988 year, the x-ray technician was absent twenty-nine times and he was terminated. He appealed the decision to the board and his termination was upheld. He filed this suit in a federal district court alleging a violation of the Federal Rehabilitation Act (act).

The act defines a handicapped person as "any person who has a physical...impairment which substantially limits one or more of such person's major life activities." A major life activity was defined by federal regulation as the functions of "caring for one's self, performing manual tasks, walking, seeing, hearing, speaking, breathing, learning and working." The court stated that in this case the condition was not of the type which interfered with the employee's ability to perform in the workplace. Further, the court noted that even if a worker was handicapped, he must be otherwise qualified to do the job. The court noted that excessive absenteeism would not be accommodated and the x-ray technician was not otherwise qualified. The court upheld the termination. *Santiago v. Temple Univ.*, 739 F.Supp. 974 (E.D.Pa.1990).

An Alabama letter-sorting-machine (LSM) distribution clerk experienced wrist pains as a result of bilateral carpal tunnel syndrome. This disease was caused and aggravated by the LSM and by manual sorting of mail, and the office of workers' compensation thus informed the postal service that it considered him temporarily disabled. The employee had surgery on both wrists, but continued to suffer substantial pain and could not engage in work activity. After being gone from work for over two years, the postal service discharged the employee on charges that he was physically unable to perform the duties of his position. He appealed to the Merit Systems Protection Board (MSPB) which affirmed the department's decision. He then sued the postal service in the U.S. District Court, S.D. Alabama, alleging discrimination under the Rehabilitation Act.

The district court determined that the employee was barred from seeking additional compensation because the federal workers' compensation program is a comprehensive scheme which is intended to exclusively and preemptively remedy an employee for all work-related injuries. The law clearly stated that, while the employee was receiving workers' compensation payments, he could receive no additional compensation. Further, the court held that the postal service could properly fire the employee if he could not perform the essential functions of his position, and it was not required to reassign him. Moreover, he was still unable to return to work, so such a remedy would not be effective. The court affirmed the MSPB's decision and granted summary judgment to the postal service. *Black v. Frank*, 730 F.Supp. 1087 (S.D.Ala.1990).

An employee of the Department of Housing and Urban Development (HUD) was discharged from her position for unsatisfactory work performance. At the time, she suffered from a chronic alcohol problem. She sued HUD in a federal district court alleging handicap discrimination. The trial court determined that HUD had an obligation to try and accommodate the woman's needs. The court granted a preliminary injunction which required HUD to reinstate the woman on a leave without pay basis. The preliminary injunction also directed HUD to reinstate the woman once it was demonstrated that she was fit for duty. Because the woman was participating in an aftercare treatment program and was performing satisfactorily, the court denied the defendant's motion for reconsideration. The court found that the woman was in fact discriminated against due to her alcohol problem. She was also awarded attorney's fees. *McElrath v. Kemp*, 741 F.Supp. 245 (D.D.C.1989).

The Pennsylvania Department of Transportation revoked the driving privileges of a school bus driver who had worked for eighteen years at a public school district. The license revocation occurred nearly two years after the driver was diagnosed as a diabetic and found incompetent to drive a school bus under a Pennsylvania statute. The driver appealed to a Pennsylvania trial court, which ruled that the transportation department's action violated § 504 of the Rehabilitation Act of 1973, 29 U.S.C. § 794. The court reinstated the driver's driving privileges, but also ordered the district to perform a blood prick test on the driver each day she was scheduled to drive and to suspend her immediately if her condition was not under control. The district was also ordered to supply copies of blood tests to the transportation department. The department appealed to the Pennsylvania Commonwealth Court.

The commonwealth court considered the trial court's decision in view of the U.S. Supreme Court's decision in *School Bd. of Nassau County v. Arline.* The *Arline* case held that in Rehabilitation Act cases, courts were to evaluate the condition of the individual handicapped person who was otherwise qualified to perform the job duties. In each case, the inquiry must be into whether the employee was able to perform the job duties. In this case, the driver's diabetes had been under control since her release from the hospital. Because the school district and transportation department would not suffer a great burden by accommodating the school bus driver, the trial court had properly reinstated her. The transportation department's argument that diabetics present a risk to the safety of bus passengers was speculative. Because the transportation department was solely authorized to make department rules and regulations, the commonwealth court affirmed the driver's reinstatement, but not the extra testing requirements. *Comm. of Pennsylvania v. Tinsley*, 564 A.2d 286 (Pa.Cmwlth.1989).

A federal employee with multiple sclerosis was hired pursuant to an affirmative action plan for the handicapped. After receiving satisfactory work reviews, the employee stated that commuting to work caused her great stress. She requested permission to work at home. The employer explained that because of the employee's duties it was not feasible to allow her to work at home. Notice of successive unsatisfactory work reviews followed, and the employee was eventually terminated. The employee contended that the unsatisfactory performance was caused by the stress of commuting and then claimed discrimination based on handicap. Appeals to the Equal Employment Opportunity Commission and Merit Systems Protection Board resulted in decisions against the employee, and further appeal reached the federal district court.

The court explained that employees must show that they were qualified for the position in spite of their handicap. If this is shown, the employer must make reasonable accommodations for the employee so long as it does not create undue hardship. The element in question was whether the employee's health impaired her ability to commute to work. Unless the difficulty in commuting was shown, the unsatisfactory work reviews eliminated the employee's assertion of being otherwise qualified. The employee did not have medical substantiation of her condition. It was also uncontested that the declining work performance was the result of a preoccupation with attempting to gain approval to work at home. Because the employee's burden was unsatisfied, the court granted summary judgment to the employer. *Langon v. U.S. Dep't of Health and Human Services*, 749 F.Supp. 1 (D.D.C.1990).

A naval reserve member tested positive for the AIDS antibody. He was released from active duty and sued the Secretary of the Navy and his commanding officer of the naval air reserve. He contended that his release resulted from testing positive with the AIDS antibody and that this violated his rights under the Federal Rehabilitation Act, 29 U.S.C. §§ 791(b), 794 and 794(a), and the Due Process Clause of the Fifth Amendment. The Federal District Court for the Middle District of Florida stayed the case pending his exhaustion of administrative remedies. He then filed an application for correction of his naval record before the Board for Correction of Naval Records (BCNR). The BCNR corrected his records and awarded compensation to which he would have been entitled had he not been released from active duty. He returned to the federal district court claiming that the results obtained before the BCNR failed to provide him complete relief.

The district court held that he had no claim for discrimination under the Rehabilitation Act for his release from active duty. The court noted that the Rehabilitation Act does not include uniformed military personnel. As a member of the naval reserve, he was included under uniformed military personnel and had no remedy under the act. Further, he was not deprived of any property or liberty interest under the Fifth Amendment. He was accorded complete relief for his wrongful release from active duty by the BCNR. *Dole v. Ball*, 725 F.Supp. 1210 (M.D.Fla.1989).

A New York City man passed the city's civil service examination and his name was placed on the police department's list of candidates eligible for appointment. He completed a written psychological profile and had a screening interview with a doctor from the Police Department's Psychological Services Division. Although he was never diagnosed as having any psychological problem, the doctor concluded that his profile indicated that he showed "poor judgment, irresponsible behavior and poor impulse control" which rendered him "unsuitable to be a police officer." Upon learning of his disqualification, he appealed to the New York City Civil Service Commission. His appeal was denied by the commission and he appealed to a federal district court, claiming that his disqualification violated the Rehabilitation Act. The district court dismissed the claim and the applicant appealed to the U.S. Court of Appeals, Second Circuit.

The appellate court noted that the Rehabilitation Act protects handicapped persons from employment discrimination solely by reason of their handicap if the employment involves a state program receiving federal funding. The appellate court held that the applicant's psychological profile did not make him handicapped within the meaning of the Rehabilitation Act. The appellate court affirmed the district court decision. *Daily v. Koch*, 892 F.2d 212 (2d Cir.1989).

A hearing-impaired toolmaker performed satisfactorily his first five years at a naval shipyard. However, his productivity declined after he was not given an outstanding performance award. After he was diagnosed as suffering from chronic paranoia, the Navy's Office of Personnel Management retired him. The toolmaker filed a complaint with the Equal Employment Opportunity Commission (EEOC), alleging handicap discrimination in violation of the Rehabilitation Act. After the EEOC dismissed his claim, the toolmaker sued the shipyard in a federal district court for violation of §§ 501 and 504 of the Rehabilitation Act. After the district court found for the shipyard, the toolmaker appealed to the U.S. Court of Appeals, Ninth Circuit.

The court of appeals noted that § 501 obligates federal employers to provide reasonable accommodations for the handicapped and to implement affirmative action plans for those employees. Section 504 also prohibits the exclusion of otherwise qualified individuals from activities or programs receiving federal funds solely by reason of their handicap. The court upheld the district court's decision, ruling that although § 501 creates a cause of action for federal employees against their employers, the toolmaker had failed to file the lawsuit naming the appropriate head of the naval department within thirty days after receiving the EEOC's decision. The toolmaker had erroneously named the commander of the shipyard instead of the Secretary of the Navy. The court also ruled that the toolmaker could not recover under § 504, since that section did not create a private cause of action for handicap discrimination against federal employers. Therefore,

§ 501 was the exclusive remedy for all federal employees. The court dismissed the case. *Johnston v. Horne*, 875 F.2d 1415 (9th Cir.1989).

The U.S. Military Academy at West Point employed a mason's helper who was also a volunteer firefighter in a nearby town. The employee suffered from dyslexia and could read only at a first grade level. West Point twice rejected his applications for the firefighter position and rejected a third application for a temporary transfer to a summer firefighter's position. The employee filed complaints with West Point's Equal Employment Opportunity Office (EEO), complaining that West Point had illegally discriminated against him on the basis of his handicap. West Point claimed that its firefighters must read at the twelfth grade level. Meanwhile, the employee was rejected by the academy a fourth time, and he filed a second EEO complaint. The army found no merit to the employee's second claim of hiring discrimination and issued a right-to-sue letter. The employee then sued the academy in a federal district court, seeking injunctive relief and damages under civil rights statutes, and §§ 501, 503 and 504 of the Rehabilitation Act of 1973, as well as the New York Human Rights Law. The employee's counsel served the U.S. Attorney General with the complaint. Later, the employee attempted to sue the Secretary of the Army.

The court determined that because the U.S. Attorney General was the army secretary's agent for service of process, the secretary could be joined in the lawsuit. Service was in time to meet the Army EEO's thirty day statute of limitations. The court noted that the employee's claims were invalid because he was a federal employee. Only the § 501 Rehabilitation Act complaint survived because it was the federal employees' exclusive remedy for employment discrimination based on handicap. The § 504 claim could not be brought against the individual officials. Title VII complaints could only be brought against agency heads in their official capacities. Therefore, all the complaints were dropped against West Point and its officials, leaving the army's secretary as the only defendant in the lawsuit.

The court stated that the employee could bring a Title VII lawsuit for surmountable barriers discrimination upon proving a prima facie discrimination case. In order to do so, the employee would have to show that his dyslexia made him a handicapped person under the Rehabilitation Act, that but for the dyslexia he would be qualified for the firefighter jobs, that the twelfth grade level reading requirement disproportionately affected dyslexic persons and that the academy could accommodate him as a firefighter. Conversely, the secretary would have to show that firefighting duties at West Point were different from the employee's voluntary firefighting duties with the town. Because neither party had sufficient evidence to compel a summary judgment, a trial on the merits would follow. *DiPompo v. West Point Military Academy*, 708 F.Supp. 540 (S.D.N.Y.1989).

A blind District of Columbia man was hired by the Department of Health, Education and Welfare as a public affairs assistant. The employee was then transferred to the same position in the Department of Education (DOE). The employee was originally hired to transcribe printed matter into Braille. Upon his transfer, however, his duties consisted of analyzing and answering correspondence. The employee sued the DOE claiming it had not reasonably accommodated his handicap. Thereafter the employee received a notice from his supervisor stating that his job performance and attitude were unsatisfactory. He was advised that he had thirty days to improve his performance or face termination. Four months later his employment was terminated. The employee sued the DOE under § 501 of the Rehabilitation Act in a federal district court. The district court held for the DOE. It found that the employee had been provided reasonable accommodation for the performance of his duties. The employee then appealed to the U.S. Court of Appeals, District of Columbia Circuit.

The appeals court held that the DOE had not assigned the employee to a position in which it was impossible to reasonably accommodate his visual handicap. The position required only basic skills such as making phone calls and correspondence. The court held that the DOE had reasonably accommodated the employee. The employee was provided two part-time readers and efforts had been made to secure a full-time reader. Even after the DOE provided a reader, the employee's work remained unsatisfactory. While other people in the office drafted up to twelve letters per week, the employee's workload had been reduced to six letters per week. The department had made accommodation which made it possible for the employee to perform his essential duties. The court of appeals affirmed the lower court's decision. *Carter v. Bennett*, 840 F.2d 63 (D.C.Cir.1988).

B. State Handicap Discrimination Laws

A Wisconsin man applied for employment as a police officer and was orally offered the position subject to a physical examination. One of the physical tests measured back strength and flexibility, and the applicant received a "B" rating where it was recommended that he undergo a back conditioning program before undertaking heavy labor. The police and fire commission then recommended that the applicant not be hired because of the rating. He later took a second test where he received an "A" rating. Nevertheless, the city chose not to hire him because he had "failed" the first test. The applicant filed a handicap discrimination complaint charging that he was denied employment because of an alleged weak back. The labor and industry commission ruled that the applicant had been discriminated against because of a perceived handicap and recommended he be hired and given backpay. The city sought judicial review in a Wisconsin trial court, which affirmed, and the city successfully appealed to the Wisconsin Court of

Appeals. The commission then further appealed to the Supreme Court of Wisconsin.

The supreme court held that the applicant had been discriminated against because of a perceived handicap, and that he had in fact been qualified to perform the job requirements. Even though the applicant had not been handicapped, because of the perception that he was, he was entitled to the protections of the Fair Employment Act. The court reversed the court of appeals' decision, but remanded the case for a determination on the issue of backpay for the applicant. *City of La Crosse Police and Fire Comm'n v. Labor and Industry Review Comm'n*, 407 N.W.2d 510 (Wis.1987).

A Michigan man applied for employment as a firefighter. He successfully completed a written examination and certain agility tests, and was then informed that a position was available. Prior to being hired, he submitted to a physical examination where it was discovered that he was suffering from a narrowing of certain disc-spaces in his spine. He was given a "Class IV" back rating and was not hired because of his condition. He filed a complaint with the civil rights commission under the Handicappers' Civil Rights Act (HCRA) asserting that his back condition was a congenital birth defect and that he had been discriminated against because of it. The commission agreed with the applicant and ordered that he be offered employment as a firefighter. However, it found that the applicant's back condition was not actually a handicap, but only a perceived handicap. The fire department appealed successfully to a Michigan trial court, and the applicant then appealed to the Court of Appeals of Michigan.

The appellate court noted that both parties agreed the applicant had a determinable characteristic arising from a congenital condition of birth. However, there was a dispute as to whether this condition was a true handicap and related to the applicant's ability to be a firefighter. Because the trial court did not address this question, the court reversed and remanded the case for a determination on this issue. A concurring opinion was filed which asserted that those who are discriminated against because of a mere perception of a physical disability or mental deficiency are protected by the HCRA. *Bay City Fire Dep't v. Dep't of Civil Rights*, 451 N.W.2d 533 (Mich.App.1989).

The Minnesota Human Rights Act defines a disabled person as one who has a physical or mental impairment substantially limiting one or more major life activities or who is regarded as having an impairment. A former Marine Corps administrative assistant with a college degree and experience in social services sought a position in law enforcement or corrections. He applied for a detention deputy job with a county law enforcement agency and was one of thirty finalists among 900 applicants. However, he was rejected because he failed the department's uncorrected vision requirements and had high tone hearing loss in one ear. The applicant filed a discrimination complaint with the state human rights department, which then sued the county. An administrative law judge ruled for the county and the department appealed to the Minnesota Court of Appeals. The court of appeals affirmed the administrative law judge's decision and the department appealed to the Minnesota Supreme Court.

The supreme court ruled that the applicant had no substantial limitation on any major life activity because his hearing and vision problems did not substantially affect his ability to see and hear. He had never been rejected for employment on this basis and was qualified to obtain other law enforcement jobs. The county had not falsely perceived the applicant as disabled or based its decision on a perception of disability. The applicant had simply failed to meet the job qualifications required for employee and prisoner safety. The supreme court affirmed the lower court's decision for the county. *State by Cooper v. Hennepin County*, 441 N.W.2d 106 (Minn.1989).

A Minnesota man worked for several years as a county probation officer and an at-will employee. It was later discovered that he had been hospitalized for paranoid schizophrenia and had been periodically counseled after his release. However, in his application, he had stated that his health was excellent and had made no mention of his hospitalization. He had poor working relationships with other employees and experienced difficulty in doing his job adequately. Subsequently, the county sent him a letter notifying him of his dismissal and the reasons for it. He then sued the county in a Minnesota trial court, asserting that he had been discriminated against because of disability in violation of Minnesota law. The trial court dismissed the case, and he appealed to the Court of Appeals of Minnesota.

The court of appeals first recognized that he had set forth a preliminary case of discrimination because he had shown that he was a member of a protected class of disabled people and because he had the basic qualifications for his position at the time of his discharge. However, the county had shown that he had misrepresented himself on his application, and that his job performance had been poor. Further, the employee had not been able to show that the county's reasons for discharging him had been a pretext for discriminatory intent. The employee had not really even disputed the fact that he had poor working relationships with his coworkers. Accordingly, the court affirmed the trial court's dismissal of the case. *Rutherford v. County of Kandiyohi*, 449 N.W.2d 457 (Minn.App.1989).

A Kansas man applied for a police officer's position and passed all the tests required except for an uncorrected visual acuity test. The minimum physical standard for such a test was 20/50 for each eye and applied only to new recruits. He tested at 20/70 and 20/100, and the city refused to hire him even though he was then employed with another city as a police officer and had performed all his duties satisfactorily. He sued the city in a

Kansas trial court, asserting that its refusal to hire him was a violation of his constitutional right to equal protection. The court invalidated the visual acuity requirement and ordered that the applicant be considered as qualified. The city appealed to the Supreme Court of Kansas.

The supreme court held that the city's minimum uncorrected vision requirement was rationally related to a legitimate state end. Emergency situations might arise where an officer would be required to act without glasses and a minimum visual requirement would be of importance to the city. The court further held that the applicant was not a handicapped person as defined by statute because he did not have a physical impairment which substantially limited his ability to find satisfactory employment. Thus, the city did not violate his rights by failing to hire him. The court reversed the trial court's decision, and upheld the city's visual acuity requirement. *Padilla v. City of Topeka*, 708 P.2d 543 (Kan.1985).

Two applicants were rejected for firefighter positions by a Colorado fire protection district. Both applicants had passed written and personal exams and strength and agility tests. They were placed on an eligibility roster and ranked among the top ten applicants. When the top ten applicants were physically examined under civil service commission rules, the district determined that one applicant had an injured right knee and that the other's uncorrected vision did not meet district requirements. When the district removed the applicants from the eligibility roster, they filed employment discrimination charges with the Colorado Civil Rights Commission. The commission determined that probable cause of handicap discrimination existed against the district. A commission hearing officer determined that both applicants were handicapped under Colorado civil rights statutes and ordered a hearing on the reasonableness of the medical disqualifications. The commission reviewed the hearing officer's decision and determined that both applicants were handicapped under the statute and that the district's disqualifying factors were unrelated to safety and therefore discriminatory.

The district appealed to the Colorado Court of Appeals, which reversed the commission's decision. The commissioner appealed to the Colorado Supreme Court which ruled that the court of appeals had incorrectly interpreted the statute's provision that persons who were considered handicapped by an employer were handicapped under the act. The district had treated both applicants as substantially limited in a major life activity even though neither actually had a substantial limitation. The court remanded the case to the commission to determine whether the applicants were removed from the eligibility roster because of their handicaps. A genuine fact issue also existed about the reasonableness of the district's medical disqualifying factors. *Colorado Civil Rights Comm'n v. North Washington Fire Protection Dist.*, 772 P.2d 70 (Colo.1989).

A laborer worked in a federally-funded program in Pittsburgh. He sought a transfer to a similar position with the city, which required a pre-employment medical examination. The laborer was thirty-seven pounds overweight and did not meet the city's height and weight standards. The city notified the laborer that he would be allowed to transfer if he successfully completed a weight reduction program. Several months later he was suspended without pay because his progress was insufficient. During his suspension, the laborer received unemployment compensation. Two months later, the city notified the laborer that an order had been issued in another case which required it to discontinue use of its height and weight standards. The laborer could therefore resume his employment. Meanwhile, the laborer had filed a complaint with the Pennsylvania Human Relations Commission (PHRC), claiming that the city had unlawfully regarded him as handicapped due to his obesity. The PHRC determined that the city had unlawfully discriminated against the laborer when it suspended him without pay. It ordered the city to award backpay without an offset for the unemployment compensation he had received. The city appealed to the Commonwealth Court of Pennsylvania.

On appeal, the city argued that the laborer's obesity was not a handicap, and that his unemployment compensation recovery should be deducted from the award. The commonwealth court noted that a handicap was any physical or mental impairment which substantially limited one or more major life activities, including work. Regardless of whether obesity constituted a handicap, the laborer had been treated as having such an impairment. A single rejection from an employer due to impairment of a major life activity such as work qualified a person as handicapped if the employer rejected the applicant for that reason. The court affirmed the PHRC's decision for the laborer. *Civil Service Comm'n of Pittsburgh v. Pennsylvania Human Relations Comm'n*, 556 A.2d 933 (Pa.Cmwlth.1989).

In another lawsuit alleging obesity discrimination, a 400-pound New York bus driver sued the Central New York Regional Transportation Authority and its wholly-owned subsidiary. The subsidiary stated that the driver was terminated because he had failed to pass a physical examination and was not physically qualified to drive its buses. The driver filed a complaint with the New York State Division of Human Rights (DHR), claiming that he had been terminated because of his race, color and disability. The DHR found probable cause for employment discrimination and determined that it had jurisdiction over both the authority and its subsidiary. The authority sought a declaration from a New York trial court that the DHR had no jurisdiction, and an order to compel the DHR to dismiss a pending hearing. The trial court refused to prohibit a substantive hearing on the driver's complaint. The DHR had jurisdiction over the subsidiary and the DHR could proceed to hold a hearing on the merits of the driver's case. However, because the authority was not the driver's employer, the DHR had no jurisdiction over it. *Central New York Centro v. State Div. of Human Rights*, 539 N.Y.S.2d 626 (Sup.1989).

A white female worked for the Michigan Department of Treasury as a clerk. She received a promotion, but was later denied further promotions. She had asthma and the Michigan civil service department certified her as handicapped. The clerk was not promoted to two supervisory positions which became available although she had degrees in areas of study unrelated to her employment. There was evidence that the department had attempted to accommodate her need for a smoke-free environment. She sued the department in a Michigan trial court, which dismissed the matter for lack of jurisdiction. The clerk appealed to the Michigan Court of Appeals, which reversed and remanded the case. On remand, the trial court granted the employer's motion for summary judgment and the employee again appealed.

The court of appeals ruled that although employers have a duty to accommodate handicapped employees under the Michigan Civil Rights Act, this was limited to alteration of physical structures to accommodate handicapped persons to allow them to perform their jobs. There was no duty to extend job placement or rehabilitation services. In this case, the individuals selected for supervisory jobs had more seniority than the clerk. One of the positions would have placed the clerk under the immediate supervision of her mother which was against an established departmental policy. Higher education degrees in unrelated fields did not qualify her for positions over persons holding only high school educations because the positions required only a high school degree. Accordingly, the appeals court affirmed the trial court's dismissal of the lawsuit. *Marsh v. Dep't of Civil Serv.*, 433 N.W.2d 820 (Mich.App.1988).

An employee of the Greater Cleveland Regional Transit Authority, who had undergone unsuccessful treatment for alcoholism, returned to his workplace while off-duty and intoxicated. He struck a fellow employee, and later returned and engaged in a fight. The personnel director discharged the employee, concluding that the employee was beyond rehabilitation. The employee claimed discrimination based on the handicap of alcoholism, and appealed his termination. The Ohio Civil Rights Commission ordered him reinstated. The reinstatement order was reversed by a trial court, and the employee appealed to the Supreme Court of Appeals of Ohio.

The employee first needed to show the three elements of a prima facie handicap discrimination case. The first element is showing a handicap. The employee's alcoholism was shown by records from a hospital and a treatment center. The second element is showing that the discharge was due in part to the handicap. This was shown by the personnel director's noted conclusions, and by the events leading to the termination being caused by alcohol consumption. The last element is proving that an employee can safely perform his job. The employee showed that he did not drink at work, and that the fights occurred while off-duty. The transit authority argued that his employment posed a safety threat to other employees when his alcoholic behavior manifested itself in fights. The court held that this danger should lead to discharge only if a reasonable accommodation of the handicap could not avoid the danger and did not place an undue hardship on the employer. An employer with knowledge of alcoholism must offer a "firm choice" of reentering alcohol treatment or facing discipline. In this case the court ruled that the employer must allow another chance at treatment. The court warned that future allowances for treatment are not always mandatory, and limited the burden on the employer by making reinstatement of the employee subject to both successful completion of the treatment program and medical approval. The decision of the trial court was reversed. *Greater Cleveland RTA v. Ohio Civ. Rights Comm'n*, 567 N.E.2d 1325 (Ohio App.1989).

A female patrol officer with the Denver police department suffered an injury which rendered her a quadriplegic. She had no movement in her legs, fingers or lower arms. She received disability leave at full pay for one year following the accident. She was then retired from active service after the fire and police pension association determined that she was totally disabled. Claiming that there were positions open within the department which she could fill, the officer filed a complaint with the Commission on the Disabled alleging discrimination on the basis of her handicap. The hearing officer concluded that the department had in fact discriminated against the officer. The city then appealed the decision to the Colorado Court of Appeals.

The city contended that the officer did not make a prima facie showing of discrimination because she did not prove that she was otherwise qualified for the jobs in question. An otherwise qualified person is one who is able to meet all requirements of a program in spite of his or her handicap. The court determined that the woman could not comply with the department's weapon-firing and forceful arrest policy. The woman then argued that granting an exception to this policy would be a reasonable accommodation for several positions within the department for which she was otherwise qualified. A reasonable accommodation, the court noted, is one that strikes a balance between the legislative intent of protecting handicapped persons from employment discrimination and the legitimate concern of an employer for ensuring the safety of its employees and those with whom they are in contact. The court determined that an officer who cannot fire a weapon or make a forceful arrest was a danger to herself, other officers, and the public. Because there was no reasonable accommodation that would allow the woman to perform the essential functions of an officer, she was not otherwise qualified to hold that position. Therefore, the court determined that the department had not discriminated against her on the basis of her handicap. The appellate court reversed the decision of the commission. *Coski v. City and County of Denver*, 795 P.2d 1364 (Colo.App.1990).

An Illinois community college hired a secretary to serve under three administrators. Several months after her hiring, the college notified her that unless her work performance improved she would be terminated. During the next two months her performance improved. Later, the college learned that the secretary was pregnant. One of the administrators allegedly stated "here we go again." Ten days later the administrators informed her that they were recommending termination to the college board of trustees. They notified her that she had a right to appeal their decision, but she did not appeal. Within two weeks she was suspended without pay pending a final board determination. The board denied her attendance at the meeting and later voted to terminate her employment. The secretary filed an Equal Employment Opportunity Commission (EEOC) complaint in which she was unsuccessful.

The secretary then filed a civil rights lawsuit in a federal district court claiming she was discriminated against because of her pregnancy. Her lawsuit was brought under Title VII, 42 U.S.C. § 1983 and state antidiscrimination laws. The district court refused to dismiss the Title VII complaints because there was sufficient evidence that the college discriminated against her. A jury should determine whether termination might have been based on her pregnancy. The court also refused to dismiss the § 1983 complaints. However, the secretary failed to follow state law procedural requirements by not filing an action with the state human rights department. The state claims were dismissed. The college's qualified immunity defense was insufficient to bar a trial because it was clear that discriminating against pregnant women violated constitutional and statutory law. Trial would proceed on the federal claims. *Suarez v. Illinois Valley Comm. College*, 688 F.Supp. 376 (N.D.Ill.1988).

III. RACE DISCRIMINATION

One of the leading cases on race discrimination is *U.S. Postal Service Board of Governors v. Aikens*, below, which sets forth the standard to be used in determining if the employer has acted discriminatorily. The lawsuit in *Aikens* was brought under Title VII, one of the two most frequently used statutes for the enforcement of employment civil rights. The other federal statute often used is § 1983 of the Civil Rights Act. Section 1983, along with § 1981, provides for monetary relief instead of just injunctive remedies.

A black Washington, D.C. post office employee was turned down for a promotion. Although he possessed the minimum qualifications necessary, the postal service selected a nonminority candidate. It asserted that he was not promoted because he had turned down several lateral transfers which would have broadened his postal service experience. He filed suit against the post office under Title VII, 42 U.S.C. § 2000e <u>et</u> <u>seq</u>., claiming he had been discriminated against by race. The federal district court ruled in favor of the postal service, but the court of appeals reversed. It held that the district court had erred in requiring the employee to offer direct proof of discriminatory intent.

On appeal, the U.S. Supreme Court noted that once the employee established a prima facie case that the postal service had discriminated against him, and the postal service had produced a legitimate, nondiscriminatory reason for not promoting him, the burden fell on the employee to show that the reason given for rejecting him was pretextual. However, it was not necessary for him to submit direct evidence of discriminatory intent. Rather, he merely had to persuade the judge that the postal service's reason was not the real reason for his rejection. Because the district court had used the wrong standard to determine whether the postal service was liable, the Court vacated the court of appeals' decision and remanded the case to the district court for a proper determination. *U.S. Postal Service Bd. of Governors v. Aikens*, 460 U.S. 711, 103 S.Ct. 1478, 75 L.Ed.2d 403 (1983).

Certain black employees of the North Carolina Agricultural Extension Service and the United States sued the service in a federal district court, alleging a pattern and practice of racial discrimination in employment and provision of services. The district court found no pattern to certify the action as a class action, and further held that no individual discrimination had taken place. The U.S. Court of Appeals, Fourth Circuit, affirmed, and a further appeal was taken to the U.S. Supreme Court. The Supreme Court held that, under Title VII, the service had a duty to eradicate salary disparities between white and black workers which had their origin prior to the enactment of Title VII. Here, the employees had shown by a preponderance of the evidence that discrimination had occurred, even though they had not proven it with scientific certainty. Since it was more likely than not that discrimination had played a part in the salary discrepancies, the Court determined that the employees were entitled to the relief they sought. The Court thus affirmed in part and reversed in part, and remanded the case for a proper determination of damages. *Bazemore v. Friday*, 478 U.S. 384, 106 S.Ct. 3000, 92 L.Ed.2d 315 (1986).

The Equal Employment Opportunity Commission brought an action in a federal district court against the Federal Reserve Bank of Richmond, Virginia, alleging that one of the bank's branches had violated Title VII by engaging in discriminatory employment practices. Four black employees were allowed to intervene and received certification as a class. They then notified other class members who joined in the suit. The court found discrimination with respect to employees in certain specified pay grades, but not with respect to employees above those grades. The court denied other employees' motions to intervene because they were in the higher grades, and they then filed separate actions under 42 U.S.C. § 1981. The U.S. Court of Appeals, Fourth Circuit, reversed the district court's finding of discrimination in the class action and further determined that the judgment in the class action precluded the individual suits from being litigated. The U.S. Supreme Court granted certiorari.

The Court noted that, while the class members were bound by the judgment against them in the class action, they were not precluded from bringing individual claims against the bank. Even though it had not been shown that the bank had systematically engaged in a discriminatory pattern of conduct, the individuals might be able to show isolated cases of discrimination. The Court thus reversed the court of appeals' decision and allowed the individual claims to be brought. *Cooper v. Federal Reserve Bank of Richmond*, 467 U.S. 867, 104 S.Ct. 2794, 81 L.Ed.2d 718 (1984).

A white male was employed by the Dallas Independent School District (DISD) as a teacher, athletic director and head football coach at a predominantly black high school. After numerous problems with the school's principal over school policies, the principal recommended that the teacher be relieved of his duties as athletic director and coach. The district's superintendent reassigned the teacher to a teaching position in another school. The teacher sued the school district and the principal, claiming that they had discriminated against him on the basis of race in violation of 42 U.S.C. §§ 1981 and 1983. A federal district court held in the teacher's favor. The U.S. Court of Appeals, Fifth Circuit, reversed in part and remanded, finding that the jury instructions as to the DISD's liability under § 1983 did not make clear that the district could be liable only if the officials had been delegated policy-making authority or had acted pursuant to a well settled custom or policy. And even if the superintendent could be considered a policy-maker for purposes of the transfer of personnel, the jury made no finding that his decision to transfer the teacher was either improperly motivated or consciously indifferent to the principal's improper motivations. The court of appeals also rejected the district court's conclusion that the district's liability for the principal's actions under § 1981 could be predicated on a vicarious liability theory or that the municipality could be liable for its employees' acts. The court noted that Congress did not intend that municipalities be subject to vicarious liability under § 1983. The teacher then appealed to the U.S. Supreme Court.

The Supreme Court stated that a municipality may not be held liable for its employees' § 1981 violations under a vicarious liability theory. The express "action at law" provided by § 1983 for the deprivation of rights secured by the Constitution and laws provides the exclusive federal remedy for the violation of rights guaranteed by § 1981 when the claim is pressed against a state actor. A municipality cannot be held liable under § 1983 on a vicarious liability theory. The Supreme Court affirmed part of this decision and remanded the case in order to determine if the superintendent possessed final policy-making authority in the area of employee transfer and whether a new trial was required to determine the DISD's responsibility for the principal's actions in light of this determination. *Jett v. Dallas Indep. School Dist.*, 109 S. Ct. 2702, 105 L.Ed.2d 598 (1989).

The town of Harrison, New Jersey, had hiring and application policies which limited public employment to town residents. Because the town was 99.8% non-black, this resulted in no blacks being considered for employment. Several branches of the National Association for the Advancement of Colored People (NAACP) challenged the town's requirements as being racially discriminatory, and sought an injunction in a federal district court.

A prima facie case was shown by the NAACP by comparing the town's workforce of zero blacks to the private sector's employment of twenty-two percent blacks. Additionally, the last law enforcement officer hired had an examination score of seventy, while many available nonresident black applicants had higher scores. The court explained that Title VII goes beyond purposeful discrimination and extends to prohibit policies which have a disparate impact on any group of people. The court concluded that the disparate impact was caused by the residency requirement. The town then argued that the policies were justified by local interests. These interests included avoiding expensive employment investigations, desiring a local presence and participation, and that residents would be more loyal and less likely to be absent or tardy. The court found these justifications too insubstantial to justify the disparate impact. The final argument by the town was that resident law enforcement officers or firefighters could be more readily called during off-duty hours. The court found that other criteria, such as a minimum response time requirement, could achieve the town's goals without having the disparate impact on blacks. The court granted injunctive relief to the NAACP and ordered the town to alter its policies. *N.A.A.C.P. v. Town of Harrison, New Jersey*, 749 F.Supp. 1327 (D.N.J.1990).

In May of 1974 the city of Cincinnati entered into a consent decree which was designed to increase the hiring and promotion of blacks in the city's fire department. The consent decree modified the city's practices to vary from Ohio Civil Service Law, and set the final goal of eighteen percent blacks in the department by 1980. In 1988, after the eighteen percent quota had been reached, white applicants who took the exam were placed on a "majority" list. They were not appointed. Applicants from the "minority" list were appointed, however, even though they had lower scores than some of the white applicants. Various white applicants challenged their non-appointment in a federal district court.

The court noted that a consent decree which provides favored treatment for minorities is not per se unlawful. However, such decrees must be carefully examined and strictly construed. When the goals of a decree have been reached, the decree (or a portion of it) is at an end. In this case, the goal of eighteen percent black firefighters had been reached. Therefore, the city was in violation of Ohio Civil Service Law for continuing to maintain the practices outlined in the decree. Since only the hiring practices under the decree were challenged, the court severed the promotional practices and did not address them. The white applicants were added to the next hiring list which their exam scores warranted, and were granted attorney's fees. *Jansen v. City of Cincinnati*, 758 F.Supp. 451 (S.D.Ohio 1991).

A Puerto Rican woman, employed by the Federal Aviation Administration (FAA), attained the position of air traffic assistant. Her performance was evaluated as exceeding the requirements of the position and her work was found to be fully acceptable. Subsequently, a new supervisor was appointed who subjected her to racial and ethnic slurs. He continuously monitored her, using subjective and vague performance standards, and eventually decertified her. Later, upon discovering that the employee had been recertified, he again decertified her. She then received at least ten recommendations for recertification, but her supervisor refused to provide her with an opportunity to be recertified. Another supervisor was appointed who also bore an animosity toward Puerto Ricans and the employee in particular, and he demoted her to a secretary's position. She then filed a Title VII action against the government, asserting race and national origin discrimination, in the U.S. District Court, D. Puerto Rico.

The court first noted that the employee had shown direct proof that she had been discriminated against. Further, the FAA's reasons for her demotion were clearly pretextual. The court found the rationale behind the demotion to be unlawful and not justified by any rational basis. Accordingly, it awarded the employee backpay of $25,000 for what she would have made if she had not been demoted, and ordered her immediate reinstatement as an air traffic assistant. *Cardona v. Skinner*, 729 F.Supp. 193 (D.Puerto Rico 1990).

A black man served in an Alabama city's police department until it was learned that he had assaulted another police officer. Subsequently, he received a pardon, was certified as a police officer and was hired by a county sheriff's department. The city then advertised for the position of chief of police and the officer applied for the job. He met with the mayor who told him he was over-qualified. He later reapplied for the position and also applied for police officer positions, but was not hired by the city. He then sued the city in a federal district court under Title VII, asserting that it had failed to hire him on account of his race. The district court ruled for the city, and the officer appealed to the U.S. Court of Appeals, Eleventh Circuit.

The appellate court held that the district court erred in refusing to consider the testimony of a witness who heard the mayor make a racial slur.

Although it was up to the district court to determine whether the statement was direct evidence of discrimination, the appellate court did not feel that the lower court had properly considered its probative value. The court thus reversed the district court's decision and remanded the case for a complete determination based on all the evidence. *Wilson v. City of Aliceville*, 779 F.2d 631 (11th Cir.1986).

A black California woman graduated from a police officer training program and applied for an entry-level position with a city. An opening existed when she applied and, after oral and written examinations, she was placed on an eligibility list, but the city was still hiring off the previous eligibility list and hired a male for the job. During the time her name appeared on the list, no openings occurred. She filed a complaint with the Equal Employment Opportunity Commission (EEOC) and received a right-to-sue letter. She then brought a suit in federal district court, asserting race and sex discrimination in violation of Title VII and violations of 42 U.S.C. §§ 1981 and 1983. The court granted summary judgment in favor of the city and she appealed to the U.S. Court of Appeals, Ninth Circuit.

The court of appeals first noted that because the woman had not filed a sex discrimination claim with the EEOC, she could not bring a Title VII sex discrimination claim in court. The court then stated that a claim for racial discrimination might exist because the city had no blacks on its police force, and a supervisor told the applicant that she should apply for a position in Los Angeles, where they "were begging for minorities and especially females." The court further held that the §§ 1981 and 1983 claims presented triable issues and that the district court should not have granted summary judgment. It thus affirmed the dismissal of the Title VII sex discrimination claim, but reversed the dismissal of the others and remanded the case for a factual determination. *Lowe v. City of Monrovia*, 775 F.2d 998 (9th Cir.1985).

Two black male applicants and one black female employee of the Mississippi Governor's Highway Safety Program brought suit against the program in a federal district court, alleging discrimination on the basis of race and sex. The two black male applicants specified a preference to work in Jackson, but the agency instead hired a white male acquaintance of the governor who was not certified for the work. The black female employee worked as a secretary and was passed over for promotion in favor of two men, at least one of whom was unqualified. When the federal government notified the agency that its funding would be cut off and the staff had to be reduced, the agency discharged the secretary rather than another white clerical employee with less seniority. After filing complaints with the Equal Employment Opportunity Commission, the three agreed to a trial by federal magistrate, who found insufficient evidence of discrimination. They then appealed to the U.S. Court of Appeals, Fifth Circuit.

The court of appeals held that the magistrate's finding did not meet specificity requirements for showing that he had properly reached his conclusions. Without specific findings of fact, the court of appeals could not be certain that he had properly decided the cases. Because of the insufficiency of the federal findings and the errors of law, the court vacated the magistrate's decision and remanded the case for a complete determination. *Ratliff v. Governor's Highway Safety Program*, 791 F.2d 394 (5th Cir.1986).

A group of private plaintiffs brought suit against the Mississippi State Department of Public Welfare and its local agencies, alleging racial discrimination in hiring practices. Suit was commenced in a federal district court under Title VII of the Civil Rights Act of 1964. The United States also brought suit against the department. The district court ruled against the state department and found it liable under Title VII. The department appealed to the U.S. Court of Appeals, Fifth Circuit.

The court of appeals found that the plaintiffs had been discriminated against on the basis of invalid written examinations. Further, the subjective selection of candidates from the eligibility lists had resulted in a discriminatory hiring practice. However, even though the federal government had provided substantial funding to the state department, the court did not feel it could be held liable for costs and backpay to the other plaintiffs. The court thus affirmed the district court's decision for the most part, reversing only with respect to a finding of federal governmental liability. *Walls v. Mississippi State Dep't of Public Welfare,* 730 F.2d 306 (5th Cir.1984).

Two Hispanic males had been working in the position of Analyst III for at least ten years. Both applied for and were qualified for promotion to Analyst IV but neither was selected for advancement. The positions sought were filled by temporary appointees who were white and who were eventually given the positions permanently. The provisional or temporary appointments prevented the interruption of work during the hiring process. They also provided the appointees with on-the-job training. Since the temporary appointments were not within the civil service merit system, they were made by individual department heads and were reviewed by the Office of Equal Employment Opportunity Management; that office, however, had no veto power over the decisions. The county's director of Equal Employment Opportunity Management stated that temporary appointments were used to advance majority employees; he further stated that the system was changed in 1986 so that the temporary appointment system was equally applicable to all employees. He also testified that generally the temporary employee ultimately was hired to fill the job on a permanent basis. The two Hispanic male employees commenced this action for racial discrimination against the county in a federal district court.

In order to prevail on a claim of racial discrimination, the plaintiffs had to prove that the acts of the defendant were intentionally discriminatory. The court determined that the evidence presented was sufficient to raise an inference of illegal discrimination. In each position at issue, the temporary appointments were used, and the white appointees were eventually given the jobs on a permanent basis. When making these appointments, the department heads were acting outside the normal civil service merit system and knew that their decisions could not be challenged by the Equal Opportunity Management Office. Since the court was satisfied that the plaintiffs proved a case of discrimination, the county was then required to state a legitimate reason for its course of action. The county had not met its burden of producing a legitimate reason for excluding the plaintiffs from the pool of potential temporary employees. The court ruled for the Hispanic males and awarded back pay and retroactive promotions. *Bua v. County of San Diego*, 731 F.Supp. 962 (S.D.Cal.1990).

A black employee at a prison was disciplined and demoted. The employee's supervisor then provoked the employee, and the employee threatened the supervisor. The employee was subsequently terminated. A lawsuit was filed in a federal district court in which the employee alleged that he had been subjected to racial discrimination.

The employee was able to show a prima facie case by proving that he was from a protected class of persons, that he had demonstrated his qualifications by working successfully for over three years, and by showing that his position was filled by a person from outside his protected class. The supervisor then needed to show valid and nonpretextual reasons for the termination. He argued that the misconduct and threats were severe enough to justify the demotion, and the eventual termination. The employee, however, was successful in showing that the supervisor's reasons for discipline were pretextual. Many other employees had violations which were at least as severe as the employee's but these employees were not disciplined. Nevertheless, the employee failed on the last element of proof. Even though the reasons for termination were shown to be pretextual, it was not shown that the actions were taken because of racial animus. Other employees who were not disciplined included fellow black employees, and the supervisor had a record of hiring blacks. The court held that the employee may have been treated unfairly, but he was not discriminated against because of his race. Judgment was granted for the supervisor. *Hicks v. St. Mary's Honor Center*, 756 F.Supp. 1244 (E.D.Mo.1991).

A black lieutenant in a North Carolina correctional facility applied for a promotion to captain. The black lieutenant had the highest score on a qualification examination, had longer work experience than a white employee being considered for the promotion, and had received "excellent" ratings on performance evaluations. The state based its entire decision on an interview, however, and promoted a white lieutenant. The black lieutenant then filed an appeal, charging discrimination, with the State Personnel Commission. The administrative law judge found that the state's reasons for promotion of the white lieutenant were pretextual and ordered the state to promote the black lieutenant into the next vacant captaincy and to pay him back and front pay. The state appealed to the Court of Appeals of North Carolina.

The state asserted that the sole determining factor was the interview process and that it had rejected all other criteria. The court found that the state's exclusive consideration of the interviews "contravened its own system of promotion" and affirmed the administrative law judge's finding of the state's reasons as pretextual and discriminatory. The court upheld the ruling. *N.C. Dep't of Correction v. Hodge*, 394 S.E.2d 285 (N.C.App.1990)

The Ohio Adult Parole Authority hired a black male as a parole officer (level 2). He remained in this position for four years until Ohio implemented a statewide reclassification when he was reclassified as level 1. A level 2 position opened up one year later which he applied for, but the department selected a white male instead. After another year, the parole officer resigned. He then sued the department in a federal district court, alleging that he had been discriminated against on the basis of race. The district court ruled for the parole officer, and the department appealed to the U.S. Court of Appeals, Sixth Circuit.

The appellate court first noted that the burden of proof of discrimination lay with the parole officer. Further, the department had given a legitimate nondiscriminatory reason for not promoting the black parole officer. A supervisor had testified that the white male who had been promoted was more qualified, and that was all the department needed to show. It was then up to the parole officer to prove that the department's reason was pretextual. The court reversed the district court's decision and remanded the case for a determination on the pretext issue. *Burton v. State of Ohio, Adult Parole Authority*, 798 F.2d 164 (6th Cir.1986).

A black food manager at a Washington state hospital reported to the hospital superintendent that he had seen his supervisor stealing food. After the supervisor had been cleared of the charges, he charged the black employee with improper conduct. An administrative hearing was held in which fellow employees testified against the black employee. The black employee agreed to a two-day suspension and then filed suit against the hospital supervisor in a federal district court, alleging racial discrimination under

Title VII, 42 U.S.C. § 2000e-2 and interference with contractual opportunity under § 1981. The district court dismissed the employee's claims and he appealed to the U.S. Court of Appeals, Ninth Circuit.

The employee argued that the supervisor had restricted his supervisory duties as a food manager on the basis of his race. He offered evidence of several racially derogatory statements made to him by the supervisor. The court of appeals reversed the district court's dismissal of the employee's claim. It held that Title VII protected the existence of supervisory duties because they were part of the employee's job as food manager. It noted that employees who have the opportunity to supervise are most likely to advance in their careers. However, the court rejected the employee's § 1981 claim, concluding that the employee's job description did not create contractual expectancies. Finally, the court ruled that the employee's agreement to the two-day suspension did not bar his civil rights claim. The court reversed the dismissal and remanded the case for trial. *Judie v. Hamilton*, 872 F.2d 919 (9th Cir.1989).

A woman of Chinese ancestry who had been employed by the U.S. Department of Health and Human Services filed a formal administrative complaint of discrimination with an Equal Employment Opportunity (EEO) counselor. In her complaint she alleged that her supervisor harassed her by continually assessing her performance, denying her a within-grade salary increase, and by throwing a pen or pencil at the employee during a conference about her performance. Although the department accepted her complaint for investigation, it had not completed its investigation more than four years later. The employee then appealed to the Equal Employment Opportunity Commission (EEOC) which affirmed the department's rejection of the salary increase claim and also failed to address the other complaints. The employee then filed suit in a federal district court for full administrative processing and investigation of her complaint.

Before the district court, the department claimed that its dismissal of the salary increase claim was valid because the employee had failed to raise the matter with the EEO counselor within thirty days of the decision to deny her salary increase. The district court ruled that federal regulations require federal agencies to review and investigate any employee complaints. The department's rejection of the employee's salary increase claim was wrong because the evidence indicated that the employee told her EEO counselor about the salary denial within thirty days. The court noted that employees complaining to an agency are not required to articulate their claims to a specific degree, and that an agency must construe administrative complaints liberally. The court granted the employee's request and remanded the case back to the department. *Young v. Bowen*, 714 F.Supp. 764 (D.Md.1989).

A black teacher was appointed head basketball coach at an Alabama high school. When the coach started, the school's basketball program was disorganized and the players were undisciplined. The coach worked to improve the team, but its record was 2-38 the first two years. The school's principal twice tried to remove the coach from that position in violation of the Alabama Tenure Law. After the end of the coach's second year, the principal removed him in favor of a white teacher. The coach sued the board of education in the U.S. District Court for the Northern District of Alabama. The principal argued that the coach was removed because of his losing record and because a better coach had become available. The coach argued that he was dismissed for discriminatory reasons. Other coaches with losing records had not been dismissed after two years. A school official also testified that academic achievement and discipline are far more important in determining good coaching than a win-loss record. Students also overwhelmingly stated that the coach was better than his replacement. The principal admitted that one reason the coach was removed was that an all white parents club wanted a white coach so that more white students would be attracted to the basketball program. The district court held that the reasons given for the coach's removal as varsity basketball coach at the high school were not credible. They were a pretext for racial discrimination. The board of education was ordered to pay damages and to reinstate the coach. *Jackson v. Birmingham Bd. of Educ.*, 695 F.Supp. 1164 (N.D.Ala.1988).

A black woman, employed by a Maryland county's department of social services, applied for a promotion which she was denied. She sued the department and the state in a federal district court, alleging that she had been denied the promotion because of her race. She asserted both a Title VII claim and a §1983 claim and sought a jury trial on the §1983 claim. The district court dimissed her claim under §1983 because it believed that Title VII provided the exclusive remedy for employment discrimination claims by a state employee. It then denied her request for a jury trial because Title VII does not grant a right to trial by jury. The judge then found the employee's witnesses not credible and determined that the county had shown a legitimate nondiscriminatory reason for denying the employee the promotion. The court ruled for the county and state, and the employee appealed to the U.S. Court of Appeals, Fourth Circuit.

The appellate court first noted that Title VII claims and § 1983 claims provide for different remedies and have different procedural requirements. The court then stated that the Congress had clearly not intended to make Title VII an exclusive remedy. Further, although the U.S. Supreme Court had not addressed the issue directly, it had expressly stated that in its view Title VII did not preempt an action under § 1983. However, the appellate court deemed it necessary to remand the case to the district court for a determination as to whether the county was a state or local government unit. If the county was a state entity, it could not be sued under § 1983. Thus, the court reversed the district court's decision and remanded the case for a complete determination. *Keller v. Prince George's County*, 827 F.2d 952 (4th Cir.1987).

The Virginia Department of Mental Health and Mental Retardation hired a black man as an assistant commissioner. Two years later, a vacancy opened up in the office of deputy commissioner. The black assistant commissioner applied for the position and made it through the first two screening procedures. He was one of five finalists for the position, but a white man was eventually selected for the job. The black assistant commissioner sued the commissioner and the department in a federal district court, asserting violations of Title VII and 42 U.S.C. § 1983. The district court dismissed his claim and the court of appeals affirmed. He petitioned for further review which the U.S. Court of Appeals, Fourth Circuit, granted.

On appeal, the assistant commissioner acknowledged that all five finalists had been "very well qualified," but contended that because there were so few blacks in executive management positions in the department, he should have been given a preference when being considered for promotion. The court, however, disagreed. It noted that the man selected by the department had more experience in dealing with municipalities and local governments. Further, the assistant commissioner had not been able to show any direct or indirect evidence of discrimination. He had merely shown that he did not get the position and that he was black. The court held that he had presented insufficient evidence and, accordingly, it affirmed the district court's dismissal of the case. *Holmes v. Bevilacqua*, 794 F.2d 142 (4th Cir.1986).

A Missouri city hired a black male to work in its refuse department. He eventually attained the position of superintendent of the department and served in that capacity for fifteen years. He was then demoted to the position of heavy equipment operator by the city manager because of an inability to maintain the municipal sanitary landfill in compliance with state requirements, and for poor management of the department. He sued the city and city manager in a federal district court, and a magistrate determined that he had failed to show he had been discriminated against. He then appealed to the U.S. Court of Appeals, Eighth Circuit.

The court of appeals first noted that the city manager had hired a greater percentage of minorities during his tenure than actually lived in the surrounding county. Further, the city had shown that the ex-superintendent had poorly run the department and had even used city vehicles and equipment for personal use. Thus, a legitimate reason for the demotion had been presented and the employee had failed to prove that it was a pretext for race discrimination. The court of appeals affirmed the magistrate's decision and determined that the employee had not been demoted because of his race. *Henderson v. City of Mexico,* 798 F.2d 320 (8th Cir.1986).

A black postal service employee worked as a parttime flexible mail handler. He received a letter of warning concerning his job performance, and then refused to obey his supervisor's order to "dump mail." He received a second warning letter, but then left work early without permission. He was suspended, returned to work late, left without permission again and was eventually discharged. He then filed a complaint with the EEOC, alleging race discrimination and sued in a federal district court under Title VII. He asserted that three white employees with spotty attendance records had not been fired, and that his situation was similar to theirs. The district court disagreed, finding that their situations were different. He appealed to the U.S. Court of Appeals, Seventh Circuit.

The court of appeals noted that there were plenty of nondiscriminatory reasons for the employee's discharge, and that the district court had correctly concluded that no discrimination had been present. The employee here had been unable to show that he was treated differently than white employees because his attendance problems were too dissimilar to theirs. The court affirmed the district court's decision. *Yowell v. United States Postal Service*, 810 F.2d 644 (7th Cir.1987).

A Hispanic male worked for the U.S. Army as a civilian equipment repair inspector at an army base in Oklahoma. A higher position became available on the base and the employee applied for it. Though rated as one of the three best candidates for the job, another employee was chosen for the position. After an investigation, an army official recommended to the base commander that a finding of discrimination be made. However, an Equal Employment Opportunity officer disagreed, finding no evidence of discrimination. Thereafter, the commander denied relief to the employee who then sued in a federal district court under Title VII, alleging that he had been denied the promotion because of his Puerto Rican heritage. The district court ruled against him, and he appealed to the U.S. Court of Appeals, Tenth Circuit.

The appellate court held that the evidence clearly indicated that the other employee had been selected because of his superior administrative experience and skills. Further, even if the employee selected had not been better qualified, the army had believed that he was when it offered the position to him. Since the unsuccessful applicant had been unable to show that the army's reasons were just a pretext for discrimination, the court ruled in the army's favor, and affirmed the decision of the district court. *Colon-Sanchez v. Marsh*, 733 F.2d 78 (10th Cir.1984).

A black Pennsylvania man was employed by a county prison for approximately nineteen months. Because of two citations issued to the employee, and numerous suspensions and reprimands, the prison conducted a disciplinary hearing. The two citations related to excessive absenteeism and failure to attend training sessions. At the conclusion of the hearing, the warden gave the employee a chance to resign rather than than be fired. The employee refused and was discharged. He then filed a complaint with the state human relations commission and another hearing was conducted. The commission found that the employee had been justifiably terminated because of the accumulation of prior offenses and citations, and the employee then appealed to the Commonwealth Court of Pennsylvania.

On appeal, the court found that a prima facie case of discrimination had been established because the employee was a member of a protected minority with a desire to remain employed. However, it further found that the county prison's actions in discharging him were based on substantial evidence and were reasonable. The prison's reasons for discharging him were not pretextual, and he had been treated no less favorably than other white employees who were guilty of the same offenses. The court affirmed the commission's decision, and upheld the employee's dismissal. *Thomas v. Human Relations Commission*, 527 A.2d 602 (Pa.Cmwlth.1987).

A black employee worked for a North Carolina city park and recreation department. He applied for two job openings on the department's ground maintenance crew, either of which would have been a promotion. Three whites and one other black applied for the positions. Following interviews and tests, two white applicants were selected for the openings. Although the applicants selected scored the highest on interviews, one was a department crew supervisor's son and the other was a nephew of one of the interviewers. The interviewers allegedly relied on their knowledge of the applicants, but not upon their personal or work records. The black employee, who had more experience than either selected applicant, claimed that the promotions were motivated by racial discrimination. After exhausting his administrative remedies, he sued the city in a federal district court. The court determined that the employee had made out a prima facie case for race discrimination under Title VII of the 1964 Civil Rights Act. The city argued that the panelists had a legitimate concern that the employee was not trustworthy. They also claimed he had a poor attendance record. The employee countered with evidence that his attendance had improved after a warning. A court magistrate then ruled that the city had successfully rebutted the employee's prima facie case based upon the interview scores. The employee appealed to the U.S. Court of Appeals, Fourth Circuit.

The appeals court acknowledged that nepotism had played a role in the city's selection process. However, it ruled that Title VII did not permit courts to invalidate all unfair employee decisions. Title VII forbade only specific acts of employment discrimination based upon race, color, religion, sex and national origin. Because the employee had not proven discriminatory intent by the city, nepotism by itself was insufficient to warrant a finding of racial discrimination. Finding no error in the magistrate's determination, the court affirmed his decision. *Holder v. City of Raleigh*, 867 F.2d 823 (4th Cir.1989).

A black female teacher was employed by an Arkansas school district for fourteen years. On the recommendation of the superintendent of schools, the school board voted not to renew her contract. The nonrenewal was based on an allegation that she taught her students the actual questions from a standardized achievement test. A white male teacher also did not have his contract renewed for the same reason. The black teacher challenged her nonrenewal in an Arkansas federal district court on two grounds. She claimed that she was discriminated against because of her race and that the school board failed to comply with the Arkansas Teacher Fair Dismissal Act. The district court held for the school board on both counts and the teacher appealed to the U.S. Court of Appeals, Eighth Circuit. The appeals court affirmed the district court's decision. It reasoned that because a white male teacher was dismissed for the same reason, the charge of racial discrimination failed. It also affirmed the district court's conclusion that the school board complied with the Arkansas Fair Dismissal Act. It required the superintendent to notify the teacher that her contract was not recommended for renewal. The superintendent had in fact sent a notice of nonrenewal to the teacher. Therefore, her nonrenewal was upheld. *Scoggins v. Bd. of Educ. of Nashville, Ark. Pub. Sch.*, 853 F.2d 1472(8th Cir.1988).

IV. SEX DISCRIMINATION

One of the leading cases in this area is *Texas Department of Community Affairs v. Burdine*, below, which is frequently cited by other cases involving sex discrimination. The case demonstrates the rule that once a plaintiff establishes a prima facie case of discrimination by the employer, and the employer articulates a legitimate nondiscriminatory reason for its actions, the plaintiff must then prove that the employer's reason was pretextual.

A. Employment Decisions

A Texas woman, with several years experience in employment training, was hired by the state's department of community affairs. She received one promotion, and subsequently applied for a supervisor's position, which she did not receive. The department then fired her in a staff reduction. However, it later rehired, transferred and promoted her, keeping her salary commensurate with what she would have received had she gotten the first promotion. She nevertheless sued the department in a federal district court, asserting that the failure to promote and the decision to terminate her were based on gender discrimination. The district court ruled for the department and she appealed to the U.S. Court of Appeals, Fifth Circuit, which held that she had not been discriminated against in the nonpromotion, but that she had been discriminated against in the termination. The department petitioned the U.S. Supreme Court for review.

The Supreme Court first stated that the employee had the burden of showing a prima facie case of discrimination, namely: that she belonged to a protected minority, that she was qualified for the job, that she was rejected despite her qualifications, and that after her rejection the department continued to look at candidates with the same qualifications. The burden would then shift to the department to "articulate some legitimate, nondiscriminatory reason for the employee's rejection." If it was successful, the employee would then have to prove that the reasons given by the department were a pretext for discrimination. Because the court of appeals had not used this standard, the Supreme Court vacated its decision and remanded the case for a determination based on this. *Texas Dep't of Community Affairs v. Burdine*, 450 U.S. 248, 101 S.Ct. 1089, 67 L.Ed.2d 207 (1981).

A North Carolina city developed a new job for managing the city's recreational facilities. Four men and one woman composed the mayoral committee responsible for selecting an applicant. After considering eight applicants, the four men voted to hire a twenty-four-year-old man who had recently graduated from college with a physical education degree. The sole female committee member voted to hire the only female applicant, a thirty-nine-year-old teacher with degrees in social studies and education. The female applicant filed a sex discrimination complaint under Title VII against the city, claiming that she had not been hired solely on the basis of her sex. The federal district court in which the matter was filed held in the applicant's favor, finding that she had a broader range of experience than the selected applicant.

The court also held that the male committee members were biased against the female applicant and that one male committee person had stated that he would not have wanted his wife to perform the recreation director's job duties. There was also evidence that the committee had actively solicited male applicants but had made no attempt to recruit females. Finally, the reasons given for hiring the male applicant were pretextual. The city appealed to the U.S. Court of Appeals, Fourth Circuit, which reversed the lower court's decision. The applicant appealed to the U.S. Supreme Court, which held that the court of appeals had improperly weighed the district court findings by attempting to conduct a new evaluation of the evidence. There was sufficient evidence of sex bias and discrimination in the district court record and the court of appeals should not have denied relief to the applicant. The Court reversed the court of appeals' judgment. *Anderson v. Bessemer City*, 470 U.S. 564, 105 S.Ct. 1504, 84 L.Ed.2d 518 (1985).

A Texas woman worked for the state's department of water resources as a secretary. Shortly after her hiring, she applied for an engineering aide position because of her technical background. She was assured that the position would be more technical and not involve secretarial duties. She received the job, but when she reported for work the divisional director requested that she relieve his secretary on a daily basis for thirty minutes each morning and afternoon. She asked for time to think about this request, and the director then terminated her. She sued the department and director in a federal district court, alleging sex discrimination in violation of Title VII, and the court ruled for the department. She appealed to the U.S. Court of Appeals, Fifth Circuit.

The court of appeals determined that although the department did not hire anyone to replace the aide, it could not automatically be assumed that no discrimination had occurred. Evidence had been presented showing that male aides were not required to perform any secretarial duties, while females did have to serve as parttime secretaries. Further, even though the aide was a probationary employee who could be terminated at will, that termination could not legally be the result of sex discrimination. The court thus vacated the district court's decision, and remanded the case for more specific findings on the facts. *Smith v. Texas Dep't of Water Resources*, 799 F.2d 1026 (5th Cir.1986).

A New York mathematics teacher sued her school district and superintendent in a New York trial court, alleging that they had discriminated against her on the basis of her sex by denying her request for educational leave and relief from an administrative assignment. The trial court denied the district's summary judgment motion and the district appealed to the Supreme Court, Appellate Division. The appellate division held that summary judgment should have been granted because the teacher had failed to establish a prima facie case of sex discrimination. The appellate division court noted that the fact that two male teachers were granted educational leaves did not create an inference of sex discrimination against the female teacher. The two male teachers' requests for educational leave were significantly different than the female teacher's request. Specifically, the personnel needs in the math department were more pressing than in the music and English departments where the two male teachers taught and it was easier to secure a replacement for one year than for a semester, which the female teacher had requested. The appellate division reversed the trial court decision. *Baker v. West Irondequoit Cent. School Dist.*, 550 N.Y.S.2d 762 (A.D.4th Dep't 1989).

A woman was the only eligible candidate for promotion at a Maryland correctional facility. The only prior contact between the woman and the warden had been during a disciplinary meeting which resulted from the woman's refusal to wear pants because of her religious beliefs. Instead of promoting her, the warden waited for an updated list of eligible candidates. The warden then appointed men to the next four vacancies. The woman was more experienced than all the men, and alleged discrimination based on gender. A lawsuit was filed in a federal district court.

From the above evidence, the woman was able to produce a prima facie case of discrimination. The burden then shifted to the warden to produce valid and non-discriminatory reasons for his decision. The warden presented a list of nine factors which were used in his promotional decisions. He also put on record his notes and computations using these factors from the time when each decision was made. Although each candidate had small problems in certain areas, the court found that the neutral criteria given and demonstrated by the warden were valid. The final responsibility to persuade the court remained with the woman, and she was unable to prove that the promotion decisions were based on gender. The court ruled that no discrimination had occurred. *Colbert v. State of Maryland, Dep't of Corrections*, 736 F.Supp. 75 (D.Md.1989).

A female Arkansas postal worker applied for a clerk position. She was the least senior of four candidates for the position; the other three were men. The senior applicant received the position. Another position opened up and the other two men refused the position. The postmaster did not contact the female. Instead he went to the hiring roster and chose a male parttime rural relief carrier who had no prior clerking experience. The woman then filed a complaint with the Equal Employment Opportunity Commission against the postal service alleging sex discrimination. After a hearing, an administrative law judge found that she had established a prima facie case of sexual discrimination, but that the postal service had demonstrated a legitimate nondiscriminatory reason for the challenged employment decision. There was an alleged one year residency requirement for all clerks which the female employee did not meet. The woman then filed an action in a federal district court. At trial the postmaster offered another explanation of the decision not to transfer her. The court affirmed the hearing officer's decision. The woman then appealed to the U.S. Court of Appeals, Eighth Circuit.

On appeal, the court determined that the record revealed inconsistent and contradictory explanations set forth by the postmaster. Such a finding is viewed as evidence establishing the explanations as pretextual. The postmaster testified as to five reasons why he did not transfer the female. This testimony supported a finding that all the explanations were really only a pretext for discrimination. Therefore, the court determined that in light of the record it could find no legitimate, nondiscriminatory basis for the challenged action. The district court's contrary finding was erroneous. Accordingly, the court of appeals reversed its decision. *Edwards v. U.S. Postal Service*, 909 F.2d 320 (8th Cir.1990).

A Michigan woman was hired by a county sheriff's office in its corrections division. She sought a transfer to the road patrol division, but the sheriff refused to grant it. He allegedly maintained an unwritten separate career ladder policy for all employees hired after a certain date. Because the employee had been hired afterward, she was denied a transfer. She then brought a Title VII action in a federal district court, where the judge granted partial relief. Both parties appealed to the U.S. Court of Appeals, Sixth Circuit.

The appellate court first noted that there was no evidence that the sheriff had engaged in discriminatory practices against women in general. It further held that since no pattern of discrimination had been found, the sheriff could not be ordered to implement a written career ladder policy. However, the court then stated that since the district court had made a finding of intentional discrimination against the employee alone, it would uphold the lower court's order to transfer the employee to an available position in the road patrol division. However, the court denied her request for backpay because she had been employed in the corrections division the whole time and there was no difference in pay between the two assignments. The court of appeals thus affirmed in part and reversed in part, and remanded the case to the district court for implementation of its orders. *Kent County Sheriff's Ass'n v. County of Kent*, 826 F.2d 1485 (6th Cir.1987).

A woman worked for a Nebraska city for ten years before the city terminated her employment. The employee, who was white, had a relationship with a black man and bore his son. After taking maternity leave, she requested additional sick leave because of medical complications. The city denied her request, although it allowed white women with white children to take sick leave in conjunction with maternity leave. The employee sued the city and the local union in a federal district court alleging civil rights violations. The court found that the employee had not been discriminated against for dating the black man and having his child, nor for exercising her First Amendment rights. However, the court found that the union and the city conspired to deny her a promotion based upon her sex. The union moved for a directed verdict and for judgment notwithstanding the verdict. The court denied the motion and the union appealed to the U.S. Court of Appeals, Eighth Circuit.

The court of appeals held that the evidence was insufficient to support the finding that the city and union conspired to deny the employee a promotion because of her sex. The employee failed to allege with particularity or to demonstrate with material facts that the city and union had agreed to violate her civil rights. Even if the union had known that the city discriminated against women and failed to take appropriate measures, that alone would have been insufficient to hold the union liable as a conspirator. The court of appeals reversed the district court's decision. *City of Omaha Employees Betterment Ass'n v. Omaha*, 883 F.2d 650 (8th Cir.1989).

A Connecticut police department employee was sent to the state police academy for training. During her training she had problems with her coordinator, and failed to pass enough courses to be certified. She was later discharged as a patrol officer by the board of police commissioners for her "bad attitude." The employee filed a grievance under the applicable collective bargaining agreement. She alleged that her dismissal was based on sex discrimination. The employee's labor association submitted the grievance to the Connecticut board of mediation and arbitration. The board found that the discharge was based on sex discrimination and that her coordinator disliked her. The board ordered her reinstated with no loss of pay or seniority. She would be allowed to return to the academy to complete her training under a different coordinator. The city applied to a Connecticut trial court to vacate the award. The state trial referee denied the application and the city appealed to the state appellate court. The Supreme Court of Connecticut transferred the appeal to its court for consideration.

The supreme court held that the arbitrators had the authority to order the employee back to the police academy to complete her training under a different coordinator. The court noted that the award did not order a non-party, the academy, to perform an act necessary to enforce the award. The arbitrators had not exceeded their powers by rendering a remedy that was enforceable only against the city. The supreme court found no error in the arbitrators' decision. *Town of East Haven v. AFSCME*, 561 A.2d 1388 (Conn.1989).

A school board employee worked as an elementary school teacher and received superior work evaluations. She received a master's degree and an educational specialist degree and achieved Kentucky's highest professional teacher rating. The state certified her as a qualifed elementary school principal and instructional supervisor. Upon receiving this rating the employee actively sought promotion to an administrative post. In a six year period in which nine administrative positions became available the school board hired men for each position. The employee filed a discrimination complaint with the U.S. Equal Employment Opportunity Commission (EEOC) and the Kentucky Human Rights Commission. Meanwhile, the school board employed a new superintendent who promoted the employee to one of the lowest paying administrative jobs in the school system. The employee continued to apply for better paying administrative positions. Of the four administrative positions which became available during the next three years, each was filled by a man less qualified than the employee. Following a successful probable cause determination by the EEOC, the employee filed a lawsuit in a federal district court. The court noted that the school board had failed to seriously consider the employee for any of the administrative positions she sought and that she was better qualified than the men hired. The school district failed to promote her because of her sex and was guilty of discrimination. The court awarded back pay to the employee from the point at which she obtained the state's highest teacher rating. The school board appealed to the U.S. Court of Appeals, Sixth Circuit, which affirmed the judgment but modified the damage award. The employee had shown unlawful discrimination and the school board had failed to show nondiscriminatory reasons for hiring men. The court modified the damages so that back pay was awarded from the date the employee actively began to seek a promotion. *Spears v. Bd. of Educ. of Pike County, Kentucky*, 843 F.2d 882 (6th Cir.1988).

A Minnesota woman, employed by a county assessor's office, attempted to reach the position of deputy assessor. She completed all the coursework necessary and received her certification in appraising. However, her supervisor refused to promote her, keeping her in the office and requiring her to do only clerical work. Eventually, she was allowed to do field work, but was not classified as a deputy assessor. Subsequently, several problems arose between the employee and her supervisor, and she initiated a complaint with the Minnesota Human Rights Department. Her complaint was dismissed, and she then sued in a Minnesota trial court, alleging sex discrimination in employment practices in violation of the Minnesota Human Rights Act. An advisory jury concluded that she had been discriminated against but the trial judge disagreed, finding no discrimination. The court of appeals affirmed, and the employee appealed to the Supreme Court of Minnesota.

The supreme court stated that the trial court should have used the three-part analysis presented in *McDonnell Douglas Corp. v. Green,* 411 U.S. 792 (1973) and subsequently followed in cases like *Texas Department of Community Affairs v. Burdine*, 450 U.S. 248 (1981). Since it could not determine if the trial court had in fact used that analysis, it reversed and remanded the case, ordering the trial court to explicitly outline its analytical procedure in arriving at its decision. Further, the court stated that even if the employee lost on her claim, she could not be liable for attorney's fees because such a liability would discourage people from bringing discrimination suits. *Sigurdson v. Isanti County*, 386 N.W.2d 715 (Minn.1986).

A Tennessee woman applied for an administrator's position at a county nursing home. She possessed a health care facilities license and had two-and-a-half years of experience as a nursing home administrator. After the interviews with the nursing home committee, it selected instead the current assistant administrator, a male, for the position even though he was not yet licensed. The woman applicant then sued the state, the county, the committee and various officials in a federal district court, asserting that she had been discriminated against on the basis of gender in violation of Title VII and 42 U.S.C. § 1983. The district court ruled in favor of the defendants, but refused to award them costs in defending the action, and both parties appealed to the U.S. Court of Appeals, Sixth Circuit.

The court of appeals first noted that the committee had probably preselected the male candidate for the position. However, such preselection does not violate Title VII when it is based on the candidate's qualifications and not on some prohibited basis. Further, there was little evidence to show that the reason for the committee's selection was gender-based. More likely, it had chosen the man out of a patronage system. Thus, the court determined that the woman applicant's claim had failed. The court also held that because the defendants had prevailed in the suit, a determination had to be made as to the extent of the appropriate attorney's fees. The court affirmed the district court's decision, holding the defendants not liable, but reversed and remanded on the question of attorney's fees. *Goostree v. State of Tennessee*, 796 F.2d 854 (6th Cir.1986).

A female Wisconsin attorney was hired by the Milwaukee office of the U.S. Department of Human Services' Office of Hearings and Appeals as an attorney advisor. She was to assist administrative law judges in drafting their decisions. However, less than a year later, she was discharged for poor work product, failure to return timely drafts of decisions, poor performance, failure to draft decisions as requested, and poor attitude. She then sued the office in a federal district court, alleging violations of Title VII. The case was tried before a magistrate, who ruled against her, and she appealed to the U.S. Court of Appeals, Seventh Circuit.

The court of appeals held that even though the employee had made out a prima facie case of discrimination, the office had set forth legitimate nondiscriminatory reasons for her discharge. She had thus been unable to ultimately prove that the office had discriminated against her. The court affirmed the magistrate's decision, and denied relief to the employee. *Germane v. Heckler*, 804 F.2d 366 (7th Cir.1986).

A female psychologist was employed by the Illinois Department of Mental Health and Developmental Disabilities. She sought a promotion to a higher pay level on two occasions, but was told that she needed a Ph.D. to receive the promotion. When she received her Ph.D., she asked for an audit so that she could be considered for promotion. However, in the audit, civil service personnel determined that because she did not supervise other psychologists she was not eligible for the promotion. Meanwhile, the department promoted four male psychologists, two without Ph.D.s. She then complained to the EEOC, received a right-to-sue letter, and sued the department in a federal district court under Title VII. The district court expressed doubts about the reasons given by the department for the nonpromotion, but held that the employee had failed to prove that the department's reasons were a pretext for discrimination. She appealed to the U.S. Court of Appeals, Seventh Circuit.

The appellate court agreed with the district court that the department had probably not given the real reason for its nonpromotion of the employee, but stated that, by itself, that was insufficient to show discrimination. The department could have engaged in its promotional process out of personal or political favoritism, a grudge, or an error it did not choose to admit to, but unless the reason for the nonpromotion was discrimination based, it was beyond the court's power to address it. The court thus affirmed the district court's decision. *Benzies v. Illinois Dep't of Mental Health*, 810 F.2d 146 (7th Cir.1987).

A Wisconsin school principal applied for an assistant superintendent position in the Madison school district. The principal was the only female among four applicants. She rated third by district criteria and was not selected for the position. She initiated sex discrimination proceedings against the district. She accused the district of failing to follow its own affirmative action plan. Shortly thereafter she applied for a curriculum development position within the school district. The assistant superintendent selected in the first employment matter conducted the interviews for the curriculum development position. The principal was not selected. The principal claimed that she was rejected for the first position because she was a woman and that her nonselection for the second position was in retaliation for her sex discrimination charges. The principal filed a lawsuit in a federal district court against the school district claiming violation of federal civil rights statutes. The district court ruled for the school district and the principal appealed to the U.S. Court of Appeals, Seventh Circuit, which affirmed the district court decision. The district did not violate its affirmative action plan by failing to hire the principal. Refusal to place an underqualified person in a vacant position does not constitute sex discrimination. The principal's due process rights were not violated because she had no property interest in either position. *Yatvin v. Madison Metropolitan School Dist.*, 840 F.2d 412 (7th Cir.1988).

A black female teacher at a North Carolina elementary school made an application to be promoted to assistant principal or principal. She was denied promotion and the positions were instead awarded to white job applicants. She then sued the school board in U.S. district court alleging that the board had failed to promote her because of her race and sex. The evidence showed that the teacher had more teaching certificates than the other applicants, had taught within the school system for a longer time and had consistently received satisfactory performance evaluations from her superiors. However, the district court agreed with the school board, finding that the white job applicants were more qualified than the black teacher because one had previously held the position of assistant principal and one had experience with computers. The U.S. Court of Appeals, Fourth Circuit, upheld the decision. The appeals court held that although Title VII may raise a presumption of discrimination, the board was able to convince the court that it had made its promotions based solely on ability. *Love v. Alamance County Bd. of Educ.*, 757 F.2d 1504 (4th Cir.1985).

In a Nebraska case, when a school district promoted a male accountant in the school district's business office over a female accountant, the latter sued on the grounds of sexual discrimination. A U.S. district court in Nebraska ruled that while the female had established a *prima facie* case of sexual discrimination, the school district had successfully satisfied its burden of showing that its decision to promote the male was based on legitimate, nondiscriminatory reasons. The record showed that objective and subjective testing and evaluations had been performed on the two candidates over a period of years and, presumably, prior to the time the position became open. In these tests and evaluations, the male had scored the same or higher in the critical categories. *Cummings v. School Dist. of City of Lincoln*, 508 F.Supp. 20 (D.Neb.1980).

A Georgia public school teacher, a white female, applied for two administrative vacancies in the school district. When both positions were eventually filled by men, she brought suit in federal district court under Title VII alleging that she had been discriminated against on the basis of sex. At trial, the superintendent of schools contended that although the teacher was qualified academically, she was lacking in subjective and tangible criteria such as leadership ability and a willingness to be cooperative and flexible. He testified that she "lacks interpersonal skills which are necessary for an administrator to have" and that "she is perceived as inflexible, overly aggressive, and abrasive." The trial court concluded that she would not have been appointed to any administrative position had she been a man, and therefore that the school board did not discriminate against her because of her sex. On appeal by the teacher, the U.S. Court of Appeals, Eleventh Circuit, noted that since the teacher had relied mainly on circumstantial evidence to raise an inference of discriminatory intent, "the employer need only articulate (not prove) a legitimate, nondiscriminatory reason for its actions." At that point, the burden was on the teacher to prove that the school board's actions had been undertaken for discriminatory reasons. Since the school board had proven that the teacher would not have been hired even if she were a man, the teacher could not meet her burden of proof and the decision of the district court in favor of the school board was upheld. *McCarthney v. Griffin-Spalding County Bd. of Educ.*, 791 F.2d 1549 (11th Cir.1986).

B. Equal Pay

Female guards at an Oregon county jail were paid substantially less than male guards at the same facility. The county eliminated the female section of the jail, transferred its prisoners to a neighboring county and terminated the employment of the female guards. The terminated guards sued the county in a federal district court under Title VII of the 1964 Civil Rights Act, 42 U.S.C. Section 2000e et seq., seeking backpay and alleging that they had been unlawfully paid unequal wages for substantially similar work as that performed by the male guards. The court held that the male guards supervised over ten times as many prisoners and did less clerical work than their female counterparts. It ruled that the females were not entitled to equal pay because they did not perform substantially similar work, and that the pay inequity was not attributable to sex discrimination. The court held that because the females had not met the standard of the 1963 Equal Pay Act, 29 U.S.C. Section 206(d), no Title VII action was possible. The female employees appealed to the U.S. Court of appeals, Ninth Circuit, which reversed, holding that alleged sex discrimination victims were entitled to Title VII protection. The county appealed to the U.S. Supreme Court.

The Court first noted that the case did not involve a comparable worth analysis, but was simply a sex discrimination case. It stated that the court of appeals had correctly ruled that Title VII wage discrimination claims could be brought in this situation, and that the female guards were not limited to remedies under the Equal Pay Act. Title VII by its terms barred sex-based wage discrimination but permitted differentials which could be justified under the Equal Pay Act. This included seniority, merit, quantity or quality of work or other bona fide factors. Title VII claims for sex-based wage discrimination were thus permissible. In this case, the county had evaluated the female guards' job worth at ninety-five percent of the male guards; yet had paid them only seventy percent as much. The court of appeals had correctly ruled that this presented a viable Title VII complaint for sex discrimination. *County of Washington v. Gunther*, 452 U.S. 161 (1981).

A female who coached girls' track and girls' tennis was paid substantially less than the males who coached boys' track and boys' tennis at the same school. As assistant coach of the girls' basketball team, she was paid less than the male assistant coach of the boys' track team. Another woman who coached girls' basketball, softball and volleyball was paid less than the male coaches of boys' basketball, baseball, and soccer. As assistant coach of the girls' track team she was paid less than the assistant coach of the boys' track team. The EEOC filed a lawsuit against the school district alleging that these practices violated the Equal Pay Act. After a U.S. district court ruled in favor of the EEOC the school district appealed. The U.S. Court of Appeals, Seventh Circuit, concluded that "[a]n employer cannot divide equal work into two job classifications that carry unequal pay, forbid women to compete for one of the classifications, and defend the resulting inequity in pay by reference to a factor other than the sex of the employees." The court of appeals affirmed the district court's decision that the Act had been violated with respect to the coaching of the following sports: 1) boys' and girls' track, 2) boys' and girls' tennis, and 3) boys' baseball and girls' softball. However, it reversed the district court's finding that the following comparisons could be made under the Act: 1) boys' soccer to girls' volleyball, 2) boys' soccer to girls' basketball, and 3) boys' track to girls' basketball. The court ruled that the coaching of these sports could not be said to require equal skill, effort and responsibility. *EEOC v. Madison Comm. Unit School Dist. No. 12*, 818 F.2d 577 (7th Cir.1987).

A female Illinois college graduate went to work for the state department of public health. Five years later, she was a supervisor and had more than doubled her salary. However, three male employees who worked under her made more than she did. She requested a salary adjustment, which was denied, and she then sued the department head in a federal district court, asserting that she had been discriminated against on the basis of sex. The district court granted summary judgment for the department head, and the employee appealed to the U.S. Court of Appeals, Seventh Circuit.

The court of appeals held that the fact that her male subordinates received more money then she did was suspicious enough to warrant a trial to determine if discrimination had been present. The court doubted that discrimination could be proven because the male subordinates did not do strictly the same work she did, and two of them were accountants. However, it determined that a trial should be held to uncover all the facts. It thus reversed the district court's grant of summary judgment, and remanded the case for further proceedings. *Riordan v. Kempiners*, 831 F.2d 690 (7th Cir.1987).

C. Sexual Harassment

A man and a woman were hired as Internal Revenue Service (IRS) trainees and were assigned to the same California office. The man later began to write "weird" letters to the woman. The woman became frightened and requested that her supervisor transfer her or the man. The supervisor then told the man that he was to have no contact with the woman, and later transferred him out of California. The man filed a grievance, and the IRS and the man's union settled on a transfer back to California. The woman then became "frantic," and requested a temporary transfer to be effective when the man returned. The man subsequently wrote another letter to the woman. After exhausting administrative remedies, the woman filed a sexual discrimination action against the IRS in a federal district court. Summary judgment was granted to the IRS, and the woman appealed to the U.S. Court of Appeals, Ninth Circuit.

A sexual discrimination claim can succeed upon a showing of a hostile environment. Under Equal Employment Opportunity Commission guidelines, this requires showing that an employee was subjected to unwelcome sexual conduct that was severe or pervasive enough to alter the conditions of employment or create an abusive working environment. The first issue for the court was whether the conduct was severe. The court disagreed with the standards of severity in other federal circuits, and wished to adopt a lower standard. To do this, the court set out a new legal standard; the severity of the conduct must be judged by the "reasonable woman" standard. The court found that the conduct in this case would be considered severe. The second issue was the determination of what actions needed to be taken by the IRS in order to shield itself from liability. The court stated that the remedy taken by the employer must be reasonably calculated to end the harassment without changing the status of the victim. Further, the employer must send a strong message of intolerance; transfer alone will not suffice. The employer's actions are also to be judged under the reasonable woman standard. The appeals court remanded this case for a determination of whether a reasonable woman would find that the man's mere presence would create a hostile environment. *Ellison v. Brady,* 924 F.2d 872 (9th Cir.1991).

After a female police officer began working in the Des Moines Police Department in 1981, she was assigned to work with two fellow male officers. The female officer complained to her superiors of sexually suggestive language and other sexual harassment from her two fellow officers, but no action was taken by them. She then filed a formal complaint with the internal affairs unit of the police department, which determined that the officers were guilty of conduct in violation of the Des Moines police department conduct code. Both officers were suspended and reassigned. The female officer was also reassigned but to an allegedly lower position. She then filed an administrative complaint with the Iowa Civil Rights Commission (ICRC) in which she alleged that the city had discriminated against her on the basis of her sex and in retaliation for her complaint. Subsequently, the ICRC issued the female officer a right to sue letter. She instituted this action in an Iowa trial court, which found for the female officer. The city of Des Moines appealed to the Supreme Court of Iowa.

In order to establish a valid claim of a sexually hostile work environment, it must be proven that 1) the officer belonged to a protected class, 2) the officer was subject to unwelcome sexual harassment, 3) the harassment was based on sex, 4) the harassment affected a condition of employment, and 5) the employer knew or should have known of the harassment and failed to take prompt action. The court determined that the female officer was subject to unwelcome harassment based on her sex because of the particularly lewd comments made by her fellow officers. The court also determined that since her only option was to quit working to escape the hostile environment, the harassment did affect a condition of employment. Finally, the court found that her reassignment to a less desirable job after her filing of a complaint was in retaliation for the formal complaint. The supreme court affirmed the trial court's decision. *Lynch v. City of Des Moines*, 454 N.W.2d 827 (Iowa 1990).

A captain in a Texas county sheriff's department received notice that he was accused of sexual harassment. The notice contained the acts and statement that made up the complaint, but did not include the names of the complainants. The department denied a request for the names and held a pretermination hearing which resulted in the captain's dismissal. The captain appealed to the civil service commission, which held a formal hearing. Again the county refused to disclose the complainants' names prior to their testimony. The hearing covered parts of twenty-two days, allowed the captain's lawyers to cross-examine the government's witnesses including four female complainants, and included the captain calling eighteen of his own witnesses. Both the commission and a later trial court upheld the dismissal. However, a Texas Court of Appeals reversed. The commission then appealed to the Texas Supreme Court.

At issue was whether the captain should have been given the names of the complainants either before the pretermination hearing or before the complainants took the stand at the commission's posttermination hearing. The nondisclosure of the complainants' names was found not to violate due process. The court noted the captain's defense was adequate and included cross-examination and ample time to prepare. Further, there were only eight women in the captain's department and the problems of surprise or nonpreparation were minimized. The government's interest included the flexibility to not report names, which would hopefully foster reporting of sexual harassment because the complainants would not fear harassment from coworkers. The court cited other cases which have held that supplying the names of accusers is an absolute minimum requirement of due process, and noted that it did not disagree with those cases but felt that the facts of this case were distinguishable. The captain's dismissal was upheld. *Bexar Cty. Sheriff's Civ. Serv. v. Davis*, 802 S.W.2d 659 (Tex.1990).

A female correctional officer at an Iowa reformatory received three discipline citations: for filing an inappropriate disciplinary report against an inmate, for being inattentive or sleeping while on guard duty, and for offering an inmate unrestricted access outside the reformatory by leaving two security gates unlocked. Following the gate incident she was discharged. She then sued the state and various officials in a federal district court, asserting a Title VII sex discrimination claim and a sexual harassment claim. The court found that she had been subjected to some unwelcome on-the-job sexual remarks, but that they were not severe enough to warrant a legal action. It further held that she had not been discriminated against on the basis of sex and dismissed her claims. She appealed to the U.S. Court of Appeals, Eighth Circuit.

The court of appeals noted that the state had articulated legitimate, nondiscriminatory reasons for the officer's discharge. Only after committing three serious breaches of security was she let go. Although some males seemed to have received more lenient treatment, others had received harsher treatment, for similar although not identical offenses. Accordingly, the court ruled that the record supported the district court's finding that the officer was discharged solely for legitimate business reasons unrelated to her sex. The court affirmed the district court's decision. *Minteer v. Auger*, 844 F.2d 569 (8th Cir.1988).

V. AFFIRMATIVE ACTION

Affirmative action plans will generally be upheld if they have been instituted to remedy some prior discrimination. The employers, however, must not set quotas or hire strictly minorities in their attempts to rectify past wrongs. A prospective employee's minority status may only be used as one factor in the hiring process.

In 1972, a federal district court determined that the Alabama Department of Public Safety had systematically excluded blacks from employment as state troopers in violation of the Fourteenth Amendment and issued a hiring quota order. By the early 1980's, there were still no blacks who had been promoted to the rank of corporal. The district court determined that the test used for promotions had an adverse impact on blacks and ordered the department to promote at least fifty percent blacks to the rank of corporal if qualified black candidates were available. It also ordered the department to submit a realistic schedule for the development of promotional procedures for all ranks above the entry level. The United States appealed the order, asserting that it violated the equal protection clause of the Fourteenth Amendment. The court of appeals affirmed the order and the question came before the U.S. Supreme Court.

The Supreme Court held that the one-black-for-one-white promotion requirement was permissible under the Fourteenth Amendment. There was a compelling governmental interest in eradicating the department's pervasive and continuing discriminatory exclusion of blacks. Further, the order provided for promotions only when openings were available and did not require gratuitous promotions. Also, the requirement could be waived if no qualified black troopers were available. Finally, the requirement was only a temporary measure and was contingent on the department's successful implementation of valid promotional procedures. Accordingly, the Court found that the requirement did not impose an unacceptable burden on whites and was thus constitutional. The Court affirmed the lower courts' rulings. *United States v. Paradise*, 480 U.S. 149, 107 S.Ct. 1053, 94 L.Ed.2d 203 (1987).

A California county transportation agency voluntarily adopted an affirmative-action plan. The plan allowed the agency to consider, as one factor, the sex of an applicant in making promotions. The long term goal of the plan was to achieve a workforce whose composition reflected the proportion of women and minorities in the area labor force. When a road dispatcher position opened up, the agency promoted one of the qualified female applicants. A male employee who was passed over sued the agency in a federal district court. The court found that the woman had been selected because of her sex and invalidated the agency's plan. The court of appeals reversed this decision, and the man further appealed the case to the U.S. Supreme Court.

The Supreme Court held that the agency had appropriately taken the woman's sex into account as one factor in determining that she be promoted. It found that the agency plan was flexible and presented a case-by-case approach to effecting a gradual improvement in the representation of women and minorities in the agency. Thus, the plan was fully consistent with Title VII. Even though the male candidate had shown a prima facie case of discrimination on the part of the agency, the agency had shown a nondiscriminatory rationale for its decision, namely the affirmative-action plan. Further, the Court noted that an employer need not point to its own prior discriminatory practices to justify its adoption of such a plan. It need only point to a conspicuous imbalance in traditionally segregated areas of employment. Since the plan had taken into account distinctions in qualifications to provide guidance, the agency had not merely engaged in blind hiring by the numbers. The Court affirmed the court of appeals' decision and upheld the affirmative-action plan. *Johnson v. Transportation Agency, Santa Clara County*, 480 U.S. 616, 107 S.Ct. 1442, 94 L.Ed.2d 615 (1987).

In 1974, the NAACP and seven black persons entered into consent decrees with an Alabama city and a county personnel board. The decrees stated that the city and board had practiced discriminatory employment practices in violation of Title VII and other civil rights statutes. They mandated an extensive remedial plan, including annual hiring and promotional goals for black firefighters. A federal district court approved the decrees, which were then challenged by the city firefighters' labor organization in a reverse discrimination lawsuit. The court ruled against the firefighters' association and its decision was affirmed by the U.S. Court of Appeals, Eleventh Circuit. A second group of white firefighters then sued the city and board in a federal district court, claiming that they had been denied promotions in favor of less qualified blacks. The district court dismissed their lawsuit, ruling that the city was required to promote blacks under the consent decree. The firefighters appealed to the Eleventh Circuit Court of Appeals, which ruled in favor of the firefighters. It found that they had not participated in the consent decrees and were bringing independent racial discrimination claims. The court rejected the doctrine of impermissible collateral attack, which had been used by other U.S. circuit courts to immunize parties participating in consent decrees from reverse discrimination complaints by nonparties. The U.S. Supreme Court agreed to hear the appeal of the city and a group of intervening black firefighters.

The Supreme Court noted that nonparties are not bound by judgments and decrees among parties to a lawsuit. Moreover, Rule 19(a) of the Federal Rules of Civil Procedure required mandatory joinder where parties to the lawsuit had inconsistent obligations to persons claiming an interest in the action. Litigants are presumed to know the nature and scope of their litigation, and they should bear the burden of bringing in additional parties when required. The Court rejected the argument that this burden would discourage civil rights litigation because of the perceived difficulty in identifying numerous adverse claimants. This difficulty was an effect of the broad remedial relief that resulted from consent decrees in racial discrimination cases. Parties seeking the aid of courts to change existing employment policies and employers were best able to bear the burden of identifying potentially affected third parties. The Supreme Court affirmed the court of appeals' decision. *Martin v. Wilks*, 490 U.S. 755, 109 S.Ct. 2180, 104 L.Ed.2d 835 (1989).

The U.S. Supreme Court ruled on the validity of an affirmative action (or "affirmative retention") plan implemented by the Jackson, Michigan, board of education, which called for the layoff of nonminority teachers with greater seniority than some minority teachers. The case arose after the Jackson board of education entered into a collective bargaining agreement with the local teachers' union. Article XII of the agreement read as follows: "In the event that it becomes necessary to reduce the number of teachers through layoff from employment by the Board, teachers with the most seniority in the district shall be retained, except that at no time will there be a greater percentage of minority personnel laid off than the current percentage of minority personnel employed at the time of the layoff. In no event will the number given notice of possible layoff be greater than the number of positions to be eliminated. Each teacher so affected will be called back in reverse order for positions for which he is certificated maintaining the above minority balance." The district court ruled that the importance of providing minority teachers as "role models" for minority students as a remedy for past "societal discrimination" justified the layoff provision. The U.S. Court of Appeals, Sixth Circuit, affirmed the district court's decision and the nonminority teachers appealed to the Supreme Court. By a 5-4 vote the Supreme Court reversed the lower court decisions and held that the nonminority teachers had been unfairly discriminated against in violation of the Equal Protection Clause. A total of six different opinions were filed in the case as the justices failed to agree on an appropriate standard of review for government affirmative action programs.

The school board's argument that race-based layoffs were necessary to remedy the effects of societal discrimination was rejected by the majority, which held that clear and convincing evidence must be presented that the government entity in question had engaged in past racial discrimination.

Similarly, the Supreme Court rejected the "role model" justification for retaining minority teachers (i.e., minority children benefit from having minority teachers) on the ground that such a theory would allow racially based layoffs long after they were needed to cure the ills of past discrimination. The majority held that even if the Jackson school board had sufficient justification for engaging in remedial or "benign" racial discrimination, layoff of white teachers was too drastic and intrusive a remedy. While hiring goals and promotion policies favorable to minorities are acceptable under the Equal Protection Clause, the actual laying off of a certain race of employees was held to be unconstitutional. "Denial of future employment is not as intrusive as loss of an existing job," observed the Court. The lower court rulings were reversed. *Wygant v. Jackson Bd. of Educ.*, 476 U.S. 267, 106 S.Ct. 1842, 90 L.Ed.2d 260 (1986).

In 1969, persons seeking employment with the Los Angeles County Fire Department were required to take a written examination as well as a physical test. Applicants were ranked according to their performance on the tests and selected for interviews on the basis of their scores. Those who passed the oral interviews were placed on a hiring-eligible list. Because blacks and Hispanics did poorly on the written exams, this method resulted in disparate impact on minority hiring. In 1972, the county administered a new test it had designed which was graded on a pass-fail basis solely to screen out illiterates. It then intended to select 500 passing applicants at random to interview. However, prior to doing so, the county was sued because its random selection process was violative of Civil Service regulations. A hiring freeze was instituted, and as a result of the ensuing manpower shortage, the county next sought to use a prior graded test to meet the needs of the fire department. At this point, a class action suit was filed on behalf of present and future black and Mexican-American applicants in a federal district court. It was alleged that the hiring procedure violated 42 U.S.C. § 1981. The court found violations had occurred and ordered affirmative-action efforts. The court of appeals affirmed this decision, and the U.S. Supreme Court agreed to hear the case. However, by the time the case reached the Court, the district court had found an efficient and nonrandom way to screen applicants and increase minority representation in the fire department. Because the Supreme Court determined that a successful system was being used and the chances of reverting to the old invalidated system were now very slim, it held that the case should be dismissed on grounds of mootness. Accordingly, it dismissed the case. *County of Los Angeles v. Davis*, 440 U.S. 625, 99 S.Ct. 1379, 59 L.Ed.2d 642 (1979).

The Chicago Fire Department (CFD) implemented an affirmative action plan where nonrank-order minorities were promoted based upon a goal of promoting twenty percent black and five percent Hispanic firefighters until a new promotion examination could be devised to reduce the discriminatory effect upon minorities taking the exam. White firefighters sued the CFD in a federal district court alleging a violation of the Equal Protection Clause of the U.S. Constitution. Both parties moved for summary judgment.

The Equal Protection Clause provides that every citizen shall enjoy "equal protection of the laws." Specifically, the white firefighters contended that the CFD did not have a compelling governmental interest to justify an affirmative action plan and that the plan was not narrowly tailored to remedy the effects of past discrimination. The court, however, disagreed, stating that the examinations had a severe, discriminatory impact upon minority candidates and therefore could not be used to rank candidates for promotion. Further, the past promotion practices that had been unfair to minorities provided a sufficient governmental interest to justify an affirmative action plan. The court also held that the plan was narrowly tailored to remedy the effects of the past discriminatory practices as it only provided for qualified firefighters to be promoted and it did not excessively burden white candidates. The court granted summary judgment to the CFD. *Chicago Firefighters v. Washington*, 736 F.Supp. 923 (N.D.Ill.1990).

The New Jersey Department of Civil Service administered tests to rank candidates for promotion to the position of fire captain. The United States filed suit against the state alleging that it was engaging in race and national origin discrimination with respect to hiring and promotion practices. The federal district court did not find discriminatory practices, but ordered the state to take affirmative action to increase substantially the proportion of blacks and Hispanics in the fire departments and to conduct analyses of all promotional classifications to ensure that they were job-related. The United States then determined that the tests used by the state seemed to exhibit adverse impact and sued to enforce the prior judicial order. The court held against the state which appealed to the U.S. Court of Appeals, Third Circuit.

The court of appeals found that the tests employed by the state were not appropriate for ranking candidates because they did not adequately measure necessary skills. The court prohibited the state from making appointments to the position of fire captain based on the invalidated exam's eligibility lists. Further, it required the state to rotate acting captains until a new examination process could be created and administered. The court affirmed the district court's decision. *Vulcan Pioneers v. New Jersey Dep't of Civil Service*, 832 F.2d 811 (3d Cir.1987).

The Michigan Department of Treasury posted an opening for an Auditor X position. Several employees qualified for the position after oral and written examinations. A male candidate received a "highly qualified" rating, but the department hired a "qualified" female for the position under its affirmative action plan. The male candidate sued the department in a Michigan trial court, asserting that he had been discriminated against on the basis of sex. The court ruled that because the department had not gotten the plan approved by the Civil Rights Commission, it was void. The court ordered that the man be appointed to the position in a summary disposition, and the department appealed to the Court of Appeals of Michigan.

The appellate court, while noting that the department should have had its affirmative action plan approved, determined that the failure to seek approval of the plan did not void it. Instead, the failure just meant that the male candidate was allowed to bring the lawsuit. The court could then make a determination as to whether there was a valid reason for the presumptively discriminatory action. Since the state had an affirmative duty to eradicate the effects of past discrimination, there was a factual issue for the lower court to decide. The court reversed the trial court's decision and remanded the case to the lower court to consider the department's justification for its action. *Ruppal v. Dep't of Treasury*, 413 N.W.2d 751 (Mich.App.1987).

An employee of the Michigan Department of Treasury applied for a promotion to an Auditor IX position. He had taken two tests to be eligible for this position. He scored "highly qualified" on the written exam and was the highest scored applicant in the oral examination. A female coworker also applied for the position. She scored a "qualified" on the written test and never received her oral exam score. The female coworker was hired to fill the position. The department promoted her on the basis of her sex pursuant to an affirmative action plan which was designed to rectify the underrepresentation of woman and minorities in upper level positions within the department. However, the plan was not approved by the Civil Rights Commission (CRC). The male employee then sued the department challenging the employer's affirmative action plan in a trial court. The trial court found for the male employee, and the department appealed to the Court of Appeals of Michigan.

On appeal, the issue was whether a voluntary affirmative action plan which did not have the prior approval of the CRC was automatically invalid. In *Ruppal v. Department of Treasury* (see above), a panel of the Michigan appellate court held that noncompliance with the CRC did not render a voluntary affirmative action plan void. The *Ruppal* court reasoned that to find an unapproved plan completely void ignores the overall purpose of the Civil Rights Act and fails to take into account the public employer's affirmative duty under the U.S. Constitution. In another decision, however, *Van Dam v. Civil Service Board of Grand Rapids*, 162 Mich.App. 135, 412 N.W.2d 260 (1987), a panel of this court held that an affirmative action plan for which no CRC approval had been sought was void. The *Van Dam* court found that the language of the Civil Rights Act was clear and unambiguous and that an affirmative action plan may be implemented only if prior commission approval is given. Rejecting the *Ruppal* court's decision and accepting the *Van Dam* reasoning, the court concluded that the affirmative action plan was void and affirmed the lower court's decision. *Victorson v. Department of the Treasury*, 454 N.W.2d 256 (Mich.App.1990).

In 1974, a Michigan city implemented an affirmative action plan to hire more minorities and women. However, the plan was ineffective due to hiring freezes. In 1980, the police department laid off seventeen police officers with the agreement that they would be recalled by seniority before any recruiting of new officers. In 1982, the city and the police union entered into an agreement that permitted the department to employ one minority applicant from an affirmative action list for every recalled officer. The laid off officers instituted an action in a federal district court. The court granted summary judgment to the police department and the officers appealed to the U.S. Court of Appeals, Sixth Circuit.

The appellate court determined that an affirmative action program must have convincing proof of prior discrimination to be constitutional. The court noted that no recorded complaint had been lodged by any local, state or federal administrative agency charging the police department with overt discrimination in hiring practices. The statistical evidence offered was insufficient to justify the plan. Therefore, the court reversed the trial court's decision and found the affirmative action plan void. *Long v. City of Saginaw*, 911 F.2d 1192 (6th Cir.1990).

A male employee of the Michigan Department of Transportation (MDOT) filed a discrimination suit when a female employee was promoted to the position of property specialist in compliance with an affirmative action plan. A U.S. district court sought to determine if there was a need for the affirmative action plan, and if the plan "unduly trammeled" the rights of the male workforce.

Women were currently underrepresented at MDOT and there were no female employees holding the position of property specialist. The court looked to the current workforce of real estate salespersons (the nongovernment job most closely related to property specialist), and from that was able to discern that a need existed for the plan. Because the nongovernment workforce was forty-eight per cent female and fifty-two percent male, there should have been some female employees in the government position. The court next looked at the male's rights. The type of plan used by MDOT included "augmented certification." Augmented certification requires separating all candidates into one of three categories: unqualified, qualified, and highly qualified. When a particular group, in this case women, is underrepresented in the highly qualified group, members from the qualified group are added to the highly qualified group for consideration. During consideration there are no affirmative action requirements. The court found that this plan did not "unduly trammel" the male employee's chance for employment and promotion. Further, there was evidence that the appointed woman was preferred to the male employee after the interview process. The court dismissed the complaint. *Conlin v. Blanchard*, 745 F.Supp. 413 (E.D. Mich.1990).

Eleven minority present and former employees of the New York City Transit Police Department who had been subjected to one or more internal disciplinary proceedings sued the transit authority and various officials under Title VII and 42 U.S.C. § 1981, alleging claims of intentional employment discrimination. Sixty-eight percent of the officers were white and the rest were minorities. Of the disciplinary citations issued which were in question, whites received 58% and minorities 40%. The federal district judge found no racially motivated disciplinary procedures, but did conclude that intentional discrimination existed in the initiation of disciplinary proceedings. It ordered the transit authority to create new rules addressing racial favoritism on the issuance of disciplinary citations. The transit authority appealed to the U.S. Court of Appeals, Second Circuit.

The appellate court found that the district court's conclusions were clearly erroneous. No evidence of discrimination existed in the statistics shown regarding whites versus minorities. Further, the court noted that the transit authority had instituted affirmative-action and minority recruitment programs which were significant indicators of nondiscriminatory treatment. Because the court could not find support in the record for the district court's holding of intentional discrimination, it reversed that decision. *Woodbury v. New York City Transit Authority*, 832 F.2d 764 (2d Cir.1987).

The Florida Governor's Council on Indian Affairs (FGCIA) hired a non-Indian woman as a staff assistant. The following year, both acting directors resigned and she assumed the task of running the council office. She ran the office for three years until the board of directors voted to change its staff structure. The board determined that it wanted only Indians to run Indian programs, and accordingly voted to replace the woman as director with an Indian. She then sought administrative relief, and when an indefinite stay was granted, she successfully sued in a federal district court. The decision was reversed by the court of appeals on immunity grounds, and the administrative proceeding was resumed. The hearing officer found that she was a victim of race discrimination and recommended she be reinstated with backpay. The board of directors rejected the finding and the woman appealed to the District Court of Appeal of Florida.

The appellate court held that even though the law provided for affirmative action programs for Indians, it also intended to allow preferential treatment for women. Thus, she was just as protected as an Indian or other minority would be. Since she was a member of a protected class and the better qualified applicant, and since the FGCIA failed to state why it rejected these facts, the court ordered that the woman be reinstated with full backpay. *Tuveson v. Florida Governor's Council on Indian Affairs*, 495 So.2d 790 (Fla.App.1st Dist.1986).

Three separate employment discrimination actions filed in an Atlanta federal district court were consolidated so that the court could determine the validity of entry-level tests used by a city and a state personnel board to screen applicants for firefighting and police officer positions. The court determined that the tests were discriminatory in violation of Title VII. The court then approved two consent decrees which provided remedial schemes for the hiring and promotion of blacks. Seven white male firefighters sued to prevent the enforcement of the consent decrees on the grounds that the decrees would discriminate against them. The city and personnel board admitted they had made race conscious promotion and employment decisions, but asserted that they were lawful because they were in compliance with the consent decrees. The district court entered a judgment for the city and personnel board and appeal was taken to the U.S. Court of Appeals, Eleventh Circuit.

The court of appeals held that the firefighters were not bound by the consent decrees which had been issued. In fact, their claim of reverse discrimination did not even arise until the consent decrees took effect and they were denied promotions. The court thus reversed the district court's decision and remanded the case to allow the firefighters to bring their discrimination claims. *Birmingham Reverse Discrimination Employment Litigation*, 833 F.2d 1492 (11th Cir.1987).

A Virginia city posted a notice announcing three vacancies in the rank of major within the police department. Eight captains were considered for the three openings, seven of whom were white. The eighth candidate was black and finished last in a performance test. Nonetheless, he was promoted to major ahead of several of the white captains. One of the white officers sued the city and various officials under 42 U.S.C. § 1983 in a federal district court, which ruled in his favor. The city then appealed to the U.S. Court of Appeals, Fourth Circuit.

The court of appeals found that the black officer had been qualified for the position of major and that his race had been only a factor in his promotion. The evidence clearly showed that the director of public safety had on previous occasions promoted officers "out of order" according to the test rankings. Further, there would be no need for the city to consider eight candidates for the three spots if they could only promote the top three. The court recognized that there were other legitimate factors besides just the test score to be considered in making the promotions. The black candidate, for instance, had been an acting major for more than a year, and this experience was another reason the director had chosen to promote him. The court thus determined that the city's promotion for the first time of a qualified black officer to a top level policy-making position to benefit a city whose population was approximately fifty percent black was legitimate because the promotion had not been primarily racially based. The white officer failed to show that discrimination was a motivating factor, and the court therefore reversed the district court's decision and upheld the promotion. *Talbert v. City of Richmond*, 648 F.2d 925 (4th Cir.1981).

In 1973, the federal government filed a Title VII civil rights action against the Chicago Police Department, claiming that its hiring and promotion practices discriminated against black and hispanic officers. A federal district court ordered the department to hire forty percent of its sergeants from eligible black and hispanic officers. The lawsuit went through a series of appeals to the U.S. Court of Appeals, Seventh Circuit, which approved a minority promotion quota of twenty-five percent for minorities and five percent for women. In 1986, the city informed the district court that it was making eighty promotions, including fifty-six white males. While the fifty-sixth rated white male applicant was awaiting promotion, the city found an error in the rating computation of the fifty-seventh rated white male and placed him ahead of the fifty-sixth rated officer on the promotion list. The fifty-sixth rated officer intervened in the discrimination lawsuit, claiming that he had been passed over for promotion because of the city's failure to comply with the court-ordered quota. He also claimed that the city was required to notify him of the error on the fifty-seventh rated officer's status. The district court ruled for the fifty-sixth rated officer and the city appealed to the Court of Appeals, Seventh Circuit.

The court ruled that the officer had no property or liberty interest in a promotion to sergeant. The Chicago Municipal Code gave the city authority to choose from among the five highest rated applicants for promotion. Thus, the city had the right to promote the fifty-sixth rated officer or any of the next four who were in line for promotion. Because the officer ratings were based in part upon subjective performance ratings and the rankings were always subject to change, no candidate had a right to promotion. There was no evidence that the complaining officer's total score was higher than that of the fifty-seventh rated officer. Nor had the city created any property interest by publishing the rankings. The appeals court reversed the district court's decision. *U.S. v. City of Chicago*, 869 F.2d 1033 (7th Cir.1989).

The city of Detroit sought to increase the number of blacks in its police force. Because of widespread alienation of black residents from the police department and the fear of a recurrence of civil disturbances such as the tragic occurrences of 1967, it instituted an affirmative action plan. Essentially, the plan required a minimum exam score in promotion tests and then allowed for individualized selection of officers for promotion. Further, it modified the entry level exams to compensate for racial bias inherent in the written tests. The police officers' association sued the city in a federal district court, alleging that the affirmative action plan violated Title VII because the city had not previously discriminated against blacks so it could not undertake a race-conscious remedy now. The district court agreed with the association and issued an injunction to prevent a continuation of the affirmative action plan. The city then appealed to the U.S. Court of Appeals, Sixth Circuit.

The court of appeals held that Title VII did not require past discrimination to justify an affirmative action plan. Further, it noted that the statistical evidence pointed to statutory violations and that prior discrimination had almost certainly been present. It could find no reason for the statistical disparity other than an intent to systematically exclude blacks. Even if discriminatory acts which did not give rise to legal liability were present, a voluntary remedial affirmative action plan could be initiated. The court also held that it was unnecessary for the persons receiving preferential treatment to show more than that they were within a general class of persons likely to have been discriminated against. The city's legitimate interest in having its police force reflect the makeup of its community should have been given greater weight by the district court. The court reversed the district court's ruling and remanded the case for further consideration of constitutional issues. *Detroit Police Officers' Ass'n v. Young*, 608 F.2d 671 (1979).

Two rejected black applicants for firefighter positions in an Ohio city filed a suit in federal district court seeking affirmative relief for past discriminatory practices and asking for injunctive relief on their employment rejections. The district court eventually entered a consent decree that both parties agreed to in order to hire and promote minorities in proportion to the community. Even though the city denied it had engaged in discriminatory acts, it conceded that certain tests presented the appearance of past discrimination. One of the sections of the consent decree dealt with promotions and required every sixth vacancy in the rank of lieutenant to be "double-filled." The firefighters' union opposed the order and sued to prevent its enforcement. The district court required compliance with the consent decree, and the union appealed to the U.S. Court of Appeals, Sixth Circuit.

The appellate court held that "double-filling" was an allowable means of achieving greater racial balance. Essentially, on each sixth lieutenancy that opened up, a new position was created by the city and the highest ranked minority was given that position. This way, no whites lost seniority or were skipped over because the positions created were new and would not exist but for the minorities. Since this was not a quota system and since the consent decree was being correctly complied with, the court held that it was valid as a narrowly tailored method to furthering a compelling governmental interest. The court affirmed the district court's decision. *Youngblood v. Dalzell*, 804 F.2d 360 (6th Cir.1986).

A white Virginia woman worked for the Federal Aviation Administration (FAA) and applied for a specialist position along with eighteen other applicants. The applicants were interviewed and the top five were referred to the selecting official. He selected two black women for the openings even though one did not have a current required certificate at the time of her selection. The white applicant sued under Title VII in a federal district court, which dismissed her complaint. She then appealed to the U.S. Court of Appeals, Fourth Circuit.

The appellate court determined that the evidence sufficiently presented a question of fact as to whether the employee had been discriminated against. There was evidence of a subjective interviewing process, and there were indications that the black uncertified applicant had been previously promoted to a temporary position ahead of some other employees who were not even notified of the opening. The court thus ruled that the possibility of discrimination was present, and reversed and remanded the case to the district court. *Lucas v. Dole*, 835 F.2d 532 (4th Cir.1987).

A group of senior New York parole officers sued the state's parole division, claiming that it had instituted an affirmative action plan which violated their constitutional rights. The plan was instituted because the parole division believed that women and minorities were underrepresented in positions outside of the New York City area. Although parole officers were hired on a state-wide basis, they were not able to select their assigned locations.

At the time the affirmative action plan was instituted, there was a marked demographic disparity between parole officers who worked in New York City and those who worked in the rest of the state. Women and minorities comprised less than twelve percent of all state parole officers, but comprised over forty percent of New York City officers. The affirmative action plan made seniority a factor in reassignment, but also took into consideration race and gender. Priority for reassignment was previously based solely upon seniority. Senior employees generally requested reassignment from New York City to upstate or Long Island locations. A federal district court found that the plan was constitutional and granted the division's motion for summary judgment. The employees appealed to the U.S. Court of Appeals, Second Circuit.

The appeals court ruled that the statistical evidence was insufficient to provide an inference that the division engaged in past discriminatory practices. However, the court affirmed the district court's determination that the aggrieved employees' request for summary judgment in the district court was properly denied. They had presented no evidence that past discrimination was not a factor contributing to the imbalance of women and minorities throughout the parole division. The district court had correctly ruled that the plan was a constitutional attempt to integrate its workforce. Despite the affirmative action provisions, one-half of the reassignments were still to be made on the basis of seniority. On remand, the parole division would not have to justify the constitutionality of the plan, but would be required to establish that the demographic disparity was the result of past discrimination. *Barhold v. Rodriguez*, 863 F.2d 233 (2d Cir.1988).

The Tennessee Valley Authority (TVA) employed a research chemist of Chinese descent. She held a Ph.D. in an applicable field of study and had five years of experience. The TVA had adopted an affirmative action plan targeting vacancies for women or minorities because of their underrepresentation in agricultural sciences and engineering. The plan did not contain any provisions governing termination during cutbacks. Four years after the chemist was hired, the TVA suffered budget cuts and was forced to reduce its workforce. The chemist was designated as the least experienced researcher in her department and was fired. She filed a sex and race discrimination charge with the TVA's internal equal opportunity office. The office found that she was terminated for legitimate, nondiscriminatory reasons and its findings were adopted by the Equal Employment Opportunity Commission (EEOC).

The chemist sued the TVA in a federal district court, alleging sex discrimination in retaliation for her complaints. The court ruled that the TVA had violated its own affirmative action plan and, as a result, it had violated Title VII. The court relied on *Johnson v. Transportation Agency*, 480 U.S. 616 (1987), in which the U.S. Supreme Court found an employer was required to adhere to its own affirmative action plan despite its voluntary adoption. The TVA appealed to the U.S. Court of Appeals, Eleventh Circuit. On appeal, the TVA argued that its plan concerned only hiring practices and not termination practices. The chemist argued that regardless of the plan's specific provisions, Title VII created an affirmative action obligation on all federal departments. The court ruled that *Johnson* did not make deviations from voluntary affirmative action plans a Title VII violation. Title VII required a showing of discrimination in order to prove a violation. Failure to follow an affirmative action plan by itself was insufficient. The appeals court reversed the district court's decision. *Liao v. Tennessee Valley Authority*, 867 F.2d 1366 (11th Cir.1989).

A white New York man took the state civil service examination for legal assistants. After the examination results were certified, a class action suit was brought on behalf of blacks and Hispanics who had taken the test. They alleged discrimination in the testing and grading of the examinations. The court entered a consent decree, which invalidated the test results and required new selection procedures providing for equal employment opportunities. The man took the new legal assistant examination as well as a civil service examination for beverage control investigator trainee. Although the man remained on the eligible employment list, he was not hired. He sued the state civil service department in a New York trial court, alleging that the governor's executive order, which imposed affirmative action requirements on state agencies, was improper because appointments were based on sex, race and ethnic background rather than merit and fitness. The court granted the man's motion for summary judgment. The civil service department then appealed to the New York Supreme Court, Appellate Division.

The appellate division court found that the trial court had improperly interpreted the executive order as having implemented an affirmative action program where merit and fitness were judged by sex, race or ethnic background. The executive order mandated only permissible executive affirmative action to enlarge pools of persons eligible for employment based on discrimination-free merit selection. The executive order did not make reference to quotas or preferential treatment in hiring practices. Rather, it mandated programs to ensure "full and equal employment opportunity" which, in the absence of any reference to hiring practices, referred merely to expanding the pool of applicants. The appellate division court reversed the trial court's decision. *Hase v. NYS Civil Serv. Dep't*, 554 N.Y.S.2d 387 (A.D.3d Dep't 1989).

An Indian part-time tutor-counselor learned that federal funds had been made available to fund a full-time tutor-counselor position. The funding was made under a federal grant with express conditions that the district utilize the best available talent. The school district then advertised for applicants, stating that "Indian preference" would be given. The Indian teacher applied but a non-Indian with better credentials won the job. The Indian applicant sued, declaring the Indian preference should have raised him above all other candidates regardless of their qualifications. The Washington Supreme Court held that the mandates of the federal grant required that the best available talent be hired. The school district had attempted to give effect to the right of Indian preference. However, it was required to hire the best available talent even if that talent was possessed by a non-Indian. *Johnson v. Cent. Valley School Dist.*, 645 P.2d 1088 (Wash.1982).

VI. RELIGIOUS DISCRIMINATION

In a U.S. Supreme Court case, a Connecticut high school teacher sued his school district under Title VII. He belonged to a church which required members to refrain from secular employment during designated holy days. This required the teacher to miss approximately six school days each year for religious purposes. The district's collective bargaining agreement allowed only three days of paid leave for religious observation. The agreement also allowed three days paid leave for "necessary personal business" which, the district said, could not be used for religious purposes. The teacher took either unauthorized, unpaid leave for the extra three religious days he required, scheduled his hospital visits on church holidays, or was forced to work on those holidays. He repeatedly asked to be granted permission to use three days of his "necessary personal business" leave for his religious purposes. He also offered to pay for a substitute teacher if the school board would pay him for the extra days that he missed. These alternatives were turned down by the school board. When all administrative alternatives were exhausted, he filed a lawsuit alleging that the school board's policy regarding "necessary personal business" leave was discriminatory on the basis of religion. A U.S. district court dismissed the teacher's lawsuit and he appealed. The U.S. Court of Appeals, Second Circuit, said that the school board was bound to accept one of the teacher's proposed solutions unless "that accommodation causes undue hardship on the employer's conduct of his business." On appeal, the U.S. Supreme Court modified the appellate court's decision. It decided that the school district was not required to accept the teacher's proposals even if acceptance would not result in "undue hardship." The school board was only bound to offer a fair and reasonable accommodation of the teacher's religious needs. The bargaining agreement policy of allowing three days paid leave for religious purposes, but excluding additional days of "necessary personal business" leave if needed for religious purposes, would *not* be reasonable, explained the Court, if paid leave was provided "for all purposes *except* religious ones." Because none of the lower courts had decided whether "necessary personal business" leave policy had been administered fairly in the past, the case was remanded for a determination of that question. *Ansonia Bd. of Educ. v. Philbrook*, 479 U.S. 60, 107 S.Ct. 367, 93 L.Ed.2d 305 (1986).

The Minnesota Supreme Court found the St. Paul School District liable for damages in a discrimination suit arising out of the district's failure to promote a Jewish teacher despite his outstanding qualifications. The teacher had been employed by the district for twenty-four years and had for nineteen years repeatedly applied for administrative positions. The teacher had successfully completed an administrator internship program conducted by the district to give minorities a chance to gain administrative experience, had received a specialist's degree in educational administration and had received letters of recommendation from his supervisors stating his qualifications to be superior to those of other applicants. In reversing a district court which found no inference of discrimination, the Minnesota Supreme Court said the teacher had presented a *prima facie* case of discrimination, thus shifting the burden of proof to the school district to show why its actions were not discriminatory. The school district offered absolutely no evidence to show that its repeated failure to promote this teacher was not discriminatory. *Kaster v. Indep. School Dist. No. 625*, 284 N.W.2d 362 (Minn.1979).

VII. EMPLOYER DEFENSES

A. Bona Fide Occupational Qualifications

A firefighter began work for a Wisconsin fire department in 1949 and rose to the post of assistant chief, which he held until 1978 when he was involuntarily retired. The city maintained a compulsory retirement age of fifty-five for all protective service employees, including assistant fire chief. The city notified the employee that he would have to retire and it later denied his application for an extension of employment. The employee brought an unsuccessful administrative appeal with the Equal Employment Opportunity Commission and then filed an age discrimination lawsuit against the city in a federal district court, charging that his forced retirement violated the Age Discrimination in Employment Act (ADEA). The city argued that the age fifty-five compulsory retirement did not violate the ADEA because the age restriction was a bona fide occupational qualification (BFOQ). It also argued that the ADEA was unconstitutional in its application to state and local governments. The federal magistrate appointed by the district court found that the employee was in excellent physical and mental health and that the department made no claim that he was personally incapable of performing fire department duties. The magistrate held for the employee and awarded him damages. However, the employee was required to deduct his unemployment and pension benefit income from the damage award. The magistrate also refused to award damages for pain and suffering, holding that these damages were precluded by the ADEA. The city appealed to the U.S. Court of Appeals, Seventh Circuit, arguing that the magistrate had incorrectly held that age fifty-five was not a BFOQ for firefighters.

The court of appeals noted that the ADEA made age discrimination against persons between the ages of forty and seventy illegal, except where a BFOQ existed. Under the ADEA, compulsory retirement policies were required to be rational and reasonably necessary to the operation of the business of the department. Unlike federal employers, which were subject to direct regulation by the Congress, municipalities were required to show strong evidence in support of their policies. Thus, the city had no legitimate argument that it was bound to obey a state mandatory retirement at fifty-five requirement based on a similar law for federal firefighters. The court held that although Wisconsin law stated that the "normal retirement date" was age fifty-five, individual municipalities were entitled to extend employment beyond that age. State laws were not presumptively invalid in the face of an ADEA challenge. In order to prevail on a BFOQ defense, an employer was required to show that the age qualification was reasonably related to an essential business operation and also to demonstrate that there was either a factual basis for drawing the age limit based on inability to perform job duties, or that an individualized job fitness determination was impossible or impracticable. Economic factors were not a legitimate basis for establishing a BFOQ defense. Because the city had failed to show any legitimate justification for not rehiring firefighters at age fifty-five, the employee was entitled to bring his ADEA claim and the court affirmed the magistrate's ruling. The court also upheld the damage award. *Orzel v. City of Wauwatosa,* 697 F.2d 743 (7th Cir.1983).

A Wisconsin women's maximum security prison promoted its treatment director to the position of superintendent. She then began discussions with her superiors and personnel regarding the prison's staffing needs. She felt that many of the positions at the prison should be staffed only by female correctional officers. Ultimately, her plan was adopted and three male officers were reassigned with no loss in pay. They were unhappy with the demotions and sued the superintendent and the department of health and social services in a federal district court, alleging sex discrimination in violation of Title VII of the Civil Rights Act of 1964. The district court found that the department and supervisor had not established a valid bona fide occupational qualification (BFOQ) to justify discriminating against males and ordered the male officers reinstated at their old positions. The defendants appealed to the U.S. Court of Appeals, Seventh Circuit.

The court of appeals first stated that sex discrimination would be valid only when the essence of the business operation would be undermined by not hiring members of one sex exclusively. So long as it was reasonably necessary to the normal operation of the prison, a classification based on sex would be upheld as a valid BFOQ. The court then noted that because rehabilitation of the female inmates was essential to the "business" of running the prison, and because the superintendent and department had believed female correctional officers were reasonably necessary to achieve that goal, a valid BFOQ had been demonstrated. However, the court noted that this holding was narrow in scope and based on the superintendent's professional expertise and experience and that the decision was not intended to open the way for sex discrimination. In most cases, no valid BFOQ could be demonstrated. The court reversed the district court's decision and remanded the case for a full consideration of the superintendent's decision to be certain the BFOQ was valid. *Torres v. Wisconsin Dep't of Health and Social Services*, 859 F.2d 1253 (7th Cir.1988).

In a companion case to *EEOC v. Kentucky State Police Dep't*, the U.S. Court of Appeals, Sixth Circuit, struck down the Tennessee Wildlife Resources Agency's mandatory age fifty-five retirement policy. The agency was responsible for licensing and enforcing fish and game laws. Duties of its enforcement officers included investigating violations and arresting violators. Tennessee law allowed extensions of the age limit without testing for physical fitness. Evidence indicated that some officers received extensions without regard to job performance or physical abilities. Some of the extensions were granted on the basis of the employee's economic situation or for political reasons.

The court noted that the statute violated the ADEA because the exceptions to the state mandatory retirement policy were not based on physical fitness and failed the BFOQ test. The age policy was unjustified as it contained no evaluation for fitness for employees either over or under age fifty-five. There was no evidence that employees over fifty-five could not perform their job duties. The policy was struck down as unrelated to health reasons. *EEOC v. Tennessee Wildlife Resources Agency*, 859 F.2d 24 (6th Cir.1988).

In a U.S. Supreme Court case, an Alabama woman sought employment as a prison guard with the state board of corrections. The board rejected her application. Although she had graduated from college with a degree in correctional psychology, the applicant failed to meet the department's minimum height and weight requirements which were five feet two inches and 120 pounds. The applicant filed a Title VII discrimination complaint with the Equal Employment Opportunity Commission (EEOC), which resulted in a federal district court decision in her favor. The court found that the state's restrictions would exclude forty percent of all female applicants but only ten percent of male applicants. This constituted unlawful sex discrimination by the corrections department. The state appealed to the U.S. Supreme Court.

The Court noted that Title VII was an effort by Congress to remove artificial, arbitrary and unnecessary barriers to employment such as race and sex. The district court had committed no error in finding that the height and weight restrictions were discriminatory as applied to female applicants. The state had failed to justify the correlation between height and weight and strength or to show that height and weight were essential to job performance. However, the Court noted that a state regulation enacted after the commencement of the lawsuit was not a violation of Title VII. The regulation, which described prisoner contact jobs in male penitentiaries as too dangerous for women, was permissible as a measure of controlling inmates and safety at male prisons. The Court held that the state regulation outlined a BFOQ and reversed that part of the district court's judgment. *Dothard v. Rawlinson*, 433 U.S. 321, 97 S.Ct. 2720, 53 L.Ed.2d 786 (1977).

B. Business Necessity/Job Related Decisions

A Tennessee woman was hired by the Tennessee Valley Authority (TVA) as a carpenter apprentice. The construction site she worked on covered three acres and contained two portable toilets for women, one at each end of the work area. There were also twenty-one other portable toilets on the site which were not sex-designated, but which were used primarily by men. All the toilets were dirty, without running water and without locks or bolts. One had a hole punched in the side. The employee subsequently developed a urinary tract infection and began using a sanitary "off-limits" restroom in a nearby powerhouse. She was eventually terminated for "unsatisfactory conduct"in her work area because she had been using the off-limits restroom, and she filed a complaint with the EEOC, which issued her a right to sue letter. She then sued the TVA in a federal district court, asserting violations under Title VII. The court ruled for the TVA and she appealed to the U.S. Court of Appeals, Sixth Circuit.

The court of appeals, while noting that the TVA had not intentionally discriminated against her or other female employees, found evidence of discriminatory effect based on the TVA's failure to furnish adequate and sanitary facilities to its female workers. They had suffered identifiable health risks from that failure. Further, because the TVA had not offered any necessary business reasons for its actions, she was entitled to recover on her discrimination claim. The court thus reversed the district court's decision. *Lynch v. Freeman*, 817 F.2d 380 (6th Cir.1987).

In 1985, employment qualification examinations given for the position of sergeant in a municipal police department were found to be discriminatory against blacks. There was no such finding on examinations given for other positions, partly because there were few black applicants. The court granted injunctive relief outlining a procedure for review. The court also mandated an affirmative action plan for the position of sergeant. The class of black police officers next challenged the test for the rank of lieutenant. After an examination, the test was found to have an adverse impact on blacks. However, the federal district court did not find the test to be discriminatory. The class then appealed to the U.S. Court of Appeals, Sixth Circuit.

In an adverse impact discrimination suit, the burden is on the class to show that a particular practice or procedure has an adverse impact on that class. The results of the lieutenant examination clearly showed that black officers had comparatively less success. The burden then shifted to the city to show that the exam was job-related. The court noted that the skills required and tested for did not need to be absolutely essential to the position as long as they were found to be sufficiently job-related. The skills tested for were found to be sufficiently job-related. The exam also passed a court adopted test to determine whether the exam justified rank ordering. The court's test required a sufficient spread among candidates, and a reliability analysis of the test and its components. The court determined that although the test did have an adverse impact on blacks in this instance, it did not discriminate. The district court's nondiscriminatory ruling was upheld. *Police Officers v. City of Columbus*, 916 F.2d 1092 (6th Cir.1990).

C. Standardized Tests

A Mississippi city used a standardized test to assess qualification for promotion in its police department. Fourteen black officers sued the city in a federal district court, asserting that it engaged in discriminatory employment practices by its use of the exams. The court ordered two of the officers promoted to lieutenant and awarded them backpay, but dismissed the claims of the other twelve officers. Appeal was taken to the U.S. Court of Appeals, Fifth Circuit.

The appellate court held that the twelve officers' complaints should not have been dismissed. It further held that the burden of showing that the standardized test was job-related should have rested on the city and not on the officers. Here, the officers had made a prima facie showing of discrimination on the part of the city and it was now up to the city to demonstrate that its practices were not discriminatory. The court thus affirmed the district court's decision to promote the two officers, but reversed and vacated the remainder of the lower court's rulings. *Bunch v. Bullard*, 795 F.2d 384 (5th Cir.1986).

The city of Jacksonville, Florida, administered a written examination to firefighters seeking promotion. Those firefighters who scored seventy or higher on this examination were ranked on the basis of their score and their tenure in the department. A black firefighter scored below seventy and was not promoted. He then filed a complaint in a federal district court for injunctive relief alleging that the examination had a disparate impact on minorities in violation of Title VII of the Civil Rights Act. The trial court found that the test was job-related and therefore valid. The firefighter appealed to the U.S. Court of Appeals, Eleventh Circuit, which vacated the decision and remanded the case to the trial court to enter judgment for the firefighter. The city appealed to the U.S. Supreme Court which vacated the Eleventh Circuit's holding and remanded the case for reconsideration in light of its decision in *Wards Cove Packing Co. v Atonio*, 109 S.Ct. 2115 (1989).

On remand, the Eleventh Circuit noted that the Supreme Court in *Wards Cove* determined that the statistical evidence of a lack of minorities in skilled jobs was not sufficient to make out a case of disparate impact; rather the aggrieved party must also show the racial composition of the pool of qualified applicants. The Court also reduced the burden on employers to justify an employment practice. Employers are only required to show a legitimate interest in pursuing the particular practice. The Eleventh Circuit determined that the city had failed to prove the necessity of the exam since supervisory skills were the primary qualification for promotion and the exam failed to test supervisory skills. The court remanded the case to the trial court to enter judgment for the firefighter. *Nash v. City of Jacksonville, Duval County, Fla.*, 905 F.2d 355 (11th Cir.1990)

CHAPTER SIX
EMPLOYEE BENEFITS

I. FEDERAL EMPLOYEES' BENEFITS

Federal employees seeking benefits will generally be governed strictly by federal law. If benefits are available from a federal source, they often will not be awarded by a state as well.

A U.S. Navy welder applied for disability retirement with the Office of Personnel Management (OPM). OPM determined that the welder's poor eyesight prevented him from performing his job and made him eligible for a disability annuity under 5 U.S.C. § 8337(A). Section 8337(a) provides that the benefits for disabled federal employees shall be restored to an earning capacity comparable to the current rate of pay of that position. After taking disability retirement, the welder had the opportunity to earn more money by working overtime on a parttime job. The welder contacted an employee relations specialist at the Navy Public Works Center's Civilian Personnel Department, seeking information on how much he could earn without losing his benefits. The specialist gave the government welder erroneous information from an old handbook. The welder relied on the information and took the overtime work. He then lost his disability benefits by going over the statutory limit. The welder sought review of the decision from the Merit Systems Protection Board (MSPB) which held that the OPM could not be prevented from enforcing a statutory requirement. The welder then appealed to the U.S. Court of Appeals, Federal Circuit. The court of appeals reversed the MSPB's decision, stating that the use of an out-of-date handbook was "affirmative misconduct" and could prevent the government from denying benefits. The OPM appealed to the U.S. Supreme Court.

The Court noted that Congress had not authorized a money remedy for misinformation and the government, therefore, could not be prevented from denying benefits. The Court also noted that awarding benefits for misinformation would invite endless litigation over real and imagined claims and impose an unpredictable and substantial drain on the public funds. The Supreme Court reversed the decision of the court of appeals. *Office of Personnel Management v. Richmond*, 110 S.Ct. 2465 (1990).

In 1973, a federal employee designated his wife as the beneficiary of his Federal Employees Group Life Insurance (FEGLI). Although the designation form stated that the form must be free of erasures or alterations, the employee had mistakenly printed his own name in the place where the beneficiary should be indicated. His name was lined out and his wife's name was printed on the next line. The form was witnessed and returned to the proper office. Approximately four years later, the couple divorced and shortly thereafter the employee remarried. After he had been married to his second wife for four years, the employee died. Both the first and second wives filed claims to receive FEGLI proceeds. After a Georgia trial court held for the current wife, the first appealed to the Court of Appeals of Georgia.

The second wife challenged the validity of the first wife's designation as beneficiary. The court of appeals held that under the applicable federal law, all that was required in order to properly designate a beneficiary was that the employee designate a person in a signed and witnessed writing received in the proper office. The code section did not contain any provisions on erasures and alterations on the form. Therefore, the first wife had properly been designated as beneficiary of the FEGLI. The court also observed that the employee had died almost ten years after he designated his first wife as beneficiary and four years after his second marriage. Therefore his act was voluntary and he intended that his first wife be the beneficiary. The court held that the first wife was entitled to the FEGLI proceeds. *Law v. Law*, 384 S.E.2d 891 (Ga.App.1989).

A U.S. Air Force sergeant retired from active duty in 1976. The sergeant had elected not to participate in the survivor benefit plan (SBP). The sergeant then died in 1980. His widow filed suit in 1988 seeking to recover SBP annuity benefits allegedly due her from the date of her husband's death. She alleged the government failed to notify her of her husband's decision not to participate in SBP, as required by federal law. The government moved to dismiss the suit contending that the claim was barred by the statute of limitations. The claims court denied the government's motion holding that the claim for SBP annuity benefits was a continuing claim and therefore not time barred. Thereafter, the court granted the widow's motion for summary judgment, except for the benefits which accrued more than six years before the suit was filed. The government then appealed to the U.S. Court of Appeals, Federal Circuit.

A claim first accrues "when all the events have occurred which fix the liability of the government and entitle the claimant to institute an action." Persons retiring from the military were automatically enrolled in the plan unless they elected not to participate. The military was then required to notify the member's spouse of the election. The military's failure to notify the spouse voids the member's election not to participate. Upon the sergeant's death, the statute of limitations began to run because all of the events had occurred that fixed the liability of the government. The widow had six years to institute an action to receive the annuity benefits. Since suit was brought after the six years she was not allowed to continue the action. The court reversed the trial court's decision and dismissed the case. *Hart v. U.S.*, 910 F.2d 815 (Fed.Cir.1990).

After working for a proprietary company of the CIA, a lawyer took employment with the U.S. Air Force. He subsequently died, and his wife then applied for survivor's benefits to the Office of Personnel Management (OPM). OPM determined that the lawyer was not an appointed civil servant during the time that he worked at the CIA's proprietary company and refused to pay survivor's benefits to his widow. She then appealed to the Merit Systems Protection Board which affirmed the OPM's decision. She further appealed to the U.S. Court of Appeals, Seventh Circuit.

The court noted that, at the time of the lawyer's employment with the proprietary company, social security was not taken out of civil servants' pay. However, since social security had been taken out of the lawyer's pay, the lawyer was not considered a civil servant and was not entitled to civil service benefits. The court of appeals affirmed the district court's decision to deny survivor's benefits to the wife. *Bevans v. Office of Personnel Management*, 900 F.2d 1558 (Fed.Cir.1990).

An employee of the U.S. Postal Service received coverage under a Federal Employees Group Life Insurance policy, naming his wife as the beneficiary. Subsequently, the couple divorced and the employee, in the settlement agreement, stated that he would maintain his ex-wife as the beneficiary under the postal service insurance policy. The employee then remarried and named his new wife as the beneficiary. When he died, both women sought to collect the policy proceeds. The case was brought to the U.S. District Court, N.D. Georgia, for a determination as to who was entitled to the proceeds.

The district court first noted that had this been a privately contracted insurance policy, the settlement agreement would have precluded the insured from changing his named beneficiary. However, the policy in question was a federal policy administered under federal law. Further, the law stated that a change of beneficiary could be made at any time and without the knowledge or consent of the previous beneficiary. The law also stated that the right could not be waived or restricted. Accordingly, the court determined that the widow, and not the ex-wife, was entitled to the policy proceeds. *Knowles v. Metropolitan Life Ins. Co.*, 514 F.Supp. 515 (N.D.Ga.1981).

A Tennessee man was a member of the Tennessee Air National Guard. The guardsman was ordered by the Air Force to navigate an aircraft to an airbase in Panama. The mission was described as federal active duty for training. The guardsman suffered a serious back injury during an episode of air turbulence while returning from Panama. He was treated first at a Navy hospital and then by a private physician. A line of duty determination was made by the Air Force and substantial incapacitation pay and medical expenses were awarded. The guardsman filed a claim for permanent disability benefits with the Tennessee Division of Claims Administration. The commissioner ruled that the guardsman was on federal active duty at the time of his injury and therefore not acting as an employee of the state. The commissioner denied the guardsman's claim for workers' compensation benefits. The guardsman then appealed to the Supreme Court of Tennessee.

The supreme court held that the guardsman was injured while exclusively on federal active duty and was not a state employee at the time of his injury. The court noted that the state had no control over the guardsman's military activities under orders given by the Air Force. The guardsman was denied workers' compensation benefits. The supreme court affirmed the commissioner's decision. *Yount v. State*, 774 S.W.2d 919 (Tenn.1989).

A Louisiana National Guard member was injured while attempting to lift a portable toilet into a military truck during an annual training exercise. As a result, the guardsman received federal benefits during his period of disability until he was discharged from the National Guard. He then sought state workers' compensation benefits for his injury and sued in a Louisiana trial court which ruled in his favor. The state appealed to the Court of Appeal of Louisiana.

The appellate court noted that the National Guard has both a state and a federal mission. However, under 32 U.S.C. § 502(a), annual training is required as part of the exclusively federal mission of the guard. Further, since the guardsman had been in the service of the United States at the time of his injury, under the allocative aspect of workers' compensation law, no state benefits should have been paid. The court also noted that the guardsman could not have been in the service of both the federal and the state governments; the two were mutually exclusive. The court thus reversed the trial court's decision, and disallowed further benefits to the guardsman. *Lucas v. Military Dep't*, 498 So.2d 161 (La.App.1st Cir.1986).

An Ohio National Guardsman, participating in annual summer training exercises near Fort Knox, Kentucky, died as a result of injuries sustained in an army jeep accident. His widow then filed a workers' compensation claim for death benefits which a hearing officer denied. The hearing officer determined that the guard member's death had not occurred while pursuing Ohio employment, and the widow, after several unsuccessful administrative appeals, filed suit in an Ohio trial court. Again she was unsuccessful and again she appealed to the Court of Appeals of Ohio. When the lower court decision was affirmed, she sought review from the Supreme Court of Ohio.

The supreme court noted that if the guardsman had been on "state active duty," his widow would be entitled to death benefits. However, here the widow had already received death benefits from the federal government and, under Ohio law, persons for whom federal benefits are provided are excluded from the definition of "state active duty." Thus, the guardsman had not been involved in Ohio employment at the time of his death and his widow was not entitled to further compensation. The supreme court affirmed the lower courts' decisions. *Farrier v. Connor*, 466 N.E.2d 557 (Ohio 1984).

The National Capital Transportation Agency (NCTA) was created as a temporary federal agency to aid in coordinating the transportation systems in the Washington metropolitan area. Federal law authorized Maryland, Virginia and the District of Columbia to organize a permanent agency to take over these tasks. Accordingly, the Washington Metropolitan Area Transit Authority (WMATA) was created. The NCTA was then abolished, all its assets were transferred to the WMATA, and all NCTA employees were discharged and offered employment with the WMATA. Various employees,upon their acceptance of the new "comparable" positions with the WMATA, sought severance pay for their separation from Federal Service. However, the Civil Service Commission proffered a regulation which disallowed severance pay to employees who were offered comparable positions within ninety days of their previous employment. The employees then sued in the U.S. Court of Claims for their benefits.

The court of claims noted that the law was valid and that the employees did not satisfy the necessary requirements because they had all been offered comparable positions within the ninety days. This regulation put these employees in the same situation as other NCTA employees who had accepted different federal jobs rather than move to the WMATA. Thus, it was fairly applied to all. The court of claims ruled for the government and denied benefits to the employees. *Akins v. United States*, 439 F.2d 175 (1971).

A fifty-nine-year-old Colorado man was employed as a physicist for twenty-nine years by the U.S. Department of Commerce. The employee was notified that he would be separated from his employment by a reduction in force. He was advised that he would not receive severance pay as he was immediately eligible for a retirement annuity. After complying with all administrative procedural requirements, the employee sued the department's secretary in a federal district court for severance benefits under the Age Discrimination in Employment Act (ADEA) 29 U.S.C. § 633(a).

The employee contended that the secretary's denial of severance pay violated the ADEA because it discriminated against employees who were at least forty years of age. The secretary alleged that at the time of separation, the employee had fulfilled the requirements for an immediate annuity under the civil service retirement statute. The court held that the employee was precluded from receiving severance pay by Congress because he was statutorily eligible for a retirement annuity at the time of his severance. It further noted that the monetary relief afforded by the ADEA is aimed at federal employees who, after years of federal service, are without work or retirement pay. The employee was eligible for a retirement annuity and did not have an ADEA claim. The district court dismissed the case. *Geltman v. Verity*, 716 F.Supp. 491 (D.Colo.1989).

A WWII veteran developed a gastrointestinal ulcer while an officer in a German prisoner of war camp in Virginia. He began receiving military disability retirement pay in 1945. Later, he served twenty-five years in the civil service and retired in 1981. His military service length was originally included in the creditable service used to determine his civil service retirement annuity. He was then notified four years later by the Office of Personnel Management (OPM) that since he was receiving military retirement pay, the inclusion of his military service was unlawful. The OPM told him the error resulted in a $10,000 overpayment, which would be deducted from his annuity payments. The veteran sought a waiver of the overpayment recovery from the Merit Systems Protection Board. The board denied his request for an exemption since he was receiving military retirement pay. The veteran then appealed to the U.S. Court of Appeals, Federal Circuit.

On appeal, the veteran contended that his military retirement pay was received for a medical condition caused by war and was therefore exempted from the double credit restrictions. The court of appeals affirmed the board's decision, ruling that the veteran did not fall within the exemption provided for those disabled by an instrumentality of war. The veteran had not shown that a prisoner of war camp is an instrumentality of war. Nor had he shown that the disability was directly caused by the instrumentality of war. Finally, the court ruled that he had not exhausted his administrative remedies by appealing to the Army's Board for the Correction of Military Records. The appeals court affirmed the exemption denial. *Noguera v. Office of Personnel Management*, 878 F.2d 1422 (Fed.Cir.1989).

II. DENIAL OF BENEFITS

Often, when an employee seeks benefits for disability, the employee will have to prove that he or she was engaged in the employer's business

or that the disability occurred as a result of an accident to recover benefits. An employee will also be forced to comply with any applicable statutes of limitation or other regulations required to receive benefits.

A New Orleans police officer had some drinks at a local lounge after playing baseball. Later that evening he died in a single car accident while driving a police vehicle at approximately 59 m.p.h. His survivors sued the New Orleans Police Department and the city of New Orleans for worker's compensation death benefits. The trial court dismissed the claim and the survivors appealed to the Court of Appeal of Louisiana, Fourth Circuit, claiming that the trial court erred in its finding that the officer was not acting in the scope of his employment at the time of the accident.

The appellate court noted that workers' compensation death benefits cannot be recovered when the decedent is pursuing his own business or pleasure, instead of his employer's business, at the time of the accident. The appellate court held that the officer was not acting in the scope of his employment when the accident occurred because he was on a personal mission, indicated by his driving in the opposite direction from his residence and place of employment. The appellate court affirmed the trial court decision. *Lawless v. New Orleans Police Dep't*, 550 So.2d 252 (La.App.4th Cir.1989).

A Smithsonian Institute employee was hired in 1961 as a private roll employee. Private roll employees were paid from private trust funds rather than from the federally appropriated funds. During his time on the private roll he did not contribute to the Civil Service Retirements System (CSRS). He was appointed to the federal roll six months later. He then eventually obtained employment with the State Department. As an employee of the State Department, the employee participated in the Foreign Service Retirement and Disability System. The man wished to get credit for his Smithsonian private roll employment. He took up his case with the Office of Personnel Management (OPM) which denied his request. The employee then appealed to the Merit Systems Protection Board which upheld the OPM's decision. The man then instituted this action in a federal district court which also upheld the OPM's decision. The employee finally appealed to the U.S. Court of Appeals, Federal Circuit.

The employee contended that since a 1947 Civil Service Commission minute entry allowing thirty-five private roll employees to be considered federal employees for CSRS purposes, he should be considered one as well. However, in 1970, the Civil Service Commission ruled that that while the original thirty-five employees and their successors (who had been paying into the retirement system) appointed prior to March 2, 1970, were entitled to credit for time served for civil service retirement purposes, all future Smithsonian private roll employees would not be a part of CSRS. Therefore, the government was not estopped from denying his credit for the time he served as a private roll employee. The court of appeals affirmed the district court's decision. *Bisson v. Office of Personnel Management*, 908 F.2d 947 (Fed.Cir.1990).

A Minnesota police officer, while walking down a building's steps, slipped and nearly fell. He avoided a fall by grabbing a railing, but in the process suffered a heart attack. He was off work for several months and received disability compensation benefits during that time. Approximately one year later, he suffered a second heart attack while walking a half block to work through heavy snow. The officer again obtained benefits. He finally retired and had a third, and fatal, heart attack. His widow sought death benefits from the city and the police officers' benefit fund. After an administrative hearing the widow was granted an award of $50,000. The benefit fund sought review of that decision from the Supreme Court of Minnesota.

The supreme court held that the widow could only recover benefits if her husband had been "killed in the line of duty." This was something more than just being on the job. It required that the death result from an officer's performance of duties peculiar to a police officer which expose the officer to the hazard of being killed. Here, when the officer suffered his first heart attack, he had merely been walking down a set of steps. He had not, therefore, been "killed in the line of duty." The supreme court reversed the administrative decision, and disallowed death benefits to the widow. *Kramer v. State, Peace Officers Benefit Fund*, 380 N.W.2d 497 (Minn.1986).

A policeman for a Florida city was on duty when he heard a radio call dispatching a county sheriff's deputy to the scene of a fight. Aware that he was the closest patrol vehicle to the scene and that the deputy had no one to back him up, the officer went to the fight, which was outside the city limits. The officer suffered a heart attack immediately after he helped the deputy apprehend a suspect in the fight. The city police's deputy commissioner determined that the heart attack resulted directly from the stress of the incident and awarded the officer workers' compensation benefits. He also concluded that the city, rather than the county sheriff's department should pay the benefits. The city appealed the award to the Florida District Court of Appeal.

The court ruled that there was competent and substantial evidence to support the commissioner's finding that the officer's heart attack was due to the stress of the situation. The court also ruled that the commissioner had practically determined that the city should pay for the benefits. The city had authorized the officer to back up the deputy and the two departments had routinely backed each other up regardless of whether the incident was within the city limits. The court ruled that the officer had therefore been acting within the course and scope of his employment with the city. The benefits award was upheld. *City of Maitland v. Heatwole*, 546 So.2d 63 (Fla.App.1st Dist.1989).

An electrician, employed by the Louisiana Department of Highways, was responsible for maintaining electrically operated traffic signals throughout the state. He was occasionally put on stand-by duty for twenty-four-hour periods, which required him to be at home to answer calls concerning "downed" traffic signals. One night, while on such duty, the electrician drove to a friend's house located thirty-five miles away. There were no calls pending at this time. When the electrician later drove home, he lost control of the truck, crashed and died two weeks later as a result of injuries sustained in the accident. His widow sought workers' compensation benefits which a Louisiana trial court granted, and the state's insurer appealed to the Court of Appeal of Louisiana.

On appeal, the court noted that the electrician had removed himself from the area wherein he could receive work calls in order to engage in a purely personal mission. Even though he was in the course of his employment, he had not been engaged in his employer's business. Thus, the accident did not arise out of his employment, and the widow had been improperly awarded benefits. The court of appeal reversed the trial court's decision. *Bush v. Houston Fire and Cas. Ins. Co.*, 152 So.2d 377 (La.1963).

An Albany fireman accidentally slipped on ice, causing him to fall on his chest. His widow claimed that this accident caused him to have a fatal heart attack and filed an application for accidental death benefits with the New York State Policeman's and Fireman's Retirement System (NYSPFRS). NYSPFRS denied her application because she failed to prove that her husband's death "was the natural and proximate result of an accident sustained in the performance of his duties." Her application was brought before the New York Supreme Court, Appellate Division.

The supreme court noted that the widow was entitled to a presumption that her husband's heart attack was incurred in the performance of duty and was a natural, proximate result of an accident. The widow's expert witness testified that a severe blow to the chest might cause a heart attack. However, the witness was not absolutely certain whether the heart attack caused the fall, or whether the fall and the blow to the chest were the cause of the heart attack. NYSPFRS' expert witness testified that even if such a blow had occurred it would not have produced the heart attack. Further, the expert stated that the widow's husband had a history of cigarette smoking, high cholesterol, and other risk factors which led to the development of a degenerative atherosclerotic condition. This was the ultimate cause of the heart attack and not the accident. The supreme court held that NYSPFRS' expert witness rebutted the presumption that the accident caused the fireman's heart attack. The supreme court affirmed the decision of

NYSPFRS denying the widow accidental death benefits. *Nearney v. Police and Firemen's Ret. Sys.*, 549 N.Y.S.2d 198 (A.D.3d Dep't 1989).

A fire fighter employed by the City of Rochester, New York, was injured by the inhalation of toxic fumes after responding to a fire. The fire fighter applied for accidental disability retirement benefits, which were denied. The fire fighter sought a redetermination and a subsequent hearing was held. The hearing officer denied the application for benefits, concluding that the injury was not an accident within the meaning of the state Retirement and Social Security Law. The fire fighter appealed to the New York Supreme Court, Appellate Division.

The appellate court held that in order for the fire fighter to be eligible for accidental disability retirement benefits, he must prove that the injury was a "sudden, fortuitous mischance, unexpected [and] out of the ordinary" within the meaning of the state Retirement and Social Security Law. The court concluded that the presence of toxic fumes at a fire is an inherent risk of a fire fighter's duties and in this instance the inhalation of such fumes was not accidental. The appellate court affirmed the hearing officer's decision denying benefits to the fire fighter. *Huether on behalf of Hauser v. Regan*, 548 N.Y.S.2d 114 (A.D.3d Dep't 1989).

A mental health worker at a Connecticut state hospital was attacked and injured by a patient. He claimed that the attack had left him permanently physically and psychologically disabled. The worker applied to the state employees retirement commission for service-connected permanent disability retirement benefits. The commission's medical examining board held two hearings on the worker's application during which the worker presented medical reports. Following the second hearing, the board denied the worker's application and the worker appealed to a Connecticut trial court. The court dismissed the worker's appeal, finding that the board had not acted illegally or arbitrarily. The worker then appealed to the Connecticut Appellate Court which reinstated the worker's application, stating that the decision of the board was contrary to evidence that the worker suffered from a permanent psychological disability. The commission appealed to the Connecticut Supreme Court.

The court noted that a court reviewing administrative proceedings such as this one was limited to a substantial evidence standard of review. In this case, the medical examining board had found that the worker suffered from chronic post-traumatic stress disorder, but had failed to present sufficient evidence that the condition was permanent. Although the worker's psychiatrist had testified that the worker was permanently disabled, the board had rejected this finding. According to the supreme court, the board was not bound by the testimony of the worker's psychiatrist and the board's determination satisfied the substantial evidence standard. The court reversed the appellate court's decision and reinstated the board's denial of the claim. *Briggs v. State Employees Retirement Comm'n*, 554 A.2d 292 (Conn.1989).

A 73-year-old Hungarian refugee misrepresented his age as 57 and was hired by the New York State Department of Motor Vehicles. He worked there as a clerk for ten years and then sought benefits from the New York State Employees' Retirement System. In the process of applying, the clerk submitted a birth certificate with his true age. The retirement system notified the clerk that no benefits were payable because his retirement would have been mandatory when he joined the retirement system. The clerk exhausted his administrative remedies, then initiated two lawsuits, one in a state trial court for a determination that the right to his pension was contractual, and another in a state court of claims for breach of the pension contract. Both lawsuits were dismissed. The clerk appealed to the New York Supreme Court, Appellate Division, First Department.

The appellate division court disagreed with the clerk's contention that his lack of a remedy against the retirement system violated his constitutional rights. Although the appellate division court upheld the system's determination, it noted that the clerk could still apply for retirement benefits under the state social security law. *Kutas v. New York State Employees' Retirement System*, 537 N.Y.S.2d 30 (A.D.1st Dep't 1989).

While the New York appellate division court considered the case, the clerk filed a third lawsuit against the state retirement system in a federal district court, based upon 42 U.S.C. § 1983. The clerk's case was publicized by a New York newspaper, which led to a state enactment allowing him to receive a full pension. The clerk applied for and received his full pension and the state court vacated its decision. The clerk then sought attorney's fees under 42 U.S.C. § 1988, claiming that his federal lawsuit had precipitated the pension award, making him a prevailing party under the statute. The court ruled that the publicity surrounding the case had led to the clerk's success, rather than the filing of the federal lawsuit. The application for attorney's fees was unwarranted and the court denied it. *Kutas v. Regan*, 712 F.Supp. 445 (S.D.N.Y.1989).

Family support investigators for a California county investigate allegations and prepare complaints for civil actions to establish and enforce child support obligations. Although it is a crime in California to violate child support requirements, the district attorney pursues only civil remedies against violators. The county, because of this policy, requested that family support investigators not be classified as county peace officers. They would then lose their entitlement to enhanced retirement benefits. The Public Employees' Retirement System (PERS) determined that the employees were peace officers. A hearing was conducted, and an administrative law judge also ruled that the family support investigators were peace officers. The county appealed to a California trial court which overruled that decision.

PERS appealed to the California Court of Appeal, Third District.

On appeal, PERS argued that because the investigators' duties include the investigation of crime, those employees were within the legal definition of county peace officer. The county argued that, in instances where the district attorney chose to criminally prosecute violators, criminal investigators were assigned to the cases, which were then reassigned to the criminal division. The court ruled that family support investigators did not qualify as county peace officers because their "principal duties" did not include the investigation of crime and criminal cases. Since the county's policy was to use civil enforcement, the investigators' goal was not the gathering of evidence for use in prosecution of criminal cases. The court denied enhanced retirement benefits to the family support investigators. *County of Sutter v. Bd. of Admin., Pub. Employees' Retirement System*, 264 Cal.Rptr. 233 (Cal.App.3d Dist.1989).

A Texas university professor and his wife divorced. As part of the property settlement, the wife was awarded $54,000 worth of assets from the professor's retirement plan. She requested the money from the insurer who maintained the plan and her request was denied. She then sued in a Texas trial court, seeking to garnish that amount from her ex-husband's future benefits. The trial court ruled for the insurer, and she appealed to the Court of Appeals of Texas.

On appeal, the court noted that, prior to the divorce, the professor was unable to withdraw any retirement funds from his account because he was still teaching. In fact, he was still teaching after the divorce. Thus, the wife could not be awarded retirement benefits in a divorce settlement if her husband had no right to receive such benefits. Further, the wife could not invoke the Employee Retirement Income Security Act (ERISA) to have the divorce decree declared a "qualified domestic relations order," and avoid the requirements of the retirement plan. The court determined that the professor's retirement plan was a governmental plan and therefore exempt from ERISA. Accordingly, it affirmed the trial court's decision. *Dyer v. Investors Life Ins. Co. of North America*, 728 S.W.2d 478 (Tex.App.-Fort Worth 1987).

A New York man worked as a clerk for the Long Island Railroad (LIRR). Although eligible for retirement and vested in the LIRR pension plan, he continued to work up until his death. Under the terms of the plan, he could have elected a survivorship option which would have reduced his payments upon his retirement, but upon his death would have continued to pay his spouse for her lifetime. He never elected this option. When he died, his widow applied to the LIRR for survivorship benefits, which were denied because the employee had not chosen that option. The widow then sued in a federal district court, asserting that the plan was in violation of the Employee Retirement Income Security Act (ERISA) which required that all

ERISA covered retirement plans provide benefits to surviving spouses unless expressly waived. The district court ruled against the widow, and she appealed to the U.S. Court of Appeals, Second Circuit.

The court of appeals first determined that because the Metropolitan Transit Authority had acquired all the LIRR's outstanding stock, the LIRR was owned by a political subdivision of the state. Accordingly, the LIRR pension plan was a governmental plan and was exempt from the requirements of ERISA. The court thus affirmed the decision of the district court, and held that the widow was not entitled to survivorship benefits. *Rose v. Long Island Railroad Pension Plan*, 828 F.2d 910 (2d Cir.1987).

A California city employee and his wife were insured under a group benefits plan purchased by the city. The insureds submitted several claims to the insurer resulting from the birth and care of their daughter. When the insurer rejected some of their claims, the insureds sued the insurer in a California state court. The insurer removed the lawsuit to a federal district court contending that the health plan was within the scope of the Employee Retirement Income Security Act of 1974 (ERISA). The insurer then moved to dismiss the insureds' claim, arguing that ERISA preempted state law. The district court granted the insurer's motion to dismiss and certified the dismissal of state law claims as a final judgment. The insureds then appealed to the U.S. Court of Appeals, Ninth Circuit.

The court of appeals held that the group benefits policy purchased by the city for its employees was a "governmental plan," which was exempt from ERISA even though it was offered and administered by a private insurer. The court noted that a governmental plan was a plan established or maintained for its employees by a state government or its political subdivision. The city, as a political subdivision of the state, automatically provided the insurer's plan to its employees. The city itself paid the insurance premium directly to the insurer. The court of appeals reversed the district court's decision and remanded the case to the state court. *Silvera v. Mutual Life Ins. Co. of New York*, 884 F.2d 423 (9th Cir.1989).

A New York civil service employee worked as a telephone operator with a school district. She left paid service with the district when she sustained an injury in the district's parking lot. She received workers' compensation benefits for a year and, after that, was paid disability benefits by the district's insurer. Approximately three years later, the district notified her that her employment had been terminated according to New York law. She then applied for accidental and ordinary disability retirement benefits, which the state retirement system denied. Her administrative attempts for relief were unsuccessful, and she appealed to the New York Supreme Court, Appellate Division.

On appeal, she argued that her service to the district did not end until she was notified by the district. The district, however, asserted that its notification reflected its understanding that the employee was absent from work and free to return to the district's employ. The court agreed with the district, noting also that the employee did not seek or receive an authorized medical leave of absence. The employee's claim was thus time barred because the date at which she left paid service, without an authorized medical leave, was the date which triggered the statute of limitations. Since her application was not filed within 2 years of her last day of paid service, she was not entitled to accidental disability benefits. The court affirmed the administrative determinations and dismissed the employee's claim. *Matter of Triolo v. New York State Employees' Retirement System*, 499 N.Y.S.2d 493 (A.D.3d Dep't 1986).

III. CONSTITUTIONAL CHALLENGES AND COLLECTIVE BARGAINING AGREEMENTS

A commonly litigated issue in the area of employee benefits is the constitutionality of benefits programs. If benefit plans arbitrarily discriminate against certain classes of employees, they will generally be struck down. Also, employees challenging benefit plans, if those plans fall within collective bargaining agreements, must generally comply with the provisions of the agreement before bringing suit.

The Los Angeles Department of Water and Power required its female employees to make larger contributions to their retirement pension funds than those made by male employees. Upon retirement, each employee eligible for monthly retirement benefits received an amount computed as a fraction of salary multiplied by years of service, funded entirely by their own contributions. The department justified the disparity in contribution by the use of mortality tables and experience which showed that females lived longer than males, necessarily increasing the average pension of retired females. The monthly pension contribution required of female employees was $14.84 higher than that of male employees.

A group of aggrieved female employees filed a Title VII discrimination complaint against the department in a federal district court, seeking an injunction against the disparate contributions and a refund of their excess contributions. Meanwhile, the California state legislature enacted a law prohibiting municipal agencies from requiring higher contributions based upon sex. The department then amended its plan so that both sexes paid the same retirement contribution. The court then granted the employees' motion for summary judgment on federal law grounds and ordered restitution of the excess funds. The department appealed to the U.S. Court of Appeals, Ninth Circuit, which affirmed the district court decision. The department appealed to the U.S. Supreme Court, which granted a writ of certiorari.

Before the Supreme Court, the department argued that the difference in required contributions was based upon mortality tables, which constituted a factor other than sex under the 1963 Equal Pay Act, and therefore was not unlawful discrimination. The Court held that while there was a legitimate basis in fact for the distinction drawn by the department, the distinction involved a generalization which was not true in each individual case. Not every individual female lived longer than every individual male. Because Title VII prohibited unlawful discrimination against any individual with respect to compensation, terms, conditions or privileges of employment, courts were required to focus on alleged discrimination against individuals and to disregard generalizations about classes of persons. The lower courts had correctly ruled that the distinction drawn by the department was unlawful discrimination based upon sex. However, the lower courts had inappropriately awarded restitution of excess contributions to the aggrieved female employees. The pension fund had taken the disparate contributions in the good faith belief that the mortality tables would justify them. Employers should be given time to adjust to the requirements of Title VII and there was no reason to penalize the funds and possibly jeopardize them for a good faith error. The Court remanded the case for proceedings consistent with its opinion. *City of Los Angeles Department of Water v. Manhart*, 435 U.S. 702, 98 S.Ct. 1370, 55 L.Ed.2d 657 (1978).

A male Connecticut teacher took an early retirement from his position with a city's school system. He was required, under Connecticut law, to participate in a retirement benefits program. He began receiving benefits, but they were actuarially reduced by the use of sex-based actuarial tables. Because of the use of these tables, females received a larger percentage of their average salary than similarly situated males. Over a year later, however, a "unisex" table was adopted and the teacher began receiving benefits equal to similarly situated females. He then filed a complaint with the commission on human rights and opportunities, which found that the use of gender-based tables had discriminated against the teacher, and ordered that he be paid the difference between what he had received and what early retiring females had received. The state appealed to a Connecticut trial court which held that the teacher had been discriminated against and ordered him compensated for the difference between what he had received and what females had received. The state appealed to the Supreme Court of Connecticut.

The supreme court first noted that each payment to the teacher had been a separate act of discrimination on the part of the state. It then ruled that, according to state antidiscrimination statutes, the teacher could only be compensated for each of the payments he had received within 180 days prior to his filed complaint. Further, since the teacher had only sought to be compensated for the "unisex" amount, he was not entitled to the full difference that had been awarded him. The court thus remanded the case to the trial court for a proper determination of the correct increase amount due the teacher. *State v. Comm'n on Human Rights and Opportunities*, 559 A.2d 1120 (Conn.1989).

In 1983, Oregon's legislature amended its public employee retirement system to exclude some teacher benefits and earnings for computing their employment retirement credits and employer contributions. The Oregon Constitution permits its governor to sign legislation into law while simultaneously vetoing emergency riders to preclude taxpayer referendums for a period of ninety days. The governor signed the legislation with an emergency clause. He then attempted to make his veto applicable to the entire bill. The legislature treated the vetoes as legally ineffective but the executive branch continued to make employee contributions as though the act was vetoed. Taxpayers sued the department of higher education for an order to declare the contributions illegal. An Oregon trial court ruled in favor of the taxpayers and this decision was affirmed by the Oregon Court of Appeals and Oregon Supreme Court. The supreme court noted that the emergency provision referred only to emergency legislative riders. The governor could not veto the entire legislation under this portion of the constitution and the act was valid as enacted by the legislature. The taxpayers were granted an order discontinuing the employee contributions. *Lipscomb v. State Bd. of Higher Educ.*, 753 P.2d 939 (Or.1988).

Several postal employees were injured and killed when an emotionally disturbed fellow employee began shooting inside the post office. City police were summoned to the scene and a hostage situation developed. The police took no action for more than an hour and a half as the shooting and suffering of the hostages continued. The injured employees and relatives of the deceased employees (employees) brought a 42 U.S.C. § 1983 suit against the city, its police chief and the postmaster. The employees alleged that they were deprived of associational and familial relations in violation of the due process clause. A federal court dismissed the action and the employees then appealed to the U.S. Court of Appeals, Tenth Circuit.

The employees argued that the appeals court should view their complaint in light of inferences which could be drawn from its facts. The lower court explained that ordinary negligence does not give rise to relief under §1983. However, the Supreme Court has left open the question of whether gross negligence may be actionable. The appeals court denied the inference of gross negligence here because this distinction must be specifically pled, and because the employees failed to amend their complaint as the district court allowed. The employees alternatively pled that the questioned conduct was carried out intentionally. The appeals court found that no set of facts could be shown to support this claim. Finally, the court held that a state's failure to protect citizens from private violence does not violate the due process clause unless the state helped to create the danger. The appeals court affirmed the dismissal of the case. *Bryson v. City of Edmond*, 905 F.2d 1386 (10th Cir.1990).

A retired Oregon civil service employee sued the state Public Employees Retirement Board challenging the constitutionality of an Oregon statute requiring mandatory retirement at sixty years of age for police and firefighters, and sixty-five years of age for general service employees. In order to compensate police and firefighters for early retirement, the statute provided higher pensions than those afforded general service employees with the same seniority and final pay. A retired civil service employee claimed that the difference in pay violated his right to equal protection under the Fourteenth Amendment of the U.S. Constitution. He sued the retirement board in a federal district court which dismissed the complaint. The employee appealed to the U.S. Court of Appeals, Ninth Circuit.

The court of appeals held that the statute did not violate the employee's equal protection rights. The difference in pension benefits was rationally related to the goals of aiding recruitment into hazardous professions, rewarding performance of hazardous duties, and encouraging retirement before the physical ability required in police and firefighting were diminished with age. The court of appeals affirmed the district court's decision. *Shaw v. Oregon Pub. Employees' Retirement Bd.*, 887 F.2d 947 (9th Cir.1989).

The Rhode Island legislature enacted legislation permitting Providence municipal employees to make contributions toward their retirement system. The Rhode Island Constitution permits legislation regarding its cities only where the laws apply to all cities or where legislation is ratified by a majority of the subject city's voters. A Providence city employee applied to begin making payments into the retirement system, but the state retirement board rejected his and all other applications filed under the act. The employee then sued the board in a Rhode Island court for a declaration on the statute's validity. The trial court judge determined that the legislation was unconstitutional under the state constitution and the employee appealed to the Rhode Island Supreme Court.

The supreme court ruled that the state maintains sovereignty over police affairs and business where they are matters of statewide concern. The city's employee pension plan was not a matter of statewide concern. Because the legislation did not concern other Rhode Island cities, nor was it approved by a majority of Providence voters, it was unconstitutional under the state constitution. The supreme court affirmed dismissal of the lawsuit. *Bruckshaw v. Paolino*, 557 A.2d 1221 (R.I.1989).

The Alaska Public Employees' Retirement System (PERS) provided that a state employee with at least five years of credited service could elect early retirement at age fifty, subject to an actuarial adjustment of the amount of PERS benefits the employee would have received upon normal retirement at age fifty-five. Essentially, the application of the new actuarial tables adjusted the payments to retirees downward from 70% of earnings to 67% of earnings. The state public employees' association and various individual employees then sued the state in an Alaska trial court, asserting that the adjustment of actuarial tables for presently vested employees (who were expecting the higher payments) was a violation of Alaska's constitution. The trial court agreed, and the state appealed to the Supreme Court of Alaska.

The supreme court first noted that a diminution in an employee's accrued right to benefits was constitutionally invalid unless it was outweighed by comparable advantages. The court then held that a vested right was essentially an accrued right, and determined that the employees involved here would not receive any comparable advantages upon the decrease in their expected payments. It thus held that computation of early retirement benefits according to actuarial factors adopted after employees' hiring by the state, and before their retirement, violated the state constitution. The supreme court affirmed the trial court's decision. *Sheffield v. Alaska Public Employees' Ass'n, Inc.*, 732 P.2d 1083 (Alaska 1987).

An Illinois lawyer worked as a city attorney for six years. At the time of his hiring, the city had in force an ordinance which allowed most city employees to earn sick leave with pay up to six days for each six months of service at a rate of 25% of regular pay. Shortly before the attorney left the city's employ this ordinance was amended to provide a rate of 75% of regular pay for retiring employees (except for appointed employees). This amended ordinance repealed all ordinances in conflict with it. When the attorney resigned to take a job elsewhere, he sought sick leave benefits for forty-eight days of accumulated time, which the city refused to pay. He then sued in an Illinois trial court which held for the city, and he appealed to the Appellate Court of Illinois.

The appellate court first noted that the attorney came within the "appointed personnel" exclusion of the city's sick leave ordinance. It further held that even if the attorney had had a right to unused sick leave benefits by the earlier ordinance, he could not claim those benefits until he left the city. Essentially, they could not be determined until his employment was terminated. Thus, the attorney was subject to the later ordinance which denied him benefits. The appeals court therefore affirmed the trial court's decision. *McCarty v. City of Rockford*, 421 N.E.2d 576 (Ill.App.1981).

A California lawyer was employed by the state controller as an inheritance tax attorney. He became a member of the Public Employees' Retirement System (PERS). In 1974, he was placed on mandatory retirement because he had reached the age of 67. However, up until 1971, the mandatory retirement age had been 70. The employee sued in a California trial court, seeking to hold the reduction in mandatory retirement unlawful and asking to be reinstated to his former position. With standard promotions, this would have increased the employee's benefits by over $500 per month. The trial court ruled against the employee, and he then appealed to the Supreme Court of California.

The supreme court noted that although the employee's pension rights had vested prior to his retirement, and thus could not be destroyed, they were not immutable. The government could make reasonable modifications and changes in the pension system. Here, although the employee received less than he would have had he worked to the age of 70, under the modified PERS plan he received more than he would have at voluntary retirement under the old system at age 67. The court further noted that the employee had no constitutionally protected right to stay in public employment until the age of 70. The court thus affirmed the trial court's decision and denied further relief to the employee. *Miller v. State*, 135 Cal.Rptr. 386 (Sup.1977).

A group of over 2,000 disabled military retirees, entitled to receive either longevity retirement pay or disability compensation from the Veterans Administration, sought to receive both benefits at the same time. However, 38 U.S.C. §§ 3104-3105 precluded them from doing so. It required them to waive retirement pay in order to be eligible for disability benefits. They sued the United States in the U.S. Claims Court, asserting that the law violated the equal protection clause of the Fourteenth Amendment. The court ruled for the government, and the retirees appealed to the U.S. Court of Appeals, Federal Circuit.

On appeal, the court noted that the retirees had not shown that they had been unfairly treated in relation to another similarly situated group. Under 38 U.S.C. § 3105, the retirees were permitted to opt for the tax-exempt disability pensions over the regular retirement benefits, and this was not unconstitutional. The court found that the classification used here for the retirees, which gave them an option, was sufficiently fair and rationally related to the legitimate federal goal of saving money. The court thus affirmed the claims court's decision and upheld 38 U.S.C. §§ 3104-3105. *Absher v. United States*, 805 F.2d 1025 (Fed.Cir.1986).

A California deputy district attorney resigned after ten years as a county employee. Upon his resignation the employee withdrew his pension contributions from the county retirement system. For the following six years he was employed as a city attorney and a member of the statewide Public Employees' Retirement System (PERS). The employee then became a municipal court judge and a member of the judges' retirement system. In 1987 the employee applied to the county board of retirement for permission to redeposit the contributions he had withdrawn and for reinstatement in the county retirement system. The board denied the employee's request for reinstatement. It found that he was not eligible for reinstatement because he was not currently employed by a reciprocal retirement system. The employee petitioned a California trial court to set aside the board's decision and reinstate him upon redeposit of his past contributions. The trial court granted the petition and the board appealed to the Court of Appeal, First District.

The appeals court noted that the statute governing redeposit of retirement contributions and reinstatement of county employees was enacted after the employee had left the county position. The statute provided that individuals who had left county service and withdrawn retirement contributions could be reinstated. Later the statute was amended to add that the statute would not apply to members who were not covered by a reciprocal system. The court of appeal held that the employee was not entitled to redeposit funds and reinstatement into the county retirement system because he was not currently enrolled in a reciprocal plan. The court also found that the amendment did not deny the employee any vested right. The court of appeal reversed the trial court's decision. *Piombo v. Bd. of Retirement*, 262 Cal. Rptr. 624 (Cal.App.1st Dist.1989).

A Massachusetts assistant court clerk missed work due to illness for an extended period. When he had exhausted all his sick leave and vacation days, the employer ordered that the clerk's salary be discontinued until he returned to work. The clerk claimed that he had a protected property interest in his accumulated benefits under the Due Process Clause of the Constitution. The Supreme Judicial Court of Massachusetts disagreed, ruling that he had no enforceable right to future employment benefits. At most, the clerk had only an expectancy interest in future benefits. His job was not guaranteed. The court ruled that the clerk had no right to notice and a hearing before his salary was terminated. *Glynn v. Clerk of the Superior Court*, 533 N.E.2d 1025 (Mass.1989).

An Iowa man was employed by a city for thirty-two years, the last seventeen as a deputy health officer. His employment was appointive in nature and not subject to a collective bargaining agreement. Eventually, the employee accepted a similar position with another city and made a claim for, among other benefits, unused sick leave in the amount of $10,600. The city acknowledged that he was entitled to some of the other benefits he claimed, but disputed his entitlement to unused sick leave, and refused to pay him any benefits until it could be determined exactly what benefits were owed. He then sued the city in an Iowa trial court, which granted him the benefits the city had admitted owing him, along with partial attorney's fees, but denied him the unused sick leave benefits. He appealed to the Court of Appeals of Iowa.

The appellate court noted that the employee had been treated similarly to other employees who had been in the same position he was in when he left.

Further, since he hadn't been subject to a collective bargaining agreement, he was bound by the city council's resolution which mandated the maximum amount due an employee for unused sick leave upon the employee's separation from the city. However, the city had improperly withheld payment of all benefits to the employee, so the court of appeals awarded liquidated damages to him as compensation for the city's actions. The court thus affirmed the trial court's decision as modified on the liquidated damages. *Jackson v. City of Ottumwa*, 396 N.W.2d 794 (Iowa App.1986).

An Iowa city altered its employee sick leave policy several times. Before 1974, the city permitted up to sixty days of unused sick leave to accumulate and paid employees upon termination for the unused sick leave to that limit. The city then passed a resolution permitting employees to accumulate sick leave of up to sixty days but disallowed payment for unused sick leave upon termination. In 1978, the city negotiated collective bargaining agreements with its employees permitting payment of up to thirty days of accumulated sick leave upon termination. The pay out applied only after five years of employment. Accumulated sick leave prior to 1978 was disregarded. In 1980, the collective bargaining agreements permitted 120 days of sick leave accumulation but still permitted only thirty days to be paid out upon termination. In 1980, a city council resolution extended all fringe benefits available to the bargaining units to other city employees. However, the extension omitted any reference to sick pay accumulated from 1974 to 1980.

Three long-term city employees who were not covered by the collective bargaining agreements sued the city in an Iowa trial court claiming that they were entitled to be paid for their accumulated sick leave. They also sought money damages and an order directing the city to modify its sick leave policy. The court ruled for the city and the employees appealed to the Iowa Court of Appeals. The appeals court rejected the employees' argument that sick pay was a vested benefit which they were entitled to immediately. Sick pay did not vest until retirement or termination. Sick leave benefits were not wages under Iowa law and the value of the benefit was not ascertainable until termination. Because the employees were employed at will, the city was permitted to vary the employment agreement. This included disregarding sick leave benefits during the period from 1974 to 1980. The appeals court affirmed the trial court's dismissal of the lawsuit. *Willets v. City of Creston*, 433 N.W.2d 58 (Iowa App.1988).

Two retired Kentucky fire fighters sued the city which had employed them in a Kentucky trial court, claiming that the calculation of their retirement annuities was erroneous. Both fire fighters questioned the city retirement fund board of trustees' interpretation of Kentucky statutes and a collective bargaining agreement with the city requiring payment of terminal leave pay upon retirement from accrued unused vacation and sick leave. The employees maintained that terminal leave pay was salary and should therefore be included as part of annual salary for the computation of their retirement annuities. This would increase the amount of the annuity by increasing the salary rate for one of the three years of service used to compute highest annual average salary. The board determined that unused accrued terminal leave pay was a onetime retirement bonus. The trial court returned a judgment for the employees. The city appealed to the Kentucky Court of Appeals.

The appeals court agreed with the employees that terminal leave paid under the collective bargaining agreement was part of annual salary for computing retirement annuities. Both employees were to get credit for unused accrued sick and vacation pay with full back benefits and interest. However, the trial court had erroneously issued judgment against the city. Under Kentucky law, pension fund administration was vested in the board of trustees rather than the city. The case was dismissed and remanded with instructions to enter an identical judgment for the employees against the retirement fund board. *City of Covington v. Peare*, 769 S.W.2d 761 (Ky.App.1989).

A Connecticut police officer completed training and was working as a probationary patrol officer when a medical examination revealed that he had a heart condition. The officer was hospitalized for tests and received sick pay. For the next six months, however, the officer was not permitted to resume full active duties. The officer filed a claim for nonpayment of wages in accordance with the first step of the grievance procedure under the applicable collective bargaining procedure. The department denied the claim because it considered the officer to be on "indefinite sick leave without pay." The officer then sued the department in a Connecticut trial court. The department moved to dismiss the officer's claim alleging that he had failed to pursue the grievance procedure mandated under the collective bargaining agreement. The trial court granted the department's motion to dismiss and the officer appealed to the state appellate court. The appellate court set aside the judgment finding the collection of wages an inappropriate subject for collective bargaining. The department then appealed to the Supreme Court of Connecticut.

The supreme court held that under state law, the employee was not allowed to recover from the municipality for the accrued unpaid wages. The municipality exercised distinctive governmental functions which afforded it immunity from civil liability. The court also held that the employee could not recover the unpaid wages without having first exhausted the grievance procedure. The collection of wages was a proper subject of arbitration under the collective bargaining agreement. The supreme court reversed the appellate court's decision and remanded to the trial court to find for the department. *Shortt v. New Milford Police Dep't*, 562 A.2d 7 (Conn.1989).

A Rhode Island state trooper was injured while on vacation and was unable to return to work because of his injuries. Initially, he was placed on paid sick leave by the state police department, but was eventually removed from the payroll. The trooper's employment contract stated that he would "receive unlimited sick leave with the approval of the superintendent." In arbitration which followed, an abitrator restored all but two weeks of the trooper's sick pay. The department maintained that the arbitrator exceeded his power in restoring any benefits to the trooper, but a Rhode Island superior court affirmed the arbitration award. The department then appealed to the Supreme Court of Rhode Island.

On appeal, the department argued that the department superintendent had unlimited discretion in the award of sick leave under the trooper's contract. Hence, the arbitration award, which ran counter to the superintendent's determination, exceeded the arbitrator's power. The supreme court disagreed. It stated that so long as the arbitrator used the proper sources for resolving the conflict, namely the employment contract and surrounding circumstances, the award would stand. The court would not impose its interpretation of the contract upon the arbitrator. *Rhode Island v. Pontarelli*, 564 A.2d 572 (R.I.1989).

IV. MULTIPLE BENEFIT AWARDS

Generally, multiple benefit awards are not allowed. When an employee can receive several types of benefits, the employee will usually have to choose only one of the benefits. Even if eligible to receive more than one type of benefit, an employee will often have the benefits set off to ensure fairness.

An Indiana public employee was injured during the course of his employment with the Indiana Department of Corrections. The injury totally disabled him and the state paid him his full salary for a year pursuant to Public Law 35 salary benefits. At the end of the first year, the state paid him thirteen weeks of temporary total disability payments. During this time the employee filed his application for benefits with the workers' compensation board. A single hearing judge found the employee to be permanently totally disabled and ordered the state to pay him $166 per week for his period of permanent total disability commencing with the date of the accident. The board unanimously affirmed the single hearing judge's decision. The employee filed a copy of the board's award with the trial court and requested judgment. The board claimed that it should have received a credit for the money the employee received pursuant to Public Law 35 salary benefits. The employee instituted this action in an Indiana trial court. The trial court ordered the state to pay the worker $166 per week for the disputed first year of disability without a credit for the Public Law 35 salary benefits, but allowing a credit for the payments made thereafter. The state appealed to the Court of Appeals of Indiana.

In construing a statute, the court of appeals looks to the statute as a whole and attempts to give effect to the intent of the legislature. Even though the statute on its face referred only to credit for benefits against temporary total disability benefits, the court ruled that the intent of the legislature was to give credit for benefits received under temporary and permanent total disability status. The court of appeals was guided by the expertise of the workers' compensation board and reversed the trial court's decision. *State v. Doody*, 556 N.E.2d 1357 (Ind.App.1st Dist.1990).

A Michigan police officer was injured in an automobile accident which arose out of his employment with the police department. Although he was eligible to receive workers' compensation benefits, he instead elected to receive charter benefits under the city charter which he was eligible for because of a collective bargaining agreement. After full payment of those benefits, he sought to recover no-fault benefits from the city. It denied his claim and he then sued the city in a Michigan trial court. The court ruled for the city, and the officer appealed to the Court of Appeals of Michigan.

The appeals court noted that the officer would be allowed a windfall if he obtained both no-fault and charter benefits. It then stated that the purpose of allowing charter benefits was to ensure that officers would be able to recover benefits under either that regulation or under workers' compensation law. The court held that charter benefits were one of two types of benefits required to be provided under state law. Thus, since setoff of workers' compensation benefits was required with respect to no-fault payments, so also was setoff of charter benefits. The court affirmed the trial court's decision. *Krygel v. City of Detroit*, 353 N.W.2d 116 (Mich.App.1984).

Two Miami police officers suffered permanent work-related injuries. Both officers received workers' compensation benefits and disability pension benefits. A city ordinance required the offsetting of pension benefits against workers' compensation benefits. Florida law had permitted public employers to make such reductions, but the statute was repealed in 1973. Both officers pursued administrative appeals, and their cases were consolidated and certified by the Florida Court of Appeals to the Florida Supreme Court.

The court ruled that workers' compensation claimants were entitled to workers' compensation as well as pension benefits, but that total benefits could not exceed the employee's weekly wage. Following repeal of the special rule for public employees, public and private employers were subject to the same workers' compensation statute. The Miami city ordinance providing for the pension benefits offset was invalid under state law. The supreme court quashed the lower court decisions and remanded the cases. *Barragan v. City of Miami*, 545 So. 2d 252 (Fla.1989).

An Iowa police officer was hospitalized for psychological problems caused by job-related stress. Two years later, his superiors believed he was having a recurrence of his earlier problems. The officer was placed on involuntary sick leave and ordered to see a psychologist. During this time, he continued to work two outside security jobs. The officer had previously received approval for off-duty employment. A month after being placed on sick leave, the chief of police ordered the officer to cease his off-duty employment. Under the department's rules, off-duty employment would not be approved if an officer was on sick leave. The officer knew of this rule. The department suspended him for violating the rule. The officer appealed the suspension to the city's Civil Service Commission. The commission affirmed the suspension and the officer appealed to an Iowa district court. The court reversed the commission's decision and vacated the officer's suspension. The commission then appealed to the Court of Appeals of Iowa.

On appeal, the commission argued that the rule should be read to revoke prior permission for off-duty employment while an officer is on sick leave. The officer contended that he did not believe the rule applied because he had not asked to be placed on sick leave. The court of appeals held that the officer was not in violation of the department's off-duty employment rule. The rule's wording did not give the officer notice of when approval ended. The court of appeals affirmed the district court's decision. *Post v. Sioux City Civil Serv. Comm'n*, 445 N.W.2d 425 (Iowa App.1989).

Three North Carolina police officers voluntarily participated in a separate pension system which provided coverage in the event of death, disability or retirement. This was in addition to their automatic participation in the Asheville Policemen's Pension Disability Fund. The state legislature directed that all funds from the voluntary pension system be transferred to the North Carolina State Retirement System. The three officers did not contest this transfer. Less than a year later, the city's police officers elected to participate in the state retirement system. The automatic fund was merged into the state system, and the city council assured all members that their benefits under the new system would remain the same. The three officers then sued the board of trustees, seeking to prevent the merger of the automatic fund with the state retirement system. The court awarded summary judgment to the defendants, and the officers appealed to the North Carolina Court of Appeals.

The police officers argued that under the old dual system they would have been entitled to receive two pensions, and that under the new system, a significant portion of their rights would be destroyed without compensation or consideration. Essentially, they asserted that the terms of a pension plan may not be amended when its members were voluntary participants. The court ruled that because the officers did not contest the transfer of their voluntary contributions into the state retirement system, they could not now attack the merger of the automatic fund with the state retirement system. It further stated that if the state system impaired the officers' rights, they might have an action against the state. The court affirmed the trial court's ruling against the officers. *Mathews v. Board of Trustees of the Asheville Policemen's Pension and Disability Fund*, 385 S.E.2d 343 (N.C.App.1989).

A Florida man, employed by the city of Miami, sustained a compensable back injury. The city accepted his claim of permanent total disablement and began paying him benefits. Five years later, however, it asserted that he was then able to work and it discontinued benefit payments. The ex-employee sued in a Florida trial court seeking reinstatement of the benefits and, after a modification of the benefits payable to the employee, both parties appealed to the District Court of Appeal of Florida.

On appeal, the city presented evidence that the ex-employee had worked as an investigator while receiving disability benefits, looking into taxicab accidents and handling the resulting insurance claims. The appellate court agreed that the ex-employee was no longer permanently totally disabled, but stated that the payments by the city could only be halted as of the date of the modification order, even though the ex-employee had been working for a longer period of time. The court affirmed the lower court's decision in part, upholding the modification of benefits to offset the ex-employee's new wages. *City of Miami v. Knight*, 510 So.2d 1069 (Fla.App.1st Dist.1987).

An employee with thirty-two years of service in a Pennsylvania school district suffered a job-related injury and was unable to work for ten months. The school district decided to pay the employee his full salary "in relief of his disability," which gave the district the legal right to offset the employee's workers' compensation benefits against the salary it paid him. The employee informed the district that he would rather use his 245 days of accumulated sick leave during his absence, which would give him the legal right to retain his workers' compensation benefits with no corresponding right on the part of the school district to offset those benefits against his sick leave pay. The school district refused his request so he sued. The Pennsylvania Commonwealth Court held that the school district had acted wrongfully in forcing the employee to accept his full salary "in relief of disability" with an offset for workers' compensation benefits received. Sick leave was a benefit of employment earned by the employee, said the court, and the employee had a contractual right to use it if he so desired. The employee was entitled to collect both his sick leave pay along with workers' compensation benefits with no deduction. *Allegheny Valley School District v. Allegheny Valley Education Association*, 528 A.2d 690 (Pa.Cmwlth.1987).

A tenured Philadelphia teacher worked concurrently as a fulltime police officer. He was injured on police duty and while recuperating worked a desk job for the police department. At the same time he received six weeks of

school district adopted a policy prohibiting teachers from accepting compensation while taking sick leave from the district. When the teacher returned to his classroom the district notified him of his violation. The district dismissed the teacher and refused his offer to return his sick pay. He appealed to the state secretary of education. The teacher argued that the district failed to notify its employees about the sick leave policy. The district stated that the policy prohibiting remuneration during sick time was known to the teacher and that he had acted willfully in accepting sick pay benefits. Because the policy was adopted at a public meeting the teacher should have been aware of it. The secretary affirmed the district's decision and the teacher appealed to the Commonwealth Court of Pennsylvania. The court stated that the district had not taken reasonable steps to advise its employees of the sick leave policy. The district presented no evidence that it had posted the policy on bulletin boards, mailed information to teachers or kept the information for review at individual schools. He had not willfully violated the district's sick leave policy and his leave was for a legitimate medical reason. The court ordered the secretary to reinstate the teacher to his former position. He was also entitled to back pay. *Cowdery v. Philadelphia Bd. of Educ.*, 531 A.2d 1186 (Pa.Cmwlth.1987).

A Washington school teacher announced her retirement, and elected to receive a lump sum of her accumulated retirement contributions, together with a reduced monthly retirement allowance. She designated her husband as her beneficiary upon death. The teacher died before the end of the month in which she announced her retirement. The state retirement system stated that because the teacher did not survive until her first retirement payment became due, the husband was limited to receiving either the lump sum or an unreduced monthly allowance, but not both. The husband sued the retirement system in a Washington trial court, which granted summary judgment to the system. He then appealed to the Washington Court of Appeals.

The court of appeals initially reversed the trial court's decision, but granted the system's motion for reconsideration. On reconsideration, the court noted two Washington statutes whose ambiguities had led to the dispute. RCW 41.32.498 entitled surviving beneficiaries to receive elected retirement benefits with no survivorship requirement. However, the state legislature had added language to RCW 41.32.520 reinstating a survivorship requirement. The legislative scheme as a whole gave effect to the survivorship requirement where retirement system members failed to survive until the first installment became due. Because the teacher had not survived until the end of the month, when pension payments became due, the survivorship requirement governed the husband's benefits. He was therefore to receive either the full monthly allowance or a lump sum, but not both. The court affirmed the trial court decision. *Knack v. Dep't of Retirement Systems*, 776 P.2d 687 (Wash.App.1989).

A Colorado fire fighter was injured and forced to exhaust his accrued sick leave and vacation days. After a maximum ninety-day temporary disability leave was expended, the fire fighter was placed on leave without pay for one year. On learning that the fire fighter was permanently disabled, the city terminated the fire fighter's employment. In accordance with its health coverage plan, the city offered the fire fighter the right to maintain group health coverage at group rates for ninety days. It sent the fire fighter a notice of his right to elect coverage under Subchapter XX of 42 U.S.C. § 300bb-1, a federal statute providing for continuation coverage of group health plans for state and local employees. The fire fighter never returned the required form for electing continuation coverage. He became covered under his wife's separately-maintained group health plan. The fire fighter remained covered under his wife's plan and the city did not extend continuation coverage.

The firefighter sued the city in the U.S. District Court for the District of Colorado, claiming that his status as a covered dependent under another health plan did not terminate his continuation coverage rights. The court ruled that group health plan coverage could be terminated on the day in which the beneficiary became covered under any other group health plan or became entitled to Medicare benefits. The court noted that 42 U.S.C. § 300bb-1 was intended to provide health benefits to qualified beneficiaries who were not covered by other plans. The statute did not require overlapping or dual coverage as the fire fighter contended. The court granted the city's motion for summary judgment. *Oakley v. City of Longmont*, 701 F.Supp. 800 (D.Colo.1988).

The firefighter then appealed to the U.S. Court of Appeals, Tenth Circuit. The court held that the lower court's interpretation of § 300bb-1 did not reflect Congress' true intent. It stated that § 300bb-1 was the result of congressional concern with the growing number of Americans without any health insurance coverage. The court considered congressional debates over the continuation coverage rules. The purpose of § 300bb-1 was to reduce the extent to which certain events could create a significant gap in health coverage. The court stated that the fire fighter's case presented the precise type of gap in coverage which troubled Congress, since he was terminated because of the catastrophic car accident. The court held that the city could not terminate continuation coverage on the basis that he was covered under his wife's policy. It reversed and remanded the case to the district court. *Oakley v. City of Longmont*, 887 F.2d 249 (10th Cir.1989).

A St. Louis police officer became permanently disabled after being shot in the line of duty. The Police Retirement System (Pension System) determined that he was totally disabled. The officer began receiving monthly pension payments. However, the payments did not cover his medical and nursing costs. He then filed a claim against the St. Louis Police Department under Missouri's Workers' Compensation Law for the payment of his medical and nursing care expenses. The department agreed to pay a lump sum as compensation for past nursing care and a monthly annuity to cover the cost of his future nursing care. These payments were given in consideration of his release of any further claim for medical and nursing benefits and his wife's claim of any survivor death benefits. The pension system claimed it had a right to set off the pension payments made to the disabled police officer from any payments made by the police department because of Missouri law, § 86.297 RSMo 1986. The law provided that any amounts paid under workers' compensation to a public employee on account of death or disability would be offset against any funds provided by the city to the employee. The trial court found the law inapplicable and allowed no setoff. The court of appeals reversed and the officer appealed to the Supreme Court of Missouri.

The supreme court held that the pension system could not set off its payments to the officer with workers' compensation payments from the police department for his nursing care. The court reasoned that the intent of the legislature was to allow only workers' compensation lost wages payments to be set off from pension payments. Otherwise, a retired officer who was not injured in the line of duty would be put in a financially better position than one who retired because he was injured in the line of duty. This result would occur because although both would be receiving the same benefits, the injured officer would have more expenses than the uninjured officer. The supreme court reversed the court of appeals. *Sheldon v. Board of Trustees of Police Retirement Sys.*, 779 S.W.2d 553 (Mo.1989).

A Michigan township employee was injured in a car accident while on the job. He was unable to return to his job and received workers' compensation benefits. He also received the difference between his workers' compensation benefits and his base pay under the collective bargaining agreement between his labor association and the township. The employee also applied for no-fault personal injury protection work loss benefits from the township's insurer. The insurer refused to pay benefits for work loss, claiming that the employee's receipt of wage continuation benefits precluded him from recovering work loss benefits. Alternatively, the insurer argued that wage continuation benefits should be subject to a set-off against the other governmental benefits received by the employee.

The employee sued the insurer in a Michigan trial court under the state no-fault act. The court ruled for the employee and the insurer appealed to the Michigan Court of Appeals. The appeals court ruled that the employee had suffered a work loss which was not subject to a mandatory set-off provision under Michigan law for receipt of governmental benefits. The employee's benefits had been received pursuant to a collective bargaining agreement. Under the statute, this was not a benefit provided under state or federal law. The Michigan legislature had not intended no-fault benefits to coordinate with other benefits which might be available to produce a duplicate recovery. The trial court had not erred in ruling that the employee was entitled to receive both wage continuation benefits under the collective bargaining agreement and no-fault benefits from the township's insurer. *Spencer v. Hartford Accident and Indemnity Co.*, 445 N.W.2d 520 (Mich.App.1989).

V. BENEFITS FOR ILLNESSES

Benefits will infrequently be awarded to employees who suffer illnesses unrelated to their jobs. Often, it is difficult to discern whether an illness has arisen out of an employee's occupation. Thus, lawsuits in this area have become fairly common.

A New York county police officer filed an application for ordinary disability retirement which stated that he was permanently disabled from his employment because of severe gastrointestinal disorders. The state police officers' and fire fighters' retirement system had him examined by a physician and, as a result of that examination, the officer's application was denied. The state comptroller, who made the decision, determined that the officer was not permanently incapacitated for the performance of his duties. An administrative hearing was conducted at the officer's request, and the comptroller's decision was confirmed. The officer then appealed to the Supreme Court, Appellate Division.

The appeals court noted that the medical evidence introduced at the hearing was conflicting. The officer's physician stated that the condition would persist until the officer left the police department or was given other duties, and the retirement services' physician asserted that there was no proven relationship between the officer's physical complaints and his job, and that the officer wasn't permanently disabled. The court thus determined that it must support the hearing officer's determination because the weight of the evidence was not clearly against it. The appellate court affirmed the hearing officer's decision, and denied benefits to the officer. *Matter of Rovegno v. Regan*, 478 N.Y.S.2d 114 (A.D.3d Dep't 1984).

A California woman worked for a county sheriff's department as a jail matron for nine years. Her duties were to take care of female prisoners' needs. Eight years after she started, the jail facilities were moved and the employee was "locked in" at the the new jail and given split shifts to work which resulted in irregular working hours. She allegedly suffered severe nervousness as a result of the change, and because of the additional "dirty work" assignments she was given. Eventually, after attempting to take tranquilizers before going to work, she left her job on her doctor's advice. She then filed for disability retirement benefits and a hearing officer determined that her disability had arisen out of and in the course of her employment. The county retirement board nevertheless denied her benefits, and she sought an enforcement order in a California trial court. The court granted her request and the board appealed to the Court of Appeal, First District.

The court of appeal first noted that the employee's disability had arisen out of a variety of causes, but that a part of the cause arose from her employment. California law allowed disability retirement benefits only if the disability arose out of an employee's job. The court then stated that the job related injury which caused the disability need not be the sole cause of the incapacity. So long as the job was a contributing cause of the disability, the court would find that benefits were payable. The court affirmed the trial Court's decision. *Heaton v. Marin County Employees Retirement Board,* 133 Cal.Rptr. 809 (Cal.App.1st Dist.1976).

In 1982, after undergoing a required medical examination, a New York man was appointed to a position with a city's police department. Approximately three years later, he was hospitalized complaining of chest pains. He then applied for retirement because of a "disability incurred in performance of duty" under New York's Retirement and Social Security Law. He asserted that he was permanently disabled from performing his duties because of coronary artery disease. The state police officers' and fire fighters' retirement system denied him benefits, and a hearing officer affirmed that determination. The employee then appealed to the Supreme Court, Appellate Division.

On appeal, he contended that New York law did not require that his incapacity be the natural and proximate result of a disability sustained in the performance of his duties. He argued that because he was employed and performing his duties at the time he became disabled, he should be entitled to disability retirement benefits. The appellate court disagreed. It noted that although the law's requirements had been lessened to help employees show that their disabilities were work-related, the law still required some connection between the employment and the injury. Here, there was substantial evidence that the injury was not work-related, and the employee had not introduced any evidence to the contrary. Accordingly, he had been properly denied benefits and the lower court's determination was affirmed. *Ashley v. New York State Policemen's and Firemen's Retirement System,* 521 N.Y.S.2d 845 (A.D.3d Dep't 1987).

A New York corrections officer injured his back when he slipped on a wet surface while on duty at a county correctional facility. The officer filed a claim for workers' compensation benefits and submitted to the county a "disability certificate" prepared by a doctor which certified that he was unable to return to work. Subsequently, the officer received weekly payments equal to his regular wages from the county and was awarded benefits by the workers' compensation board. However, four months later the county terminated his weekly payments. The officer then sued the county in a New York trial court claiming that he was entitled to receive payments equal to his regular wages as statutory disability benefits according to general municipal law from the county. The trial court dismissed the case as premature because the county had not yet made a determination as to whether the officer's disability arose from performance of his work. The officer appealed to the Supreme Court, Appellate Division.

The appellate court noted that according to General Municipal Law § 207-C(1) any corrections officer injured in the performance of his duties is entitled to the full amount of his regular wages until his disability has ceased. The appellate court held that the Workers' Compensation Board, in rendering its award to the officer, determined that the officer had suffered an injury in the line of duty. Thus, the officer was entitled to the weekly payments as statutory disability benefits. The appellate court reversed the trial court decision. *Crawford v. Sheriff's Dep't*, 548 N.Y.S.2d 734 (A.D.2d Dep't 1989).

A New York police officer fell down a flight of stairs injuring his back, hips and shoulders, after being attacked by a dog. Two years later, the officer returned to work where he was assigned to light duty desk work. After one month of performing these duties he went on sick leave until his retirement some two years later because sitting aggravated his back. He filed a claim for accidental and performance of duty disability retirement benefits. A hearing officer recommended that the benefits be denied because the officer did not prove that he was permanently incapacitated and unable to perform the duties of a police officer. The comptroller affirmed the hearing officer's decision, and the police officer appealed to a New York trial court which transferred the case to the Supreme Court, Appellate Division.

The appellate court held that the comptroller was free to rely on the testimony of the the retirement system's physician who determined that the officer could return to light duty work, rather than relying on the police officer's treating physician's testimony that the officer could not return to light duty work. Thus, the police officer was not entitled to accidental and performance of duty disability retirement benefits. The appellate court affirmed the comptroller's decision. *Rubinski v. Police and Fire Ret. Sys.*, 550 N.Y.S.2d 107 (A.D.3d Dep't 1989).

A man was employed by a California county as a deputy marshal. Because of an off-duty motorcycle accident, the man became permanently and totally disabled. A nonservice disability pension was applied for and denied. The reasons for denial included that the disability was caused by "intemperate use of alcohol" and a "violation of the law." A hearing upheld the pension denial, and an additional appeal was taken to the California Court of Appeal, Fourth District.

Issues for the appeals court were trimmed to one: can a single occasion constitute the "intemperate use of alcohol." This language comes directly from a California statute and must be given its usual meaning. The court disregarded the officer's argument and found that "intemperate" does not imply habitual. The fact that the conduct occurred only once was ruled to be irrelevant. The court felt that the intent of the legislature was not to force the public to finance a disability caused by an employee's willful behavior. The denial of the disability pension by the hearing board was upheld. *Keith v. San Bernardino County Ret. Bd.*, 271 Cal.Rptr. 649 (Cal.App.4th Dist.1990)

A New York police officer suffered nerve deafness to both ears when a co-worker placed a firecracker under the door of a bathroom where the officer was present. He filed claims for accidental and performance of duty disability retirement benefits. The New York State Police and Fireman's Retirement System determined that the officer's disability did not occur while in performance of his duties and denied his claims. The officer appealed to the Supreme Court, Appellate Division.

The appellate court noted that the officer must be doing his job when the injury occurred in order to be eligible for benefits. The incident took place fifteen minutes before the officer's tour of duty was to begin, but it was a long standing informal department practice that officers reported early to prepare for work. The appellate court held that the officer sustained his injury when he was performing his job duties. *De Zago v. Police and Fireman's Ret. Sys.*, 550 N.Y.S.2d 214 (A.D.3d Dep't 1990).

A New York firefighter worked for thirteen years before he was suspended for misconduct. During his suspension, the fire fighter was diagnosed as having coronary artery disease. As a result, he was unable to return to work. The fire fighter then sought salary and medical benefits under state law from the Board of Fire Commissioners. The board denied his request, concluding that the heart condition was not the result of his employment. The New York Supreme Court, Appellate Division, reversed, finding that the board had to rebut the statutory presumption that the fire fighter's disease had developed in the line-of-duty. The board then appealed to the Court of Appeals of New York.

The firefighter maintained that the statutory line-of-duty presumption found in New York's retirement and social security law applied to fire fighters seeking disability benefits under another state law which provided sick-leave benefits to fire fighters. He argued that the legislature intended to have a line-of-duty presumption for firefighter benefits since it had amended the applicable law to that effect after the appellate court had entered its decision. The court, however, determined that the legislature had not intended that the line-of-duty presumption be applied to the statute providing firefighter benefits. It noted that the legislature could have easily amended the law to include the presumption, but did not. The board's denial of the firefighter's benefits was reinstated. *Sutka v. Conners*, 541 N.Y.S.2d 191 (Ct.App.1989).

Illinois law requires firefighters to contribute toward disability pension funds. They receive sixty-five percent of their salary rates for disability for injury in the line-of-duty, and fifty percent for disability not in the line-of-duty. A veteran firefighter began to experience chronic back pain. Three years later, the fire fighter injured his lower back while lifting an accident victim onto a stretcher. He did not seek medical attention but filled out an injury report with his employer. On the same day, his symptoms worsened and he contacted his family doctor. He was put in a back brace and underwent surgery. He was physically unable to return to work as a fire fighter or paramedic. The fire fighter applied for a line-of-duty disability pension and the hearing board determined that disability was due to the preexisting condition, rather than the performance of his job duties. The fire fighter appealed the board's decision to an Illinois circuit court which affirmed the board's decision. He then appealed to the Illinois Appellate Court.

The appellate court stated that preexisting physical disabilities did not automatically bar line-of-duty disability pensions if the act aggravated a preexisting condition. However, pension claimants had the burden of proving they were entitled to line-of-duty pensions. In this case, the fire fighter did not seek medical attention and the evidence indicated that the injury was a temporary aggravation of an ongoing degenerative process. The testimony of the fire fighter's doctor indicated that the lifting injury might have been a factor in the disability, but did not unequivocally indicate that his present physical condition resulted from the injury. The court affirmed the board and circuit court decisions. *Evert v. Bd. of Trustees*, 536 N.E.2d 143 (Ill.App.2d Dist.1989).

The Age Discrimination in Employment Act of 1967, 29 U.S.C. § 621 et seq., prohibits age-based discrimination by public and private employers, subject to some exceptions, found in ADEA § 623(f)(2), and permits employers to maintain bona fide employee benefit plans which are not enacted as a subterfuge to evade the act. The Public Employees Retirement System of Ohio (PERS) administered public retirement and disability benefits. The PERS maintained separate retirement benefit rates, one of which awarded disabled employees who retired under the age of sixty to collect substantially higher benefits than disabled persons retiring after age sixty.

A speech pathologist worked for an Ohio county board of mental retardation for seven years. The board's employees were covered under PERS. The pathologist suffered medical problems, and was forced to retire at age sixty-one. Although she qualified for age and service retirement benefits under PERS, she was denied disability retirement benefits because she was over age sixty. The pathologist filed an age discrimination complaint against PERS with the Equal Employment Opportunity Commission (EEOC) and sued PERS in a federal district court. The court determined that the PERS's retirement system was discriminatory on the basis of age. PERS appealed to the U.S. Court of Appeals, Sixth Circuit, which affirmed the district court's decision. PERS then appealed to the U.S. Supreme Court.

The Court noted that plans in existence before the ADEA's enactment could not possibly be characterized as subterfuges to evade the act. The PERS system was established in 1933 and the provision governing disability retirement benefits for employees retiring after age sixty had been unchanged since 1959. Thus, the PERS statutory scheme was not a subterfuge. The Court rejected the pathologist's reliance on a Department of Labor regulation interpreting the Act, 29 C.F.R. § 1625.10, which stated that age-based reductions in employee benefits must be justified on a cost basis. The statute itself made no such requirement, and no deference was due to the agency's interpretation of the statute. Employees bore the burden of proving that benefit plans constituted subterfuge under the Act. Because the pathologist had not met her burden of proof, the lower courts had incorrectly ruled in her favor. The Court remanded the case to the district court for further consideration. *Public Employees Retirement System of Ohio v. Betts*, 109 S.Ct 1111, 106 L.Ed.2d 134 (1989).

A Philadelphia police officer suffered numerous back injuries and missed substantial time at work due to on-duty accidents which arose from being poked by a seatbelt, riding over a bump, and looking out the back window of a car. After a medical examination, the officer was ordered to return to work. He refused, and was terminated. The officer then applied to the city board for a disability retirement pension. It was denied because the officer could not establish that the injuries were solely the result of his duties. The officer successfully appealed to a state court, and the city appealed to the Commonwealth Court of Pennsylvania.

The dispute centered over the effect of a doctor's opinion that the officer suffered from a disease in his back. The issues were identifying the correct injury causation requirements for a pension, and determining how a preexisting condition should be viewed. The court construed the applicable causation ordinance to require "a complete and exclusive nexus between the performance of work duties and the resultant disability." On the preexisting injury issue, the officer argued that the court should not allow the denial of a pension based on a "statistical proposition."

The officer cited an earlier Pennsylvania case which involved an employee who suffered a heart attack. The court in that case refused to infer a preexisting condition from the statistical proposition that heart attacks are usually preceded by coronary artery disease. However, the court felt that the denial in this case was based on more than a statistical proposition. The doctor's expert testimony revealed that the officer suffered from a preexisting back disease, that he had probably exaggerated his symptoms, and that the employment duties were not the sole cause or trigger of the back problem. The appellate court reversed the trial court's decision and reinstated the board's denial of the pension. *DeBerry v. Bd. of Pensions & Retirement*, 585 A.2d 616 (Pa.Cmwlth.1991).

An Illinois city firefighter had a long history of on-the-job injuries and many of the incidents included back injuries. After receiving treatment and being placed on disability several times, the firefighter was later found to be permanently disabled. An administrative hearing was held which resulted in a determination that the injuries may have been preexisting. A partial disability pension which paid fifty percent of the firefighter's salary was granted. An appeal to an Illinois circuit awarded the full pension of sixty-five percent of the firefighter's salary and found that the injuries were caused on the job. The city then appealed to the Appellate Court of Illinois.

The issue on appeal was whether the trial court was correct in overruling the administrative board. This should be done only when the decision is against the manifest weight of the evidence or when the decision is legally erroneous. Under Illinois law, a preexisting condition aggravated by normal on-the-job duties does not disqualify an employee from receiving a full pension. Although the evidence was inconclusive, there was no incident other than on-the-job accidents causing the injuries. The fact that the firefighter's back may have been weak was irrelevant as long as on-the-job duties caused the injuries. Therefore, the decision of the administrative board to deny full pension was clear legal error. The appeals court upheld the decision of the trial court and the firefighter was granted a full pension. *Kellan v. Fireman's Pension Fund,* 551 N.E.2d 264 (Ill.App.1st Dist.1990).

A fire captain began experiencing symptoms of heart disease nineteen years after becoming a member of the New York City Fire Department. After the Pension Fund Board of Trustees denied him accidental disability pension benefits, the captain sought review of the board's decision in a New York trial court. The trial court found for the fire captain and the board appealed to the Supreme Court, Appellate Division of New York.

On appeal, the board contended that the captain's condition was psychosomatic and therefore he was not entitled to benefits. The court noted that there was ample evidence that the condition was induced by stress, as well as by exercise, and that his condition was disabling. The New York legislature passed a "heart bill" which gives disability benefits to those public employees who, because of their line of work, have a higher incidence of heart disease. The "heart bill," the court noted, affords a presumption that any disabling heart condition is service-related. Since the board failed to produce evidence that the heart condition was psychosomatic, the appellate court affirmed the lower court's decision. *Liston v. City of New York*, 555 N.Y.S.2d 757 (A.D.1st Dep't 1990).

VI. RETIREMENT BENEFITS

Generally, retirement benefits are awarded in accordance with contract law. However, in situations where denial of benefits would be egregious, the court will modify the contract, awarding benefits.

The sheriff of a West Virginia county was convicted of the felony of accepting bribes. The crime occurred shortly before the sheriff's retirement. When the sheriff applied for his pension earned from over thirty-five years of service, he was denied any benefits because of the conviction. The sheriff appealed the Public Employees Retirement System's decision to a West Virginia trial court. The denial of benefits was upheld and the sheriff appealed to the Supreme Court of Appeals.

On appeal, the sheriff argued that the punishment was unconstitutional. The original penalty for the conviction was $3,000 and three years probation. To deny the pension benefits in addition to the original penalty was argued to be cruel and unusual punishment. However, an explicit West Virginia statute called for exactly that punishment. The court brought to light the importance of the trust between the public and their servants. This was shown to be public policy as evidenced by the legislature's acts calling for public service to be honorable "throughout the service." The denial of the pension was not found cruel and unusual because of the sheriff's glaring breach of trust: specifically, the failure of a law enforcement officer to enforce the law. The court upheld the lower court's denial of a pension. *Public Emp. Retirement System v. Dodd*, 396 S.E.2d 725 (W.Va.1990).

A woman was hired in 1958 by an Alabama county for a position titled Court Clerk III, and promoted to supervisor in 1968. In April, 1977, a survey was held which was designed to reclassify county employees according to their actual duties. The woman was then reclassified as deputy sheriff for the last five years that she worked. Six years after her retirement the woman applied for a pension paid to law enforcement officials. The woman was denied the pension because she had not been classified as deputy for the required twenty years. The woman filed a lawsuit seeking the pension and was granted summary judgment. The county then appealed to the Court of Civil Appeals of Alabama.

The woman argued that despite her classification she had performed as a law enforcement officer for longer than the required twenty years. The woman showed that no classification as deputy was available for a female prior to 1977, and that her duties for over twenty years were exclusively that of a deputy. Additionally, she was not forced to undergo the training required for new deputies upon her reclassification. She contended that this was because she was grandfathered in. The county failed to directly refute the woman's evidence. The woman was ruled to have performed as a law enforcement officer for the requisite twenty years despite her classification, and was again awarded summary judgment and a pension. *Mobile County Law Enf. v. Wainwright*, 571 So.2d 1205 (Ala.Civ.App.1990).

The retirement benefits of teachers and employees of the state of Georgia (teachers) had been exempt from state income tax. In September, 1989, the Georgia legislature removed that exemption. The teachers felt that this amounted to an unconstitutional impairment of their contract with the state.

The first question was whether the income tax exemption had become part of the teachers' contracts. The court found that since all the teachers had either contributed toward the benefits or had performed the services during the active period of the exemption legislation, the exemption had become part of their contracts. The state then argued that a permanent exemption was unlawful and, therefore, the teachers' contracts were unlawful and unenforcable. An examination of the 1877 Georgia Constitution provides that no legislation shall permanently restrict the state's powers of taxation. The teachers argued that allowing them to retain the exemption did not amount to a permanent restriction of the state's powers; the state could begin to tax future retirees. However, the court failed to follow this reasoning. The supreme court affirmed the trial court's decision, and the retirees will now be subject to state income taxation. *Parish v. Employees' Retirement System*, 398 S.E.2d 353 (Ga.1990).

A city engineer, appointed by township officials, was indicted for official misconduct. After resigning, the engineer was convicted and ordered to pay a fine and costs. He sought to recover his early retirement benefits and appeared before the board of trustees of the public employee retirement system. The board recommended that he forfeit all pension benefits. The engineer appealed to the Superior Court of New Jersey, Appellate Division.

On appeal, the court noted that deferred compensation benefits have been earned by an employee and are not a gratuity. The court ruled that when considering forfeiture of vested rights, strict construction of the statute is required. Since the city engineer was not removed from office, the court found nothing to preclude his voluntary retirement before being convicted so as to attain pension benefits. The court reversed the decision of the board and gave the city engineer early pension benefits. *Widdis v. Public Employee Retirement System*, 568 A.2d 1227 (N.J.Super.A.D.1990).

A Florida police officer began working in the police department in 1960. After retiring in 1988, he submitted an application to the division for retirement benefits. On the application the police officer designated his three sons as beneficiaries. The officer died two days before he was to receive his retirement benefits. The Division for Retirement Benefits determined that the beneficiaries were not entitled to receive the accumulated contributions. The beneficiaries appealed to a Florida trial court.

The court noted that under the Florida Retirement System a member is entitled to obtain retirement benefits when he reaches his normal retirement date. The section also allows for special risk members to achieve retirement status upon the completion of twenty-five years of service, regardless of age. Since law enforcement officers are special risk members, the police officer had achieved retirement status by completing twenty-five years of service in 1985. The court determined that the officer's benefits accrued in 1985 since a worker may reach retirement status and elect not to retire at that time. The district court reversed and remanded the decision of the Division of Retirement Benefits and awarded retirement benefits to the police officer's sons. *O'Connell v. State Department of Administration*, 557 So.2d 609 (Fla.App.3d Dist.1990).

A Philadelphia city employee married in 1962 and named his wife as his beneficiary to receive death benefits. The couple separated and the city employee began paying support to the first wife pursuant to a court order. Then, he was "married" a second time and executed a change of beneficiary in which he named his second wife as his beneficiary. Up until his death, he had been making the required support payments to his first wife even though they were never divorced. After the city employee died, both wives applied to the pension board for death benefits. The board denied both applications. The first wife then requested a hearing before the board. Following the hearing, the board awarded benefits to the second wife. The first wife appealed to the Court of Common Pleas of Philadelphia which reversed the board's order and awarded her benefits. The board appealed to the Commonwealth Court of Pennsylvania.

The court noted that § 214 of Philadelphia's Municipal Retirement Ordinance provides benefits for a spouse who was living with the employee at the time of death or entitled to support by him. The court determined that the board erred in awarding benefits to the second wife because they were not married. Since the first wife was entitled to support, the court reasoned that she was entitled to death benefits. The commonwealth court affirmed the trial court's decision and awarded the first wife death benefits. *Bd. of Pension and Retirement v. Boelter*, 572 A.2d 867 (Pa.Cmwlth.1990).

CHAPTER SEVEN
LABOR RELATIONS

I. DEVELOPMENTS UNDER THE FLSA

The courts have made a substantial swing over the last twenty years with respect to interpreting how the Fair Labor Standards Act, 29 U.S.C. § 201 et seq., applies to public employees. Eventually, the law became rather well settled with the U.S. Supreme Court's decision in *Garcia v. SAMTA*, third case below, decided in 1985, which required state and local employers to comply with the FLSA.

In 1961, Congress amended the Fair Labor Standards Act, extending protection to employees of businesses involved in interstate commerce regardless of whether the individual employees were themselves engaged in commerce or production for commerce. This amendment also applied to hospitals and schools. Subsequently, the state of Maryland and twenty-seven other states sued the Secretary of Labor to prohibit enforcement of the amended act. They contended that the expansion of coverage was beyond Congress' power under the commerce clause, and that schools and hospitals should be exempt because they were not related to interstate commerce. A three-judge district court determined that the amended law was valid, and the states appealed directly to the U.S. Supreme Court.

On appeal, the Court first noted that the extension of coverage to all employees of businesses engaged in interstate commerce was constitutional. Since substandard labor conditions tended to lead to labor disputes and strikes, the whole country's flow of goods could be affected by low wages and nonpayment of overtime. The Court further held that the extension of the act to schools and hospitals was valid as well because regardless of whether they were engaged in interstate commerce they purchased a vast range of out-of-state goods and thereby affected interstate commerce a great deal. The Court thus affirmed the lower court's decision and upheld the act as valid. *Maryland v. Wirtz*, 392 U.S. 192, 88 S.Ct. 2017, 20 L.Ed.2d 1020 (1968).

The Fair Labor Standards Act of 1938, 29 U.S.C. § 201 et seq., required certain employers to pay their employees a minimum hourly wage and to pay time-and-a-half for hours worked over forty in a given workweek. In 1974, Congress sought to amend the act and broaden its coverage to include almost all public employees. Various cities and states and the National League of Cities brought an action in a federal district court to challenge the validity of the amendments, asserting that intergovernmental immunity prevented Congress from so amending the act. A three-judge district court was convened, which dismissed the complaint. Further appeal was taken to the U.S. Supreme Court.

On appeal, the Supreme Court held that the 1974 amendments operated to obstruct the states' abilities to structure their employer-employee relationships with respect to areas of traditional government functions. In this respect, the amendments were invalid because they impaired the states' abilities to function effectively in a federal system. Essentially, the Court determined that Congress could not directly force the states to utilize only Congress' means of conducting integral governmental functions. To do so would usurp the states' authority as separate entities. The Court thus reversed the three-judge court's decision and held the amendments invalid. *National League of Cities v. Usery*, 426 U.S. 833, 96 S.Ct. 2465, 49 L.Ed.2d 245 (1976).

The San Antonio Metropolitan Transit Authority (SAMTA), a public mass-transit authority, provided transportation to the San Antonio area with the help of substantial financial assistance under the Urban Mass Transportation Act. In 1979, the Wage and Hour Administration of the Department of Labor issued an opinion that SAMTA's operations were not immune from the minimum wage and overtime requirements of the Fair Labor Standards Act (FLSA). SAMTA filed a suit in federal district court, asserting, under *National League of Cities v. Usery*, see above, that it was exempt from the requirements of FLSA. The district court agreed, and appeal was taken directly to the U.S. Supreme Court.

The Supreme Court noted that drawing boundaries between areas of traditional governmental functions and those areas which were not traditionally run by the government was not only unworkable, but inconsistent with established principles of federalism. Forcing local governments to comply with FLSA in areas not traditionally governmental, and allowing state immunity for functions which were deemed traditionally governmental would lead to inconsistent results. Further, the Court noted that the FLSA requirements were not destructive of state sovereignty nor violative of the constitution. Accordingly, the Court overruled *National League of Cities* and reversed the decision of the district court. *Garcia v. San Antonio*

Metropolitan Transit Authority, 469 U.S. 528, 105 S.Ct. 1005, 83 L.Ed.2d 1016 (1985).

Eleven supervisory housing inspectors employed by the District of Columbia unsuccessfully made considerable efforts to be compensated for overtime work in accordance with the Fair Labor Standards Act (FLSA). The inspectors then filed an action against their employer in a federal district court. Despite the city's arguments that an administrative exception applied, the suit resulted in an order for the city to pay the contested overtime compensation. Two post-trial motions were then filed by the inspectors seeking liquidated damages and a declaration that the city had wilfully violated the FLSA.

A court is vested with discretion by the FLSA to order a wilful violator to pay, in addition to the backpay it owes, liquidated damages equal to the amount of compensation withheld. These additional damages are commonly awarded unless the violator can show that it acted in good faith. This heavy burden requires evidence of an effort to determine the law, and showing that the decision was based on reasonable grounds. In this case, good faith was not found. The city had made no effort to determine the inspectors' duties. It had classified them based solely on job title, despite notice that it should classify based on actual duties. Further, the city was shown to be aware of the requirements of the FLSA. It had been involved in earlier litigation over the issue. The court accordingly declared a wilful violation. This extended the statute of limitations and allowed the inspectors damages for an additional six months. Both post-trial motions were granted and liquidated damages were awarded to the inspectors. *Harris v. District of Columbia*, 749 F.Supp. 301 (D.D.C.1990).

Various present and former employees of a water utility department for a Florida county sued the department in a federal district court, asserting that it had violated 29 U.S.C. §§ 206-207 of the FLSA. The district court dismissed their complaint, and they appealed to the U.S. Court of Appeals, Eleventh Circuit.

The issue on appeal was whether the Supreme Court's decision in *Garcia v. San Antonio Metropolitan Transit Authority*, see above, should be applied retroactively and whether FLSA barred the suit because it came within the grace period granted by FLSA. The appellate court first held that retroactive application should not be extended to the present case because, prior to *Garcia*, public employees' benefit packages and monetary compensation were based on the presumption that overtime would not be paid and that the public employers were not required to comply with FLSA with respect to "traditional governmental functions" jobs (tgf jobs). To hold the county liable retroactively would change the employment relationship which had previously existed. The court then noted that if the employees had not held tgf jobs, their suit would not be barred by the amendments to FLSA.

The grace period granted by FLSA applied only to tgf jobs and not all public employment. The court thus remanded the case to the district court for a determination as to whether the employees held tgf jobs. *Ackinclose v. Palm Beach County, Florida*. 845 F.2d 931 (11th Cir.1988).

District of Columbia department of corrections foremen and teachers sued the District of Columbia for overtime pay under the Federal Labor Standards Act (FLSA). Under § 13(a)(1) of the FLSA, 29 U.S.C. § 213(a)(1), overtime provisions are inapplicable to "any employee employed in a bona fide executive, administrative or professional capacity."

The U.S. District Court, District of Columbia, determined that in order for the foremen to be exempt from the FLSA overtime provisions, they must be executives who regularly supervise two or more employees. Since the persons the foremen supervised were prisoners, the foremen were not exempt from the FLSA overtime provisions. As for the teachers, the district court held that they were exempt from the FLSA overtime provisions, because they were professionals within the meaning of the FLSA. *Wilks v. District of Columbia,* 721 F.Supp. 1383 (D.D.C.1989).

Alien detainees of the Immigration and Naturalization Service (INS) were employed in grounds maintenance, cooking, laundry and other services at the rate of one dollar per day. The detainees filed suit in a federal district court and alleged that this practice was a violation of the Fair Labor Standards Act (FLSA), 29 U.S.C. §§ 201-219, seeking unpaid minimum wages and an injunction against the INS. The INS filed a motion to dismiss the case. The federal district court granted the INS's motion to dismiss and the detainees appealed to the U.S. Court of Appeals, Fifth Circuit.

Under the FLSA, an employee is defined as any individual employed by an employer. Since the INS is not an employer the alien detainees were not employees within the meaning of FLSA. The court noted that the FLSA was enacted to protect the standard of living and the general well-being of the worker in American industry. Since the detainees were not in American industry, they were not in the group Congress sought to protect in enacting the FLSA. The court determined that minimum wage provisions were not applicable and affirmed the district court's decision. *Lavarado Geuvera v. INS*, 902 F.2d 394 (5th Cir.1990)

Minnesota paramedics and ambulance workers could not come to an agreement with a county medical center on a new contract. The employees had been working twelve hour shifts for seven days and then were off for seven days. When the U.S. Supreme Court decided *Garcia v. San Antonio Metropolitan Transit Authority*, 469 U.S. 528 (1985), see above, the county informed the employees they would have to work regular shifts. Otherwise the county would have to pay them overtime under *Garcia*. The employees asked that the matter be submitted to mediation and when that failed, to arbitration. The arbitrator decided that the county should reinstate the twelve hour shift and give employees a three percent raise. The county appealed to a Minnesota trial court. The trial court reversed the arbitrator's decision because this was a determination of regular shift length, not maximum hours, and therefore was not included in the collective bargaining agreement. The employees appealed this decision to the Minnesota Court of Appeals.

The court of appeals stated that the arbitrator could not make decisions on questions of internal management. It also decided that determination of shift lengths and normal work hours were matters of managerial concern, and outside the scope of the arbitrator's power. The court affirmed the trial court's decision. *Hennepin Cty. Ambulance Ass'n v. Hennepin Cty.*, 394 N.W. 2d 206 (Minn.App.1986).

The U.S. Bureau of Prisons established a standard national uniform for all its guards. The Federal Correctional Institute in Morgantown, West Virginia, was a low-security prison populated by inmates convicted of nonviolent crimes. The facility did not strictly observe the bureau's uniform requirements. In 1985, its management drafted regulations that more strictly complied with federal standards. The proposed regulations generally called for a standardized uniform featuring neckties and blazers. The union representing prison guards requested negotiations over the regulations. The prison warden responded that he would negotiate only on the impact and implementation of the uniform changes and not on the substance of the proposal. The union claimed it had the right to negotiate the proposal's substance and attached a set of counter-proposals. The warden reiterated the nonnegotiability of the proposed regulations and the union filed an unfair labor practices complaint against the bureau with the Federal Labor Relations Authority (FLRA)'s general counsel. Meanwhile, the revised regulations went into effect.

An administrative law judge determined that the bureau had not engaged in unfair labor practices and dismissed the complaint. This decision was affirmed by the FLRA and the union appealed to the U.S. Court of Appeals, District of Columbia Circuit. The appeals court considered the Federal Service Labor-Management Relations Statement, 5 U.S.C. § 7106(b)(1), which defined matters about which agencies were not permitted to bargain. These included decisions concerning these "methods, and means of performing work." Federal agencies were permitted but not required to negotiate with labor organizations in those cases. The court determined that the uniform requirements involved a "means of performing work" under the statute and were exempt from the bureau's duty to bargain. The union's counter-proposal would directly interfere with the warden's proposal. This was based on testimony that uniformed guards would interact better with the inmates and the public. The proposal was designed to improve the guards' performance and was a "means of performing work." The court affirmed the FLRA's dismissal of the unfair labor practices charge. *American Federation of Gov't Employees, AFL-CIO, Local 2441 v. FLRA*, 864 F.2d 178 (D.C. Cir.1988).

The Federal Labor Relations Authority (FLRA) ordered the Immigration and Naturalization Service (INS) to bargain over a decision to alter the practice of allowing border patrol agents on rough duty in the San Diego sector to wear green, levi style jeans instead of the INS's standard green drill uniform trousers. The border patrol agents' union, the American Federation of Government Employees, intervened and the FLRA moved for enforcement of the order in the U.S. Court of Appeals, Ninth Circuit.

The court of appeals held that the INS was not required to bargain with the employees' union over its official service uniform. The designation of the components of the official uniform was a management right reserved to the employing agency by federal statute. The court noted that under the Federal Service Labor-Management Relations Act, agencies such as the INS were empowered to govern the appearance of their public contact employees. The right to control the actual uniform components was inherent in the INS's unquestioned right to require border patrol agents to wear a uniform. The court of appeals denied the enforcement of the FLRA's order. *U.S. Dep't of Justice v. FLRA*, 881 F.2d 636 (9th Cir.1989).

In four separate cases, labor unions which represented federal employees sought to have different government agencies provide them with the names and home addresses of agency employees working in relevant bargaining units. The unions stated that they needed the information to perform their representational duties effectively. The agencies refused and the Federal Labor Relations Authority (FLRA) ordered them to comply with the unions' requests. The FLRA stated that the unions were entitled to the disclosure under 5 U.S.C. § 7114(b)(4). Section 7114(b)(4) requires agencies to furnish information which is necessary for full discussion, understanding and negotiation of subjects within the scope of collective bargaining so long as such disclosure is not prohibited by law. Each of the agencies appealed the decision to the U.S. Court of Appeals, District of Columbia Circuit.

On appeal, the agencies contended that the information was not "necessary" within the meaning of § 7114(b)(4) and that, in any case, the disclosure was prohibited by the Privacy Act, 5 U.S.C. § 552a, which prohibits disclosure of personal information about federal employees without their consent unless such a disclosure is necessary under the Freedom of Information Act (FOIA) or for a "routine use." The court of appeals first stated that it would accept the FLRA's interpretation of what was "necessary" under § 7114(b)(4) since the FLRA is generally given deference on such matters. The court agreed, however, with the agencies that the disclosure was prohibited by law. The disclosure was not required by the FOIA since the Act's purposes would not be served by releasing the home addresses of government employees. Nor was the disclosure for a "routine use" as defined by the Office of Personnel Management. Such a use cannot include disclosure to a labor organization so long as an adequate alternative method of contacting employees exists. The court of appeals denied an order forcing disclosure. *FLRA v. U.S. Dep't of Treasury*, 884 F.2d 1446 (D.C.Cir.1989).

Two federal employee labor organizations requested the names and addresses of all their bargaining unit employees from their respective federal agencies. After the agencies refused to divulge the requested information, the labor associations brought separate unfair labor practice complaints against them with the Federal Labor Relations Authority. In both cases the authority reversed its own initial decisions and ruled that the agencies must disclose names and home addresses to the labor organizations. The authority agreed with the labor organizations' argument that the information was necessary for collective bargaining purposes under the Federal Service-Labor Management Relations Act (FSLMRA). The agencies petitioned the U.S. Court of Appeals, Eighth Circuit, for review of the decisions, and the authority cross-petitioned for enforcement.

The court of appeals considered the cases together. It noted the FSLMRA's requirement for agency disclosure of data reasonably necessary for the collective bargaining process. It also noted the conflict between the Privacy Act, which prohibits disclosure of federal employee personnel files without consent, and the Freedom of Information Act, which generally requires disclosure of government records. The court ruled that employees have cognizable privacy interests in their home addresses, which must be weighed against the public interest in disclosure. The competing interests of privacy and disclosure could best be served by requiring disclosure of the names and addresses of those employees who did not request confidentiality. The court affirmed the authority's cross-petition in part, limiting the disclosure to those employees who consented to disclosure. *U.S. Dep't of Agriculture v. FLRA*, 836 F.2d 1139 (8th Cir.1988).

The FLRA petitioned the U.S. Supreme Court for review. The Supreme Court vacated and remanded the appeals court decision because both agencies had meanwhile issued new regulations requiring disclosure of employee names and addresses where necessary for union representation. *FLRA v. U.S. Dep't of Agriculture*, 109 S.Ct. 831 (1989).

On remand, the appeals court noted that the federal agencies had voluntarily complied with what the labor associations had sought in the litigation. All parties had agreed that the appeals court's initial ruling barring disclosure of those individuals not opting for disclosure should not stand. There was little risk of further litigation and the legality of disclosure had been established. The court dismissed the case as moot. *U.S. Dep't of Agriculture v. FLRA*, 876 F.2d 50 (8th Cir.1989).

II. DISCRIMINATION

One area of labor relations which seems to invoke less litigation today is that of discrimination with respect to wages. This subject is also covered in Chapter Five (Discrimination).

A Georgia state college was found to have violated the Equal Pay Act with regard to male and female custodial workers at its facility. Thereafter, the U.S. Department of Labor (DOL) began investigating for possible equal pay violations among the faculty and determined that the college had violated the act in six specific instances. It then brought suit against the college in a federal district court, which held for the DOL. The college appealed to the U.S. Court of Appeals, Eleventh Circuit.

On appeal, the college contended that the female teachers receiving less pay were not doing substantially the same work as the male teachers who were paid more. The court, however, disagreed, finding that all the teachers who were compared were within the same academic division. Further, the teachers all taught students at approximately the same level and had similar course loads. Unless there was a valid seniority system, a merit system, a system which measured earnings by productivity or a system differentiated by a factor other than sex, the difference in pay for female teachers would be violative of the act. The court then determined that the college had failed to show a valid system for paying male and female teachers differently, and affirmed the district court's decision. *Brock v. Georgia Southwestern College*, 765 F.2d 1026 (11th Cir.1985).

A female faculty member of an Illinois university filed a complaint with the regional Office of Civil Rights (OCR), contending that the university had discriminated against its female faculty in salaries, promotions and assignments. The OCR investigated and determined that the university had discriminated against females, and it offered the university a chance to remedy its past practices. The university further investigated, agreed with the OCR, and devised a formula for incremental pay increases raising females' salaries to the same level as males' with similar experience and abilities. A class of male faculty members then sued the university in a federal district court, asserting that they had been discriminated against because the incremental pay increase formula should also have been applied to them. The court held for the university, and the male professors appealed to the U.S. Court of Appeals, Seventh Circuit.

The court of appeals first noted that the equity increase provided an accurate remedy for a clear wage violation and, as such, was valid. Further, it stated that the equity increases were not calculated as rates of pay for given female professors, but were merely incremental adjustments to remedy past discrimination. To allow the formula to apply to males would essentially continue the effects of discrimination at a higher level by giving men higher salaries and keeping women beneath those levels. The court thus held the salary adjustment valid and affirmed the district court's decision. *Ende v. Board of Regents of Regency Universities*, 757 F.2d 176 (7th Cir.1985).

Six teachers at the Indiana State Prison filed grievances against the state, asserting that they were not being compensated in compliance with Indiana law. Indiana law requires that teachers at the state prison be compensated according to the teacher salary structure of the largest school system in the county. An arbitrator ordered the state to correctly compensate the teachers, and also awarded them back pay. The state complied after unsuccessfully appealing the order. Subsequently, four other teachers filed complaints because they were being discriminated against by the state. They were being paid less than the six teachers who had won their arbitration awards, and were doing the same work with the same status. An Indiana trial court determined that the four teachers must be compensated in the same manner as the previous six, and the state appealed to the Court of Appeals of Indiana. The appellate court held that to allow the four teachers who had not originally filed complaints to be paid less than the other six was discriminatory and created unsatisfactory working conditions. The court thus affirmed the trial court's decision and granted similar awards to the remaining four teachers. *State v. Martin*, 460 N.E.2d 986 (Ind.App.4th Dist.1984).

The Fort Buchanan Installation Club System (FBICS) provided food and beverage services at the Fort Buchanan military base in Puerto Rico. The FBICS was a nonappropriated fund instrumentality (NAFI) of the United States government. Accordingly, its funds did not come from congressional appropriation but rather primarily from its own activities, services, and product sales. A group of employees of FBICS brought an action in a Puerto Rico trial court for back pay and damages under the Fair Labor Standards Act (FLSA) against the government. The government removed the case to a federal district court, then successfully sought a dismissal. The employees appealed to the U.S. Court of Appeals, First Circuit.

The appeals court stated that because the FBICS was a NAFI, it was suable in its own right to the extent of its nonappropriated funds. It then held, however, that because the employees were covered by FLSA, they could not seek benefits greater than those they were entitled to under FLSA. Even though private Puerto Rican employees might be better paid than federal employees because of the Puerto Rican minimum wage law, the employees had failed to show that that minimum wage law was intended to include federal employees. Accordingly, the court affirmed the lower court's dismissal of the case. *Cosme Nieves v. Deshler*, 786 F.2d 445 (1st Cir.1986).

A disabled veteran applied for a job with a Minnesota city. The veteran was among the top fifteen applicants but was not hired for the position. The city did not use a civil service system nor a competitive civil service examination in hiring. After the veteran was notified that he had not been chosen for the position, he filed a claim with the commissioner of veterans affairs alleging that he was denied his veterans preference rights under Minnesota law. An administrative law judge held that the city denied veterans preference rights and that the veteran would have been hired if given the advantage of veterans preference points. The judge recommended that the city immediately hire the veteran. The commissioner affirmed the judge's decision and ordered the city to hire the veteran. The city appealed to the Court of Appeals of Minnesota.

On appeal, the city argued that the veterans preference statute only applied to governmental units that used a civil service system of hiring. Since the city used a personnel ordinance hiring system, it was not required to give preference to veterans. The appellate court held that the veterans preference statute recognized veterans for their experience, loyalty and sacrifice. This statute applied uniformly throughout the state and included governmental units which used a personnel ordinance hiring system. The appellate court affirmed the commissioner's decision. *Hall v. City of Champlin*, 450 N.W.2d 613 (Minn.App.1990).

III. OVERTIME WAGES

The provision of the Fair Labor Standards Act which governs overtime wages is 29 U.S.C. § 207 which states that an employer may not work an employee more than forty hours per week unless the employee is paid at least one and one-half times his regular wage. The following cases illustrate that FLSA can be difficult to interpret.

The Fair Labor Standards Act (FLSA) requires all employers to pay their employees for overtime, but allows public employers to provide their employees compensatory time under a collective bargaining agreement or other agreement between the public agency and employee representatives. Where employees are unrepresented, public employers and their employees may reach agreement before the performance of any work. A Colorado fire protection district paid its employees compensatory time rather than overtime pay. The fire fighters appointed a labor organization, which the district did not officially recognize. The parties failed to reach an overtime compensation agreement. The labor organization then sued the district in a federal district court, claiming that the district was required to pay overtime pay under the FLSA. The court ruled for the labor organization and the district appealed to the U.S. Court of Appeals, Tenth Circuit.

The appeals court noted an ambiguity in FLSA § 207(o), which in one clause permitted payment of compensatory time under collective bargaining agreements but in another clause permitted preexisting agreements between public employers and unrepresented employees. The fire protection district argued that because it had not recognized the labor association as its employees' representative, the second clause of § 207(o) permitting preexisting agreements controlled. Under that theory, the district compensatory policy was legal under the FLSA. The appeals court disagreed, ruling that the clause permitting collective bargaining agreements to control was triggered when employees designated their representatives. Therefore, the district was required to negotiate a new compensation agreement with the labor organization. After rejecting the district's alternative theory that the FLSA requirements violated the Tenth Amendment, the appeals court affirmed the district court's decision for the labor association. *Local 2203 v. West Adams County Fire Protection Dist.*, 877 F.2d 814 (10th Cir.1989).

Kansas firefighters were required to be on on-call status whenever a unit was called out when the fire department was operating at minimum acceptable staffing levels. On-call status shifts were twenty-four-hours in length. During these shifts, firefighters could be called into the station at any time. On-call firefighters did not have to remain on station house premises but were required to reach the fire station within twenty minutes from the time they were contacted. When a firefighter was actually called in, he was paid overtime compensation. If on-call firefighters were late or missed a callback, they were subject to disciplinary action including possible termination. The firefighters sued the city in a federal district court, alleging that the city had violated the Fair Labor Standards Act (FLSA) by failing to pay overtime compensation for on-call hours when they were not called in.

The city argued that its policy of not compensating firefighters for on-call hours when they were not called in did not violate the FLSA requirements because the firefighters did not have to be on the station house premises while they were on-call. Also, the firefighters were free to engage in personal activities while on-call. The district court noted that the test under the FLSA is whether the time is spent predominantly for the employer's benefit or for the employee's. The court held that although on-call firefighters were not required to remain on the station house premises, the conditions of the on-call status restricted the employee from using the time for personal pursuits. Thus, under FLSA the city was required to pay the firefighters overtime compensation for on-call time. *Renfro v. City of Emporia*, 729 F.Supp. 747 (D.Kan.1990).

A Virginia city's administrative regulation gave its chief of police the power to establish overtime and regularly scheduled hours. The regular schedule for uniformed patrol officers was eight hours and fifteen minutes. After years of not enforcing a policy which required patrol officers to report for work fifteen minutes before their scheduled shifts, the police chief reaffirmed the policy, requiring the patrol officers to work an eight hour, fifteen minute day with no compensation for overtime. A group of patrol officers sued the city for breach of the city's administrative regulation, implied breach of contract and violation of their state and federal constitutional Equal Protection rights. A Virginia trial court dismissed the lawsuit and the officers appealed to the Virginia Supreme Court.

The supreme court found that there was no requirement under state law for overtime compensation for work in excess of eight hours a day. The officers had also failed to prove any right to overtime pay under the applicable city regulation or under an implied contract. The police chief had the authority to establish regularly scheduled hours and there was evidence that the eight hour, fifteen minute day without overtime pay was reasonable. Although patrol officers worked fifteen minutes longer than other uniformed officers, this compensation dispute was simply a contract dispute which did not implicate either the state or federal constitution. The supreme court affirmed the trial court's dismissal of the lawsuit. *Buchanan v. city of Chesapeake*, 375 S.E.2d 736 (Va.1989).

A Kansas man was employed by a county as an undersheriff for four years. During his employment, he was often required to work overtime. The county compensated him for the overtime at time-and-a-half until, two years into his employment, he waived his right to overtime pay. The undersheriff was eventually terminated when a new sheriff was elected, and he then sought compensation for the overtime he had worked and for accrued vacation time. A Kansas trial court ruled that he was entitled to vacation pay, but not overtime compensation, and both parties appealed to the Supreme Court of Kansas.

On appeal, the court first noted that although the undersheriff might not fall within the provisions of FLSA, he might be covered by the Kansas Minimum Wage and Maximum Hours Law (KMWMH). Only if the undersheriff was considered an administrative employee would he be excluded from the KMWMH. Since the trial court had neglected to ascertain whether the KMWMH applied, the supreme court determined that the case must be remanded for proceedings consistent with the KMWMH. The court then affirmed that part of the trial court's decision which had awarded the employee vacation pay. *Dollison v. Osborne County*, 737 P.2d 43 (Kan.1987).

A Colorado city employee worked as a mechanic and laborer from 1983-1985. He was required to work a substantial amount of overtime for which he was not compensated other than by his regular salary. After the U.S. Supreme Court decision in *Garcia v. SAMTA*, the employee sued the city in a Colorado trial court, asserting that the city had violated the Fair Labor Standards Act (FLSA) and Colorado Statute § 8-13-105(2) which both required that time-and-a-half be paid to employees who had to work overtime. The trial court dismissed his claim, holding that *Garcia* did not apply retroactively, and the employee appealed to the Colorado Court of Appeals.

On appeal, he dropped the FLSA claim and argued that § 8-13-105(2) clearly was intended to provide overtime compensation for all public employees. The city contended that the statute applied only to county employees, and not city employees, because it stated that the Board of County Commissioners would determine whether an employee should be compensated. The court of appeals determined that the employee was correct in his reading of the statute. It noted that the statute, as originally written, did not make a distinction between city and county employees, but included all public employees. The inclusion of the words "Board of County Commissioners" was merely an oversight. The court thus reversed the trial court's decision and remanded the case for trial. *Olin v. City of Duray*, 744 P.2d 761 (Colo.App.1987).

A group of New York teamsters worked on a maintenance crew in New York. The union had a collective bargaining agreement with the New York Thruway Authority (the Authority) which stated that during Winter Maintenance Patrol the crew would be fully staffed. During this time the crew was not to receive overtime pay on the weekdays but would receive such pay on the weekends and holidays. However, the Authority did not fully staff the crew on the weekends or holidays so they did not receive any overtime pay. By staffing a smaller crew on the weekends, the Authority was able to avoid overtime by working only those employees with less than forty hours during the week. The union filed a claim that was submitted to binding arbitration. The arbitrator held that the authority violated the agreement. The arbitrator decided that the phrase stating there would be full-time crews on weekdays also included weekends and holidays. The authority appealed the decision to a New York trial court which reversed the arbitrator's decision and ruled in favor of the Authority. The union appealed.

The New York appellate court stated that there was sufficient evidence to support the arbitrator's decision. It held that the clause was in the agreement to ensure that the crew would receive some overtime hours. It also stated that if the trial court's decision was followed, the Authority would have complete discretion over all staffing. It reversed the trial court's decision and reinstated the arbitrator's decision. *New York State Thruway Auth. v. Local 72*, 499 N.Y.S.2d 495 (A.D.3d Dep't 1986).

A New Jersey police officer was forced to be on stand-by duty for twenty-four hours, every other day. The officer would be on patrol duty for six hours and then on call for the next eighteen hours every other day. This was due to budget cuts in the New Jersey city, forcing the chief to fire three other police officers, keeping only the plaintiff. The police officer brought an action to recover additional compensation for the overtime he worked. The New Jersey trial court dismissed the case. It stated that since *Garcia v. San Antonio Metropolitan Transit Auth.*, 469 U.S. 528 (1985), see above, should not be given retroactive application, the officer did not have a claim. It also stated that overtime pay could not be given because New Jersey state wage and hour law did not apply to this employment relationship since there were specific statutes to govern the employment of police officers. The police officer appealed to the New Jersey Appellate Court.

The appellate court agreed with the trial court. Further, it stated that the issue of payment for excessive hours of work should not recur in the future unless the Federal Fair Labor Standards Act was amended to include police officers who were already covered by state law or the U.S. Supreme Court again reconsidered the applicability of the Garcia case to local government units. The appellate court affirmed the trial court's decision. *Perry v. Borough of Swedensboro*, 520 A.2d 410 (N.J.Super.A.D.1986).

A Washington police officer was told to work only eight hours a day with some "on call" duty. The officer worked twelve hour shifts, eight hours of duty and four hours on call. The officer later changed to forty-eight hour shifts to alleviate physical demands. When the officer was on call he had to remain in the city. Thus, he couldn't go home since he lived in another city. The police officer told the mayor and a city council member that he could not get everything done in eight hours and asked for additional compensation. The mayor and the city council member agreed that the officer should be given additional compensation. However, the full council rejected his request. Subsequently, the officer was dismissed and he filed a complaint in a Washington trial court. The trial court awarded the officer $25,399.03, overtime pay plus double compensation. The city appealed to the Court of Appeals of Washington.

The city argued that the Washington Minimum Wage Act (MWA) did not apply here because the officer was under an exclusion clause which states that employees who spend a substantial portion of their worktime on call and not in active duty are not under MWA. The court of appeals stated that to determine if the employee is on call or on active duty depends on the employment agreement, whether the employee is required to remain on the premises, whether the employee can engage in his own activities, and whether the time spent is for the employer's benefit. Further, it stated that the "on call" time must be a substantial portion of the duty. It also stated that MWA exclusions must be strictly construed in favor of the employee since MWA is intended to benefit the employee. However, the court stated that the trial court did not give adequate instructions or definitions to allow the jury to properly apply the exclusion. Thus, the court of appeals reversed the trial court's decision and remanded the case for a new trial. *Goff v. City of Airway Heights*, 730 P.2d 691 (Wash.App.1986).

Other Washington police officers from a different county also brought a claim for compensation for "on call" time. These officers were paid overtime if actually called for duty while on call. When these officers were on call they could not leave the county and they had to remain at a location where they could be reached by radio or phone. The trial court in Washington decided these officers were entitled to receive overtime for all "on-call" duty, even if sleeping and eating. The court of appeals affirmed the trial court's decision.

The Supreme Court of Washington consolidated this case with *Goff v. City of Airway Heights*, 730 P.2d 691 (Wash.App.1986), see above. The court decided that both cases centered on whether the officers' "on call" duty was a substantial part of their employment and whether this time was active duty. It stated that to determine if on call duty was substantial it must determine if the time spent was benefitting the employee or employer, if the employee was required to remain at a particular place, and the degree to which the employees were allowed to engage in their own activities.

In the instant case the court decided the case must be remanded to the trial court, to decide if sleeping was active duty and if other on call time was active duty under MWA. Thus, the Supreme Court reversed the trial court's decision and remanded the case. In the *Goff* case it decided that the trial court's instructions to the jury were adequate. Even though the instructions were not labeled and explained under the MWA, the judge still set forth the applicable rule. However the court decided that there was no evidence to support awarding the officer double compensation. Thus, the supreme court affirmed the trial court's decision, reversing only the award of double compensation. *Deputy Sheriffs Ass'n v. Chelan County*, 745 P.2d 1 (Wash.1987).

The New Jersey Transit Corporation, an instrumentality of the state of New Jersey that operates commuter rail service, was sued by the transit police officers' benevolent association for failure to comply with the provision of the Fair Labor Standards Act (FLSA) that requires employers to pay their employees time-and-a-half for overtime hours. The transit corporation sought to dismiss the claim, asserting that its employees fell within the categorical exemptions from the overtime rules because of 49 U.S.C. § 10504 which, after the Interstate Commerce Commission relinquished control of commuter railroads to the states' executive officers, retained the overtime exemption to FLSA. The district court denied the corporation's motion, but allowed a direct appeal to be taken to the U.S. Court of Appeals, Third Circuit.

The court of appeals noted that § 10504 had been intended to relieve certain subclasses of railroads from redundant rate control mechanisms because the fares were subject to control by the chief executives of states anyway. However, the court then determined that Congress did not intend to alter the regulatory environment under which these commuter railroads operated. Instead, Congress intended to maintain the status quo with respect to safety, collective bargaining, and dealings between employees and employers. Thus, the overtime exemption that applied prior to § 10504's taking effect was still in place. The court reversed the district court's decision and allowed the case to be dismissed. *N.J. Transit Policemen's Benevolent Ass'n Local 304 v. New Jersey Transit Corp.*, 806 F.2d 451 (3d Cir.1986).

Various Indiana state police officers filed a complaint in a federal district court, seeking to recover overtime compensation pursuant to FLSA, 29 U.S.C. § 207. However, one month after the lawsuit was begun, Congress amended FLSA to grant states a grace period of one year before they could be held liable for violations of FLSA. The district court then determined that the amended act barred the officers' claim, and that it was constitutional. The officers appealed to the U.S. Court of Appeals, Seventh Circuit.

The appellate court acknowledged that the officers may have consented to work overtime because of the Supreme Court's decision in *Garcia*, above, but it also noted that the state had relied on earlier law when it negotiated contracts for the officers. The court stated that the amended act was rationally related to a legitimate legislative purpose, namely, achieving the desired results of FLSA without financially overburdening the states. No one would be helped by reducing the states to financial instability. Because the officers had failed to show that the legislation was harsh or oppressive, the court upheld it, and affirmed the district court's decision. *Rhinebarger v. Orr*, 839 F.2d 387 (7th Cir.1988).

An Arizona woman worked for the Tucson Air Museum as an after-hours security guard for four years. She moved her mobile home onto museum grounds so that she could provide after-hours security services on a regular basis. She was paid to make three two-hour patrols of the museum grounds between sundown and sunrise every other day. When disputes arose between her and the museum, she resigned. She then sued in an Arizona trial court, seeking to recover unpaid minimum wages and overtime under FLSA. The museum moved the case to a federal district court, and sought summary judgment because it was not an enterprise engaged in interstate commerce or in the production of goods for commerce. The court agreed, and the security guard appealed to the U.S. Court of Appeals, Ninth Circuit.

The court of appeals acknowledged that the museum performed activities similar to those of a public agency. Further, it was a nonprofit corporation which had entered into an exclusive management agreement with the county within which it was situated. However, it then determined that even with this public control, the museum was not a public agency because it was only indirectly responsible to public officials and the general public. The court thus held that the museum was a private corporation not subject to FLSA, and affirmed the district court's decision. *Powell v. Tucson Air Museum Foundation of Pima County*, 771 F.2d 1309 (9th Cir.1985).

IV. DISCHARGE OF EMPLOYEES

The subject of termination is covered in Chapter Two of this volume, but when an employee is subject to a collective bargaining agreement, or is a member of a labor association, and is discharged, she or he will generally have greater rights, albeit with more structured remedies.

The Defense Language Institute (DLI) is a federal agency. A course developer for the DLI was demoted to instructor when his position was abolished. Five years later, the DLI reopened and advertised the position. The former course developer did not reapply and another instructor was awarded the job. The developer filed a grievance against the DLI, asserting that he should have been assigned the position and that there should have been no competitive application process. The developer's labor organization accepted his claim and successfully arbitrated the matter. The developer was reassigned to the job. The previously-selected instructor was demoted. The employees' labor organization then refused to handle the instructor's grievance, claiming that it had a conflict of interest because it had previously represented the developer.

The instructor filed an unfair labor practice charge with the Federal Labor Relations Authority (FLRA) claiming that the DLI had violated its collective bargaining agreement and that the labor organization had breached its duty of fair representation. The FLRA's general council upheld only the fair representation claim. The FLRA and labor organization reached an agreement in which the labor organization posted notice that it would represent all employees. The instructor contended that this settlement gave him no relief and sued the DLI and labor organization in a federal district court. The court dismissed the charge against the DLI but permitted the unfair labor practice charge against the labor organization as a private action for breach of the duty of fair representation. The labor organization appealed to the U.S. Court of Appeals, Ninth Circuit, which reversed the district court's decision. The court ruled that the federal Civil Service Reform Act (CSRA) created no private cause of action against the labor organization. The U.S. Supreme Court granted the instructor's petition for certiorari.

The Supreme Court ruled that although the CSRA was patterned after the National Labor Relations Act (NLRA), it did not imply a private right of action. Because Congress expressed no intention to provide a private legal remedy to enforce the duty of fair representation, the instructor had no recourse. Because the FLRA had final authority to issue unfair labor practice complaints, the appeals court had correctly denied the instructor's private action against the labor organization. *Karahalios v. Nat'l Federation of Federal Employees, Local 1263*, 489 U.S. 527, 109 S.Ct. 1282, 103 L.Ed.2d 539 (1989).

A U.S. Postal Service employee, following an altercation with a fellow employee, was suspended without pay. He was a member of the American Postal Workers Union. After the employee was formally terminated, he filed a grievance with the union as provided by the collective bargaining agreement (CBA). The union chose not to take his grievance to arbitration, and he then sued the union and the postal service in a federal district court, asserting that the postal service had violated the CBA by dismissing him without just cause, and that the union had breached its duty of fair representation. A jury found for the employee and against both defendants and apportioned the damages between the two. On appeal to the U.S. Court of Appeals, Fourth Circuit, the court affirmed except for the award of damages against the union. The postal service then appealed to the U.S. Supreme Court.

The Supreme Court held that where damage had been caused by both the employer and the union, it was proper to apportion liability between the two according to the damage each had caused. Here, requiring the union to pay damages would not impose on it a burden inconsistent with national policy, but rather would provide an additional incentive to unions to process members' claims where warranted. The Court thus reversed the court of appeals' decision, and allowed apportionment of the damages between the postal service and the union. *Bowen v. United States Postal Service*, 459 U.S. 212, 103 S.Ct. 588, 74 L.Ed.2d 402 (1983).

The U.S. Postal Service employed a Washington man as a part-time substitute rural letter carrier. After a year, and pursuant to a new contract agreement, the employee was made a full-time rural carrier. He then joined the National Rural Letter Carriers Association which entered into a collective bargaining agreement (CBA) with the postal service. The CBA provided for arbitration upon an employee's discharge. Subsequently, the employee was arrested for stealing air pressure regulators from a railroad yard while off duty. He pleaded guilty to the misdemeanor offense and, following his conviction, was discharged from employment. He filed a grievance with his union which unsuccessfully appealed his dismissal through two stages of arbitration. The union's attorney then determined not to proceed further because of the slim chance of success. The employee sued his union and the postal service for reinstatement and damages for breach of the CBA and violation of the union's duty to fairly represent him. A federal district court held for the defendants, and the employee appealed to the U.S. Court of Appeals, Ninth Circuit.

On appeal, the court noted that the union had made a rational decision not to further arbitrate based on experience and the criminal conviction.

Further, the decisionmakers within the union bore no animosity toward the employee and did not discriminatorily refuse to pursue the employee's claims. The court also noted that the postal service had a legitimate concern about the public's trust in the employee after his conviction and had validly discharged him. Accordingly, it affirmed the district court's decision. *Johnson v. United States Postal Service*, 756 F.2d 1461 (9th Cir.1985).

In another postal service case, a Missouri employee was discharged for submitting fraudulent documents to obtain paid leave. He gave his supervisor documents which were supposedly signed by his military commanding officer, stating that his active duty had been extended one day because of the eruption of Mount St. Helens. In reality, he had returned in time to report for work. He went through arbitration where his discharge was upheld by the arbitrator. Even though the CBA made arbitration decisions final and binding, he sued the postal service in a federal district court, seeking reinstatement. His complaint was dismissed, and he appealed to the U.S. Court of Appeals, Eighth Circuit.

The appellate court first recognized that the applicable statute of limitations for bringing charges of unfair labor practices under the National Labor Relations Act was six months, so the employee had timely filed his claim. The court then noted, however, that the employee's claim had been properly dismissed because it sought review of the arbitrator's award without asserting that the union had unfairly represented him. Without such a claim, the CBA precluded review of an arbitrator's award, presuming that the award was a final determination not to be overturned unless the employee had not received fair representation. The court thus affirmed the district court's decision to dismiss the case. *Abernathy v. United States Postal Service*, 740 F.2d 612 (8th Cir.1984).

A Minnesota employee, working as a human services technician at a state hospital, allegedly slapped an epileptic patient who was blind and retarded. The employee was suspended for ten days while the incident was investigated. Subsequently, the hospital discharged him, informing him that he could proceed with arbitration under the collective bargaining agreement (CBA) or could request an administrative hearing. The employee proceeded under the CBA, and the arbitrator found in favor of the hospital. The employee's union did not appeal, and the employee then sued the state in a Minnesota trial court, seeking to have the arbitration award vacated. The court vacated the award, and the state appealed to the Supreme Court of Minnesota.

On appeal, the court noted that the union had actively represented the employee at the arbitration hearing. When it made its determination not to appeal the award, the employee's rights against the state, apart from the union, were lost. If the employee felt that the union had not adequately represented him, he could sue the union for breach of duty. Since he was notified of his choices and had selected the CBA route, the employee could not now alter the means by which he sought redress. The supreme court reversed the trial court's decision and reinstated the arbitrator's award. *Eisen v. State Dep't of Public Welfare*, 352 N.W.2d 731 (Minn.1984).

A veteran, employed by a Minnesota regional corrections board as a corrections agent, was served with a notice of intent to dismiss on grounds of misconduct, following an incident at his office. The local branch of AFSCME filed a grievance objecting to the employee's dismissal, and the board informed AFSCME that the employee would have to choose between a veteran's preference hearing, to which he was entitled, or go through AFSCME in an arbitration proceeding. The employee chose the veteran's preference hearing, where his discharge was upheld. AFSCME then sued in a Minnesota trial court, seeking to compel arbitration for the dismissal, and the court acceded in that request. The board appealed to the Supreme Court of Minnesota.

The supreme court held that veterans have a statutory right to both a veteran's preference hearing and to arbitration. The legislature clearly intended veterans to be secure in their employment, and thus both avenues had to be kept open. Further, the trial court ruled that even though the hearings and arbitration proceedings would be somewhat duplicative, collateral estoppel and res judicata would not apply to bar reexamination of the facts and issues involved. The court therefore affirmed the trial court's decision and allowed the veteran both avenues of review. *AFSCME Council 96 v. Arrowhead Regional Corrections Board*, 356 N.W.2d 295 (Minn.1984).

The Southeastern Pennsylvania Transportation Authority (SEPTA) discharged one of its employees, alleging that he had made improper fare collections. Under a CBA, the labor association processed the employee's grievances through three grievance hearings which all resulted in decisions against the employee. The labor association then declined to seek impartial arbitration which the CBA authorized. As a result, the employee sued both the labor association and SEPTA, asserting breach of duty against the former and discharge in violation of the CBA against the latter. SEPTA sought to dismiss the claim against it because the employee had not exhausted contractual grievance procedures. The Pennsylvania trial court refused to dismiss the action, and the appellate court affirmed the decision. SEPTA appealed to the Supreme Court of Pennsylvania.

The supreme court acknowledged that, generally, an employee could not seek reinstatement from a court even where a labor association had failed to pursue a discharge to arbitration in bad faith. However, the court noted that the employee could bring a joint action against both the labor association and SEPTA so that an appropriate remedy could be awarded. The court then stated that the trial court could only compel arbitration to be completed; it could not fashion a remedy itself. The supreme court thus affirmed the lower courts' rulings and remanded the case to the trial court. *Martino v. Transport Workers' Union of Philadelphia, Local 234*, 480 A.2d 242 (Pa.1984).

An Illinois city public works department employed two departmental foremen, one of whom was active in the organization and certification of a labor association as the employees' bargaining representative. When the city council postponed recognition of the labor association, it petitioned the Illinois State Labor Relations Board for recognition. The board certified the labor association as the exclusive bargaining representative for city employees. Meanwhile, the city council enacted an ordinance restructuring the public works department, which resulted in the elimination of the prounion foreman's position and a promotion for the other foreman, who was anti-union.

The labor association filed an unfair labor practices complaint against the city, claiming that the ordinance was enacted to terminate the prounion foreman's position. A hearing officer agreed with the labor association, finding that the city's actions were intended to subvert the Illinois Public Labor Relations Act. The city appealed to the Illinois Appellate Court which affirmed the board's decision, and the city appealed to the Illinois Supreme Court. The supreme court ruled that employers could not reorganize departments to evade the state labor relations act. The evidence indicated that the city had reorganized to discourage union activities. The strongest evidence was the timing of the prounion foreman's discharge, together with the elevation of the antiunion foreman to a new job title with the same duties. The court affirmed the board's decision for the labor association. *City of Burbank v. Labor Relations Bd.*, 538 N.E.2d 1146 (Ill.1989).

A county worker who was employed as a probation officer resigned her permanent position to take employment as a childcare social worker. After a performance evaluation, she was terminated from the position because of unsatisfactory performance. She tried to gain reinstatement to her former position of probation officer, but the county probation department refused. The worker filed a grievance seeking reinstatement to her former position, arguing that she was a probationary employee entitled to be restored to her former position according to her collective bargaining agreement. The county rejected her grievance, stating that the agreement only covered permanent employees, and that the childcare social worker position was provisional. The worker then filed a demand for arbitration in a New York trial court, seeking reinstatement to her former position of probation officer. The trial court denied the county's petition for a stay of the arbitration and the county appealed to the Supreme Court, Appellate Division.

The supreme court held that she was not entitled to arbitration because the collective bargaining agreement only covered permanent employees. Her job as a childcare social worker was provisional because her employment was not the result of a competitive examination. Thus, she was not entitled to reinstatement to her former position of probation officer. *Thrasher v. Civil Service Comm'n*, 549 N.Y.S.2d 258 (A.D.4th Dep't 1989).

The Illinois Department of Children and Family Services employed security officers under the state personnel code, paying them $10 per hour. Citing a shortage of funds, the department laid off two officers and contracted with a private service to employ new personnel at $6.40 per hour. The former security personnel and their employees' association sued the department in an Illinois trial court for a declaration that the department had illegally contracted for the security services. The employees' association and laid off personnel relied upon the state personnel code. They sought an order enjoining the department from continuing its policy. The court agreed with the employees' association and the laid off employees. The department appealed to the Illinois Appellate Court, Fourth District.

The appellate court noted that there was no express Illinois authority for departments or agencies to contract for services and that statutory language relied on by the employees' association did not expressly or impliedly prohibit hiring private security personnel to furnish services. However, the Illinois Purchasing Act expressly recognized authority to contract for private security services under the prevailing wage rate. Therefore, the department had a general authority to perform its function by entering into the private services contract. The court dissolved the lower court's injunction and reversed its decision. *Illinois State Employees Ass'n v. Dep't of Children & Family Services*, 533 N.E.2d 566 (Ill.App.4th Dist.1989).

V. OTHER LABOR RELATIONS CASES

Many public employees belong to labor associations, which help to promote their legal rights. Through collective bargaining, labor associations can help ensure that public employees are treated equally and fairly. Employer-employee problems can arise in myriad contexts. The following cases examine some of these situations.

A union's collective-bargaining agent, who represented the employees of two schools owned and operated by the U.S. Army, submitted proposals asking for mileage reimbursement, paid leave, and salary increases on behalf of the schools' employees. The schools refused to negotiate, stating that under Title VII of the Civil Service Reform Act of 1978 they were not required to negotiate these matters. The union filed a complaint with the Federal Labor Relations Authority (FLRA) which held that the union's proposals were negotiable. The schools appealed to the U.S. Court of Appeals, Eleventh Circuit, which upheld the FLRA's decision. The schools then appealed to the U.S. Supreme Court.

Title VII of the Civil Service Reform Act defines conditions of employment as matters "affecting working conditions" but excludes matters relating to prohibited political activities, classification of positions, and those specifically provided for by federal statute. The Court determined that the union's proposals were "conditions of employment." The Supreme Court, affirming the district court's decision, held that the schools were required to negotiate salary increases and fringe benefits. *Fort Stewart Schools v. Federal Labor Relations Authority*, 110 S.Ct. 2043 (1990).

A city council adopted a policy which required all fulltime employees to undergo a physical examination once every four years. The city administrator informed the affected employees through a memo which named all employees to be examined. Over a year had passed, and one of the city's four police officers questioned the applicability of the policy to police officers. The city explained its position, and noted that the officers were expressly named in the memo. The officer and his union challenged the policy in a Minnesota trial court alleging that the policy was subject to mandatory bargaining. The trial court held that certain aspects of the policy must be negotiated, and the city appealed to the Minnesota Court of Appeals.

Minnesota public employment law provides that the establishment of a physical examination policy which affects all employees as a matter of inherent managerial policy is not subject to mandatory bargaining. However, it is an unfair labor practice for a public employer to refuse to negotiate certain aspects of the implementation of that policy. The city argued that the establishment of the policy and its implementation were so "intrinsically interwoven" that implementation was rendered nonnegotiable. The appeals court held that the city must negotiate. The city's argument was weakened by the fact that it had negotiated implementation with the union which represented other city employees. The city lastly argued that the union had waived its right to object by failing to object to the original memo. The court held that the union's rights were statutory, and must be waived clearly and expressly; silence could not waive the union's rights. The trial court's decision was affirmed. *Law Enforcement Labor Service v. City of Luverne*, 463 N.W.2d 546 (Minn.App.1990).

The National Labor Relations Board petitioned the U.S. Court of Appeals, Seventh Circuit, for enforcement of its order requiring a nonprofit Illinois corporation to bargain with a union. The nonprofit corporation was controlled by two Presbyterian governing bodies and operated a foster home.

The foster home contended that it was exempt from the National Labor Relations Act (NLRA) under three theories: 1) that it was a political subdivision of the state and hence exempt, 2) that it was incapable of bargaining, and 3) that it was a religious organization and therefore exempt from the NLRA. The court determined that the foster home was required to bargain with the union under the NLRA. First, it was not a religious organization because it did not inquire into the religion of the children, nor did it seek to indoctrinate the children it admitted, Second, it was not a political subdivision of the state because its only connection with the state was the state subsidy. Third, the court ruled that even though the state had imposed requirements upon the foster home's employment contracts it did not so control the home so as to bar it from bargaining with the union. Therefore, the court held that the religious corporation was subject to the National Labor Relations Act. *N.L.R.B v. Kemmerer Village, Inc.*, 907 F.2d 661 (7th Cir.1990).

A Pennsylvania man, employed by a city's water department, was also a member of a labor association. The water department and labor association entered into a binding agreement with respect to a pension plan. Subsequently, the employee alleged that his pension was not being computed according to the provisions of the pension agreement, and he filed a complaint with the labor association. It did not act on the grievance to the employee's satisfaction and, when the water department did not redress the problem, the employee sued the department and the labor association in a federal district court. The district court dismissed the complaints against both defendants, and the employee appealed to the U.S. Court of Appeals, Third Circuit.

On appeal, the court held that the water department was not an employer within the meaning of the Labor Management Relations Act (LMRA) because it was a political subdivision. Further, it found that since the department was not an employer, the employee was not an employee of the department under the LMRA either. Thus, the labor association could not be considered to represent employees within the meaning of the LMRA. The court of appeals therefore affirmed the district court's decision, and denied relief to the employee. *Manfredi v. Hazelton City Authority, Water Dep't*, 793 F.2d 101 (3d Cir.1986).

Over half of the federal government's civilian and military personnel were required to sign two types of nondisclosure agreements in order to obtain access to classified and "classifiable" information. The nondisclosure agreements were standard forms describing confidentiality obligations and penalties for unauthorized disclosure. Congress enacted the Continuing Resolution for Fiscal Year 1988, Pub. L. 100-202 § 630 which prohibited federal fund expenditures for enforcing the forms, which were designed by the Information Security Oversight Office (ISOO) and the Central Intelligence Agency (CIA). Following the congressional action, the ISOO's director issued a regulation defining the term "classifiable" as information which was in the process of becoming classified. The regulation also limited violations to those disclosures which the employee knew involved information which was being classified. However, the Director of Central Intelligence (DCI) continued to require employees to sign the CIA form for an additional three months. The DCI then issued a form which eliminated the term "classifiable."

The American Foreign Service Association (AFSA) sued the ISOO's director and the DCI in the U.S. District Court for the District of Columbia claiming that use of the forms violated § 630. It sought an order that would prevent use of the forms and would nullify those forms which had been signed after the congressional action. The district court dismissed the AFSA's claim on grounds that the congressional action unconstitutionally interfered with presidential authority to protect national security. The employee association appealed to the U.S. Supreme Court, which agreed to hear the matter.

The Supreme Court observed that the ISOO's regulations remedied the vagueness in the term "classifiable." DCI had deleted the word "classifiable" from its documents and replaced it with the definition given in the ISOO's regulation. The court ordered the directors to notify their employees that the term classifiable had been defined. The Court ruled that at least for current employees, the controversy was now moot. However, the Court remanded the issue of the definition of "classified information," which the associations argued did not comply with the congressional action. *American Foreign Service Ass'n v. Garfinkel*, 490 U.S. 153, 109 S.Ct. 1693, 104 L.Ed.2d 139 (1989).

The city of Houston passed ordinances to "civilianize" its police department. The ordinances encroached upon traditional promotion by seniority within the department and police officers argued that they violated the Texas fire fighter's and police officer's civil service statute. Houston employed uniformed classified officers and civilians under different authority. Classified police officers were under the state civil service statute, while civilians were employed under the municipal civil service system. The state civil service act called for filling employment vacancies by examination and appointment from lists of classified officers having the highest grades on eligibility lists. The Houston ordinances created nine civilian positions within the police department. The city hired civilians to fill each of the positions and did not follow the state civil service statute. Six of the administrators assumed duties previously performed by uniformed officers.

The aggrieved police officers argued that they should have been promoted to fill the new positions or that the state civil service statute preempted the city ordinances. They sued the city, mayor, chief of police and civil service commission in a Texas district court. The court ruled in favor of the officers and granted their request for an order declaring the ordinance void in contravention of the state statute. The court also awarded back pay, promotion and attorney's fees. The city and officials appealed to the Texas Court of Appeals, Houston District. The appeals court ruled that no ordinance required Houston's police bureaus to be headed by classified officers. The state statute required that only law enforcement personnel be classified. According to the court, the statute did not apply to the newly-created administrative positions, which performed no law enforcement duties. The appeals court dissolved the district court's injunction and reversed its judgment. *City of Houston v. Lee*, 762 S.W.2d 180 (Tex.App.-Houston 1st Dist.1988).

A group of adjunct faculty members in Vermont sought inclusion with full-time faculty members from the state Labor Relations Board (Board) to obtain collective bargaining rights and employment protection under the State Employees Labor Relations Act. Until they achieve tenured status, full-time faculty members go through a more involved process of hiring and reappointment than do adjunct faculty members. Vermont State Colleges (VSC) hires adjunct faculty members to supplement its full-time faculty. They are hired on a per-semester basis, through a much less formal process. After several hearings, the Board determined that certain adjuncts with "a reasonable expectation of continued employment" were essentially state employees. The VSC appealed that decision to the Supreme Court of Vermont.

The supreme court ruled that, for the purposes of employment protection, the adjunct members were state employees, but that they could not be included for the purposes of collective bargaining rights. The court interpreted Vermont law to include as "state employees" part-time workers employed on a less than permanent basis. The court further held that the Board could have inferred that some adjuncts, for example, those that teach during both semesters of an academic year, would have a reasonable expectation of continued employment. However, the court concluded that, with respect to bargaining rights, the two distinct groups of full-time faculty and adjuncts would encounter a difficult and confusing bargaining process if they were included in the same bargaining unit. *Vermont State Colleges Faculty Fed'n v. Vermont State Colleges*, 566 A.2d 955 (Vt.1989).

Two certified labor organizations, the Alaska Public Employees Association (APEA) and the Public Employees Local 71, represented Alaska's union employees. The state Public Employment Relations Act (PERA) divides employees into classes. Class II employees have a limited right to strike. After an impasse in negotiations, class II employees must submit to mediation and if that fails, they can strike upon majority vote. Class III employees can strike only after an impasse in negotiations as long as a majority votes by secret ballot to strike. The unions and the state were parties to a collective bargaining agreement but were unable to agree on new contracts after their agreements had expired. The state notified the unions that it would implement unilateral changes in the terms and conditions of employment. APEA and the state had stipulated that their negotiations were at an impasse. The unions sued the state in a state trial court seeking declaratory and injunctive relief from the imposition of the unilateral contract changes. The court held that the state could change the terms and conditions of employment of class II and class III employees upon an impasse in negotiations whether or not the employees held a strike vote. It also ruled that the employees had not been unconstitutionally deprived of property. The unions appealed to the Supreme Court of Alaska.

The supreme court held that the state could implement unilateral contract changes when negotiations reached an impasse. For class II employees the impasse was reached when the mediation process had been exhausted. For class III employees the impasse was reached when negotiations were deadlocked. It also ruled that the employees had not been unconstitutionally deprived of property when the state demanded that they work longer hours for less pay. Once the collective bargaining agreement had expired, the continuation of existing terms and conditions was merely an expectancy. The supreme court affirmed the trial court's decision. *Alaska Pub. Emp. v. Dep't of Admin.*, 776 P.2d 1030 (Alaska 1989).

A labor association set its agency fee (fair share) at ninety percent of union dues and sent notice to its bargaining unit employees. Nine Illinois state and local agency employees who were in the association's bargaining unit but were not union members sued the labor association for a court order which would prevent any agency fee deduction. They complained that the association's notice had been deficient. A federal district court denied the motion and the employers deducted the fee. The district court also refused to certify a class action suit, although 10,000 nonunion employees belonged to the bargaining unit. The following year, the labor association fixed the agency fee at ninety-six percent of union dues. An arbitrator determined that the fee should have been ninety-five percent of union dues. The labor association agreed to refund the difference and to abide by future decisions by arbitrators. However, nonunion members who had not been parties to the arbitration proceedings appealed the district court's decision. The employees appealed to the U.S. Court of Appeals, Seventh Circuit.

The appeals court noted that public employers and labor associations could be held liable under 42 U.S.C. § 1983 for violating employee free speech rights if nonunion members were forced to pay union dues or agency fees that exceeded collective bargaining costs, where the excess was used to fund political goals. In this case, the district court had properly refused to certify a class action suit. A potentially serious conflict of interest was present because the nine individuals did not adequately represent the entire class. The nine employees had benefitted from the inadequate notice because the challenged agency fee was actually less than the amount the arbitrator had found correct. The appeals court affirmed the district court's decision for the labor union. *Gilpin v. AFSCME, AFL-CIO*, 875 F.2d 1310 (7th Cir.1989).

A group of 1,700 nonunion teachers objected to procedures used by some Indiana teachers' unions to collect fair share fees from nonunion employees including a state court decision allowing the union to collect the fees. The unions retained The American Arbitration Association (AAA) to select an arbitrator to determine the fair share amount for a particular school year. The arbitrator's determination of the fair share amount was binding only on the unions. If a nonmember teacher refused to pay the fair share fee, the unions' only recourse was to sue in state court. The teachers' group objected to the rate for a particular year and claimed that the arbitration procedure was constitutionally inadequate because it did not provide them with an impartial decision-maker to hear their objections. The teachers sued the unions in a federal district court, which denied the teachers' motion for a preliminary injunction against the state court decision allowing the unions to collect the fair share fees. The teachers then appealed to the U.S. Court of Appeals, Seventh Circuit.

The court of appeals stated that the teachers were not entitled to an injunction since they did not show any likelihood of prevailing on the case's merits. The court stated that the arbitrator's selection did not represent the unions' unrestricted choice, but was instead made according to the AAA's own internal selection rules without any input by the unions. The court of appeals affirmed the denial of the injunction. *Ping v. Nat'l Educ. Ass'n*, 870 F.2d 1369 (7th Cir.1989).

Many police officers in Hobart, Indiana, opposed the incumbent mayor and city council members during a primary election. The incumbents were defeated. Before leaving office, the lame-duck council enacted a city ordinance which required all city employees to work an average of forty hours per week. The mayor issued an executive order which put the ordinance into immediate effect. The ordinance did not affect most city employees, but significantly altered the police department's regular schedule. The officers previously received a three-day weekend every third week, resulting in less than a forty hour average work week. As a result, the city police union and two of its members sued the mayor and council members in a federal district court under 42 U.S.C. § 1983. They claimed that the ordinance was passed in retaliation for exercising their First Amendment rights. The court dismissed their lawsuit and the union and police officers asked to amend their complaint in order to contest the executive order and request damages. The court refused, and the union and officers appealed to the U.S. Court of Appeals, Seventh Circuit.

The appeals court ruled that courts cannot strike down otherwise constitutional ordinances simply because they appear to be enacted for suspect motives. On its face the ordinance appeared to be a routine personnel regulation that was not directed toward any particular group. It was not a bill of attainder as it applied to all city employees. Because the ordinance was lawful, the mayor was bound to put it into effect and the police were not allowed to amend their complaint to challenge the executive order. The appeals court affirmed the district court's decision. *F.O.P. Lodge No. 121 v. City of Hobart*, 864 F.2d 551 (7th Cir.1988).

Congress enacted the Flexible and Compressed Work Schedules Act (FCWSA), 5 U.S.C. §§ 6120-6133 in 1982 as an experimental program to promote federal employee productivity. It permitted federal employees alternatives to the eight-hour five-day work week. Although the act was not governed by the Federal Labor-Management Relations Act (FLMRA), the FCWSA stated that its provisions could become the subject of collective bargaining between unions and government entities. A union representing Bureau of Land Management office workers presented its management with a proposal for an alternative work schedule. The bureau objected to the proposal. It believed that sections concerning employee rights to apply for alternative work restricted management. The bureau interpreted the proposal as a limit on management powers which would preclude use of alternative work schedules only where work objectives were being damaged. The bureau refused to negotiate the proposal and the union then filed an unfair labor practices charge against it with the Federal Labor Relations Authority (FLRA). The bureau argued that the proposal pertained to nonnegotiable management rights under the FLMRA. The FLRA disagreed, ruling for the union. The bureau appealed to the U.S. Court of Appeals, Ninth Circuit.

The court stated that the purpose of the FCWSA was to limit management control over work hours in favor of employees. The correct standard for judging the proposal was the FCWSA rather than the FLMRA. The FLRA had properly ruled on the issues and the court affirmed its decision. *Bureau of Land Management v. FLRA*, 864 F.2d 89 (9th Cir.1988).

The New Jersey Public Employment Relations Commission (PERC) regulates public employee labor relations and designates appropriate bargaining units. New Jersey law does not prohibit firefighters from joining bargaining units which do not solely represent firefighters. However, a New Jersey statute provides for compulsory interest arbitration of salary disputes between police, firefighters and their public employers where the bargaining unit is comprised solely of police or firefighting employees. A firefighters' labor organization sought to represent state firefighters who were in a bargaining unit that represented many nonfirefighting state employees. The firefighters' union also sought to create separate units for supervisors and rank-

and-file firefighters. The PERC determined that the state firefighters need not be represented by a bargaining unit which represented only firefighters. It determined that the state firefighters interacted more frequently with nonfirefighters than other fire departments and therefore there was no greater community of interest in separate firefighter units. The union appealed to a New Jersey appellate division court which reversed and remanded the PERC's decision. PERC appealed to the Supreme Court of New Jersey.

On appeal, the labor organization argued that the firefighters needed a separate bargaining unit in order to enforce their statutory right to interest arbitration. The supreme court noted that state firefighters were entitled to compulsory interest arbitration because they did not have the right to strike. However, the PERC hearing officer had determined that there had been a history of stable collective bargaining negotiations in this bargaining unit. The firefighters had failed to establish a unique community of interest among themselves and there was no showing that the present labor organization had inadequately represented the firefighters. Mixed units of firefighters and nonfirefighters were appropriate if the evidence showed that labor stability would be enhanced by continuation of the bargaining unit. The supreme court reversed the appellate division's decision and reinstated the PERC hearing officer's determination. *Matters of State*, 554 A.2d 1309 (N.J.1989).

The Federal Service Labor-Management Relations Act (FSLMRA) comprehensively governs labor relations between federal employers and their employees. Some federal agencies are excluded from coverage. The President can exclude other agencies by executive order where the agency has a primary intelligence, investigative or national security function and the FSLMRA cannot be applied consistently with national security. In 1986, President Reagan issued an executive order which excluded some subdivisions of the U.S. Marshals Service from FSLMRA coverage. The marshals' labor organization contested the executive order's legality and sued the President in the U.S. District Court for the District of Columbia. The court granted the marshals' motion for summary judgment and the President appealed to the U.S. Court of Appeals, District of Columbia Circuit.

On appeal, the marshals argued that they were not engaged in protection of national security and that the order was invalid. The President argued that the lawsuit was moot, and that executive orders were presumptively valid. The appeals court noted that since 1986 the marshals had lost the advantage of their collective bargaining agreement, grievance procedures and other benefits and that therefore the lawsuit was not moot. However, the court agreed with the President's argument that executive orders were granted a presumption of regularity by reviewing courts. The presumption of regularity in favor of public officers' official acts had been recognized by courts since the War of 1812. The appeals court reversed the district court decision. *American Federation of Gov't Employees, AFL-CIO v. Reagan*, 870 F.2d 723 (D.C.Cir.1989).

CHAPTER EIGHT
EMPLOYMENT PRACTICES

I. JOB CLASSIFICATIONS

Job classifications have led to a fair amount of litigation. Usually, an employer is seeking to classify an employee at a level below that of other similarly situated employees. If the two classes of employees are too similar, however, courts will often deny the classification difference.

In 1976, the New York legislature enacted the Unified Court Budget Act which essentially converted local court employees into state employees. Subsequently, secretaries to New York judges were classified into three titles and allocated three different salary grades. Also, court clerks were similarly classed, with clerks of higher courts receiving more in wages than lower court clerks. The secretaries' and clerks' association appealed these classifications to a review board which held that the classifications for secretaries had been correct, but that the clerks all performed basically the same kinds of duties, and disallowed the classifications for them. After a series of lower court decisions, appeal was taken to the Court of Appeals of New York.

On appeal, the court recognized that the duties of secretaries working for appellate judges were substantially broader in scope and more demanding than those of trial court judges' secretaries. The court then stated that, with respect to court clerks, the levels of difficulty and responsibility were largely equivalent between trial clerks and appellate clerks. Therefore, the court affirmed the board's decisions and held that the secretaries could be classified at different levels, but that the clerks should not. *Ass'n of Secretaries v. Office of Court Admin., State of New York*, 553 N.E.2d 979 (N.Y.1990).

A Kansas man worked for the state as a Physical Plant Supervisor II. Subsequently, the state's division of personnel services (DPS) did a comprehensive classification study of certain job classes. In the study, it was determined that the employee should be classified as a Supervisor I under the new classification scheme. His salary range remained the same as before, but he nevertheless complained of his reclassification, asserting that he should have been raised to Supervisor II. The DPS performed an "on-site" review of his job to determine the most appropriate classification. The DPS again concluded that he should be classed as a Supervisor I. The employee then filed for judicial review in a Kansas trial court which reversed the agency action, ordered the employee classed as a Supervisor II and granted a back pay award. Further appeal was taken to the Court of Appeals of Kansas. The court of appeals noted that Kansas law provided for modification of classification and did not require a position-to-position study to be done whenever an employee requested one. Further, there had been substantial evidence presented showing that the employee was not doing substantially similar work to employees ranked as supervisors, level II, so it was not inequitable for him to be paid less. His duties were on the lower level of supervisory responsibilities. Thus, the court reversed the trial court's decision and reclassified the employee as a Supervisor I. *Mulford v. Dep't of Human Resources*, 790 P.2d 957 (Kan.App.1990).

The U.S. Foreign Service (FS) covered employees in at least five executive departments, including the United States Information Agency (USIA). A USIA employee, one of a substantial number of FS employees who served in the U.S. but were not available for service worldwide, fell within the Foreign Service Act of 1980. This act required domestic FS employees to convert from the FS schedule to the Civil Service General Schedule (GS). It provided that individuals would be converted to the class or grade and pay rate that most closely corresponded to the level the employee was at before the conversion. It further provided that upon conversion there should be no reduction in basic rate of salary. The USIA employee was converted to the GS, where he determined that he would no longer be eligible for within-grade pay increases because of the level he had been converted to. He filed a grievance which was upheld, and appeal was taken to a federal district court. The court ruled for the USIA, and the employee then appealed to the U.S. Court of Appeals, District of Columbia Circuit.

The court of appeals agreed with the district court that the statutory provision applied only to an employee's basic rate of pay and not to potential future increases in salary. Since the employee's pay upon conversion had been identical to his previous salary, the law had been complied with. The court thus upheld the employee's status upon conversion and affirmed the decision of the district court. *Olds v. United States Information Agency*, 896 F.2d 1371 (D.C.Cir.1990).

Montana highway patrol officers challenged the state's pay classification system. The challenged system consisted of consecutive grades which ranged from two classes of patrol officers through captain. Officers within the first class appealed for a raise in their grade, which was granted by the department. Officers within the second class were automatically upgraded, so that there was no distinction between their grade and the grade of sergeants. Officers representing the classifications of sergeant, lieutenant and captain then brought a grievance against the state personnel appeals board for reclassification of their positions. In addition to reclassifications, they sought to compel the personnel division to design new job descriptions. The personnel division audited the state patrol's job descriptions and issued a five-factor formula to reassign positions into classes. The five-factor test resulted in a grading system similar to the previous one. Officers representing sergeants, lieutenants and captains appealed to the personnel appeals board.

A state personnel appeals board hearing officer determined that the officers were aggrieved and each of the upper three grades should be raised one pay level. The personnel board affirmed the hearing examiner's factfinding and conclusions of law. The state personnel division then appealed to a Montana trial court which found that the board's order violated Montana statutes and that the board had abused its discretion by refusing to use the five-factor test. The board appealed to the Montana Supreme Court.

The supreme court found that the board had ignored the division's grade assignment, instead relying on the previous practice of maintaining one grade difference between supervisors and first and second class officers. The board's decision was erroneous because it ignored the division's proposed findings of fact. Montana law limited the board's role in reviewing the personnel division's decisions. The board had no authority to create new classifications or reassign grades. The trial court was correct and the case was remanded to the board for further findings on whether the division's recommendations were proper. *Matter of Mead*, 766 P.2d 1300 (Mont.1988).

A group of fire fighters and police officers who held supervisory positions in the city of Tulsa had been reclassified following a consulting firm's recommendation that managerial employees in the city be reorganized. The city's policy and procedures manual provided for an automatic five percent pay increase upon reclassification. The employees sued to receive the pay increase and back wages and were successful in a state trial court. The city appealed the matter to the Oklahoma Supreme Court.

On appeal, the city argued that the Oklahoma courts lacked jurisdiction. The Oklahoma constitution prohibits any municipality from becoming indebted beyond its annual revenues without consent from its voters. Oklahoma law also mandates that any judgment received against a municipality for the payment of debt is void unless the complaining party proves that the indebtedness provisions of the Oklahoma constitution have been complied with. The supreme court agreed, noting that no proof had been offered to the trial court to prove the validity of the debt. The court dismissed the action, finding that the trial court was without jurisdiction in the matter. *Baylis v. City of Tulsa*, 780 P.2d 686 (Okla.1989).

A Louisiana city's police department was authorized by civil service law to have three assistant chiefs and one police major. However, the police chief only filled one assistant chief position. Subsequently, the assistant chief retired, and the current major, and the captain with the most seniority, sought promotion. The chief refused to comply, and the two officers asked the city's civil service board to conduct an investigation into the vacancies. Eventually, after the board did not act on the officers' requests, the captain sued the city and the board, but agreed to delay the hearing until it was determined whether the major would be promoted to assistant chief so that the position of major would open up. The board eventually entered into a settlement with the major, promoting him to the position of assistant chief and opening up the major position. It then promoted the captain to major, but the city appealed to a Louisiana trial court, asserting that the board had overstepped its authority by ordering a promotion when the chief had refused to do so. The court upheld the promotion, and the city further appealed to the Court of Appeal of Louisiana.

On appeal, the court first noted that although the compromise between the board and the major would normally not be binding on the captain, because the captain had instituted a complaint and had agreed to a delay until the major's case was resolved, he was involved in the settled dispute. Further, the court stated that the board's decision to promote the captain was reasonably necessary to effectuate the civil service laws and intended to serve the public interest. Accordingly, the court determined that in limited cases the board could order promotions, and it affirmed the lower court's decision. *City of Shreveport v. Plaisance*, 559 So.2d 944 (La.App.2d Cir.1990).

Security officers in a Washington county jail system were supervised by the county sheriff. Until 1984, the security officers and other sheriff department employees were represented by the same labor organization. The county commissioners determined that union arbitration provisions did not apply to the security officers because they were not "uniformed personnel" under Washington statutes. The officers sued the commissioners in a Washington trial court for a determination of the security officers' status. The court ruled in favor of the officers and the commissioners appealed to the Washington Supreme Court.

The supreme court ruled that "uniformed personnel" in this case were law enforcement officers who served full time, received deputy sheriff's compensation, had completed civil service exams and did not serve in basically clerical or secretarial positions. The security officers were primarily obligated to keep custody of prisoners in the county jail and in courts, and did not have the broad responsibility of peace officers to make arrests, execute warrants and defend the county. The security officers were not uniformed personnel or law enforcement officers under Washington law. The supreme court reversed the trial court's decision, ruling in favor of the commissioners. *Yakima County Deputy Sheriff's Ass'n v. Bd. of Yakima County Comm.*, 765 P.2d 1297 (Wash.1989).

After an Indiana kindergarten student was sexually molested on her way to school, the school district held a meeting of its principals to remind them that the police must be notified upon the discovery of any sexual incident. Less than two weeks after the meeting, a black principal was informed that two of his students were having sexual relations on the premises. He hushed up the incident and refused to notify the police. When the district learned of his behavior, it warned him again of correct procedure. However, the very next day two more students were caught engaging in sex on the premises. The principal did not notify either the district or the police until a school counselor insisted on it. After these incidents, and several others, the district informed the principal that he would be given a negative rating and recommended that he accept a teaching position where he would have tenure. He did so, but then filed suit against the district in a federal district court, asserting violations of Title VII and 42 U.S.C. §§ 1981 and 1983. The court ruled for the school district, and the principal appealed to the U.S. Court of Appeals, Seventh Circuit.

The appeals court noted that the principal had been induced to return to the classroom because school officials had sincere doubts about his judgment. A principal must be discreet, diligent, follow administrative rules and protect the privacy of students, and the district felt that he had made errors in all of these areas. The lower court had agreed with the district, and the appeals court found that there was adequate documentation to support this view. Accordingly, it affirmed the lower court's judgment and determined that the district's demotion of the principal was allowable. *Morgan v. South Bend Community School Corp.*, 797 F.2d 471 (7th Cir.1986).

In a Missouri case, a tenured social studies teacher had been the subject of numerous complaints by parents and school administrators. After the teacher was informed of these complaints the principal's evaluations of the teacher reflected that his performance had improved substantially. However, the school board remained dissatisfied with the teacher and offered him a contract for the 1981-82 school year in which he was to be retained at his 1980-81 salary. In the following years he was rehired but he remained at his 1980-81 salary although all other teachers in his classification were given the pay increases applicable to the classification's salary guidelines. He was afforded none of the procedural protections relating to demotions or terminations under the Missouri Teacher Tenure Act. The teacher sued in state court alleging that he had been demoted within the meaning of the Tenure Act. The court held in favor of the school board and the teacher appealed. The Missouri Court of Appeals reversed and held that the teacher had been effectively demoted and thus should have received the procedural protections mandated by the Tenure Act. When all teachers in a given classification except one are given pay increases the remaining teacher has in effect suffered a demotion. The court declared that a school board has a statutory duty to fix the salary for a given classification and then stick to it. The teacher was awarded back pay for each year he was paid less than the other teachers in his classification. *Vilelle v. Reorganized School Dist. No. R-1*, 689 S.W.2d 72 (Mo.App.1985).

II. RESIDENCY REQUIREMENTS

So long as there is a rational basis for a residency requirement, it will generally be upheld. Some of the most frequently cited reasons are: diminution of absenteeism, increased promptness, greater awareness of occurrences within the community and more frequent community involvement.

The residency requirement for all future district employees of the School District of Pittsburgh was upheld by a U.S. district court in Pennsylvania. The school district enacted a resolution requiring that all future employees reside in the district within three months of the time of employment. The resolution's constitutionality was challenged by the Pittsburgh Federation of Teachers. The challenge was dismissed by the district court which noted that the U.S. Supreme Court has made it clear that there is no doubt about the general validity of residency requirements. The reasons set forth in the resolution, namely, personal knowledge of conditions in the school district, a feeling of greater personal stake in the district, the payment of taxes in the district, and diminution of absenteeism and tardiness, were all rational, legitimate and justifiable reasons for requiring employees to live in the district. *Pittsburgh Federation of Teachers v. Aaron,* 417 F.Supp. 94 (W.D.Pa.1976).

The Board of Education of Detroit adopted a policy requiring residency as a condition of employment for hiring and promotion of all employees. Subsequently, the district's Federation of Teachers filed an unfair labor practice suit complaining that this should not have been done without prior bargaining. An administrative law judge held that the resolution was contrary to the bargaining responsibilities of the board insofar as promotions were concerned but was permissible insofar as hiring was concerned. The Michigan Employment Relations Commission affirmed the administrative law judge's decision. The teachers' union then appealed to the Michigan Court of Appeals. The court affirmed the holding of the commission. The court stated that the residency requirement was only valid as to the day of hiring. Here, residency as a condition of hiring did not continue as a condition of employment since it ceased to exist as a criteria once a job applicant was hired. The court further held that residency requirements as criteria for promotions were subject to collective bargaining. *Federation of Teachers v. Bd. of Educ.*, 237 N.W.2d 238 (Mich.App.1975).

A Michigan city charter required city employees to become residents within a year of employment by the city. Violation was grounds for dismissal. A veteran police officer was promoted to sergeant and then lieutenant. A year after promotion to lieutenant, the officer moved outside the city for the safety of his family. He claimed that he needed to move because of his wife's ex-husband's residence in the city. Following an investigation, the city police chief demoted the lieutenant to sergeant because of the residency violation. The demoted officer submitted an explanatory letter in which he requested a waiver hearing. He then filed a grievance under the collective bargaining agreement. The grievance was denied following a full hearing.

The officer then filed a § 1983 lawsuit against the city in a federal district court, claiming that the residency requirement was unconstitutionally vague, that he had been deprived of due process and that the city had discriminated against him. The court granted the city's motion for summary judgment and the officer appealed to the U.S. Court of Appeals, Sixth Circuit. The appeals court ruled that the residence requirement was not unconstitutionally vague. The officer's due process right had not been violated because the city had provided adequate review procedures, which included the right to grieve the chief's decision. Although the grievance had been denied, the fact that review procedures were available made a due process complaint unviable. Finally, there was no merit to the officer's discrimination complaint. *Hawks v. City of Pontiac*, 874 F.2d 347 (6th Cir.1989).

New York law requires many state and local employees to reside within the state and, in the case of some New York City employees, to reside within certain counties. Various fire fighters, who fell within the scope of the law, sued the state in a New York trial court, seeking to have the law declared unconstitutional, and further seeking a declaration that if they lived within the state, their families could live outside the state. They asserted that the department had arbitrarily assumed that they did not live in the state so long as their children and wives resided outside it. The trial court ruled for the state, and the fire fighters appealed to the Supreme Court, Appellate Division.

On appeal, the court first noted that the Fourteenth Amendment permits the states wide latitude in enacting laws which affect some groups more than others. Only when the law requiring residency is determined to be wholly irrelevant to the achievement of the state's objective will it be struck down as unconstitutional. The court then determined that the state's reasons for requiring residency were rational, such as diminishing tardiness and promoting community loyalty. Next, the court held that the department's presumption that fire fighters were living with their families outside the state was merely a presumption and not irrebuttable. Thus, there was no legal controversy here. The court affirmed the trial court's decision, and upheld the residency requirement law. *Winkler v. Spinnato*, 523 N.Y.S.2d 530 (A.D.2d Dep't 1987).

A newly hired police officer moved to an Iowa city in order to comply with a municipal requirement that law enforcement officers, firefighters, and other "essential" employees live within 10 miles of their workplace. Two years later, the officer requested an exception to this requirement so that upon marriage she could move to her fiancee's farm which was 18 miles from her workplace. A committee denied this request. The officer then filed suit in an Iowa court contending that the regulation was both contrary to Iowa law and violated the Equal Protection clause of the U.S. Constitution. The trial court upheld the regulation, and appeal was taken to the Iowa Supreme Court.

An Iowa statute expressly allows municipalities to set maximum distance residency requirements for law enforcement officers and firefighters.The officer contended that the city must first conduct a study of factors, such as response time, before setting its regulations. The court held that the legislature intended only a reasonableness standard. The court stated that reasonable minds may differ over the choice of the ten mile limit, but found that the office failed to show that it was unreasonable. On the equal protection issue, the maximum distance requirement will be presumed constitutional unless is is patently arbitrary and bears no relationship to a legitimate governmental interest. A long line of of cases have consistently upheld maximum distance requirements. These cases cite enhanced community safety through shorter response time, enhanced local tax base and loyalty, and reduced absenteeism as legitimate government interests. The supreme court agreed with those cases, and upheld the requirement. *Clinton Police Dep't v. City of Clinton*, 464 N.W.2d 875 (Iowa 1991).

III. CONSTITUTIONAL CHALLENGES

Public employers, no less than private employers, have encountered lawsuits challenging the validity of various employment practices. The courts are careful to closely scrutinize practices which might infringe on constitutional rights, and they are quick to disallow practices which they find to be unreasonable.

Two highly experienced police officers were employed by a New York county when they were injured on duty and placed on sick leave. County regulations provided that officers who were on sick leave were required to remain in their homes from 9:00 a.m. to 5:00 p.m., unless permission to leave was granted. Permission was granted only for "reasonable" purposes. Additionally, any officers who were considered to be "sick leave abusers" were to remain in their homes for up to twenty-four hours and were subject to visitation. The two injured officers were deemed sick leave abusers. The officers contended that these regulations unconstitutionally deprived them of their rights. They filed a suit seeking compensatory and punitive damages in a federal court against the police department and the commissioner. All parties moved for summary judgment.

The court faced two issues: whether the regulations were facially unconstitutional, and whether they deprived the officers of their rights. In determining the facial constitutionality of a government employment regulation, a court uses the rational relationship standard: the regulation must be nonarbitrary and contribute toward government interests. The court first noted the absence of written regulations for determining a "reasonable purpose" or a "sick leave abuser." This absence created a great potential for arbitrary application. The fact that the regulations were incorporated into the collective bargaining agreement was ruled to be irrelevant. The regulations were held to be facially unconstitutional. The court next held that although the officers alleged general injuries, they failed to plead any specific injury. Finally, the court dismissed all punitive damage claims against the municipality. Punitive damages are available only against individuals. A later trial was scheduled to decide two issues: whether the officers suffered actual injuries, and whether punitive damages should be awarded against the commissioner with or without a showing of actual injury. *Uryevick v. Rozzi*, 751 F.Supp. 1064 (E.D.N.Y.1990).

A Nebraska human services agency which provided services to mentally disabled persons adopted a chronic infectious disease policy. It required personnel having the most frequent contact with clients to take blood tests for AIDS and hepatitis B viruses. It also required employees to notify personnel officers when they knew or suspected they had one of the diseases. The agency justified the policy by stating that it was concerned for clients who were violent or aggressive and might become infected by biting or scratching infected employees. Employees of a county subagency challenged the policy in a federal district court, claiming it violated their constitutional rights. The court accepted evidence that the chance of transmission from staff members to clients from the clients' scratching or biting or from employees' personal hygiene habits was near zero. There was no evidence of drug abuse or sexual abuse by the agency's personnel. The agency appealed to the U.S. Court of Appeals, Eighth Circuit.

The appeals court ruled that mandatory blood testing was a search or seizure under the Fourth Amendment and must comply with its reasonableness standard. This required a balance between the personnel members' privacy rights and the public and client interests and safety. The court rejected the agency's argument that employees had a reduced expectation of privacy because they worked in a highly-regulated state agency. It also accepted the district court's finding that the risk of transmission from employees to clients was miniscule. Therefore, the agency's blood testing policy was unreasonable from its inception and was unjustifiable under the Constitution. The appeals court affirmed the district court's order preventing enforcement of the policy. *Glover v. Eastern Nebraska Comm. Office of Retardation*, 867 F.2d 461 (8th Cir.1989).

A class action was brought by Houston employees who had applied for jobs in public employment areas. The class was certified for the purpose of declaratory and injunctive relief. The class representatives were applicants to the Houston Fire Department, Police Department, and Airport Police. Each of the three departments used a polygraph test in preemployment screening for jobs in security sensitive positions. A Texas trial court stated that the questions asked in the test and the polygraph procedure violated the constitutional limits of permissible governmental action established by the U.S. Constitution. Further, the preemployment polygraph procedures also violated the limits permissible under the Texas Constitution. The city appealed to the U.S. District Court, district of Houston.

The district court decided in favor of the class. It ruled that the polygraph could be used but put limits on the questions asked. It further ruled that applicants for positions in the three departments should be given a written notice of the injunction, the taped record, and their right to review and appeal the decision. The court also stated that the city should advise anyone to whom it had provided information about the polygraph tests, that they had been administered improperly and were a violation of law. It also stated that the city must publish the notice of the injunction in the Houston Post and the Houston Chronicle. It decided that the city must destroy, without copying or preserving the contents, all polygraph examination documents. Further, any member of the class could reapply to the departments before October 1, 1990, and earlier polygraph results would not be used directly or indirectly in reviewing new applications. *Woodland v. City of Houston*, 731 F.Supp. 1304 (S.D.Tex.1990).

A class action suit was brought on behalf of thirty-nine Illinois women who failed the physical agility test given by a fire department to firefighter applicants. The test used by the department consisted of a group of tasks which were to be performed consecutively by each applicant without a break, while wearing a firefighter's uniform. The department chose one standard deviation above the mean as the passing score. Different pass rates were selected from year to year. A federal district court entered judgment for the class, finding that although the test clearly related to the employer's legitimate need for physically strong firefighters, the method of scoring satisfied no legitimate purpose. The city appealed to the U.S. Court of Appeals, Seventh Circuit.

The court of appeals held that the city had not justified its method of scoring which resulted in a disparate impact on the women applicants. On remand, the city would be required to produce evidence that the method of determining who passed the test was related to the city's need for a physically capable firefighting force. The court of appeals vacated and remanded the district court's decision. *Evans v. City of Evanston*, 881 F.2d 382 (7th Cir.1989).

The U.S. Supreme Court has held that rules of school boards requiring that maternity leaves be taken at mandatory and fixed time periods violate the Due Process Clause of the Fourteenth Amendment to the U.S. Constitution. Two cases were involved in this appeal to the Supreme Court. In both cases school district rules required mandatory leaves at a fixed time early in pregnancy. The Court said that the rules were unconstitutional. The test in this case and other similar cases is that the maternity policy, in order to be valid, must bear a rational relationship to legitimate school interests. If there is a relationship the rules pass constitutional examination; if not they are unconstitutional and cannot be enforced. *Cleveland Bd. of Educ. v. LaFleur*, 414 U.S. 632, 94 S.Ct. 791, 39 L.Ed.2d 52 (1974).

The California Federal Savings and Loan Association, a federally chartered S&L, was an employer covered by both Title VII and § 12945(b)(2) of the California Government Code. Section 12945(b)(2) prohibits employers from disallowing reasonable pregnancy leaves. The S&L employed a woman as a receptionist for several years. She took a pregnancy disability leave for four months, then notified the S&L that she was able to return to work. However, it informed her that her job had been filled and that no other similar positions were available. It maintained that just because it allowed employees to take unpaid leaves of absence, it was not required to reinstate the employees if similar positions did not exist when they chose to return. The employee filed a complaint with the Department of Fair Employment and Housing which charged the S&L with violating § 12945(b)(2), but before a hearing was conducted, the S&L brought suit in a federal district court, seeking a declaration that § 12945(b)(2) was preempted by Title VII. It argued that compliance with § 12945(b)(2) would open the door for a reverse discrimination suit by disabled males who took unpaid leaves. The district court agreed with the S&L, but the U.S. Court of Appeals, Ninth Circuit, reversed. Appeal was taken to the U.S. Supreme Court.

On appeal, the Court noted that the purpose of both Title VII and §12945(b)(2) was to achieve equality of employment opportunities. By requiring reinstatement after pregnancy leaves, § 12945(b)(2) ensured that women would not lose their jobs on account of pregnancy. Further, the Court noted that the Pregnancy Discrimination Act, which amended

Title VII, did not prohibit employment practices which favored pregnant women. The federal and state laws merely established a minimum standard which employers were required to abide by. Accordingly, the Supreme Court affirmed the court of appeals' decision and held that § 12945(b)(2) was not preempted by Title VII. *California Federal Savings and Loan Ass'n v. Guerra*, 479 U.S. 272, 107 S.Ct. 683, 93 L.Ed.2d 613 (1987).

A sparsely populated rural county in Virginia elected sheriffs who were then responsible for hiring departmental staffs. Four women instituted an action against the county sheriff, which the United States joined, asserting that he and his predecessor had engaged in discriminatory employment practices against women. A federal district judge determined that the positions of road deputy, investigator deputy and supervisor deputy were within the "personal staff" of the sheriff and thus such positions were exempt from coverage under Title VII of the Civil Rights Act of 1964. The court also found that the sheriff's express prohibition against the employment of female officers in the county's all-male jail was justified as a bona fide occupational qualification (BFOQ). Appeal was taken to the U.S. Court of Appeals, Fourth Circuit.

The appeals court first noted that the positions in question did not fall within the personal staff exemption to Title VII. The positions did not entail policymaking for the sheriff, nor did they involve an intimate or sensitive working relationship with the sheriff. The court then noted that the sheriff had not offered any evidence as to why women could not function as corrections officers at the all-male facility. Since the burden was on the sheriff to show a BFOQ, the court held that the lack of evidence precluded a finding that such a BFOQ existed. The court thus reversed on these issues and affirmed on others, holding that the sheriff had engaged in discriminatory employment practices. *U.S. v. Gregory*, 818 F.2d 1114 (4th Cir.1987).

Section 13 of article XIII of the New York State Constitution, up until January 1, 1990, provided that counties could not be liable for the acts of sheriffs and their deputies. However, in November of 1989, this language was repealed by amendment. The department of civil service then issued a memorandum stating that it considered, by virtue of the amendment, the county sheriffs and their employees performing civil functions to now fall within § 45 of the Civil Service Law (which granted civil service status to individuals employed by private enterprises for more than a year when those enterprises were taken over by the state). The memorandum further stated that the department interpreted the amendment to subject these employees to competitive examination the same as most other public employees. Forty-five county sheriffs then brought suit against the department, seeking a declaration that the department's interpretation of the amendment was incorrect.

The Supreme Court, Albany County, noted that although the amendment made it clear that counties would now be liable for the torts of deputy sheriffs, the department of civil service had misapplied § 45 of the Civil Service law here. Section 45 had been intended to apply only when private institutions were taken over by government agencies. Thus, to bring deputy sheriffs into the classified civil service system, some other means would have to be used. The court held that the department's interpretation was incorrect. *Thoubboron v. New York State Dep't of Civil Service*, 552 N.Y.S.2d 1012 (Sup.1990).

A Texas legislator, a mid-term state senator, met the qualifications to be a candidate for the position of Attorney General for the State of Texas (AG) in the 1990 Republican primary, provided that the Texas Constitution did not make him ineligible. Article III, section 18 of the document stated that senators and representatives could not, during their elected terms, run for any civil office for which the "emoluments" had been increased during their terms. Emoluments were gains from employment such as salary, wages and fees. During the legislator's term of office, the AG's retirement benefits were increased. The legislator, subsequent to this event, sought to run for the AG office and brought a declaratory action in a Texas trial court, seeking a judgment that he was so qualified. The court ruled in his favor, the appellate court reversed, and appeal was taken to the Supreme Court of Texas.

The supreme court first noted that the purpose of article III, section 18 was to keep improper motivations of personal gain from influencing legislators when they established the rewards of elective office. It then determined that an increase in emoluments meant only actual monetary gain and not contingent and remote benefits. Since retirement benefits were not assured, they could not be classified as emoluments. The court thus reversed the appellate court's decision, and held that the legislator could run for the AG office. *Brown v. Meyer*, 787 S.W.2d 42 (Tex.1990).

A Connecticut high school teacher belonged to a church which required its members to refrain from secular employment during designated holy days. The practice caused the teacher to miss approximately six school days each year for religious purposes. The teacher's bargaining agreement allowed only three days of leave for religious observation. The agreement also allowed leave for "necessary personal business" which could not be used for religious purposes. He repeatedly asked for permission to use three days of his "necessary personal business" leave for religious purposes, or for permission to pay for a substitute teacher if the school board would pay him for the extra days that he missed. When these alternatives were turned down by the school board, the teacher filed a lawsuit alleging that the school board's policy regarding "necessary personal business" leave was discriminatory on the basis of religion. The U.S. Supreme Court declared that the school board was only bound to offer a fair and reasonable accommodation of the teacher's religious needs. The bargaining agreement policy of allowing three days off for religious purposes was found to be reasonable. The case was remanded for a determination of whether the policy had been administered fairly. *Ansonia Bd. of Educ. v. Philbrook*, 479 U.S. 60, 107 S.Ct. 367, 93 L.Ed.2d 305 (1986).

After a public school district received requests under the Texas Open Records Act for the "personnel file and other related public records" of one of its teachers, the school district and teacher asked a federal court for a determination of whether release would violate her rights under the Family Educational Rights and Privacy Act of 1974 (FERPA) as well as her right to privacy under the U.S. Constitution. The U.S. Court of Appeals, Fifth Circuit, pointed out that FERPA was designed to regulate the release of student records. Because records relating to individuals employed by educational agencies or institutions were excluded from FERPA's protections, the teacher could not rely on it to shield her college transcript. Even if the teacher had a privacy interest in avoiding disclosure of her college transcript, that interest was outweighed by the public's need to evaluate schoolteacher competency. Public disclosure of the teacher's teaching certificate was not a sufficient substitute for her college transcript since the quality of certified teachers had become a matter of "grave concern" in Texas. The school district could release the teacher's college transcript to the public without violating her privacy rights. *Klein Indep. School Dist. v. Mattox*, 830 F.2d 576 (5th Cir.1987).

IV. OTHER EMPLOYMENT PRACTICES

The following cases illustrate various employment practices which have been challenged by public employees.

Up until 1983, it had been the practice of the city of New Orleans to pay its police officers overtime wages based on the regular pay they received from the city alone. However, their regular pay was supplemented by the state of Louisiana and not paid solely by the city. Various New Orleans police officers filed a class action suit against the city, seeking to have their overtime wages based on the total salary they received from both city and state. A Louisiana trial court judge determined that the officers were entitled to be paid according to both regular salaries, and the city appealed to the Court of Appeal of Louisiana, Fourth Circuit.

On appeal, the city maintained that overtime compensation, according to the civil service commission's rules, should have been based on the rate of "base pay" from the city only. The city asserted that the recently decided *New Orleans Firefighters Association v. Civil Service Commission*, 422 So.2d 402 (La.1982), which involved a similar issue for firefighters and which the firefighters had been successful in, was in opposition to this case because the firefighters had been covered by a state minimum wage law and because the city had agreed to include supplemental pay when calculating the firefighters' overtime.

The court, however, disagreed. It found that the state legislature had intended to include state supplements in overtime wage calculations. The court refused to allow a narrow reading of the *Firefighters* case to deny full overtime benefits to the officers. Accordingly, it affirmed the trial court's decision and held that overtime wages must be calculated from both regular pay sources. *Bruno v. City of New Orleans*, 523 So.2d 1384 (La.App.4th Cir.1988).

A New York City Transit Authority employee sought a promotion. He received the third highest score on the required civil service examination. Less than six months after taking the test, a position became available and the employee was required to take a medical examination. The transit authority disqualified him after a psychiatric evaluation, based on medical reasons. The employee appealed to the city's civil service commission, resulting in a favorable decision. However, over a year had elapsed since the employee had become eligible for promotion and the eligibility list had expired. Because the employee had not taken a subsequent examination, his name was not on the new eligibility list. His request to be placed on a special eligibility list was denied. He then sued the city personnel department in a New York trial court, asserting due process violations under the state and federal constitutions. The court dismissed the lawsuit, but a New York Appellate Division court reversed the decision and granted the employee's request to be placed on a special list. The city's personnel department appealed to the New York Court of Appeals.

The court noted that the New York Constitution required civil service promotions to be made according to merit by competitive examination. Civil service applicants could not be appointed from expired lists. A narrow exception existed where applicants had initiated lawsuits prior to expiration of the eligibility list. Because the employee had not done so, there were no grounds for placing him on a special list. Status on an eligibility list did not create a protectable property interest. With no property interest at stake, the employee had not suffered a due process violation under either the state or federal constitutions, and the trial court had properly dismissed the lawsuit. *Deas v. Levitt*, 539 N.E.2d 1086 (N.Y.1989).

A group of New Orleans police officers formed an organization for providing security to private individuals, groups and businesses. Officers worked for the organization on their off-duty hours and received compensation from it. While one of the officers was working for the organization, he was observed not wearing his uniform cap. The officer received a letter of reprimand, telling him that not wearing his uniform cap during off-duty work was a violation of department rules regarding personal appearance. Although the letter was on the Board of Commissioners' stationery, it was signed by the police department's superintendent. The officer appealed the disciplinary action to the Civil Service Commission (CSS), seeking removal of the letter from his personnel file. The board contended that the commission lacked jurisdiction over the appeal because the officer's misconduct had occurred outside the scope of the officer's employment with the board. The board argued alternatively that if the reprimand applied to the officer's employment with the board, it was invalid because it had not been taken by the general manager of the board of commissioners, who was the proper appointing authority. A referee from the CSS rejected the board's arguments, stating that it was irrelevant that the misconduct occurred during the off-duty work. The referee concluded that off-duty work for the organization was in reality nothing more than overtime. She ordered that the reprimand letter be removed from the officer's file and awarded the officer attorney's fees. The board then appealed to the CSS, which ruled that since the reprimand dealt with the officer's work with the private organization, it lacked authority to hear the appeal. However, it upheld the attorney's fees award. The board then appealed to the Court of Appeal of Louisiana.

The court of appeal ruled that the commission did have authority to hear the appeal because the officer's off-duty misconduct could affect his employment with the board. It held that the private organization and the department were so intertwined that rule violations occurring outside the officer's employment with the board could jeopardize his employment with it. The court further held that the reprimand letter was void because it had not been written by the proper appointing authority. The court ordered that the reprimand be removed from the officer's file and affirmed the attorney's fees award. *Bd. of Comm'rs v. Livingston*, 546 So.2d 259 (La.App.1st Cir.1989).

An Iowa school district added a swimming pool and began offering swimming classes to its students. The school district required its physical education teachers to complete training in cardiac pulmonary resuscitation (CPR) and water safety. This training was to be provided by the school during working hours at no cost to the teachers. The local teacher's association sought a declaratory judgment that the physical education teachers could not be required to take the life saving training classes. The trial court held that requiring the physical education teachers to take life saving training classes was not beyond the scope of the district's powers, contractually or legally. The teacher's association appealed to the Court of Appeals of Iowa.

The appellate court held that the school district did not abuse its discretion by requiring the physical education teachers to take life saving training classes during school hours and at school expense. The requirement to take the safety-related classes was reasonable and well within the discretionary function of the school district. The appellate court affirmed the trial court's decision. *Pleasant Valley Educ. Ass'n. v. School Dist.*, 449 N.W.2d 894 (Iowa App.1989).

A surgeon was employed by a Colorado state hospital on a parttime basis. He was then designated as the hospital's fulltime chief of surgery and placed on probationary status as a state employee. Several months later he requested an unpaid leave of absence because he had been appointed a senior instructor by a Colorado university. As a university instructor he would be paid substantially more than authorized as a state employee. The hospital granted the surgeon a leave of absence. The state later terminated the surgeon's probationary status and he was certified as a state employee. As a state university instructor the physician performed the same duties as a certified state hospital employee. Several years later, following complaints about the surgeon's conduct, a hospital hearing committee revoked the surgeon's surgical privileges and medical staff membership. The surgeon appealed to the state personnel board alleging that his due process rights had been violated. The hearing officer found the surgeon an "exempt" employee and that the board had no jurisdiction. The surgeon appealed to the Colorado Court of Appeals.

The court of appeals held that the surgeon did not retain his certified state employee status when he was appointed a state university instructor. As an instructor, the surgeon's salary was greater than that authorized by state law. The court noted that one of the basic precepts of state employment is that state employees performing similar duties receive the same compensation. The surgeon performed the same duties as a university instructor that he would have as a certified state hospital employee. The court of appeals affirmed the board's decision denying the surgeon state employee status. *Fogel v. Colorado State Hospital,* 778 P.2d 318 (Colo. App.1989).

A Wyoming couple provided jailer and matron services to a county jail for nineteen and one-half months. The county and the couple had agreed that the couple would provide round-the-clock coverage for the jail. In the event they were absent, the couple was required to provide a substitute jailer at their own expense. In return, they received $2,500 per month and living quarters. No written contract was ever signed by the parties. Concerned about overtime, the husband asked the county to institute eight-hour shifts in the jail, but this was not done. He then sued the county for violating the Fair Labor Standards Act. The trial court dismissed the case, finding no legal basis for the claim. The husband then appealed to the Supreme Court of Wyoming.

On appeal, the husband contended that Wyoming law prohibits employment of more than eight hours per day unless it is for emergency purposes, in which case overtime pay is mandatory. The supreme court disagreed. The court stated that Wyoming law simply prevents government employers from requiring more than forty hours per week. Nothing prevents employees from voluntarily working more than that amount. Additionally, those who work over forty hours per week do not automatically receive overtime compensation. According to Wyoming law, county rules and regulations determined when such compensation was to be given. The county here had not adopted any regulations, so compensation was denied. *Cyr v. Bd. of County Comm.*, 780 P.2d 986 (Wyo.1989).

A village in New York maintained an all volunteer fire department. The Department of Labor (DOL) conducted an inspection of the fire department, issued a notice of six violations of the Public Employee Safety and Health Act (PESH) and ordered a correction of these violations. Upon follow-up investigations, the DOL discovered that the fire department had corrected only two of the six violations. The DOL sued the village, in a New York trial court, seeking to enforce its order to comply. The court dismissed the action holding that volunteer firefighters are not employees under the PESH Act because they do not receive compensation in exchange for work. The DOL appealed to the New York Supreme Court, Appellate Division.

The appellate division court held that the purpose of the PESH Act was to protect all employees who were not covered by the federal Occupational Safety and Health Act, and to provide safe workplaces for state public employees. The court concluded that volunteer firefighters are included within the PESH Act's definition of employees. The appellate court modified the trial court's decision and ordered the village to correct the remaining four violations of the Public Employee Safety and Health Act. *Hartnett v. Village of Ballston Spa*, 547 N.Y.S.2d 902 (A.D.3d Dep't 1989).

A New York school district prohibited smoking in the district's buildings and aboard its buses. The state Public Employment Relations Board (PERB) then ordered the district to rescind its smoking prohibition. After the school district refused, the PERB sought an order in a New York trial court to compel the district's compliance. The trial court transferred the case to the New York Supreme Court, Appellate Division.

Before the appellate division court, the PERB argued that smoking regulations affect employment terms and conditions and are subject to mandatory collective bargaining negotiations. It argued that it had authority to rescind the district's regulations. The appellate court agreed with the PERB that since it had previously held that smoking regulations affect the terms and conditions of employment, the PERB could rationally order the district to rescind its prohibition against smoking in school district buildings. However, the court ruled that the PERB could not order the district to rescind its prohibition against smoking in the district's buses, since the state commissioner of education had already established a regulation which preempted the district's obligation to negotiate such a ban with its employees. The court ordered the school district to comply with the PERB's order only in regard to smoking in buildings. *Rush-Henrietta Central School Dist. v. Newman*, 542 N.Y.S.2d 440 (A.D.4th Dep't 1989).

The Indian Health Service (IHS) sought to implement an areawide ban on smoking at its facilities in Oklahoma City. The National Federation of Federal Employees requested negotiations with the IHS and presented four alternatives to the total smoking ban. After some discussions, IHS stated that the proposals were nonnegotiable, and implemented its own smoke free policy at its facilities. Employees were forced to go outside if they wished to smoke. The labor association filed an unfair labor practice charge against IHS, and an administrative law judge ruled in favor of IHS. The case then came before the Federal Labor Relations Authority (FLRA), which ruled for the labor association. IHS appealed to the United States Court of Appeals, District of Columbia Circuit.

The court stated that, because the FLRA statute requires federal agencies to bargain in good faith with employee representatives over conditions of employment, refusal to bargain constitutes an unfair labor practice. The court ruled that smoking policy proposals involve conditions of employment and therefore are subject to negotiations between agencies and employee labor organizations unless they are in conflict with management rights. If IHS could have shown that the labor association's proposals interfered with agency objectives or management prerogative, it could have rejected the proposals. Because nothing in the record indicated that the proposals would interfere, the court upheld the ruling of the FLRA as reasonable. *Dep't of Health and Human Servs., Indian Health Serv. v. FLRA*, 885 F.2d 911 (D.C.Cir.1989).

The Kansas legislature enacted an environmental protection control which required oil and gas corporations to notify the Kansas Corporation Commission (KCC) before taking action which might cause pollution. Implementation required the KCC and other agencies to keep personnel on-call twenty-four hours per day. The agencies installed special telephones at their employees' homes and assigned employees to telephone duty on a rotating basis. On-call employees were required to field telephone inquiries and to direct emergency calls to other employees for assistance. During the three years of the program about 30,000 calls were handled involving approximately 80,000 man-hours of home duty. Employees on home duty were required to remain at home when they were on-call, but otherwise they were unrestricted. Employees received $1 per hour for each home duty hour and were given fifteen minutes of compensatory time for each call actually taken. While the program was still in effect, employees sued the KCC for time and one-half overtime compensation for home telephone duty. They sued under a Kansas statute requiring time and one-half compensation to state employees working over forty hours per week and the federal Fair Labor Standards Act (FLSA). A Kansas trial court rejected the FLSA complaint. However, it ruled that the Kansas statute applied. The court concluded that twenty-five percent of the employee's on-call hours required compensation at overtime rates. The parties reached a partial settlement compensating the employees for overtime pay for time actually spent responding to telephone calls. They appealed to the Kansas Supreme Court on the unresolved issues.

The supreme court ruled that the employees were only entitled to the $1 per hour compensation for stand-by pay under the Kansas statute. The settlement agreement compensated them for actual work time and nothing further was owed to them. The trial court's resolution was based upon an equitable approach to the problem, but had no basis in law. The FLSA did not apply and the stand-by pay and actual overtime compensation appropriately compensated the employees. The court reversed the trial court's decision, ruling in the KCC's favor. *Hickey v. KCC*, 765 P.2d 1108 (Kan.1988).

The Texas Highway Department operates a free automobile and passenger ferry across the harbor entrance for the city of Houston. One of its employees, a marine technician, was injured in the course of her employment. She fell within the status of a "seaman" under the Jones Act, which allows injured seamen to sue in federal court for the full measure of damages to which they are entitled if they can prove negligence on the part of their employer. Her options were to either sue under the Jones Act or to collect workers' compensation benefits to which she was entitled under Texas law. She chose to sue in a federal district court, which held for the state, and she appealed to the U.S. Court of Appeals, Fifth Circuit.

On appeal, the court recognized that Texas had sovereign immunity from such a suit unless it had expressly waived that immunity or unless the Jones Act forced the state to yield its immunity. The court then determined that not only had the state not waived its immunity, but Congress had not required the state to yield its immunity through the Jones Act. The employee was thus barred from bringing her suit against the state and could only receive workers' compensation benefits. The appellate court affirmed the district court's decision. *Welch v. State Dep"t of Highways and Public Transportation*, 780 F.2d 1268 (5th Cir.1986).

A Wisconsin county developed and administered certain programs funded under the Comprehensive Employment and Training Act (CETA). After the U.S. Department of Labor (DOL) received a series of complaints about the way in which the county was handling the CETA programs, it determined that the county had substituted CETA money for its own funds in violation of CETA "maintenance of effort" requirements. The DOL then ordered the county to perform a record review and provide backpay and benefits to former participants, and it disallowed costs associated with seventeen ineligible CETA participants. An administrative hearing was conducted on the matter and the law judge presiding issued his decision over two years after the hearing, affirming the DOL's order. The county then appealed to the U.S. Court of Appeals, Seventh Circuit.

On appeal, the county contended that the law judge had issued his decision too late and that the DOL had therefore been divested of authority to order it to comply. The court, however, disagreed, noting that the complaints had been timely filed and that it was only the complexity of the case which had delayed the law judge's final determination. The court then stated that the county had substituted CETA funds for local funding in connection with work that would otherwise be performed for the county. CETA was designed to create new employment opportunities and not to substitute federal funds for county funds in jobs that currently existed. The court further found that the county had used federal funds to pay seventeen ineligible participants and ordered the county to reimburse the DOL. The court affirmed the law judge's decision in large part and remanded on other issues. *Milwaukee County, Wisconsin v. Donovan*, 771 F.2d 983 (7th Cir.1985).

The state of Idaho prosecuted a defendant for failure to collect and pay sales tax. Guilty verdicts were obtained from the jury, but the trial judge granted the defendant's motion for a new trial. The state appealed the judge's decision and requested that a transcript of the case be prepared for its appeal free of cost. The trial court judge determined that the state was required to pay the costs of preparing the court reporter's transcript, and the state appealed to the Supreme Court of Idaho.

The supreme court noted that the two state laws contradicted each other with respect to paying a court reporter for a transcript. One law stated that no compensation was to be paid to state employees for performing duties for the state. The other statute allowed for payments to court reporters in preparing transcripts in both civil and criminal appeals. The court then noted that the second law had also repealed all laws in conflict with it. Thus, the state was required to pay the court reporter's costs in preparing the transcript and the trial court's decision was affirmed. *State v. McDermott*, 720 P.2d 640 (Idaho 1986).

The Chicago Zoological Society operates the Brookfield Zoo in Illinois. Following an inspection by Occupational Safety and Health Administration (OSHA) officials, a citation and $2,000 penalty were assessed against the society for safety violations occurring on zoo premises. The society contested the citation on the ground that it was a political subdivision of the state and therefore exempt from OSHA jurisdiction. An administrative law judge found against the society, but further administrative appeal resulted in a successful ruling for the society. The Secretary of Labor then appealed to the U.S. Court of Appeals, Seventh Circuit.

The court of appeals first noted that there is a two-part test for determining whether an entity is a political subdivision. First, if it is created directly by the state so as to constitute a department or, second, if it is administered by individuals who are controlled by public officials, then it classifies as a political subdivision. The court then determined that the society had not been created directly by the state. It had been designed as a private entity to be operated independently of local and state governmental agencies. Next, the court stated that although the society relied on state funds to finance its zoo operations, and although local government maintained a significant amount of control over the society's budget, because the society maintained control over personnel matters, it could not be considered a political subdivision. The court thus reversed the second administrative ruling, and held that the society was not exempt from OSHA regulations. *Brock v. Chicago Zoological Society*, 820 F.2d 909 (7th Cir.1987).

A learning disabilities consultant was hired by a New Jersey school board. Beginning in the fall of 1980, and for each academic year thereafter, the consultant was moved up one step on the salary guide. The school board and the teacher's association, however, had negotiated an agreement before the learning disabilities consultant was hired which provided that any employee hired after February 1 of any year would remain at his or her step on the salary guide during the following academic year. The school district, which had erroneously advanced the consultant on the salary guide in the fall of 1980 even though he had been hired after February 1, did not realize its error for three years. It then reduced the teacher's salary. When the consultant received his first reduced check in November, 1983, he contacted the personnel office immediately. The board sent him a letter refusing any action.

The consultant filed a complaint with the New Jersey Commissioner of Education. The case was heard by an administrative law judge (ALJ), who ruled that the complaint had not been filed within the required ninety days of the date the consultant first received notice of his salary reduction. The ALJ held that notice of the salary reduction had been accomplished by the consultant's receipt of his paycheck. The State Board of Education affirmed the ALJ's decision, and the learning disabilities consultant appealed to the New Jersey Superior Court, Appellate Division. The court found that under the New Jersey Teacher Tenure Act the consultant had a vested right in his salary. Therefore, the decision by the school district to reduce his salary violated his rights under the Act. The paycheck did not constitute proper notice that his salary was being reduced. "[I]n this computer age," stated the court, "it could simply have been an error." It was not until receipt of the school board's letter denying his request for back pay that he was put on notice that a "dispute" existed. The court remanded the case to the Commissioner of Education for resolution of the dispute on the merits. *Stockton v. Bd. of Educ. of City of Trenton*, 509 A.2d 264 (N.J.Super.A.D.1986).

The Leominster, Massachusetts, school committee had a collective bargaining agreement with the local teachers' union which stated: "After five (5) days of absence, the Committee shall have the right to require a doctor's certificate as proof of [a teacher's] illness." State law commanded that employees would not be paid when on strike. During contract negotiations, 95 of the district's 400 teachers engaged in a "sick-out," a wildcat strike where they collectively called in sick. The school committee announced that because the law prohibited it from granting sick pay to teachers who were really staging a one-day wildcat strike, the committee would require a doctor's certificate from any teacher seeking sick pay for the day in question. The teachers' union sued on the ground that the collective bargaining agreement allowed five days' absence before a doctor's certificate would be required. The Massachusetts Court of Appeals upheld the school committee. "Nothing in this record suggests that [the contract] was intended to afford teachers an opportunity for coordinated "sick-leave absenteeism for less than five days, not really caused by illness, which could not be checked by school officials." The court held that the law allowed the school committee to require a doctor's certificate as verification of illness. *School Comm. v. Labor Relations Comm'n*, 486 N.E.2d 756 (Mass.App.1985).

A black employee of a Georgia county board of education challenged a rule requiring any school system employee who became a candidate for public office to take a leave of absence without pay for the duration of the candidacy. The employee claimed the rule violated the Voting Rights Act. The school board then abolished the rule and adopted a policy which expressly denied employee leaves of absence for political purposes and required employees holding elective office to abide by the same leave policies that were applicable to all employees. The employee brought suit against the school district in a U.S. district court alleging that the new policy also violated the Act. The court said the employee had failed to prove that the board of education enacted or sought to "administer any standard, practice, or procedure with respect to voting different from that in force or effect on November 1, 1964" as required by the Voting Rights Act. The school board merely sought to reaffirm its policy of requiring employees to fulfill their contracts. *White v. Dougherty County Bd. of Educ.*, 579 F.Supp. 1480 (M.D.Ga.1984).

APPENDIX A

TABLE OF RECENT LAW REVIEW ARTICLES

Affirmative Action

Affirmative action expanded under Title VII. [Johnson v. Santa Clara County Transp. Agency, 107 S.Ct. 1442 (1987)] 18 Golden Gate U.L.Rev. 567 (1988).

An insurmountable hurdle for affirmative action. Associated General Contractors v. City of San Francisco, 814 F..2d 922 (9th Cir.1987)] 18 Golden Gate U.L.Rev. 57 (1988).

Bell, Derrick. *Xerces and the affirmative action mystique.* 57 Geo.Wash.L.Rev. 1595 (1989).

Brooks, Roy L. *The affirmative action issue: law, policy, and morality.* 22 Conn.L.Rev. 323 (1990).

Browne, Kingsley R. *Comparable worth: an impermissible form of affirmative action?* 22 Loy.L.A.L.Rev.717 (1989).

Buchanan, G. Sidney. *Johnson v. Transportation Agency, Santa Clara County: a paradigm of affirmative action.* 25 Hous.L.Rev. 229 (1989).

Civil rights: affirmative action gender-based criteria consistent with Title VII. [Johnson v. Transportation Agency, Santa Clara County, California, 480 U.S. 616 (1987)] 20 N.M.L.Rev. 219 (1990).

Constitutional law--unitariness in student assignments requires abdication of judicial intervention in the desegregation of Boston's schools. [Morgan v. Nucci, 831 F.2d 313 (1st Cir.1987)] 22 Suffolk U.L.Rev. 1249 (1988).

Constitutional law — racial classifications in municipal affirmative action program violate Fourteenth Amendment's equal protection clause. [City of Richmond v. J.A. Croson Co., 109 S.Ct. 706 (1989)] 23 Suffolk U.L.Rev 1107 (1989).

Constitutional scholars' statement *on affirmative action after . City of Richmond v. J.A. Croson Co.* 98 Yale L.J. 1711 (1989).

Cox, Paul N. *The Supreme Court, Title VII and "voluntary" affirmative action*--a *critique.* 21 Ind.L.Rev. 767 (1988).

Daly, Mary C. *Some runs, some hits, some errors--keeping score in the affirmative action ballpark from Weber to Johnson.* 30 B.C.L.Rev. 1 (1988).

Devins, Neal. *Affirmative action after Reagan.* 68 Tex.L.Rev. 353 (1989).

Finding a "manifest imbalance": the case for a unified statistical test for voluntary affirmative action under Title VII. 87 Mich.L.Rev. 1986 (1989).

Frankel, Peter. *Title VII and the Supreme Court: the evolution of affirmative action.* 8 Glendale L.Rev. 102 (1988).

Affirmative Action (continued)

Fried, Charles. *Affirmative Action after City of Richmond v. J.A. Croson Co.: A response to the Scholars' statement.* 99 Yale L.J. 155 (1989).

Graglia, Lino A. *The "remedy" rationale for requiring or permitting otherwise prohibited discrimination: how the Court overcame the Constitution and the 1964 Civil Rights Act.* 22 Suffolk U.L.Rev. 569 (1988).

Is preferential treatment justified in voluntary affirmative action programs? 12 Am.J. Trial Advoc. 99 (1988).

Lively, Donald E. *Affirmative action and marketplace freedom: a constitutional intersection of equality and liberty.* 16 J.Contemp.L. 1 (1990).

Maltz, Earl M. *Affirmative action and employer autonomy: a comment on City of Richmond v. J.A. Croson Co.* 68 Or.L.Rev. 459 (1989).

Marinelli, Arthur J. *Affirmative action: a divided Supreme Court.* J.Marshall L.Rev. 99 (1988).

Nay, Leslie A. and James E. Jones, Jr. *Equal employment and affirmative action in local governments: a profile.* 8 Law & Inequality 103 (1989).

Negotiating a slippery slope: voluntary affirmative action after Johnson. 14 J.Corp.L. 201 (1988).

Oliver, Solomon, Jr. *Litigating the constitutionality of state and local affirmative action plans: issues and approaches.* 10 Rev.Litigation 55 (1990).

Rasnic, Carol D. *City of Richmond v. J.A. Croson Co.: what does it portend for affirmative action?* 23 Creighton L.Rev. 19 (1989-90).

Rosenfeld, Michel. *Decoding Richmond: affirmative action and the elusive meaning of constitutional equality.* 87 Mich.L.Rev. 1729 (1989).

Ross, Thomas. *Innocence and affirmative action.* 43 Vand.L.Rev. 297 (1990).

The sunset of affirmative action? [City of Richmond v. J.A. Croson Co., 109 S.Ct. 706 (1989)] 12 Nat'l Black L.J. 73 (1990)

Tate, Kathryn W. *The federal employer's duties under the Rehabilitation Act: does reasonable accommodation or affirmative action include reassignment?* 67 Tex. L.Rev. 781 (1989).

Washington, Lynn C. *Minority set-aside programs after City of Richmond v. J.A. Croson Co.* 19 Stetson L.Rev. 833 (1990).

Discrimination

A case of handicap discrimination, no transfer required. [Coffman v. W. Va. Bd. of Regents, No. 17904, slip op., (W.Va.June 2, 1988)] 91 W.Va.L.Rev. 487 (1989).

Achieving equal treatment in the workplace and in places of public accommodation. 1987 Ann.Surv. Am.L. 857 (1987).

Administrative res judicata and the Age Discrimination in Employment Act. 89 Colum.L.Rev. 1111 (1989).

Discrimination (continued)

Age discrimination—extraterritorial application of the Age Discrimination in Employment Act–Equal Employment Opportunity Commission determines that a United States corporation operating in West Germany is subject to suit under the Age Discrimination in Employment Act—employer's defense based on compliance with West German law rejected. 20 Ga.Int'l & Comp.L. 207 (1990).

Aids and the law: protecting the HIV-infected employee from discrimination. 57 Tenn.L.Rev. 539 (1990).

The arbitrability of ADEA claims: Toward an epistemology of Congressional silence. 23 Colum.J.L.& Soc. Probs. 67 (1989).

Arguments appealing to racial prejudice: uncertainty, impartiality, and the harmless error doctrine. 64 Ind.L.J. 375 (1989).

Barnard, Thomas H. *The Americans with Disabilities Act: nightmare for employers and dream for lawyers?* 64 St.John's L.Rev. 229 (1990).

Baxley, James F. *Rehabilitating AIDS-based employment discrimination: HIV infection as a handicap under the Vocational Rehabilitation Act of 1973.* 19 Seton Hall L.Rev. 23 (1989).

Beyond atomized discrimination: use of acts of discrimination against "other" minorities to prove discriminatory motivation under federal employment law. 43 Stan.L.Rev. 241 (1990).

Blum, Karen M. *Section 1981 revisited: looking beyond Runyon and Patterson.* 32 How.L.J. 1 (1989).

"A book of myths in which our names do not appear": re-defining gender discrimination and defining gender. 4 Geo.J.Legal Ethics 189 (1990).

Brown, Judith Olans, Wendy E. Parmet, and Phyllis Tropper Baumann. *The failure of gender equality: an essay in constitutional dissonance.* 36 Buffalo L.Rev. 573 (1987).

Byrnes, Andrew C. *The "other" human rights treaty body: the work of the Committee on the Elimination of Discrimination Against Women.* 14 Yale J.Int'l L. 161 (1989).

Causation and burdens of proof in Title VII mixed motive cases. [Price Waterhouse v. Hopkins, 57 U.S.L.W. 4469] 21 Ariz.St.L.J. 501 (1989).

Chagares, Michael A. *Determining the validity of waivers under the Age Discrimination in Employment Act: The Third Circuit approach and the Age Discrimination in Employment Waiver Protection Act.* 19 Seton Hall L.Rev. 678 (1989).

Chamallas, Martha. *Listening to Dr. Fiske: the easy case of Price Waterhouse v. Hopkins.* 15 Vt.L.Rev. 89 (1990).

Civil rights and the disabled: a comparison of the Rehabilitation Act of 1973 and the Americans with Disabilities Act of 1990 in the employment setting. 54 Alb.L.Rev. 123 (1989).

Colton, Roger D. *Discrimination as a sword for the poor; use of an "effects test" in public utility litigation.* 37 Wash.U.J.Urb.& Contemp.L. 97 (1990).

Constitutional law -- snake pits, lion's dens and § 1983: when does

Discrimination (continued)

inaction equal action? [DeShaney v. Winnebago County Dep't of Soc. Servs., 812 F.2d 298 (7th Cir.1987), aff'd 109 S.Ct. 998 (1989)] 24 Wake Forest L.Rev. 781 (1989).

Controlling women's equal employment opportunities through federal protection policies. [Int'l Union v. Johnson Controls, Inc., 886 F.2d 871 (7th Cir.1989), en banc, cert. granted, 110 S.Ct. 1522 (1990)] 40 Am.U.L. Rev. 453 (1990)

Corbin, Peter Reed and John E. Duvall. *Employment discrimination.* 40 Mercer L.Rev. 1247 (1989).

Craver, Charles B. *The application of the Age Discrimination in Employment Act to persons over seventy.* 58 Geo.Wash.L.Rev. 52 (1989).

Crespi, Gregory S. *Efficiency rejected: evaluating "undue hardship" claims under the Americans with Disabilities Act.* 26 Tulsa L.J. 1 (1990).

Discrimination law -- defining the hostile work environment claim of sexual harassment under Title VII. 11 W.New Eng.L.Rev. 143 (1989).

Disparate treatment versus disparate impact: a distinction without a difference. [Wards Cove Packing v. Atonio, 109 S.Ct. 2115 (1989); and Waterhouse v. Hopkins 109 S.Ct. 1775 (1989)] 41 Syracuse L.Rev. 965 (1990).

Dowd, Nancy E. *Work and family: the gender paradox and the limitations of discrimination analysis in restructuring the workplace.* 24 Harv.Civ.Rts.Civ.Lib.L.Rev. 79 (1989).

Employment discrimination--business necessity and BFOQ exceptions to Title VII extended to unmarried, pregnant youth services workers serving as role models. [Chambers v. Omaha Girls Club Inc., 834 F.2d 697 (8th Cir.1987)] 11 1.Ark.Little Rock L.J. 417 (1988-89).

Employment discrimination under the Elliot-Larsen Civil Rights Act: the state of the statute. 1989 Det.C.L.Rev. 1235.

En banc approval of disparate impact analysis for subjective employment practices. [Atonio v. Wards Cove Packing Co., 810 F.2d 1477 (9th Cir.1987)] 18 Golden Gate U.L. Rev. 127 (1988).

English-only rules and "innocent" employers: clarifying national origin discrimination and disparate impact theory under TitleVII. 74 Minn.L. Rev. 387 (1989).

Ethnic origin discrimination as race discrimination under Section 1981 and Section 1982. 1989 Utah L.Rev. 741 (1989).

Fietshans, Ilise. *Confronting AIDS in the workplace: balancing employment opportunity and occupational health under existing labor laws.* 1989 Det.C.L.Rev 935.

Greene, Kenneth A. *Burden of proving handicap discrimination using federal employment discrimination law: rational basis or undue burden?* 1989 Det.C.L.Rev. 1053.

Hands across the water: Should Title VII of the Civil Rights Act of 1964 have extraterritorial application? [Boureslan v. Aramco,

Discrimination (continued)

857 F.2d 1014 (5th Cir.1988)] 12 Hous.J.Int'l L. 125 (1989).

Hebert, L. Camille. *Redefining the burdens of proof in Title VII litigation; will the disparate impact theory survive Wards Cove and the Civil Rights Act of 1990?* 32 B.C.L.Rev. 1 (1990).

Hill, Charlotte M. *The arbitrator's response to dismissal of alcoholic employees; do violations of the "last chance" agreement constitute "just cause" for dismissal?* 1989 Det.C.L.Rev. 1213.

Homosexual employee's discrimination claims subject to judicial review. [Dubbs v. Central Intelligence Agency, 866 F.2d 1114 (9th Cir.1989)] 19 Golden Gate U.L. Rev. 115 (1989).

Hostile environment sexual harassment and the imposition of liability without notice: a progressive approach to traditional gender roles and power based relationships. [College-Town, Division of Interco., Inc. v. Massachusetts Commission Against Discrimination, 400 Mass. 156, 508 N.E.2d 587 (1987)] 24 New Eng.L.Rev. 917 (1990).

Intra-racial, color-based discrimination and the need for theoretical consistency after...[(Walker v. Internal Revenue Service. 713 F.Supp. 403 (N.D.Ga.1989)] 35 Vill.L.Rev. 983 (1990).

Jarvis, Robert M. and Judith Anne Jarvis. *The continuing problem of statutes of limitations in § 1983 cases: is the answer out at sea?* 22 J.Marshall L.Rev. 285 (1988).

Justice Anthony M. Kennedy: *will his appointment to the U.S. Supreme Court have an impact on employment discrimination?* 57 U.Cin.L.Rev. 1037 (1989).

Kaminshine, Steven J. *The cost of older workers, disparate impact, and the Age Discrimination in Employment Act.* 42 Fla.L.Rev. 229 (1990).

Levels of abstraction and employment discrimination because of arrest or conviction record. [County of Milwaukee v. Labor and Industry Review Comm., 407 N.W.2d 908 (Wis.1987)] 1988 Wis.L.Rev. 891.

Lynch, Mary Kathryn. *The Equal Employment Opportunity Commission: comments on the agency and its role in employment discrimination law.* 20 Ga.J. Int'l & Comp.L 89 (1990).

Mandatory retirement of state judges and the Age Discrimination in Employment Act. 51 U.Pitt.L.Rev. 973 (1990).

Minimum physical standards--Safeguarding the rights of protective service workers under the Age Discrimination in Employment Act. 57 Fordham L.Rev. 1053 (1989).

Minnesota Supreme Court Task Force for Gender Fairness in the Courts. 64 Wm.Mitchell L.Rev. 825 (1989).

Modjeska, Lee. *Employment discrimination and the consideration of Runyan.* 78 Ky.L.J. 377 (1989-90).

More proof required for the employer's health fitness defense against age discrimination claims. [EEOC v. Mississippi State Tax Comm., 848 F.2d 526 (5th Cir.1988)] 63 Tul.L.Rev. 711 (1989).

Discrimination (continued)

A narrowing of remedies for the employment discrimination plaintiff. [Patterson v. McLean Credit Union, 109 S.Ct. 2363 (1989)] 47 Wash. & Lee L.Rev. 995 (1990).

Not any factor other than sex: a proper limit to defending the Equal Pay Act. 1989 U.Chi.Legal F. 309.

O'Brien, Christine Neylon and Gerald A. Madek. *Pregnancy discrimination and maternity leave laws.* 93 Dick.L.Rev. 311 (1989).

Precluding collateral attacks on Title VII consent decrees and judgments: will joinder of affected persons work? [Martin v. Wilks, 109 S.Ct. 2180 (1989)] 22 Ariz.St.L.J. 323 (1990).

Presentation of the Third Comparative Labor Law Roundtable: Unlawful Discrimination in Employment. 20 Ga.J.Int'l & Comp.L. 1 (1990).

Protecting persons with AIDS from employment discrimination. 77 Ky.L.J. 403 (1988-89).

Pushing plaintiffs down the ADEA path in age discrimination suits. [Zombro v. Baltimore City Police Department, 868 F.2d 1364 (4th Cir.1989, cert denied, 110 S.Ct. 147, 1989)] 68 N.C.L.Rev. 995 (1990).

Rights, wrongs and discrimination. 11 Harv.J. L.& Pub.Pol'y 805 (1988).

Section 4(f)(2) of the Age Discrimination in Employment Act; no justification? [Public Employees Retirement System v. Betts, 109 S.Ct. 2845 (1989] 24 Ind.L.Rev. 161 (1990). *Sex discrimination: the continuing war over how to achieve equality.* 1988 Ann.Surv.Am.L. 561.

Sexual harassment and Title VII--a better solution. 30 B.C.L.Rev. 1071 (1989).

Silberman, R. Gaull. *The EEOC is meeting the challenge: Response to David Rose.* 42 Van.L.Rev. 1641 (1989).

Sullivan, Charles A. and Michael J. Zimmer. *Proving a violation under the Age Discrimination in Employment Act of 1967.* 17 Seton Hall L.Rev. 803 (1987).

Swan, Peter N. *Subjective hiring and promotion decisions in the wake of Forth Worth, Atonio and Price Waterhouse.* 16 J.C.& U.L. 553 (1990).

Ter-R.I.F.-ic news for ADEA plaintiffs. [Oxman v. WLS-TV, 846 F.2d 448 (7th Cir.1988)] 67 Wash.U.L.Q. 315 (1989).

Time limits for federal employees under Title VII; jurisdictional prerequisites or statutes of limitation? 74 Minn.L.Rev. 1371 (1990).

Torrey, N. Morrison. *Indirect discrimination under Title VII: expanding male standing to sue for injuries received as a result of employer discrimination against females.* 64 Wash.L.Rev. 365 (1989).

Underkuffler, Laura S. *Discrimination on the basis of religion: an examination of attempted value neutrality in employment.* 30 Wm.& Mary L.Rev. 581 (1989).

Union liability under the Age Discrimination in Employment Act. 56 U.Chi.L.Rev. 1087 (1989).

Discrimination (continued)

Weiss, Marley S. *Risky business: Age and race discrimination in capital redeployment decisions.* 48 Md.L.Rev. 901 (1989).

When prior pay isn't equal pay: a proposed standard for the identification of "factors other than sex" under the Equal Pay Act. 89 Colum.L.Rev. 1085 (1989).

Drug Testing

AIDS drug testing legislation in California. 10 Whittier L.Rev. 467 (1988).

Alternative challenges to drug testing of government employees: Options after Von Raab and Skinner. 58 Geo.Wash.L.Rev. 148 (1989).

Balancing public interests v. individual rights; is drug testing of federal employees here to stay? [Nat'l Treasury Employees Union v. Von Raab, 109 S.Ct. 1384 (1989)] 11 Hamline J.Pub.L. & Pol'y 195 (1990).

The battle of the balancing tests in the Fourth Amendment drug testing cases: the proper balance is struck. [Skinner v. Railway Labor Executives' Ass'n, 109 S.Ct. 1402 (1989); and Nat'l Treasury Employees Union v. Von Raab, 109 S.Ct. 1384 (1989)] 15 Okla.City.U.L.Rev. 333 (1990).

Bell, Cathleen G. *Drug testing issues in arbitration.* 1989 Det.C.L.Rev. 899.

Bookspan, Phyllis T. *Jar wars: employee drug testing, the Constitution and the American drug problem.* 26 Am.Crim.L.Rev. 359 (1988).

Bradley, Gregory. *Drug testing in the workplace: a public sector concern.* 32 How.L.J. 49 (1989).

Constitutional law: keeping Pandora's box closed: the individual's rights to be free from random urinalysis drug testing. [Skinner v. Railway Labor Executives' Assoc., 109 S.Ct. 1402 (1989); and Nat'l Treasury Employees Union v. Von Raab, 109 S.Ct. 1384 (1989)] 58 UMKC L.Rev. 129 (1989).

Crain, Marion. *Expanded employee drug-detection programs and the public good: Big Brother at the bargaining table.* 64 N.Y.U. L.Rev. 1286 (1989).

Drug testing: avoiding a prospective chill on employees' rights to privacy and Fourth Amendment protection against unreasonable searches and seizures. 16 S.U.L.Rev. 417 (1989).

Drug testing in the workplace: sacrificing fundamental rights in the war on drugs? 91 W.Va.L.Rev. 1067 (1989).

Drug testing of government employees and government-regulated industries: expounding the Fourth Amendment. 25 Wake Forest L.Rev. 831 (1990).

Drug-impaired police officers/fire fighters and the reasonable suspicion standard--"Whose turn is it to give condolences to the innocent victim's family?" 22 L.Akron Rev. 677 (1989).

The Drug War in the workplace: employee drug testing under collective bargaining agreements. 5 St. John's J.Legal Comment. 1 (1989).

Drug Testing (continued)

Firing employees for refusing to submit to urinalysis: the case for a uniform standard of reasonableness. 23 U.Rich.L.Rev. 75 (1988).

Greenblatt, David J., M.D. *Urine drug testing: what does it test?* 23 New Eng.L.Rev. 651 (1988-89).

Haas, Kenneth C. *The Supreme Court enters the "jar wars": drug testing, public employees, and the Fourth Amendment.* 94 DickL.Rev. 305 (1990).

Jar wars in the Green Mountain State: Vermont's Drug Use Testing Act has the potential to be the best in the nation. 13 Vt.L.Rev. 593 (1989).

Just say maybe: a review of drug testing methods and constitutional challenges to public sector compulsory urinalysis in the Third Circuit. 18 Seton Hall L.Rev. 679 (1988).

Legislative survey--employment law--drug testing statute. 22 Suffolk U.L.Rev. 383 (1988).

Mandatory testing of public employees for the Human Immunodeficiency Virus: the Fourth Amendment and medical reasonableness. 90 Colum.L.Rev. 720 (1990).

Martin, Gordon A., Jr. *Why not understand drug testing?* 23 New Eng.L.Rev. 645 (1988-89).

Mass, Michael A. *Public sector drug testing: a balancing approach and the search for a new equilibrium.* 42 Baylor L.Rev. 231 (1990).

Rudley, D. L. *Invasion of privacy and drug testing in the workplace: a case for the application of constitutional concepts.* 20 U.West L.A.L.Rev. 43 (1988-89).

The constitutionality of federal employee drug testing. [National Treasury Employees Union v. Von Raab, 816 F.2d 170 (5th Cir.1987)] 38 Am.U.L.Rev. 109 (1988).

Testing government employees for drug use: the U.S. Supreme Court approves. 67 Denver U.L.Rev. 91 (1990).

When workers say "no" to drug testing: issues in the public and private sectors. 38 Wash.U.J.Urb&Contemp.L. 337 (1990).

Employee Benefits

Bagley, H. Michael, Daniel C. Kniffen and John G. Blackmon, Jr. *Workers Compensation.* 41 Mercer L.Rev. 429 (1989).

Changing the rules of the game: pension plan terminations and early retirement benefits. 87 Mich.L.Rev. 1034 (1989).

Clarification of retroactive relief in Title VII pension cases. [Florida v. Long, 108 S.Ct. 2354 (1988)] 67 Wash.U.L.Q. 643 (1989).

Cornell, Diane M. *Employee benefits and the employment-at-will rule.* 8 Law & Inequality 355 (1990).

Employee benefit plans' exemption from the Age Discrimination in Employment Act of 1967. [Public Employees Retirement System v. Betts, 109 S.Ct. 2854 (1989)] 64 Tul.L.Rev. 962 (1990).

Employees not covered by qualified retirement plans and those covered by inadequate plans: the need for reform. 20 Rutgers L.J. 535 (1989).

Employment law--imposing individual liability to simplify collection

Employee Benefits (continued)

and discourage delinquencies under section 1145 of the Multiemployer Pension Plan Amendments Act. [Massachusetts Laborers' Health and Welfare Fund v. Starrett Paving Corp., No. 86-0411-Z (D.Mass.July 14, 1987)] 15 J.Corp.L 135 (1989).

ERISA, employees, and creditors' rights: a search for a consistent theme. 67 Wash.U.L.Q. 461 (1989).

ERISA--the propriety of non-fiduciary liability under § 409. [Nieto v. Ecker, 845 F.2d 868 (9th Cir.1988)] 64 Notre Dame L.Rev. 271 (1989).

Federal preemption of state mandated health insurance programs under ERISA--the Hawaii Prepaid Health Care Act in perspective. 8 St.Louis U.Pub. L.Rev. 339 (1989).

Gentile, Carolyn D. *"The check is in the mail"--mastering the maze of employer contributions to ERISA plans*. 72 Marq.L.Rev. 349 (1989).

Hansmann, Henry. *When does worker ownership work? ESOPS, law firms, codetermination, and economic democracy*. 99 Yale L.J. 1749 (1990).

Keating, Dan. *Good intentions, bad economics: retiree insurance benefits in bankruptcy*. 43 Vand.L.Rev. 161 (1990).

McGee, Tracy. *Workers' compensation law*. 18 N.M.L.Rev. 579 *(1989)*.

The National Labor Relations Board's proposed rules on health care bargaining units. 76 Va.L.Rev. 115 (1990).

The participant status of sole shareholders under ERISA. [Kwatcher v. Massachusetts Service Employees Pension Fund, 879 F.2d 957 (1st Cir.1985)] 55 Mo.L.Rev. 1021 (1990).

Shell, G. Richard. *ERISA and other federal employment statutes: when is commercial arbitration an "adequate substitute" for the courts?* 68 Tex.L.Rev. 509 (1990).

Wald, Patricia M. *Government benefits: a new look at an old gifthorse*. 65 N.Y.U.L.Rev. 247 (1990).

Workers' compensationa proposal to protect injured workers for employers' shield of immunity. 20 St.Mary's L.J. 933 (1989).

Workers' compensation law--A clinical psychologist is qualified to give expert medical testimony regarding causation. [Madrid v. Univ. of California, 737 P.2d 74 (N.M. 1987)] 18 N.M.L.Rev. 638 (1988).

Employment Practices

A call for action: the burning issue of smoking in the workplace. 5 J.Contemp.Health L.& Pol'y 221 (1989).

AIDS in the workplace: a legal dilemma. 42 Sw.L.J. 837 (1988).

AIDS: Will it qualify as a handicap in the Texas workplace? 41 Baylor L.Rev. 749 (1989).

Anderson, Patrick M. *The agriculture employee exemption from the Fair Labor Standards Act of 1938*. 12 Hamline L.Rev. 649 (1989).

Barnes, Thomas J. and David E. Khorey.I. 16 J.C.& U.L. 189 (1989).

Billingsley, Robert T. Employment law. 23 U.Rich.L.Rev. 607 (1989).

Constitutional right of privacy — open records: North Dakota

Employment Practices (continued)

upholds personnel file as governmental record open for public inspection. [Hovet v. Hebron Pub. School Dist., 419 N.W.2d. 189 (N.D.1988)] 65 N.D.L.Rev. 241 (1989).

Craver, Charles B. *The implication of the elimination of mandatory retirement for professors.* 16 J.C.& U.L. 343 (1990).

Cross, Leland B., Jr. and Douglas Craig Haney. *Developments in Indiana employment law.* 22 Ind.L.Rev. 242 (1989).

Dau-Schmidt, Kenneth G. *Union security agreements under the National Labor Relations Act: the statute, the Constitution, and the Court's opinion in Beck.* 27 Harv.J.on Legis. 51 (1990).

DeShaney and the jurisprudence of compassion . [DeShaney v. Winnebago County Dep't of Social Services, 109 S.Ct. 998 (1989)] 65 N.Y.U.L.Rev. 1101 (1990).

Equal access in NLRB elections: determining the voting eligibility of economic strikers. 58 Geo.Wash.L.Rev. 549 (1990).

Fox, John C. and Bernadette M. Davison. *Smoking in the workplace: accommodating diversity.* 25 Cal.W.L.Rev. 215 (1988-89).

Fox, John C. *Smoking in the workplace: who has what rights?* 11 Campbell L.Rev. 311 (1989).

Gale, Denise E. *Employment law.* 12 S.Ill.U.L. J. 565 (1989).

Gebbie, Kristine M. *AIDS and government: regulation of sexual behavior.* 57 UMKC L.Rev. 251 (1989).

Hazardous working conditions and fetal protection policies: Women are going back to the future. 17 B.C.Envtl.Aff.L.Rev. 201 (1989).

His honor, the employer--no longer absolutely immune for hiring decisions. [Forrestor v. White, 108 S.Ct. 538 (1988)] 57 U.Cin.L. Rev. 1141 (1989).

Holdeman, Linda L. *Civil rights in employment: the new generation.* 67 Denver U.L. Rev. 1 (1990).

Is Big Brother watching?: How far can a government employer go in regulating off-duty conduct? [Grusendorf v. City of Oklahoma City, 816 F.2d 539 (10th Cir.1987)] 56 UMKC L.Rev. 757 (1988).

Kurtz, Maxine. *Recent developments in civil rights for public employees.* 20 Urb.Lawyer 1121 (1988).

Larson, Douglas E. *Model ethical code for appointed municipal officials.* 9 Hamline J.Pub.L.& Pol'y 395 (1989).

Laura, Peter F. *AIDS in the workplace.* 10 Whittier L.Rev. 39 (1988).

Legislative attempts to modify the employment at-will doctrine: will the public policy exception be the next step? 14 J.Corp.L. 241 (1988).

Local Government Law Symposium. 18 Stetson L.Rev. 510 (1989).

Moskowitz, Seymour. *Employment-at-will & codes of ethics: the professional's dilemma.* 23 Val.U.L.Rev. 33 (1988).

Pregnancy and employment: three approaches to equal opportunity. 68 B.U.L.Rev. 1019 (1988).

Public sector agency shop agreements in the Sixth Circuit after... [Tierncy

Employment Practices (continued)

v. City of Toledo, 824 F.2d 1497 (6th Cir.1987)] 17 N.Ky.L.Rev. 235 (1989).

Rutledge, Joyce S. *Monitoring the employment contract in Alaska.* 6 Alaska L.Rev. 265 (1989).

Schmall, Lorraine. *AIDS in the workplace: doctors, lawyers, and bosses.* 41 Okla.L. Rev. 685 (1988).

Shapiro, Martin M., Michael H. Slutsky and Richard F. Watt. *Minimizing unnecessary differences in occupational testing.* 23 Val. U. L.Rev. 213 (1989).

State criminal prosecutions: putting teeth in the Occupational Safety and Health Act. 12 Geo.Mason.U.L.Rev. 737 (1990).

Stroud, Donna C. *When two "rights" make a wrong: the protection of nonsmokers' rights in the workplace.* 11 Campbell L.Rev. 339 (1989).

The constitutionality of state laws providing employment leave for pregnancy: rethinking Gelduldig after Cal Fed. 77 Calif.L.Rev. 171 (1989).

Free Speech

Application of the First Amendment to political patronage employment decisions. 58 Fordham L.Rev. 101 (1989).

Banning the truth-finder in employment: the Employee Polygraph Protection Act of 1988. 54 Mo.L.Rev. 155 (1989).

Burkholder, John David. *Religious rights of teachers in public education.* 18 J.L.& Educ. 335 (1989).

Compelled self-publication in the employment context: a consistent exception to the defamation requirement of publication. 45 Wash.& Lee L.Rev. 295 (1988).

Constitutional law--First Amendment--public employees' right to free speech in the workplace expanded. [Rankin v. McPherson, 107 S.Ct. 2891 (1987)] 19 Seton Hall L.Rev. 380 (1989).

Constitutional law; religious displays on government property: where do we stand? [County of Allegheny v. American Civil Liberties Union, 109 S.Ct. 3086 (1989)] 43 Okla.L.Rev. 375 (1990).

Defamation and employment relationships: The new meanings of private speech, publication, and privilege. 38 Emory L.J. 871 (1989).

Defamation in the workplace: the impact of increasing employer liability. 72 Marq.L.Rev. 264 (1989).

Employer defamation: reasons and remedies for declining references and chilled communications in the workplace. 40 Hastings L.J. 687 (1989).

Employer defamation: the role of qualified privilege. 30 Wm.& Mary L.Rev. 469 (1989).

Estlund, Cynthia L. *Speech on matters of public concern: the perils of an emerging First Amendment category.* 59 Geo.Wash.L.Rev. 1 (1990).

Heads or tails: the Employee Polygraph Protection Act. 39 Cath.U.L.Rev. 235 (1989).

Lewis, John Bruce, Bruce L. Ottley and Gregory V. Mersol.

Free Speech (continued)

Defamation and the workplace: a survey of the law and proposals for reform. 54 Mo.L.Rev. 797 (1989).

Political patronage and the First Amendment. [Rutan v. Republican Party of Illinois, 110 S.Ct. 2729 (1990)] 14 Harv.J.L. & Pub.Pol'y 292 (1991).

Protecting public employees and defamation defendants: a two-tiered analysis as to what constitutes "a matter of public concern." 23 Val.U.L. Rev. 587 (1989).

Public employees' rights of free speech in the workplace after...[Rankin v. McPherson, 107 S.Ct. 2891 (1987)] 2 J.Contemp.Legal Issues 61 (1988).

Rynard, Thomas W. *The public employee and free speech in the Supreme Court: self-expression, public access to information, and the efficient provision of governmental services.* 21 Urb.Law. 447 (1989).

Secondary right: protection of the free exercise clause reduced by ... [Employment Division. Dep't. of Human Resources of Oregon v. Smith, 110 S.Ct. 1595 (1990)] 27 Williamette L.Rev. 173 (1991).

Shacking up with the First Amendment: symbolic expression and the public university. 64 Ind.L.J. 711 (1989).

Squire, Madelyn C. *Making sense of employment defamation litigation.* 24 Gonz.L.Rev. 1 (1988/89).

Immunity & Liability

Barring the tort claims of firefighters and police officers. [Kreski v. Modern Wholesale Electric Supply Co., 429 Mich. 347, 415 N.W.2d 178 (1987)] 1988 Det.C.L.Rev. 767.

Burke, Michael T. and Patricia A. Burton. *Defining the contours of municipal liability under 42 U.S.C. § 1983: Monell through City of Canton v. Harris.* 18 Stetson L.Rev. 511 (1989).

Cave canem — police department liability and equitable standing under 42 U.S.C. § 1983. [Kerr v. City of West Palm Beach, 875 F.2d 1546 (11th Cir.1989)] 19 Stetson L.Rev. 973 (1990). *Congressional abrogation of state sovereign immunity under the commerce clause, or living with Hans.* [Pennsylvania v. Union Gas Co., 109 S.Ct. 2273 (1989)] 58 Fordham L.Rev. 513 (1989).

Constitutional law—civil rights— state's failure to protect child from known abuse does not trigger liability under § 1983. [DeShaney v. Winnebageo County Dep't of Social Services, 109 S.Ct. 998 (1989)] 12 U.Ark.Little Rock L.J. 777 (1989-1990).

Crossing DeShaney: can the gap be closed between child abuse in the home and the state's duty to protect? [DeShaney v. Winnebago County Dep't of Social Services, 109 S.Ct. 998 (1989)] 75 Iowa L.Rev. 791 (1990).

The dangers and pitfalls resulting from narrowing the scope of judicial immunity. [Morrison v. Lipscomb, 877 F.2d 463 (6th *Defining a uniform culpability standard in § 1983.* 56 Brooklyn L.Rev. 183 (1990).

Immunity & Liability (continued)

DeGrazia, James I. *New trends in municipal liability: changing patterns in 42 U.S.C. § 1983 claims.* 1989 Det.C.L.Rev. 1415.

The deliberate indifference standard in 42 U.S.C § 1983 municipality liability failure to train cases. [City of Canton v. Harris, 109 S.Ct. 1197 (1989). 22 U.Tol.Rev. 107 (1989).

Employer liability and sexual harassment under § 1983: a comment on ... [Starrett v. Wadley, 876 F.2d 808 (10th Cir.1989)] 67 Denver U.L.Rev. 571 (1990).

Garcia, Alfredo. *The scope of police immunity from civil suit under Title 42 § 1983 and Bivens: a realistic appraisal.* 11 Whittier L.Rev. 511 (1989).

Kramer, Irwin R. *The qualified immunity vaccine: preventing and fighting § 1983 suits against public officials.* 23 Suffolk U.L.Rev. 965 (1989).

Levy, Anne C. *The change in employer liability for supervisor sexual harassment after Meritor: much ado about nothing.* 42 Ark.L.Rev. 795 (1989).

Lynch, Judy D. *Public officials, the press, and the libel remedy: toward a theory of absolute immunity.* 67 Or.L.Rev. 611 (1988).

Municipal liability under 42 U.S.C. §1983 for inadequate police training. [City of Canton v. Harris, 109 S.Ct. 1197 (1989)] 12 Geo.Mason U.L.Rev. 757 (1990).

Nahmod, Sheldon. *Government liability under Section 1983: the present is prologue.* 21 Urb.Law. 1 (1989).

The need for the special relationship doctrine in the child protection context. [DeShaney v. Winnebago County Dep't of Social Services, 109 S.Ct. 998 (1989)] 56 Brooklyn L.Rev. 329 (1990).

Nix, H.E., Jr. and Charles E. Vercelli, Jr. *Immunities available in Alabama for cities, counties and other governmental entities, and their officials.* 13 Am.J.Trial Advoc. 615 (1989).

Private party immunities to § 1983 suits. 57 U.Chi. L.Rev. 1323 (1990).

Qualified immunity for civil rights violations: refining the standard. 75 Cornell L.Rev. 462 (1990).

Schwartz, Victor E. and Liberty Mahshigan. *In the 1990's the Government must be a reasonable person in its workplaces: the discretionary function immunity must be trimmed.* 46 Wash.& Lee L.Rev. 359 (1989).

The special relationship doctrine reconsidered. [DeShaney v. Winnebago County Dep't of Social Services, 109 S.Ct. 998 (1989)] 19 Sw.U.L.Rev. 1113 (1990).

Labor Relations

Abraham, David. *Individual autonomy and collective empowerment in labor law: union membership resignations and strikebreaking in the new economy.* 63 N.Y.U.L.Rev. 1268 (1988).

Abrams, Roger I. and Dennis R. Nolan. *AIDS in labor arbitration.* 25 U.S.F.L.Rev. 67 (1990).

Agreements to arbitrate claims under the Age Discrimination in Employment Act. 104 Harvard.L.Rev. 568 (1990).

Labor Relations (continued)

Alleyne, Reginald. *Delawyerizing labor arbitration.* 50 Ohio St.L.J. 93 (1989).

Anderson, Patrick M. *The agricultural employee exemption from the Fair Labor Standards Act of 1938.* 12 Hamline L.Rev. 649 (1989).

Arbitration--Reinforcement of arbitration's role in maintaining industrial peace. [S.D. Warren Co. v. United Paperworkers International Union v. Misco, Inc., 108 S.Ct. 364 (1987)] 23 Suffolk U.L.Rev. 78 (1989).

Avery, Dianne. *Images of violence in labor jurisprudence: the regulation of picketing and boycotts, 1894-1921.* 37 Buffalo L.Rev. 1 (1988/89).

Bedikian, Mary A. *Riding on the horns of a dilemma: the law of contract v. public policy in the enforcement of labor arbitral awards.* 1988 Det.C.L. Rev. 693.

Boyle, Louis Lawrence. *Reforming civil service reform: should the federal government continue to regulate state and local government employees?* 7 J.L.&Pol. 243 (1991).

Brower, Todd. *Toward a unified accommodation of state law and collective bargaining agreements: federalism, public rights and liberty of contract.* 26 Hous.L.Rev. 389 (1989).

Celley, Walter J. *Scope of bargaining issues in Ohio's public sector: an appraisal of the Ohio statute pertaining to subjects for collective bargaining (Ohio Revised Code § 4117.085) with commentary on the confusion surrounding its interpretation by the Courts and the Board.* 14 Ohio N.U.L.Rev. 21 (1987).

Dau-Schmidt, Kenneth G. *Union security agreements under the National Labor Relations Act: the statute, the Constitution, and the Court's opinion in Beck.* 27 Harv.J.on Legis. 51 (1990).

Decision-bargaining and the NLRA-a plea for the resurrection of First National Maintenance Corp. 68 Tex.L.Rev. 625 (1990).

Dissident activity and the exclusivity principle under the National Labor Relations Act. 55 Brooklyn L.Rev. 721 (1989).

Enjoining a teachers' strike: the difficulties in defining the clear and present danger standard. 27 Duq.L.Rev. 583 (1989).

Fischl, Richard Michael. *Self, others and § 7: mutualism and protected protest activities under the National Labor Relations Act.* 89 Colum.L.Rev. 789 (1989).

Fitzgibbon, Susan A. *Sexual harassment and labor arbitration.* 20 Ga.J.Int'l & Comp.L. 71(1990).

Gregory, David L. *Labor relations law.* 40 Syracuse L.Rev. 463 (1989).

Gregory, David L. *Union leadership and workers' voices: meeting the needs of linguistically heterogeneous union members.* 58 U.Cin. L.Rev. 115 (1989).

Guendelsberger, John W. *Labor law rights of "unauthorized aliens" after the Immigration Reform and Control Act of 1986.* 15 Ohio N.U.L.Rev. 139 (1988).

Harper, Michael C. *Reconciling collective bargaining with employee*

Labor Relations (continued)

supervision of management. 137 U.Pa.L.Rev. 1 (1988).

Heldman, Dan C. *Jurisprudence, mythology, and labor relations.* 15 Ohio N.U.L.Rev. 19 (1988).

Hexter, Christopher T. *Judicial review of labor arbitration awards: How the public policy exception cases ignore the public policies underlying labor arbitration.* 34 St.Louis U.L.J. 77 (1989).

Hyde, Alan. *A theory of labor legislation.* 38 Buffalo L.Rev. 383 (1990).

Kurtz, Maxine, Stuart Levitan and Judith Toole. *Report of the Public Employees Relations Committee.* 21 Urban.Law. 949 (1989).

Labor law--the Railway Labor Act: the employee's right to minority union representation at company-level grievance hearings. 11 W. New Engl.L.Rev. 27 (1989).

Labor law—review of arbitration awards in public sector disputes. [Pennsylvania Liquor Control Bd. v. Indep. State Stores Union, 520 Pa. 266, 553 A.2d 948 (1989)] 63 Temp.L.Rev. 437 (1990).

Louisiana teachers gain the right to strike. [Davis v. Henry, 555 So.2d 457 (La.1990)] 36 Loy.L.Rev. 477 (1990).

Moberly, Robert B. *Toward labor-management cooperation in government.* 4 Ohio St.J. Dispute Resolution 29 (1988).

Peterson, Andrew A. *The implication of a private damage action from the Taylor Law's ban on public sector strikes.* 8 PaceL.Rev. 571 (1988).

Pfeiffer, Philip J. and W. Wendell Hall. *Employment and labor law.* 43 Sw.L.J. 81 (1989).

Pietrzak, Rona. *Some reflections on Mackay's application to legal economic strikes in the public sector: an analysis of state collective bargaining statutes.* 68 Or.L.Rev. 87 (1989).

Preis, E. Frederick, Jr. and Richard M. Moyed. *Labor law.* 34 Loy.L.Rev. 995 (1989).

Protecting managerial employees under the National Labor Relations Act. 91 Colum.L.Rev. 405 (1991).

Ray, Douglas E. *The changing face of labor-management confrontation in the late 1980's.* 30 B.C.L.Rev. 99 (1988).

Rothman, Andrea C. *The birth of a rule: the National Labor Relations Board's use of informal rulemaking to promulgate a rule for health care bargaining unit determinations.* 1989 Det.C.L.Rev. 1105.

Silberman, R. Gaull. *The EEOC is meeeting the challenge: Response to David Rose.* 42 Vand.L.Rev 1641 (1989).

Sockell, Donna. *The future of labor law: a mismatch between statutory interpretation and industrial reality?* 30 B.C.L.Rev. 987 (1989).

Sympathy strikes, coterminous interpretation, and the clear and unmistakable waiver standard: unweaving the tangled web. 1988 Colum.Bus.L.Rev. 793.

Symposium: Labor & Employment Law in the 1990s. 13 Harv.J.L. & Pub.Pol'y 24 (1990).

The need for a new approach to federal preemption of union members' state law claims. 99 Yale L.J. 209 (1989).

Labor Relations (continued)

Toward consistency in collective bargaining agreement preemption of state law causes of action. [Miller v. AT&T Network Systems, 850 F.2d 543 (9th Cir.1988)] 21 Pac.L.J. 201 (1989).

Weeks, Joseph R. *Continuing liability under expired collective bargaining agreements: part I.* 15 Okla.City U.L.Rev. 1 (1990).

Who is determining our national labor policy? [National Treasury Employees Union v. FLRA, 856 F.2d 293 (D.C.Cir.1988)] 63 St.John's L.Rev. 614 (1989).

Wilkinson, Jane R. *Practice and procedure before the Washington State Public Employment Relations Commission* (PERC). 24 Gonz.L.Rev. 213 (1988/89).

Wollett, Donald H. *NLRB deferral: the arbitrator's role.* 11 Whittier L.Rev. 605 (1989).

Search & Seizure

Applying a reasonableness standard to government office searches. [O'Connor v. Ortega, 107 S.Ct. 1492 (1987)] 19 U.Tol.L.Rev. 755 (1988).

Constitutional law--search and seizure--warrantless search of public employee work area for work-related purposes and seizure of personal property does not violate Fourth Amendment. [O'Connor v. Ortega, 480 U.S. 709 (1987)] 18 Seton Hall L.Rev. 1019 (1988).

Constitutional law--the Supreme Court extends the reasonableness standard to work-related searches. [O'Connor v. Oregon, 107 S.Ct. 1492 (1987)] 22 Suffolk U.L.Rev. 1241 (1988).

Reasonable searches absent individualized suspicion: is there a drug-testing exception to the Fourth Amendment warrant requirement after ... [Skinner v. Railway Labor Executives' Ass'n. 109 S.Ct. 1402 (1989)] 12 U.Haw.L.Rev. 343 (1990).

Termination

Barcia, Senator James A. *Update on Michigan's Whistleblowers' Protection Act.* 1988 Det.C.L.Rev. 1.

Bias and the Loudermill hearing: Due process or lip service to federal law? [Cleveland Board of Education v. Loudermill, 470 U.S. 532 (1985)] 57 Fordham L.Rev. 1093 (1989).

California wrongful discharge law and the public employee. 23 U.C. Davis L.Rev. 177 (1990).

Employer opportunism and the need for a just cause standard. 103 Harv.L.Rev. 510 (1989).

Federal labor law preemption of state wrongful discharge claims. 58 U.Cin.L.Rev. 491 (1989).

Freed, Mayer G. and Daniel D. Polsby. *Just cause for termination rules and economic difficulty*. 38 Emory L.J. 1097 (1989).

Hauserman, Nancy R. and Cheryl L. Maranto. *The union substitution hypothesis revisited: do judicially created exceptions to the termination-at-will doctrine hurt unions?* 72 Marq. L.Rev.349 (1989).

Hubbell, James W. *Retaliatory discharge and the economics of deterrence.* 60 U.Colo.L.Rcv. 91 (1989).

Termination (continued)

Levine, Lawrence C. *Judicial backpedaling: putting the brakes on California's law of wrongful termination.* 20 Pac.L.J. 993 (1989).

Max, Rodney A. *A new tort in Alabama: wrongful employment termination in violation of public policy.* 12 Am.J.Trial Advoc. 39 (1988).

Raday, Frances. *Cost dismissal: An analysis in community justice and efficiency.* 9 Int'l Rev.L & Econ. 181 (1989).

Raday, Frances. *Individual and collective dismissal: a job security dichotomy.* 10 Comp. Lab.L.J. 121 (1989).

Retaliatory discharge for workers' compensation: do union employees need a state tort? 11 Cardozo L.Rev. 445 (1989).

APPENDIX B

TABLE OF RECENT AND IMPORTANT SUPREME COURT EMPLOYMENT CASES

Affirmative Action

City of Richmond v. J. A. Croson Co., 488 U.S. 469, 109 S.Ct. 706, 102 L.Ed.2d 854 (1989).

Johnson v. Transportation Agency, Santa Clara County, Cal., 480 U.S. 616, 107 S.Ct. 1442 , 94 L.Ed.2d 615 (1987).

U.S. v. Paradise, 480 U.S. 149, 107 S.Ct. 1053, 94 L.Ed.2d 203 (1987).

Wygant v. Jackson Bd. of Education, 476 U.S. 267, 106 S.Ct. 1842, 90 L.Ed.2d 260 (1986).

Martin v. Wilks, 490 U.S. 755, 109 S.Ct. 2180, 104 L.Ed.2d 835 (1989).

County of Los Angeles v. Davis, 440 U.S. 625, 99 S.Ct. 1379, 59 L.Ed.2d 642 (1979).

Firefighters Local Union No. 1784 v. Stotts, 467 U.S. 561, 104 S.Ct. 2576 (1984).

Discrimination

Stevens v. Dep't of the Treasury, 111 S.Ct. 1562, 114 L.Ed.2d 1 (1991).

Price Waterhouse v. Hopkins, 490 U.S. 228, 109 S.Ct. 1775, 104 L.Ed.2d 268 (1989).

Wards Cove Packing Co., Inc. v. Atonio, 490 U.S. 642, 109 S.Ct. 2115, 104 L.Ed.2d 733 (1989).

Patterson v. McClean Credit Union, 491 U.S. 164, 109 S.Ct. 2363, 105 L.Ed.2d 132 (1989).

Public Employees Retirement System of Ohio v. Betts, 109 S.Ct. 2854, 106 L.Ed.2d 134 (1989).

Jett v. Dallas Independent School Dist., 109 S.Ct. 2702, 105 L.Ed.2d 598 (1989).

Ansonia Bd. of Educ. v. Philbrook, 479 U.S. 60, 107 S.Ct. 367, 93 L.Ed.2d 305 (1986).

School Bd. of Nassau County, Fla. v. Arline, 480 U.S. 273, 107 S.Ct. 1123, 94 L.Ed.2d 307 (1987).

Bazemore v. Friday, 478 U.S. 385, 106 S.Ct. 3000, 92 L.Ed.2d 315 (1986).

Local No. 93, Intern. Ass'n of Firefighters, AFL-CIO C.L.C. v. City of Cleveland, 478 U.S. 501, 106 S.Ct. 3063, 92 L.Ed.2d 405 (1986).

Massachusetts Board of Retirement v. Murgia, 427 U.S. 307, 96 S.Ct. 2562, 49 L.Ed.2d 520 (1976).

Vance v. Bradley, 440 U.S. 93, 99 S.Ct. 939, 59 L.Ed.2d 171 (1979).

U.S. Postal Service Bd. of Governors v. Aikens, 460 U.S. 711, 103 S.Ct. 1478, 75 L.Ed.2d 403 (1983).

Texas Dep't of Community Affairs v. Burdine, 450 U.S. 248, 101 S.Ct. 1089, 67 L.E.2d 207 (1981).

County of Washington v. Gunther, 452 U.S. 161, 101 S.Ct. 2242, 68 L.Ed.2d 751 (1981).

Dothard v. Rawlinson, 433 U.S. 321, 97 S.Ct. 2720, 53 L.Ed.2d 786 (1977).

Andersen v. Bessemer City, 470 U.S. 564, 105 S.Ct. 1504, 84 L.Ed.2d 518 (1985).

Will v. Michigan Dep't of State Police, 491 U.S. 58, 109 S.Ct. 2304, 105 L.Ed.2d 45 (1989).

Runyon v. McCrary, 427 U.S. 160, 96 S.Ct. 2586, 49 L.Ed.2d 415 (1976).

Western Air Lines, Inc. v. Criswell, 472 U.S. 400, 105 S.Ct. 2743, 86 L.Ed.2d 321 (1985).

Johnson v. Mayor and City Council of Baltimore, 472 U.S. 353, 105 S.Ct. 2717, 86 L.Ed.2d 286 (1985).

Alexander v. Choate, 469 U.S. 287,105 S.Ct. 712, 83 L.Ed.2d 661 (1985).

Discrimination (continued)

McDonnell Douglas Corp. v. Green, 411 U.S. 792, 93 S.Ct. 1817, 36 L.Ed.2d 668 (1973).

Employee Benefits

City of Los Angeles Dep't of Water v. Manhart, 435 U.S. 702, 98 S.Ct. 1370, 55 L.Ed.2d 657 (1978).

Metropolitan Life Ins. Co. v. Massachusetts, 471 U.S. 724, 105 S.Ct. 2380, 85 L.Ed.2d 728 (1985).

Central States, Southeast and Southwest Areas Pension Fund v. Central Transport, Inc., 472 U.S. 559, 105 S. Ct. 2833, 86 L.Ed.2d 447 (1985).

Rutan v. Republican Party of Illinois, 110 S.Ct. 2729, 111 L.Ed.2d 52 (1990).

Employment Practices

California Federal Savings and Loan Ass'n v. Guerra, 479 U.S. 272, 107 S.Ct. 683, 93 L.Ed.2d 613 (1987).

Attorney General of New York v. Soto-Lopez, 476 U.S. 898, 106 S.Ct. 2317, 90 L.Ed.2d 899 (1986).

Free Speech

Texas v. Johnson, 109 S.Ct. 2533, 105 L.Ed.2d 342 (1989).

City of St. Louis v. Praprotnik, 485 U.S. 112, 108 S.Ct. 915, 99 L.Ed.2d 107 (1988).

Rankin v. McPherson, 483 U.S. 378, 107 S.Ct. 2891, 97 L.Ed.2d 315 (1987).

U.S. Civil Service Commission v. Nat'l Ass'n of Letter Carriers, 413 U.S. 548 , 93 S.Ct. 2880, 37 L.Ed.2d 796 (1973).

United Public Workers of America v. Mitchell, 330 U.S. 75, 67 S.Ct. 556, 91 L.Ed. 754 (1947).

Kelley v. Johnson, 425 U.S. 238, 96 S.Ct. 1440, 47 L.Ed.2d 708 (1976).

Elrod v. Burns, 427 U.S. 347, 96 S.Ct. 2673, 49 L.Ed.2d 547 (1976).

Connick v. Myers, 461 U.S. 138, 103 S.Ct. 1684, 75 L.Ed.2d 708 (1983).

Pickering v. Bd. of Education, 391 U.S. 563, 88 S.Ct. 1731, 20 L.Ed.2d 811 (1968).

Mount Healthy City School District v. Doyle, 429 U.S. 274, 97 S.Ct. 568, 50 L.Ed.2d 471(1977).

Givhan v. Western Line Consolidated School District, 439 U.S. 410, 99 S.Ct. 693, 58 L.Ed.2d 619 (1978).

Shelton v. Tucker, 364 U.S. 479, 81 S.Ct. 247, 5 L.Ed.2d 231 (1960).

Cramp v. Bd. of Public Instruction of Orange County, 368 U.S. 278, 82 S.Ct. 275, 7 L.Ed.2d 285 (1961).

Baggett v. Bullitt, 377 U.S. 360, 84 S.Ct. 1316, 12 L.Ed.2d 377 (1963).

Elfbrandt v. Russell, 384 U.S. 11, 86 S.Ct. 1238, 16 L.Ed.2d 321 (1965).

Keyishian v. Bd. of Regents, 385 U.S. 589, 87 S.Ct. 675, 17 L.Ed.2d 629 (1967).

Whitehill v. Elkins, 389 U.S. 54, 88 S.Ct. 184, 19 L.Ed.2d 228 (1967).

Brockett v. Spokane Arcades, Inc., 472 U.S. 491, 105 S.Ct. 2794, 86 L.Ed.2d 394 (1985).

Cornelius v. NAACP Legal Defense and Educational Fund, Inc., 473 U.S. 788, 105 S.Ct. 3439, 87 L.Ed.2d 567 (1985).

Dun & Bradstreet, Inc. v. Greenmoss Builders, Inc., 472 U.S. 749, 105 S.Ct. 2939, 86 L.Ed.2d 593 (1985).

Immunity & Liability

City of Canton, Ohio v. Harris, 489 U.S. 378, 109 S.Ct. 1197, 103 L.Ed.2d 412 (1989).

West v. Atkins, 487 U.S. 42, 108 S.Ct. 2250, 101 L.Ed.2d 40 (1988).

Immunity & Liability (continued)

Westfall v. Erwin, 484 U.S. 292, 108 S.Ct. 580, 98 L.Ed.2d 619 (1988).
Forrester v. White, 484 U.S. 219, 108 S.Ct. 538, 98 L.Ed.2d 555 (1988).
Anderson v. Creighton, 483 U.S. 635, 107 S.Ct. 3034, 97 L.Ed.2d 523 (1987).
Malley v. Briggs, 475 U.S. 335, 106 S.Ct. 1092, 89 L.Ed.2d 271 (1986).
City of Los Angeles v. Heller, 475 U.S. 796, 106 S.Ct. 1571, 89 L.Ed.2d 806 (1986).
Davidson v. Cannon, 474 U.S. 344, 106 S.Ct. 668 , 88 L.Ed.2d 677 (1986).
Harlow v. Fitzgerald, 457 U.S. 800, 102 S.Ct. 2727, 73 L.Ed.2d 396 (1982).
Mitchell v. Forsyth, 472 U.S. 511, 105 S.Ct. 2806, 86 L.Ed.2d 411 (1985).
Owen v. City of Independence, 445 U.S. 622, 100 S.Ct. 1398, 63 L.Ed.2d 673 (1980).
Gomez v. Toledo, 446 U.S. 635, 100 S.Ct. 1920, 64 L.Ed.2d 572 (1980).
Hensley v. Eckerhart, 461 U.S. 424, 103 S.Ct. 1933, 76 LEd.2d 40. (1983).
Kentucky v. Graham, 473 U.S. 159, 105 S.Ct. 3099, 87 L.Ed.2d 114 (1985).
Brandon v. Holt, 469 U.S. 464, 105 S.Ct. 873, 83 L.Ed.2d 878 (1985).

Labor Relations

Texas State Teachers Ass'n v. Garland Indep. School Dist., 489 U.S.782, 109 S.Ct. 1486, 103 L.Ed.2d 866 (1989).
Karahalios v. Nat'l Federation of Federal Employees, 489 U.S. 527, 109 S.Ct. 1282, 103 L.Ed.2d 539 (1989).
Landers v. National R.R. Passengers Corp., 485 U.S. 652, 108 S.Ct. 1440, 99 L.Ed.2d 745 (1988).
FLRA v. Aberdeen Proving Ground, Dep't of the Army, 485 U.S. 409, 108 S.Ct. 1261, 99 L.Ed.2d 470 (1988).
Atchison, Topeka and Santa Fe Ry. Co. v. Buell, 480 U.S. 557, 107 S.Ct. 1410, 94 L.Ed.2d 563 (1987)
Tony and Susan Alamo Foundation v. Secretary of Labor, 471 U.S. 290, 105 S.Ct. 1953, 85 L.Ed.2d 278(1985).
Allis-Chalmers Corp. v. Lueck, 471 U.S. 202, 105 S.Ct. 1904, 85 L.Ed.2d 206 (1985).
N.L.R.B. v. Action Automotive, Inc., 471 U.S. 1049 , 105 S.Ct. 984, 83 L.Ed.2d 986 (1985).
N.L.R.B. v. International Longshoremen's Ass'n, AFL-CIO, 473 U.S. 61, 105 S.Ct. 3045, 87 L.Ed.2d 47 (1985).
Cornelius v. Nutt, 472 U.S. 648, 105 S.Ct. 2882, 86 L.Ed.2d 515 (1985).
Frazee v. Illinois Dep't of Employment Sec., 489 U.S. 829, 109 S.Ct. 1514, 103 L.Ed.2d 914 (1989).

Search and Seizure

Skinner v. Railway Labor Executives' Ass'n, 489 U.S. 602, 109 S.Ct. 1402, 103 L.Ed.2d 639 (1989).
National Treasury Employees Union v. Von Raab, 489 U.S. 656, 109 S.Ct. 1384, 103 L.Ed.2d 685 (1989).
Graham v. Connor, 490 U.S. 386, 109 S.Ct. 1865, 104 L.Ed.2d 443 (1989).
O'Connor v. Ortega, 480 U.S. 709, 107 S.Ct. 1492, 94 L.Ed.2d 714 (1987)
New Jersey v. T.L.O., 469 U.S. 325, 105 S. Ct. 733, 83 L.Ed.2d 720 (1985).
Maryland v. Macon, 472 U.S. 463, 105 S.Ct. 2778, 86 L.Ed.2d 370 (1985).
U.S. v. Montoya de Hernandez, 473 U.S. 531, 105 S.Ct. 3304, 87 L.Ed.2d 381 (1985)
U.S. v. Sharpe, 470 U.S. 675, 105 S.Ct. 1568, 84 L.Ed.2d 605 (1985).
Thompson v. Louisiana, 469 U.S. 17, 105 S.Ct. 409, 83 L.Ed.2d 246 (1985).
Winston v. Lee, 470 U.S. 753, 105 S.Ct. 1611, 84 L.Ed.2d 662 (1985).

Termination

Carlucci v. Doe, 488 U.S. 93, 109 S.Ct. 407, 102 L.Ed.2d 395 (1989).
Dep't of Navy v. Egan, 484 U.S. 518, 108 S.Ct. 818, 98 L.Ed.2d 918 (1988).
U.S. v. Fausto, 484 U.S. 439, 108 S. Ct. 668, 98 L.Ed.2d 830 (1988).
Webster v. Doe, 486 U.S. 592, 108 S. Ct. 2047, 100 L.Ed.2d 632 (1988).
Caterpillar Inc. v. Williams, 482 U.S. 386, 107 S.Ct. 2425, 96 L.Ed.2d 318 (1987).
Board of Regents v. Roth, 408 U.S. 564, 92 S.Ct. 2701, 33 L.Ed.2d 548 (1972).
Perry v. Sindermann, 408 U.S. 593, 92 S.Ct. 2717, 33 L.Ed.2d 570 (1972).
Cleveland Bd. of Education v. Loudermill, 470 U.S. 532, 105 S.Ct. 1487, 84 L.Ed.2d 494 (1985).
Bishop v. Wood, 426 U.S. 341, 96 S.Ct. 2074, 48 L.Ed.2d 684 (1976).
American Foreign Services Ass'n v. Garfinkel, 490 U.S. 153, 109 S.Ct. 1693, 104 L.Ed.2d 139 (1989).

INDEX

Use the attached order cards to order your own or extra copies of the **DESKBOOK ENCYCLOPEDIA OF PUBLIC EMPLOYMENT LAW.**

Order extra copies of the **DESKBOOK ENCYCLOPEDIA OF PUBLIC EMPLOYMENT LAW** now. The attached cards may be removed from the book for your order.

Please send me _______ copies of the **DESKBOOK ENCYCLOPEDIA OF PUBLIC EMPLOYMENT LAW**, Second Edition, at $65.00 per copy, plus $3.75 postage and handling. Total $68.75.

Name ______________________________

Title/Organization ______________________________

Address ______________________________

City ____________________ State _______ Zip __________

Purchase Order Number, if needed ______________________________

Send order and check payable to: DATA RESEARCH, INC., P.O. BOX 490, ROSEMOUNT, MN 55068

Please send me _______ copies of the **DESKBOOK ENCYCLOPEDIA OF PUBLIC EMPLOYMENT LAW**, Second Edition, at $65.00 per copy, plus $3.75 postage and handling. Total $68.75.

Name ______________________________

Title/Organization ______________________________

Address ______________________________

City ____________________ State _______ Zip __________

Purchase Order Number, if needed ______________________________

Send order and check payable to: DATA RESEARCH, INC., P.O. BOX 490, ROSEMOUNT, MN 55068

OUR GUARANTEE: If you are not satisfied with the **DESKBOOK ENCYCLOPEDIA OF PUBLIC EMPLOYMENT LAW** for any reason, we'll refund your money.